ALSO BY JULIA FLYNN SILER

Lost Kingdom: Hawaii's Last Queen, the Sugar Kings,
and America's First Imperial Adventure

The House of Mondavi:
The Rise and Fall of an American Wine Dynasty

The White Devil's Daughters

The
White Devil's Daughters

The Women Who Fought Slavery
in San Francisco's Chinatown

JULIA FLYNN SILER

ALFRED A. KNOPF   NEW YORK
2019

THIS IS A BORZOI BOOK
PUBLISHED BY ALFRED A. KNOPF

www.aaknopf.com

Knopf, Borzoi Books, and the colophon are registered trademarks
of Penguin Random House LLC.

Library of Congress Cataloging-in-Publication Data
Names: Siler, Julia Flynn, author.
Title: The white devil's daughters : the women who fought slavery
in San Francisco's Chinatown / Julia Flynn Siler.
Description: First edition. | New York : Alfred A. Knopf, 2019. |
"This is a Borzoi Book." | Includes bibliographical references.
Identifiers: LCCN 2018039985 (print) | LCCN 2018054367 (ebook) |
ISBN 9781101875278 (ebook) | ISBN 9781101875261 (hardcover)
Subjects: LCSH: Human trafficking—California—San Francisco. |
Occidental Mission Home—History. | Social work with prostitutes—
California—San Francisco—History. | Chinese—California—
San Francisco—History. | Women abolitionists—United States—History. |
United States—Emigration and immigration—History.
Classification: LCC HQ316.S4 (ebook) | LCC HQ316.S4 S55 2019 (print) |
DDC 306.3/620979461—dc23
LC record available at https://lccn.loc.gov/2018039985

Jacket images: (girl) Courtesy of Cameron House; (background)
Partnership list of Wing Lee Company, San Francisco, CA. NARA.
Jacket design by Jenny Carrow

Manufactured in the United States of America
First Edition

Slavery can only be abolished by raising the character of the people who compose the nation; and that can be done only by showing them a higher one.

— MARIA WESTON CHAPMAN, abolitionist, feminist

Contents

Preface   ix

Prologue   3
1. Queen's Room   8
2. "The Cussedest Place for Women"   16
3. Reveille Cry   23
4. "No Ordinary Person"   30
5. Victorian Compromise   38
6. Inked Thumbprints   46
7. The Celestial Quarter   53
8. "To Have a Little Chinaman"   62
9. Baiting the Hook   70
10. Life as a *Mui Tsai*   79
11. "A Worse Slavery than Ever Uncle Tom Knew Of"   88
12. Dynamite   95
13. Devil's Playground   101
14. Chinatown in Tears   110
15. Year of the Rat   116
16. Instant Fame   124
17. Municipal Storm   135
18. "Forcing Me into the Life"   143
19. "I May Go to Sleep Tonight and Then Find Myself in Hell!"   148

20. A Deathbed Promise 156
21. Taking Public Stands 162
22. Pink Curtain 169
23. Courage to Fight Evil 175
24. The Chinese Mark Twain 180
25. "'Ell of a Place!" 188
26. The Lord Is My Shepherd 196
27. "The Stress of Circumstances" 204
28. Homecomings 212
29. Municipal Crib 218
30. Paper Son 225
31. *Dragon Stories* 232
32. Tiny 239
33. Missionaries of the Home 244
34. Matchmaking 249
35. The "Joy Zone" 258
36. Fruit Tramps 266
37. "Are You Wearing a Mask and Taking Precautions?" 272
38. Quiet Defiance 277
39. "Sargy" 285
40. Bessie 290
41. Heavens for Courage 296
42. The Thwack of Bouncing Balls 303
43. Little General 311
44. Shangri-La 316
45. Broken Blossoms 325
    Epilogue: "Blessed Tien" 333

Acknowledgments *341*
Cast of Characters *345*
Timeline *349*
A Note on Names and Language *353*
A Note on Sources *355*
Notes *359*
Index *407*

Preface

A ghost story first led me to the edge of Chinatown. One crisp morning, I dodged the crowds in Union Square and walked past a pair of
stone lions up a hill. I had an address—920 Sacramento Street—and
a description. I was looking for a five-story structure built with mis-
shapen red bricks—some salvaged from the earthquake and firestorms
that razed much of the city in 1906.

Passing a church and a YMCA, I came to an old building with
metal grates on its lower windows. Above the main entryway, I peered
up at century-old raised lettering that read,

OCCIDENTAL BOARD

PRESBYTERIAN MISSION HOUSE

On a Plexiglas sign mounted onto the bricks at eye level, I read,

金美倫堂

CAMERON HOUSE

EST. 1874

I climbed the steps and pressed an intercom button. A lock clicked.
I pushed one of the tall doors open and walked into a dark, wood-
paneled foyer.

I first visited Cameron House in 2013; by then, it was mostly
famous for being haunted. A staffer would later tell me he'd once

The main entrance to 920 Sacramento Street.

sensed a ghost in its musty basement. There, he said, terrified former slaves—nearly all of them Chinese girls who'd been sold or
kidnapped—had hidden in one of its dark corners from their former
owners. The girls and young women had lived there under the care of
two remarkable immigrant women—Donaldina Cameron, the youngest daughter of a Scottish sheep farmer, and Tien Fuh Wu, a former
household slave sold by her father to pay his gambling debts. Cameron
served as legal guardian to most of the girls and teens living in the
home. They called her Lo Mo, or "Mother." She, in turn, often referred
to them as her daughters. But Cameron's enemies used a racist epithet
to describe her: the White Devil of Chinatown.

For decades, Cameron and Wu engaged in what they called "rescue
work"—freeing women and girls from sex slavery and other forms of
bondage. An unlikely pair, they defied the conventions of their time
and even, occasionally, broke laws to help other women gain their freedom. The home they ran at 920 Sacramento Street was one of the pioneering "rescue missions" in the United States, established more than a
decade before the world's first settlement house, Toynbee Hall in London's East End, and fifteen years before Jane Addams co-founded Hull
House to offer aid to Chicago's immigrants.

Starting with a trickle of women in 1874, and continuing over the
decades, thousands of mostly Chinese girls and women entered the
home. Many came from San Francisco's Chinatown, the ghetto of
roughly eight square blocks that was North America's largest and oldest Chinese settlement. In the latter decades of the nineteenth century, many women in Chinatown ended up working as prostitutes,
some because they were tricked or sold outright by their families. They
were forbidden to come and go as they pleased, and if they refused the
wishes of their owners, they faced brutal punishments, even death.

From often-dusty records, I learned that the efforts of the home's
founders, Victorian-era churchwomen, with their bustles, corsets,
and elaborate piles of hair, were driven by compassion toward these
enslaved women. They provided food, shelter, and the teachings of the
Christian faith to members of an embattled immigrant community
who faced discrimination and violence in San Francisco and across the
West. Displaying grit and ingenuity, the home's founders overcame
considerable resistance to build their rescue home at the edge of Chi-

natown, which was then considered by many to be the most dangerous section of the city.

Those who fled there were taking a leap of faith. The desperate conditions that led thousands of women to take shelter at the home are among the most searing stories from the saga of Chinese immigration to America. A decade after the Thirteenth Amendment abolished the slavery of African Americans, this "other slavery"—the trafficking of young Asian women—was flourishing in San Francisco and throughout the West. And because Chinatown was in the original heart of the city, this brazen trade in human flesh was taking place just a few blocks away from both San Francisco's financial district and its most exclusive neighborhood, Nob Hill.

Today, the barest outlines of these brave women's stories fill a large bound ledger that still sits in a small, locked archive room on its top floor. In careful handwritten script, the book lists more than eight hundred names of women and girls who took refuge at the Mission Home from its founding in 1874 until January 1909. Nearly a thousand more women's names from the decades after that are recorded in its case files. Further clues about their lives are buried in immigration records at the National Archives, and a few of its residents, such as Wu, left moving firsthand accounts.

The house at 920 Sacramento Street has a haunted history. Few people are aware of it, because human trafficking and sex slavery, until recently, have been largely unexamined corners of the American experience. Yet the story of how the home offered a gateway to so many "daughters of joy," as prostitutes were sometimes called, is contained within the lined pages of its ledger book and offers tangible proof of the astonishing journeys these women made. They escaped their bondage, they found refuge in an ungainly brick house on Sacramento Street, and they embarked on a fight for freedom that continues today.

The White Devil's Daughters

Prologue

It was nearly dusk on December 14, 1933, when a teenage girl walked toward a hairdresser's shop in Chinatown. Around her, laundry dangled from metal fire escapes, chickens squawked in bamboo cages on the sidewalk, and the scents of sizzling wok oil and dried fish drifted through a neighborhood known as Little Canton.

Even in the depths of the Great Depression, San Francisco's Chinese quarter drew tourists, who came to see its swaying red lanterns and taste its pork dumplings. But for Jeung Gwai Ying, who had arrived in America that summer, it was a place of degradation. For months, the teen had been imprisoned in a second-floor apartment and repeatedly raped.

So, as Jeung left the cold street and entered the warm beauty parlor with its acrid scents of perming agents and scorched hair, she hit upon a plan. She did not speak the language of the largely white world that surrounded Chinatown, but she realized that her brief outing to the hairdresser—one of the few instances when she was left to her own devices—gave her the chance she needed to escape.

Jeung's journey to the United States had begun that summer with hope and a ruse. The people who had arranged her trip had promised her a well-paid job in San Francisco. But for more than fifty years, exclusion laws had barred most Chinese from entering the United States, so they had also given her a story about a Chinese American family she was supposedly rejoining in the States. As she crossed the Pacific aboard the SS *President Cleveland,* Jeung studied the more than

An alley in San Francisco's Chinatown, early 1930s.

one hundred pages of a "coaching book" containing notes on her false family's history. When she arrived in July 1933, she flung the book into the sea, as instructed, and successfully passed through immigration by reciting the details she'd memorized.

She soon realized the job she'd expected was not waiting for her. Instead, she was led to an apartment in Chinatown and ordered to strip naked as bidders examined the swell of her breasts and the curve of her narrow hips. She had high cheekbones and full lips and looked several years younger than her real age of eighteen, making her a valuable prize. But the first set of potential buyers balked at closing a deal to purchase her, perhaps sensing she might cause them trouble.

Jeung endured the same humiliating ritual again, and then for a third time. The slave trader, Wong See Duck, threatened to brutally punish or kill her if she did not act meekly and comply. If she refused to submit, he warned her that he would take her to "a very dark place."

Reluctantly, Jeung abandoned her defiant stance. If she hadn't, she feared she would never be able to return home to her family. The price the buyers paid for her was $4,500—more than ten times what the procurer had given her mother in China as an advance on her supposed earnings.

Soon after her sale, Jeung was moved into a second-floor apartment on Jackson Street. Her owners, a pair of women with severely pulled-back hair and penciled brows, set about making Jeung more appealing to men in America. They outfitted her in fashionable clothes and escorted her to the beauty shop down the street, where the hairdresser bobbed her hair, tucking her black locks behind her ears. For Jeung, who was raised as a traditional Chinese girl, having her long hair cut off was the first of many violations.

Jeung's value to her owners lay in her earning potential as a prostitute. With her bobbed hair and alluring clothes, Jeung commanded $25 a night and turned over all but $4 of her nightly earnings to her owners. Twenty-five dollars a night was a high sum in Depression-era America, where the average wage for a female garment maker was just $30 a month. Put another way, Jeung could earn more for her owners in a single evening than most women, hunched over their sewing machines in tenements throughout Chinatown, could make for themselves in weeks.

. . .

JEUNG'S OSTENSIBLE PURPOSE in visiting the beauty shop that afternoon was to have her hair "marcelled," a technique named after a French hairdresser in which waves would be pressed into her hair with a hot iron. She had been instructed to get her hair done to prepare herself for a trip later that evening to San Jose, fifty miles south of San Francisco, where she would entertain a group of men at a banquet.

Was it the thought of the long evening ahead that made her run? Did she dread the prospect of stepping into her silk gown, only to step out of it hours later, entertaining the first of one or more customers that evening? Five months pregnant, she was certainly aware of the risks to the child growing inside her.

It was one of the few times she'd been left alone since arriving in America, and Jeung had just half an hour in the shop before one of the women would return to collect her.

The streets had darkened. The minutes passed. She had nowhere to go if she attempted to flee. If she were recaptured, she would likely be beaten as punishment or forced into a drugged passivity from which she might never escape. Slave owners intentionally spread rumors of girls who had run away from their owners to the homes in Chinatown run by missionaries, only to die of eating poisoned food there.

She urged the hairdresser to work faster by curling only the ends of her hair, hoping she could slip out of the shop before her owners came back for her. If there was a clock ticking on the wall, Jeung must have watched it with rising dread. She was calm enough to put her coat back on before leaving the shop, but she did not take the few extra seconds needed to button it up—perhaps because her swelling belly strained the fabric.

She darted south, through the crowded sidewalks of the quarter, her coat flying open. She had one goal in mind: to reach the place of safety that her owners had warned her not to go.

She ran a block and a half to a house on Washington Street with an arched brick entryway lit by a Chinese lantern. She climbed the steps and pressed the bell in hope of being let in. She arrived only to discover that she had come to the wrong place. Her fear and frustration were evident. The white woman who answered the door took pity on her and led her through the streets to the place she hoped to find.

They hurried toward Nob Hill, where the grand mansions of California's railroad and mining barons had been replaced by hotels with names like Fairmont and Mark Hopkins. Their size and sheer opulence were almost unimaginable to a girl raised in poverty in Hong Kong. After pushing through shoppers and workers returning home, they climbed the five steps to the bolted door of 920 Sacramento Street, a squat building straddling a steep hill.

Jeung caught her breath at the entrance to the house that had served as a door to freedom for thousands of enslaved and vulnerable girls and women. To her right, heavy metal bars protected the windows. She didn't know it at the time, but the windows of the home were barred not to keep the residents of the home inside but to prevent the women's former owners from smashing through the glass to retrieve their human property.

By now, it was nightfall and too late to turn back. Jeung had no other options. She pushed the doorbell once and then again. The doorkeeper peered through the grated window. She saw a young Chinese woman standing outside, her coat unbuttoned despite the cold, and swung open the heavy wood doors to let her in. Two women came into the foyer to meet her. One was a white woman in her sixties with a halo of silver hair, the other a bespectacled younger woman who spoke to Jeung in Cantonese. Listening carefully to the frantic girl's pleas, the Chinese woman translated her words into English.

"Protect me!" Jeung cried.

The women were the home's superintendent, Donaldina Cameron, and her longtime aide, Tien Fuh Wu, who had worked together for four decades to protect some of the city's most scorned residents. They led Jeung to an adjoining parlor, which had a comforting Chinese carpet on the floor and Cantonese hangings on the walls. The scent of Chinese food drifted through the house. Once they were seated, Wu and Cameron gently urged the teenager: *tell us your story.*

Queen's Room

On February 23, 1869, more than six decades before Jeung's dash to safety, the *China* steamed into the port of San Francisco carrying an unusual cargo. Waiting at the foot of the wharf was a crowd of Chinese merchants, customhouse officers, a health official, detectives employed by the steamship company, and gray-uniformed police along with for-hire officers known as "specials," armed with clubs and revolvers.

As soon as the ship's crew lowered the gangplank, some of the waiting men rushed forward. Police and specials brandished weapons to hold the crowd back: what had caused the excitement was the presence of four hundred Chinese women on board. It took "the united strength of the whole police force to prevent them from getting hold of the women," wrote a reporter about the crush of presumably sex-starved men.

The officers searched the female Chinese passengers and their belongings for opium or other contraband before escorting them to the horse-drawn wagons waiting for them at the base of the wharf. Customs officials seized from the ship's passengers thirty boxes of opium and 350 pounds of tobacco, which were later advertised for sale by the customs office at a public auction.

But by far the most coveted cargo on board the *China* that day was the women. Most were bound for the city's brothels, which operated openly in Chinatown. Prostitution was not a criminal offense at that time, even though some reformers condemned it, and the police and

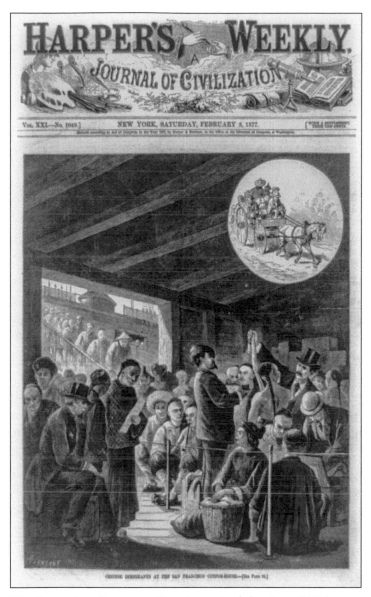

HARPER'S WEEKLY,
JOURNAL OF CIVILIZATION

Vol. XXI.—No. 1049.]   NEW YORK, SATURDAY, FEBRUARY 3, 1877.   [WITH A SUPPLEMENT.
TEN CENTS.

CHINESE IMMIGRANTS AT THE SAN FRANCISCO CUSTOM-HOUSE.—[See Page 91.]

Wood engraving of customs officers inspecting belongings of Chinese
immigrants as others enter the room from a ship; inset: Chinese on
wagon, 1877.

specials helped assure that the Chinese women disembarking from the ship did not manage to escape into the crowd or get whisked away.

Outrageously, as one newspaper reported, the officers' role was to guard the Chinese women bound for sex slavery "until the load of human freight was delivered at the destination fixed by the companies."

THE PENT-UP DEMAND for sex came largely from solitary immigrants who'd left their families behind in China. James Marshall's discovery of gold at Sutter's Mill, on the south fork of the American River, in 1848 lured tens of thousands of poor Chinese men from the Pearl River delta and Guangdong province with the prospect of getting rich in California's gold mines. They were drawn by job opportunities, because they could earn as much in one week of labor in America as it would take several months to earn in China.

Arriving in steerage class from Hong Kong and other Chinese ports, the men fanned out across the West. They found work digging for gold in the Sierra foothills. They hauled away mud to create irrigation ditches in the Sacramento–San Joaquin delta, and they swung pickaxes to build the transcontinental railroad that connected California to the eastern United States.

By the 1860s, political and economic turmoil in South China's Pearl River delta region had turned a trickle of emigrants from China to San Francisco into a torrent. As America's largest city west of the Mississippi, San Francisco had the single largest concentration of Chinese residents in America. Chinese who made their way to America in the nineteenth century called it *dai fou,* or "big city."

Upon landing, most Chinese men joined a *huiguan,* a district association founded along home-region lines, which functioned primarily as a mutual aid fraternity. Although these district associations operated nationwide, their headquarters were in San Francisco's Chinatown. Eventually, they became known as the Chinese Consolidated Benevolent Association, or the "Six Companies," and the association operated as the representative of the Chinese in America.

Joining an association was crucial for most new immigrants while they sought lodgings and work. It could also ease their loneliness. For, from the start, San Francisco's Chinatown was largely a society of men without women or children: many new arrivals were single and those who were married often left their wives at home in China. As "sojourners," or immigrants who planned to eventually return to their families in their home country, many of the Chinese men who thronged the quarter's crowded streets refused to cut off the tightly plaited single braids, known as queues, that hung down their backs.

AT LEAST A FEW Chinese women willingly followed the men to America. The first Chinese woman in San Francisco is believed to have arrived on February 2, 1848. She was a maid working for an American merchant's family that lived in a house at Dupont and Washington Streets. It is unclear whether she was enslaved or had chosen to be employed, but she ended up staying with the family for more than thirty years.

Other Chinese women followed her, often after being kidnapped, lured by traffickers, or sold by poor parents. By 1870, census workers tallied 2,018 Chinese women living in San Francisco: 1,426 of those, or some 71 percent of the total, were recorded as working as prostitutes or brothel operators. Demand for sex was intense, fueled by a glaring gender imbalance: for every ten Chinese men in San Francisco, there was one Chinese woman. The state's antimiscegenation law, prohibiting interracial marriages, which remained in force until its repeal in 1948, heightened the demand for prostitutes.

There was also a profitable market for sex from white customers who lived outside Chinatown and who enthusiastically patronized the city's commercial flesh trade. Seamen and miners visiting the city's infamous Barbary Coast, the nine-block vice district centered on Pacific Street between Montgomery and Stockton, would wander into nearby Chinatown, seeking gratification. Down narrow alleys blocked by sacks of rice and crates of live ducks, they'd find a subterranean world of opium dens and females, some as young as twelve years old, offering sexual services in small spaces known as cribs—often just four-by-five-foot slots divided by sheets.

Demand for sexual services was high. This is why the arrival of steamers carrying Chinese women was so keenly anticipated by many of the men living in and beyond Chinatown. Many of the girls and women who disembarked were bound for forced prostitution or some other form of servitude, such as household labor. By the late 1860s, Chinese criminal syndicates with their roots in China, known as triads, controlled the illegal transpacific trade in women for sex slavery. They could buy a girl from Canton (now known as Guangzhou) for as little as $100 and sell her in San Francisco for triple that amount. It didn't take long for white San Franciscans to squeeze their share of profits from this nefarious traffic. As lawyers and officials who made sure the human cargo was safely delivered, they played a crucial role.

SLAVERY HAD BEEN illegal in the United States for four years at the time the *China* unloaded its cargo of women in San Francisco. In 1865, California had ratified the Thirteenth Amendment to the Constitution, which outlawed slavery and involuntary servitude except as a punishment for crime. Originally intended to apply to black slaves, the inclusion of the term "involuntary servitude" opened the possibility that it would benefit other slaves as well—including Indian captives, Mexican peons, and Chinese "coolies" and "slave girls."

Yet in the chaotic years after the end of the Civil War, as the U.S. Supreme Court steadily restricted the scope of the Thirteenth Amendment, the widespread buying and selling of human beings continued to take place in San Francisco and many other parts of the West. Virulent anti-Chinese legislation in the United States, including immigration restrictions, ensured that trafficking of Chinese women remained a lucrative business for much of the nineteenth century. Attempts to quash it repeatedly failed.

For years, the Six Companies had worked with the police and appealed to the courts to halt the bulk import of Chinese women for prostitution, recognizing that this underworld practice would be used by their political opponents against them. Despite these efforts, criminal offshoots of the *huiguan,* known as the "fighting tongs," gained control of much of Chinese prostitution on the West Coast. Their reach stretched from Guangdong, the region in southern China where its agents bought, kidnapped, or contracted for girls and women, to brothels up and down the West Coast. Occasional police crackdowns on prostitution in the late 1860s tended to target the Chinese while ignoring white prostitutes and brothel keepers. Even so, the business thrived.

Shockingly, auctions of Chinese women took place openly on the docks, in full view of policemen and the waterfront crowds. But as San Francisco began to shed its frontier coarseness and more women began to settle there, these human sales were moved to less public locations. One of these was called the Queen's Room.

This was a bitterly ironic name, because the Queen's Room was far from royal and wasn't even a room. Essentially an outdoor paddock for the women—or, in the now archaic term, a barracoon—it was used for the temporary confinement of slaves or prisoners. "The girls and women were critically examined after the fashion of African slave-dealers not many years ago," wrote one contemporary observer.

The barracks were in Chinatown. Slave traders would strip the women naked. Potential buyers would closely examine them, looking to see whether their hymens were intact, which the men considered a sign of virginity, and whether there were discharges from the vagina or any other signs of venereal disease.

The youngest and those considered the most beautiful ended up as wives of merchants. Others were headed for "parlor houses," which were the city's more luxurious brothels. The oldest or least attractive girls and women might end up in the dark, dismal dens known as cribs. Many of these were off alleyways, and there they might service a dozen or more men each night.

THE CRUSH AT THE WHARF repeated itself in the fall of 1869. On October 20, the steamer *America* pulled alongside the dock. An unusually large crowd of men rushed down the hill from Chinatown to the wharf at First and Brannan Streets. They were drawn by the news that the ship had almost 250 Chinese women aboard.

The men saw a group of Chinese women dressed in tunics and trousers, with checked cotton handkerchiefs on their heads as a sign of their servitude or prostitution. They'd reddened their lips and cheeks with rouge. Directed by a police captain, uniformed officers marched the Chinese women to a corner of the wharf, where the mob couldn't reach them, guarding them so none of the women could escape. The officers then searched them before loading them onto horse-drawn railcars that took them to their destinations across the city.

The continuing, unabashed involvement of police officers in the slave trade caught the attention of the newspapers. *The Daily Examiner* ran a searing editorial on its front page implying that the municipal police, and specifically the police captain in charge of the operation, had been bribed to keep the women safe from the crowds and to make sure they were delivered to Chinatown.

It issued what was in effect an abolitionist cry: "No man, possessing the proud distinction of American citizenship can look upon this wholesale importation of Asiatic slaves, and for the basest purposes, in any other light than the most lurid and horrible." Calling it a "new story of slavery on this continent," the paper demanded an investigation by the police commissioners.

But the rival *San Francisco Chronicle*, which was closer to the city's administration and police force, focused instead on Chinese treatment of prostitutes who were ill and had lost their ability to attract customers. It published a shocking description in December 1869 of Chinese prostitutes who were left alone to die in dismal rooms in Chinatown called "hospitals." Chinese custom obliged relatives to pay the fare for bodies to be shipped back to China for burial, but if no one was willing to pay for transportation back to China, the corpses were abandoned in San Francisco's alleys and on its streets.

Describing one of these human dumping grounds in Cooper Alley as "loathsome in the extreme," the story noted the absence of furniture. Wooden shelves and rice mats on a dirty floor served as beds. The women were provided only with water, cooked rice, and a small oil lamp, until they died. The "doctors" tending them in these houses of horror "come for a corpse, and they never go away without it."

Outraged by these reports, California legislators in 1870 passed a law to ban the kidnapping and importation of Chinese, Japanese, and Mongolian women to the state for the purposes of prostitution. Under the new law, Asian women had to prove they were entering the United States of their own free will and offer evidence that they were persons of "correct habits and good character." If the correct paperwork was missing for the women when they landed, ship captains faced large fines.

Nonetheless, trafficking continued behind a wall of secrecy. Prostitution wasn't illegal, but slavery surely was. Lawmakers were unable to shut down the criminal organizations that operated and supplied women to the Queen's Room. But a few private citizens began their own fight against the Chinese slave trade.

2

"The Cussedest Place for Women"

On October 20, 1871, a Methodist missionary in Chinatown received a request to come to a police station near the docks. The captain held in his custody a drenched and shaken Chinese woman who'd refused to speak with anyone except a "Jesus man."

The clergyman arrived and was taken to a woman named Jin Ho. Speaking Cantonese, she told the clergyman she had left her possessions behind at a brothel where she'd been forced to work and had run six or seven blocks down the dirt slopes of Jackson Street to the waterfront. Then she flung herself into the cold waters of San Francisco Bay, hoping to drown rather than return to a life of forced prostitution she had led.

A man spotted her floundering in the water and pulled her up with a long boat hook. A policeman brought her to the station. She followed the bearded "Jesus man," who was the Reverend Otis Gibson, to the nearby mission. Along the way, she begged him, "Don't take me back to Jackson Street."

Eight weeks earlier, Gibson had helped organize the Woman's Missionary Society of the Methodist Episcopal Church in San Francisco, which set aside some rooms in its Mission House in Chinatown for rescue. The society hoped to "elevate and save the souls of heathen women on this coast," and Jin became the first woman to take refuge from her former slave owners in those third-floor rooms on Washington Street.

Six months after agreeing to accept the missionaries' help, Jin was

The population of San Francisco's Chinatown was mostly male in the nineteenth and early twentieth centuries, leading some to call it a "Bachelor Society."

so transformed that those who'd seen her at the police station in October didn't recognize her. She stayed at the Mission Home for about a year, leaving to become a servant to a local Christian family. She was baptized and soon married a Chinese man who was a Congregationalist. She became known as the first Chinese woman rescued from prostitution by the efforts of Christian missionaries in San Francisco.

Others heard about the house where Jin had gone, and more Chinese girls and women began seeking it out. The second woman to take shelter in the rooms was Sing Kum in December 1872. Unusually, she wrote her own story three years later, which was subsequently published by Gibson. Her father, whom she described as hardworking but poor, sold her when she was seven years old. She was sold three times after that and fell into the hands of an owner who whipped and mistreated her. A friend told her about the Mission House, and she ran to it one night. "I thank God that he led me to this place."

Both women ended up thanking God for their escapes, at least in the versions of their stories recorded by Christian missionaries.

IN THE SAME MONTH that Sing found safety at the Mission Home, a 240-foot-long steamer, the *Nebraska*, braved heavy rains and winds to reach the famously raucous seaport of San Francisco. The fifty-nine-hundred-mile sea journey from New Zealand took just over a month.

Among the *Nebraska*'s first-class passengers was a thirty-eight-year-old Scottish woman named Isabella MacKenzie Cameron. With straight-backed dignity, Isabella descended the gangplank from the steamer to the wharf with most of her children—her teenage daughters Annie, Helen, and Catherine, twelve-year-old Jessie, and her eight-year-old son Allan. (Her namesake, Isabella, remained in Scotland to keep her grandparents company.)

The steamer arrived on a blustery Christmas Eve in 1872 and made front-page news the next day. The *Daily Alta* noted that Mrs. Cameron had brought with her a sixth child, her youngest. Then just three and a half years old, her name was Donaldina, but the family called her Dolly.

Isabella hoped to reunite her family. Her husband, a Scotsman named Allan Cameron, had gone ahead of the rest of the family to

California, where opportunities for sheep farmers were said to be even better than those in New Zealand. He found a situation to his liking in the state's vast and fertile San Joaquin valley. The plan was that his wife and children would follow him there.

On November 21, Isabella and her progeny boarded the steamer in New Zealand, leaving the sheep ranch where they had lived and where Dolly was born on July 26, 1869. The ship stopped briefly in the city of Auckland, as scheduled, and then headed to Honolulu.

In the sultry early days of their journey to the archipelago of Pacific islands, the steamer passed over coral reefs and skirted isolated tropical islands, with swaying groves of palms, banyan, and breadfruit trees on their shores. The younger Cameron children, who had lived much of their lives on a dusty sheep ranch in New Zealand, must have marveled at the rainbow-colored underwater worlds they glimpsed from the ship's deck.

Upon arriving at the Sandwich Islands (now known as Hawaii), the ship refueled with coal and picked up passengers. On December 16, the *Nebraska* was buffeted by gale-force headwinds for a solid week, accompanied by high seas. Even the luxury of a separate ladies' drawing room couldn't have made up for eight days and nights of being tossed about by the violent swells of the North Pacific.

The *Nebraska* was uncomfortable: its fittings were old, its mattresses were lumpy, and when water splashed onto the upper deck, it would sometimes leak through the surface into the rooms below, making the matting on the saloon's floor squish as passengers stepped on it. Worse, the bread served at meals crawled with tiny ants and weevils.

A toddler, Dolly slept on poor bedding with the cockroaches skittering nearby. She might not even have felt the heaving swells as she was held in her mother's arms. The adventure of spending more than a month in snug quarters with her mother and siblings perhaps made up for the slow passage across the rough seas.

DOLLY'S FIRST GLIMPSE of San Francisco, on December 24, was cloaked in gray. It had been raining most of the day, making the streets muddy and difficult to traverse by foot. The wharves, usually lively with the sounds of longshoremen at work and crowds waiting to greet the arriving passengers, were dampened by the fog and foul weather.

"Ladies who persisted in going out yesterday presented a bedraggled appearance," the newspaper reported, "and doubtless, wished they had stayed home."

San Francisco's wharves were almost deserted, in part because of the weather but also because of the approaching holiday. "The rain was coming down nearly all day, and the result was that not a particle of work was done on any of the wharves. All the longshoremen were either at home or at their favorite resorts, enjoying a day's forced idleness," wrote a reporter for the *Daily Alta* who'd braved the foul weather to meet the incoming steamer.

The Camerons spent their first night in the American Exchange Hotel on Sansome Street, which offered moderate prices for families. After disembarking, Mrs. Cameron and the six children made their way there, perhaps in the horse-drawn carriage it provided for free to guests. Rattling over the rain-slicked streets—some of which had recently been paved with cobblestones—the carriage took them from the wharf through a rapidly expanding port city where nearly every street that year was in a state of repair, regrading, or paving. Construction in San Francisco had been constant since an earthquake struck in 1868, cracking apart pavement and toppling masonry.

They passed stately new buildings, darkened by the coal burned for heat throughout the city. At dusk, gas lamps cast their glow on the wet cobblestones and newly built sidewalks. Holiday shoppers thronged the streets, and shops laid out their glittering wares. A display of diamonds in the booming city had sparkled so brightly in one shopwindow, one newspaper reported in those years, that they "practically blinded the eye."

From the outside, the American Exchange Hotel looked respectable enough: it was a five-story brick building located across from Wells Fargo & Co.'s busy express office. But, in fact, it had declined since the tapering off of the gold rush in the mid-1850s, when it had hosted elaborate banquets offering terrapin and oyster soup, moving on to mutton saddle with cranberry sauce and plover, and ending with pineapple, ladyfingers, and jelly tarts.

In the intervening decades, it had become one of the city's many boardinghouses for seafarers and travelers from rural parts of the state. And like most boardinghouses in the city at the time, it was probably home to at least a few prostitutes. By the early 1870s, the hotel had slashed its prices for room and board to $1.50 a night, half the nightly fare at the city's best hotels at the time. The American Exchange Hotel might not have been the jolliest of places for the Cameron family to spend Christmas Eve.

IN THE EARLY 1870S, the city had far more men on its streets than women, and it retained its rough, frontier-town rowdiness. One east-erner described it around that time as "a town of men and taverns and board houses and billiard-saloons.... It is the cussedest place for women."

During their short stay in San Francisco, Dolly and the younger Cameron children pressed their noses up to the glass in their family's hotel room and gazed down on Chinese men going to work at a nearby cigar factory as the sweet, earthy scent of cured tobacco leaves floated into their window. The factory was still operating on Christmas morn-ing, irrespective of the holiday celebrated by Dolly's family—sturdy Scottish Presbyterians that they were.

Dolly accompanied her mother down Kearny, a street that led through Chinatown a few blocks from the hotel. As they walked, three-year-old Dolly noticed that Isabella was attracting a great deal of male attention. Why are those men always turning and looking back? she later remembered wondering.

Her mother, who'd attended a finishing school in Edinburgh and had learned to hold her chin high and carry herself with dignity, laughed and explained to her daughter that because there were so few women on the city's streets, the men were curious.

As a young child, Dolly wouldn't have known that her mother was the focus of their keen interest because she was an unaccompanied female. Mrs. Cameron, in her modest Victorian shirtwaist that reached up to her neck, clearly wasn't a prostitute—because women in that trade reddened their cheeks and wore dresses with plunging necklines. "I realized then it was because she was very beautiful," Dolly recalled many decades later.

If Mrs. Cameron was a novel sight to the Chinese men, the Chinese men were an unusual sight to the Cameron children, who'd grown up on sheep ranches in Scotland and New Zealand. The men shaved their foreheads and wore their hair plaited in a single long braid. The workers wore dark caps, loose cotton black pants, and jackets, while merchants wore more formal robes known as *changshan*. The scene of the Chinese men huddled under their umbrellas on their way to work that rainy Christmas day fascinated Dolly.

What she glimpsed in the streets reflected the mass migration of the Chinese to *dai fou*, or what they also called *Gum Saan* ("Gold Mountain"). By the time the Camerons arrived in San Francisco in 1872, there were more than twelve thousand Chinese people living in the city, mostly squeezed into the eight-square-block area bordered by Sacramento, Stockton, Kearny, and Pacific Streets. Chinatown's crowded conditions and poor sanitation had started to draw the attention of the city's top health official, who reported that year that the death rate among San Francisco's Chinese residents was nearly double that of the rest of the city.

When the transcontinental railroad was completed in 1869, many Chinese returned to San Francisco. They found work as cigar makers, in laundries and shoe factories, and as servants to wealthy San Franciscans. The nation's economy slumped in those postbellum years, and jobs in the city were scarce, so some frustrated whites turned against the city's newest immigrant group, the Chinese. The result was a surge in violence toward Chinatown's residents.

Dolly's family brushed up against one small sign of the city's mounting resentment during their short stay. The American Exchange Hotel proudly advertised its policy of employing only "free white labor." That meant that although Chinese men worked throughout the neighborhood, the American Exchange refused to hire them.

3

Reveille Cry

A spirited rivalry arose between missionaries to win over "heathen souls." Presbyterians, who two decades earlier had established the first Christian congregation for Asians in America on Chinatown's Stockton Street, were paying close attention to what the Methodists were doing in terms of proselytizing among the Chinese a few blocks away.

The leaders of the two Christian denominations wrote letters to their home offices, tallying up how many Chinese they'd each baptized. "Our hearts too are cheered by the application of 12 for baptism," wrote one Presbyterian missionary to his supervisor in Philadelphia in 1873. For both groups, San Francisco's Chinese "slave girls" became a new target for conversion.

Otis Gibson, the Methodist minister who had helped Jin Ho, became an outspoken advocate for the Chinese. Although a gifted linguist who'd spent a decade in a Mandarin-speaking town near Shanghai before moving to San Francisco in 1868, he nonetheless required several years to teach himself Cantonese and thus directly minister to California's Chinese immigrants, who mostly came from Guangdong, a province in southern China. As one of the few white defenders of the Chinese, Gibson rose to prominence in the 1870s by founding Sunday schools across the state in hope of converting the Chinese to Christianity.

He learned of the horrifying deaths of eighteen Chinese men in what was then the sleepy pueblo of Los Angeles—a shocking pream-

Sacramento Street in San Francisco's Chinatown, 1866.

ble to the waves of anti-Chinese violence that would soon reach San Francisco.

Gibson turned his skills as a writer and impassioned orator to defending the Chinese. Politicians, editors, and clergymen continued to blame Chinese immigrants for spreading disease and corruption. In March 1873, Gibson delivered a fiery defense of the Chinese in San Francisco's Platt's Hall. He decried what he saw every day in his work, including sex trafficking. "Chinese women are brought here as slaves, and for vilest purposes, and are daily bought and sold in this city." He denounced what he called an "abominable traffic" and "festering sore."

Thundering his outrage over San Francisco officials' complicity in the city's slave trade, his critique of societal hypocrisy echoed the arguments made by abolitionists in the years leading up to the Civil War. And like the abolitionists in Britain who brought about the end of slavery in that country decades before it ended in the United States, many American antislavery activists were motivated by their religious beliefs. For the renegade Gibson, a father of two, the enslavement of Chinese women outraged both his conscience and his sense of justice.

BY MARCH 25, 1873, the fog that had blanketed San Francisco off and on for months lifted. The skies were clear and the westerly winds gentle. A group of women made their way past Union Square's formal paths and palms to a meeting at the Calvary Presbyterian Church.

Located in a fashionable residential district about six blocks from Chinatown, Calvary Presbyterian had a reputation for civic activism. The church's first pastor, the Reverend William Anderson Scott, spoke out against local vigilante groups at the start of the Civil War and had included the Confederate president, Jefferson Davis, the Union's nemesis, in his public prayers. Both instances had provoked the pastor's local critics to hang him in effigy.

Equally outspoken pastors came and went over the following decade. Calvary Presbyterian and other churches became fertile ground for the first shoots of a new social movement. This time the cause was sex slavery. The churchwomen were gathering to hear a missionary named Emily Gulick talk about human bondage and the plight of

Chinese girls who were not valued by their parents as much as boys and were sometimes sold into prostitution.

A decade earlier, Gulick had been working as a missionary in Hong Kong when she met and married her husband, John Gulick, a member of a prominent missionary family from Hawaii. On their return to China after a yearlong leave in London, stormy weather in 1873 forced them to lay over in San Francisco. Gulick used the unexpected stop to share her stories from China.

When the small, dark-haired Emily Gulick rose to speak in the lecture hall, she looked out onto a crowd made up mostly of women in ankle-length gowns and shawls. As soon as she finished, most of her audience hurried for the exits, perhaps unsettled by her talk and discomfited by a subject that many Protestant churches did not discuss. They "silently stole away," wrote one of the eight women in the audience who stayed, quoting a popular poem by Henry Wadsworth Longfellow.

But Gulick's descriptions of conditions in China, which included famine and the sale of daughters by impoverished parents, so moved the few women who remained that they decided to form the Woman's Foreign Missionary Society, to support an orphanage and school in Shanghai.

These San Francisco women were not alone in their desire to connect with the Chinese. They were part of a swelling of Christian evangelism known as the Second Great Awakening. For Victorian-era women who did not have the right to vote and possessed almost no political or economic power outside the home, this movement held special appeal. It was one of the few areas where they could wield influence.

Women's missionary societies sprouted up throughout America, offering their members ways to expand their experience and address social problems in their communities. Devout women pushed for temperance in the consumption of alcohol. They also campaigned against prostitution and made headlines by bursting into brothels to hold prayer meetings.

San Francisco was a broad target for reformers of all types. Newly arrived Christian women saw an opportunity to help civilize the most vice-ridden city in the West by appealing to what the writer Bret Harte satirically called the "heathen Chinee"—both to stop this immigrant group from being abused and to find potential converts to Christianity.

THE WIVES OF PRESBYTERIAN MISSIONARIES, working alongside their husbands, began organizing to open a second rescue home for Chinese women in San Francisco. Among them was Samantha Condit, the new bride of one of two Presbyterian missionaries assigned to Chinatown. She and her husband lived in a dilapidated Mission House located in Chinatown, an area most privileged San Franciscans did their best to avoid.

Defying convention, Condit sought out Chinese women on the street and in the schoolroom and offered them sewing classes. She also invited them into her home before accompanying them to a church service. "They were first entertained socially in our house then a service held for them in the chapel," wrote her husband to his supervisor. "The bitterness not shown here against the Chinese is I believe working for good." By reaching out to Chinese prostitutes, Condit took on a social problem that many of her contemporaries thought was hopeless, distasteful, and potentially a liability to one's own social standing.

Gibson called the effort to help Chinese women, who were the most scorned and powerless people in the city, "a Herculean and almost hopeless task." Few San Franciscans were sympathetic to the plight of the Chinese, although many of the city's wealthier families employed Chinese servants. "So Christianity gathered up her skirts and passed by the women's plight," as Gibson wrote.

Wives of current or former missionaries were the exception. One of the women who attended that first meeting in March 1873 was Caroline Hubbell Cole, a wealthy woman from Sacramento who had once lived in China with her missionary husband. A passionate advocate for girls' education who had started a school for girls in Ningbo, in the eastern Chinese province of Zhejiang, Cole was deeply affected by an article in the influential California magazine *The Overland Monthly* on the plight of Chinese girls in San Francisco. She moved to the city in the late 1860s with her son and adopted Chinese daughter and began teaching the girls under the auspices of the Presbyterian Mission.

After visiting some of her Chinese students in the tenements where they lived, Cole reported to Gibson and others that there were probably other young Chinese women who would escape their circumstances if only they knew where to go.

About two weeks after the gathering at Calvary Presbyterian, Samantha Condit, Emily Gulick, and Caroline Cole met at the modest Presbyterian Mission House on Stockton Street, where they established a California branch of the Woman's Foreign Missionary Society. It was an offshoot of a Presbyterian women's organization headquartered in Philadelphia that had begun three years earlier to support missionaries in foreign countries.

But doubts about their decision to support a project in distant Shanghai soon crept in. And after becoming more aware of the plight of Chinese girls in San Francisco, they began questioning whether they'd chosen the right group to try to help.

At a meeting on a bleak day in December 1873, they decided to pray about it after singing "My Faith Looks Up to Thee."

> *While life's dark maze I tread*
> *And griefs around me spread,*
> *Be Thou my Guide.*

One latecomer to the prayer meeting gave voice to their thoughts. She motioned that the group change its focus from distant China. "I move that we work for the Chinese here, and that all our efforts be directed to the establishment of a Chinese home in San Francisco," she said. Her fellow Presbyterians passed the motion. Following the lead of the Methodists, the Woman's Foreign Missionary Society shifted its focus to Chinese girls and women in San Francisco.

"A *Home* is the reveille cry for our Society," wrote Condit, acting as the young group's secretary, in the organization's first annual report. "This Home is designed to be a refuge for Chinese women who may desire to lead lives of respectability and usefulness. It is also expected to furnish protection for such as may be rescued from a life of sin."

By directing their efforts toward Chinese women who were their neighbors in San Francisco, these churchwomen were at the cusp of a new movement. Until then, most missionaries went to foreign countries to try to win converts to Christianity, sometimes using cruel and insensitive methods such as forbidding potential converts to speak in their own language and teaching the inferiority of native culture. The idea of aiding recent immigrants in their own cities was just starting to take hold among women's groups in an early expression of feminism, or what they described as "woman's work for women."

4

"No Ordinary Person"

One of San Francisco's most infamous residents of the 1870s was known by several different names, including Achoy, Atoy, or Ah Toy. She was one of a handful of Chinese prostitutes who chose her profession and, for more than two decades, successfully navigated her way through San Francisco's corrupt legal system without the help of missionaries. She was renowned for her tall stature, willow-green pantaloons, and tiny bound feet, the mark of an upper-class Chinese woman.

Ah Toy had arrived in San Francisco from Hong Kong just after the 1848 gold rush. She was twenty-one. And like the vast majority of French, Mexican, Peruvian, and Chinese women who had made their way to the frontier city as prostitutes at that time, she was there in the hope of wrangling her share of the new wealth dug up by lucky miners. She began by working as a *loungei*, a vulgar Chinese term that means "woman always holding her legs up." She plied her trade in a small lean-to in an alley off Clay Street, near what would become the heart of Chinatown. She was one of the few Chinese women in the city then, and men would gather outside her tiny shack.

Almost as soon as she arrived, she sought justice through the legal system. In 1849, she appeared in court to lodge a complaint against two of her customers for cheating her out of one ounce of gold dust (worth about $16 at the time, or about $485 in today's dollars). Ah Toy was offering a sort of peep show, where the men could look at her naked body and see for themselves if the rumors were true that Chinese

A prostitute in San Francisco's Chinatown, standing in the doorway of a brothel.

women were anatomically different from white women. Some miners arriving in San Francisco on boats from Sacramento were so eager to glimpse the Chinese beauty that they'd run from the wharves to Clay Street "to gaze upon the countenance of the charming Ah Toy." More than a few of those same eager men dropped brass fittings into her bowl instead of gold dust, in an attempt to cheat her. Ah Toy had two of them arrested and brought her complaint before a judge.

Her appearance in court caused almost as much of a stir as her allegations. She stood before the judge wearing an apricot satin jacket, chartreuse pantaloons, and colorful socks covering her tiny feet. She'd arranged her dark hair in a discreet bun and patted her skin with rice powder, making it exceptionally white. When the judge asked her to detail her charges, she left the courtroom briefly and returned with a porcelain bowl filled to the brim with brass shavings. Her evidence provoked laughter, until she started pointing at other men in the court-room who she claimed had also cheated her. The judge ruled against her.

Such legal action brought her scorn. *The Annals of San Francisco*, a history of the city first published in 1855, stated that within a few years of her arrival "every body knew that famous or infamous char-acter, who was alternately the laughing-stock and the plague of the place."

In 1851, a man claiming to be her husband in Hong Kong attempted to have her sent back to China. An affidavit in the case stated that "Atoy" had "immigrated to this country for the purpose of bettering her condition; and that she is anxious to make California her permanent home, and not to return to China." This time the judge, who also heard testimony of death threats against her, ruled in her favor, requiring her adversaries to post hefty bonds.

Not long after the threats to her life and attempted deportation, Ah Toy showed up in court again—"blooming with youth, beauty and rouge" and "wearing a daring bonnet and orange-colored shawl"—this time claiming that three men had stolen a diamond brooch worth $300 from her.

The reporter relayed the questioning of Ah Toy's Chinese inter-preter in the mocking, pidgin-English style of Bret Harte's infamous "heathen Chinee" story:

RECORDER: Do you know what it is to come into Court and testify?
ANSWER: Yes, a man steal Atoy's pin.
RECORDER: Could you be punished for telling a lie?
ANSWER: Yes, Atoy tell me three men come in, steal pin.
COUNSEL: Do you know the difference between good and bad?
ANSWER: Oh yes; some men good—some men bad—man stealy Atoy's
    pin be very bad.

The court then decided the interpreter didn't understand English well enough to serve as Ah Toy's translator, so it sent for another one. The reporter noted that "Miss Atoy appeared to be highly incensed at this conclusion. . . . [Her] voice rose to so high a pitch that even the clerk, who is usually very cool under such circumstances, was considerably frightened."

Ah Toy went on a tirade that expanded to include what she considered "the corruption in the legal profession generally." The judge didn't appear to take offense. The new interpreter arrived and swore to tell the truth. The trial lasted for several days, and ultimately Ah Toy recovered her pin after the thieves offered to sell it to a jeweler.

She continued to appear in courtrooms both as a defendant and as a plaintiff. By one tally, she showed up in court at least fifty times during her first three years in San Francisco. Clearly, she was a feisty and self-assured businesswoman. Yet her time in the city also involved a great deal of suffering. She had been publicly mocked, stolen from, and treated as if she were not human. Her emotional pain from these experiences was so deep that within six years of arriving, she attempted suicide.

She survived that episode and, within a few years, was able to parlay her earnings into the capital necessary to start her own brothel. *The Annals of San Francisco* attributed the rise in the number of Chinese prostitutes in the city to Ah Toy's influence, decrying these women as "the most indecent and shameless part of the population" and condemning the main street of Chinatown, then called Dupont Street and later renamed Grant Avenue, as "thickly peopled with these vile creatures." Eventually, she became both a madam and an importer of Chinese prostitutes, shrewdly taking as a lover a man named John A. Clark who headed a special police patrol charged with investigating brothels.

She joined eighteen other women who were counted as brothel owners in San Francisco and was part of a thriving form of enterprise in the city that employed thousands of women of all ethnicities. The census for 1870 included prostitution as an occupation; it was not only legal but one of the few kinds of work, alongside being teachers, laundresses, and seamstresses, open to women at that time.

Ah Toy's public life as a madam came to an end just as a campaign against what would be called "yellow slavery" was in its infancy. Less than two years before the church ladies gathered in March 1873, determined to try to rescue Chinese women from forced prostitution, Ah Toy retired from the business. According to a two-sentence newspaper item in October 1871, Ah Toy married a man named One Ho in San Jose. Far from Clay Street, she lived a long life, dying in 1928, just before her hundredth birthday.

IN THE SPRING OF 1873, as the Presbyterian churchwomen were forming their missionary society, the Cameron family had reunited and was living about 150 miles southeast of San Francisco, on a ranch in the San Joaquin valley. Allan Cameron, Dolly's father, had grown up in a Scottish sheep-farming family and had joined a wave of Scots who left the country in the nineteenth century to seek opportunities elsewhere. In Allan's case, he had first immigrated to New Zealand before moving to the United States.

By his late twenties, Allan Cameron was enough of a catch to attract the beautiful Isabella MacKenzie, a member of an ancient clan of Highland Scots who lived near Inverness. Family lore has it that the young Allan used to visit the Royal Hotel in the town of Dingwall, which the MacKenzie family had long owned. There he met Isabella as a child, twenty-one years younger than he was. Allan used to tease Isabella that he would marry her when she grew up. He kept his promise.

Allan and Isabella married in the summer of 1853, when she was eighteen and he forty. When Isabella tied herself to Allan, he was a wealthy man who owned Dreim Farm, a sheep ranch that was part of a Highfield estate north of Inverness in the parish of Urray. By the early 1860s, the couple had four children.

A financial crisis struck the family after Allan, along with other members of the Cameron clan, invested in a business that failed. In response to these hard times, Allan boarded a schooner in Glasgow and sailed to New Zealand, where he worked as the manager of a large sheep station near Clydevale, about thirty miles inland from Molyneux Bay. The rest of the family soon joined him. In 1869, when Dolly was born, she was the only member of her immediate family not born in Scotland.

Life in New Zealand brought certain deprivations. They'd left behind in Scotland a large group of aunts and cousins who had helped care for the older Cameron children, so Dolly's care often fell to her siblings. Sister Jessie and brother Allan, charged with watching over the baby, sometimes grew bored with the job, especially given the more exciting adventures to be had. So they came up with an unorthodox solution to keep Dolly in one place.

"There weren't any roaming dangers in the way of people or animals or snakes—at least around the sheep station in New Zealand," wrote Dolly's niece, many years later, "so the children sometimes tied their baby sister with a long *manuka* rope [a kind of rope made from a native New Zealand plant] while they went about their business."

Not long after Dolly's second birthday, her father headed to California alone to try his luck, taking with him a special breed of sheep from New Zealand. He hoped to restore his family's financial stability by raising sheep that produced wool superior to the kind produced by California's predominant herds. His success would depend on the quality of the pasturelands where his sheep would graze and his skill in shearing them and marketing their wool. The family joined him, hopes high.

The ranch house where the Camerons lived at Berenda was stark, but the family found beauty in their surroundings. On clear days, they could see the peaks of the Sierra Nevada to the east, and antelope would sometimes graze in the fields nearby. In the spring, the children picked baby blue eyes and other wildflowers in the meadows. To make the hours pass more quickly in this isolated setting, they recited the works of Henry Wadsworth Longfellow, the American poet known for *The Song of Hiawatha* who was then at the height of his popularity.

But life in California also presented new challenges. The Central Valley, which was stiflingly hot in the summer and miserably cold in the winter, was a world away from both the cool Scottish Highlands and the rainy Molyneux Bay. The Camerons' ranch at Berenda was isolated, surrounded by hundreds of acres of open grassland. They had a single servant—a Chinese cook called Jim. When the younger Allan got an abscessed tooth, he had to ride his horse twenty miles to the nearest dentist, who yanked it out. He then turned back, nearly reaching home before fainting from the pain and falling off his horse. He eventually climbed back into his saddle and rode back to his family.

More serious problems had begun almost as soon as Isabella and the children joined Allan on the sheep ranch. Not only was the United States struggling from a severe economic downturn in 1873, triggered by banking failures that led to a stock market collapse, but a drought had scorched California's Central Valley for two years in a row, putting strain on ranchers like Cameron who relied on water and available grasses for their sheep. Sheep rustlers also targeted the herd managed by the Camerons. When Allan Cameron discovered the sheep were gone, he set off alone to follow the gang of men who'd stolen them.

By the time he tracked them down, the rustlers had slit the throats of most of the sheep and thrown their carcasses into a stream, perhaps to dissuade the rancher from following them. This was during the winter months, a time when rains turned dry ravines into raging streams. Drenched in the pursuit, Allan developed a bad case of pneumonia from which he never fully recovered. He ended up selling his remaining sheep at a steep discount of fifty cents a head. The failure took a permanent toll on the health and spirits of the Cameron patriarch.

Dolly's mother also suffered. She'd long experienced debilitating migraines but faced a far more serious health crisis after her appendix burst while visiting the San Francisco Bay Area to arrange the wedding of her daughter Helen.

Isabella had hoped to reverse the family's slide in fortunes by arranging a good match. But Helen balked at her mother's choice of a husband, the son of the wealthy Dutch consul who was more than twice her age. Amid this family drama, Isabella died suddenly, on May 23, 1874, in the city where she had landed with her children just seventeen months before. She was only forty, and Dolly had not yet celebrated her fifth birthday.

The family's grief was deep and lasting. Isabella's death forced the two eldest daughters, Annie and Helen, then both in their late teens, to help raise their three younger siblings, as well as to keep house for their father, brother, and sisters. Helen never did marry the groom her late mother had chosen for her. The loss of Isabella left her girls vulnerable, because it was a Victorian mother's job to guide her daughters into good marriages as they came of age. The five Cameron sisters in America were forced to rely on each other instead, knitting them even more closely together.

The extended Cameron clan mourned. Isabella's father in Scotland was bereft after Dolly's oldest sister, Annie, wrote him with the news. "My dear Isabella was my first born," wrote Dolly's grandfather Donald MacKenzie from his home in Dingwall in a July 1874 letter two months after his daughter Isabella's death.

> I loved her with more than ordinary parental affection. Perhaps too much so, and is now made to suffer for my idolatry; but your Mother was no ordinary person possessed of no ordinary talents and active courage to go through with her places, and a warm heart full of love and affection.

God "must have some important design to bring about such sore affliction on your family," MacKenzie continued, expressing a faith rooted in Scottish Presbyterianism, with its emphasis on predeterminism, the belief that all events are determined in advance. "He can bring good out of apparent evil. And this may be the method He took to bring some of you into close union with Himself."

Signing his letter as "Affectionate Grandpapa," the grief-stricken Donald MacKenzie asked after his namesake, Donaldina, whom he had never met: "And tell what is little Dolly like and how old is she?"

Dolly, the youngest of Allan and Isabella's seven offspring, had become motherless at the age most children start to read. She would never meet the "Grandpapa" Donald with whom she shared a name. But, as he expressed with a sense of hope in his letter, she would, indeed, come into "close union" with her God and remain there all her life.

＊⇒ 5 ⇐＊

Victorian Compromise

B itter racial prejudice against the Chinese had seeped into almost
every aspect of the city's life by the 1870s, so the Presbyterians' project to create a safe house for women in Chinatown faced
opposition almost immediately. When Mrs. Condit and her cohort
approached a potential donor—a woman active in other kinds of
church work—to ask for cast-off clothing or other small gifts, the
answer stunned them with its heartlessness: "I will give nothing for
such depraved women. I would not be sorry if all the Chinese women
were placed in a pile and burned."

This attitude reflected the fear and mounting anger toward the
Chinese on the part of many white San Franciscans—feelings sharp-
ened by the hard economic times. By the mid-1870s, the city had
passed a series of ordinances to harass the Chinese. A Sidewalk Ordinance banned the traditional method they used to carry vegetables
and laundry—on a pole. A Cubic Foot Ordinance required at least
five hundred cubic feet of air per person in a residence—a response
to crowded Chinatown tenements. A Queue, or Pigtail, Ordinance
required the shaving of the heads of jailed Chinese prisoners, which
meant cutting off the men's long braids.

The city also passed laws banning Chinese immigrants from working for federal, state, and local governments; from testifying in court;
and from educating their children in local public schools. Although
Chinese plaintiffs brought court challenges that succeeded in overturn-

Illustration of Bret Harte's popular poem "The Heathen Chinee," ca. 1870.

ing many of these laws, the ongoing barrage of rules and regulations amounted to a pattern of institutionalized harassment and racism.

As the economy tumbled downward, the mood toward this rapidly expanding group of immigrants darkened and turned violent. Chinese prostitution became a flash point. Anti-Chinese agitators blamed Chinese prostitutes for spreading disease and encouraging immorality. One of the key legal test cases aimed at barring the entry of Chinese prostitutes to the United States started just as the Presbyterian churchwomen were scrambling to raise money for their rescue home.

The case began in August 1874, when a Pacific Mail steamship arrived in San Francisco with eighty-nine Chinese women on board. An immigration official decided that twenty-two of the women were coming to the city for "immoral purposes" and ordered the steamship company to pay a bond of $500 in gold per woman. The company refused. The captain, John H. Freeman, was ordered to hold the twenty-two women on the ship until the issue could be resolved. One of those women was Chy Lung.

A Chinese man allegedly involved in procuring the women petitioned the court for a writ of habeas corpus, arguing that they had been illegally detained. The case wound its way through the courts over the next two years. Eventually, it reached the U.S. Supreme Court, becoming the first suit involving a Chinese litigant to be heard there. *Chy Lung v. Freeman* is now better known as the case of the "22 Lewd Chinese Women."

The Supreme Court sided with Chy Lung and the other women, ruling that Congress, not the states, had the power to regulate immigration and ordering the women to be released. But it was a Pyrrhic victory: a year before the Supreme Court decided the case, Congress had passed the Page Act, barring Chinese, Japanese, and Mongolian prostitutes, as well as contract laborers and felons, from entering the country. Just as Presbyterian women in San Francisco were organizing to create a refuge for Chinese women, Congress, the courts, and San Francisco city officials were trying to kick or keep them out.

BY SEPTEMBER 1874, the churchwomen had scraped together enough in donations to rent a tiny apartment on the edge of Chinatown, just below Nob Hill. They reached out to other middle- and upper-middle-class women who might be sympathetic to their cause. One early supporter was Phoebe Apperson Hearst, the wife of the mining baron George Hearst and mother of William Randolph Hearst, who attended a Presbyterian Sunday school as a boy.

Donors gave to the home for all sorts of reasons—not all purely charitable. More than a few gave out of an attempt at social climbing rather than a sense of social justice. Others, as newcomers to the San Francisco Bay Area, hoped to join a group of like-minded women. One even confessed to giving money because she was swayed by the attractive dress of the woman who asked her to donate, admitting, "I did not feel so much interest in those horrid heathen, but her lovely cap of lace and lavender just beguiled me into giving her some gold."

Often, the donations were domestic and modest. Mrs. Van Pelt gave the home a cake dish and a fruit dish. Mrs. J. G. Bray gave the home boxes of apples, pears, and a variety of dried fruits. Miss E. Williams gave the home an oil painting of a bouquet of flowers, which was sold for $25. Mrs. Henry Loomis gave two vases. The San Francisco–based jeweler Shreve & Co. donated half a dozen teaspoons, while the fashionable department store City of Paris gave the home fifteen yards of muslin. To launder the clothes and other items they'd make out of that fabric, a Chinese donor provided soap, starch, and bluing, an early form of fabric brightener.

The rented quarters were cramped. Over the winter, thirteen Chinese women squeezed into the second-floor apartment. They became so uncomfortable that the board decided to rent additional rooms in the same building. The many comings and goings proved bothersome to the Chinese women and their white fellow tenants. So the churchwomen began a search for a larger home and managed to line up the financing to win approval from their board's parent society in Philadelphia.

One day, the group paid a visit to a twenty-five-room boarding-house they hoped to purchase on Sacramento Street. A forceful woman named Pauline Robbins led the group and insisted on being allowed to enter the rooms to see what they would be buying, but a female tenant, realizing that she could face eviction so that these do-gooders could house Chinese prostitutes, expressed her outrage at them. The angry woman "said many insulting things to me," Robbins later wrote. "With no provocation, she spit in my face."

Being spat upon by an angry, soon-to-be-evicted tenant was just the start of their troubles. The boardinghouse at 933 Sacramento Street was run by Anna A. Key Turner, a daughter of Francis Scott Key, the composer of "The Star-Spangled Banner." For a time, 933 Sacramento had been considered one of the most elegant lodging places in the city. "You had to go up a long flight of stairs to get in," one visitor quipped, "and you had to go over a longer bill to get out."

Its location was just a few blocks east of Nob Hill, where the railroad and silver magnates were starting to build their palaces. But a few blocks farther east was where Chinatown began. By 1874, that block of Sacramento Street was no longer considered so fashionable, because the arrival of the Chinese drove wealthier whites block by block up the hill and beyond to other neighborhoods.

After the purchase of the large building was complete, the churchwomen evicted the people who were still living there. The tenants were mostly Catholics, and their forced moves sparked an outcry and threats "by a mob." Unemployment was soaring among working-class Irish Catholics in the 1870s and some formed gangs—first giving rise in San Francisco and then elsewhere to the term "hoodlums." Like the Chinese, the Irish had come to San Francisco looking for jobs after the completion of the transcontinental railroad. The evictions infuriated the neighbors, and some threatened to tear the building down.

As tensions rose between Irish Catholics and the Chinese, the churchwomen quickly decided against revealing their plans for the building to the Irish workmen they'd hired to renovate it, fearing they'd quit if they knew the building was intending to shelter Chinese women.

Almost everything needed fixing: the doorknobs, hinges, wallpaper, floors, and especially the kitchen. But there was little money for renovations. One of the male pastors, who'd balked at the project from the beginning, cautioned the women not to spend more than they had on hand. So they "hustled around" to raise funds, as one of the women later wrote. Their fears regarding the workmen were justified, at least in one instance. They hired two men to move furniture into the house.

One of them took a look at the Chinese girls and women starting to move in. "I can't stand this!" he said, and quit on the spot.

The church's Philadelphia headquarters was only slightly more helpful: it sent two staffers to Sacramento Street, but they were neither young nor in robust health. That posed a problem, because their duties required them to manage residents who were young, sometimes angry, and often traumatized. They served the Chinese girls and young women meals of American food, pouring them coffee rather than tea. The result? "They were unhappy and rebelled," wrote Robbins. Efforts to pacify them "were quite tragic."

Discipline at the home soon collapsed. Miss Cummings, one of the staffers from Philadelphia, had attempted to drag a girl up the stairs: the resisting girl bit her on the arm. Furious, Cummings threatened to quit unless the girl was removed from the home. In Robbins's view, neither Cummings nor her fellow staffer was fit for the job: "They had attempted a most difficult work—to tame barbarians," she wrote, perhaps unaware of the irony that Chinese in the nineteenth century referred to Caucasians and other foreigners as "barbarians" as well. Both missionaries quit, and the project itself teetered on the edge of collapsing.

Robbins's racist views of "barbarians" notwithstanding, she was determined to help Chinese women. She and her husband moved into the home themselves to try to restore order, bringing their own housekeeper with them. Soon, a widowed female missionary woman returning from China who spoke fluent Chinese joined the Robbinses, bringing with her a deeper understanding of the residents' preferences for food and other customs. Robbins and her husband moved out after a time, but the experience took a steep emotional toll: Robbins spent six months in a sanitorium near Rochester, New York, to restore her "exhausted nerves."

BUT HER FELLOW PRESBYTERIAN women persisted, despite roadblocks thrown up by churchmen. Some men refused to support the project at their churches, while others kept what one called "a distant reserve." The issue came to a head at a meeting of Presbyterian

Church leaders in the Bay Area; some men showed their disregard for the women's project by talking loudly during their formal presentation to the group. One church father flatly refused to come to hear the presentation because he could not "countenance women doing such things." Two ministers grew so impatient with the women's talk that they accused them of wasting time and threatened to stage a public row if they continued.

In the face of these displays of impatience and disrespect, the women refused to be bullied into cutting short their prepared remarks. They carried on as planned and detailed their lofty goals and logistical plans to the male church leaders. Ultimately, they won support.

Gaining acceptance inside the church was one thing, but outside was another. On the day that the women finally dedicated the refurbished home, they received a threat of arson. To their relief, the worst thing that happened that rainy day was a smashed window. "We feared trouble, as threats had been made to burn it down," wrote Samantha Condit, "but God was our help, and nothing worse occurred than the breaking of glass by a rude boy."

The women were acutely aware of the hostility they faced in pursuing a charity project that was radically out of step with their contemporaries' disdain for the Chinese. Yet, to their apparent surprise, they found that the Chinese women they sought to help sometimes welcomed biblical teachings. "Does it not seem marvelous that a people so ready to be taught and so anxious to hear the gospel be so persecuted?" Samantha Condit wondered.

Even so, some of San Francisco's politicians balked at having wives and daughters linked to a cause they feared would stain or reduce their own standing. Despite San Francisco's reputation as the most freewheeling of western cities and one whose recent history widely embraced and indeed celebrated prostitution and other forms of vice, some civic leaders had started to change their attitudes by the 1870s. That change coincided with the arrival of more middle-class women and families.

The Protestant churchwomen's project flew in the face of a hypocritical convention of the time politely referred to as the Victorian Compromise—the idea that police and politicians tolerated vice as long as it did not touch or otherwise intrude on ordinary family life.

While city authorities through the 1870s generally overlooked the thriving business between white prostitutes and their customers, Chinese prostitution was seen as another thing altogether. The police regularly staged crackdowns on Chinese brothels, which they blamed for outbreaks of syphilis and other venereal diseases. But this involvement by middle- and upper-class women complicated the moral equations even further.

To think that their own wives and daughters might be prowling through the back alleys of Chinatown, attempting rescues by climbing ladders and pushing through crowded tenements, was more than some Victorian-era husbands and fathers could stand. After all, who might these naive do-gooders find in the Chinese prostitutes' beds?

6

Inked Thumbprints

During state hearings on Chinese immigration in San Francisco in the spring of 1876, a police clerk presented what amounted to a bill of sale for a woman named Ah Ho for $630. The contract, translated from Chinese into English, was entered into the court transcript as evidence: "Ah Ho distinctly agrees to give her body to Mr. Yee for service of prostitution for a term of four years," after which time she would "be her own master." Because most of the women being sold were illiterate, they left their thumbprints at the bottom of such documents.

Criminal tongs—particularly the Suey Sing Tong and Hip Yee Tong—controlled the trafficking of most of the Chinese women intended for prostitution. The tongs entered into formal contracts with the women, who stated that they agreed to sell their bodies for a period of three or four years, after which they would be free. If legally challenged, tong members could present these contracts as evidence that the women had become prostitutes of their own free will. In fact, many, if not most, were forced into the sex trade.

The brutal reality was that few of the women trafficked into the United States under these agreements lived long enough to win their freedom, succumbing instead to disease, violence, and poverty. "In the sale of these girls, there is always a written contract, or a bill of sale, such as there would be in the sale of any dumb brute," wrote the Reverend Ira Condit, husband of the Mission Home co-founder Samantha Condit, alongside a reproduction of one of these contracts. "The

Drawing by H. A. Rogers of the anti-Chinese sandlot riots led by Denis Kearney of the Workingmen's Party in 1877.

one exhibited here has the impress of the slave-girl's inked finger. The original is sometimes sealed in blood."

Condit's fellow clergyman Otis Gibson also detailed the role of criminal tongs in prostitution, noting that these organizations often used the American courts to protect their human property. As in the case of the "22 Lewd Chinese Women," the criminal tongs did this by demanding that officials produce a writ of habeas corpus, to justify holding the women in custody. For prostitutes who attempted to flee, the tongs hired lawyers who'd arrange to have them arrested on trumped-up charges and then have them released into their custody. "The women, as a general thing, are slaves. They are bought or stolen in China and brought here," said Gibson.

Violence surrounded the trafficking in women, beginning from the moment they were purchased or kidnapped in China and continuing through their years of forced prostitution in San Francisco. In a hearing in 1876 on immigration, a Chinese interpreter, Ben Wong, named several traffickers and testified that they would put murder contracts on women who attempted to escape as well as on the people who tried to aid them. The importers posted these contracts on the walls of buildings on Jackson Street for everyone to see. Indeed, Wong told the court he'd seen a contract on his own life posted on a wall the day before his testimony. From the perspective of the police, violence was one of the things that distinguished prostitution in Chinatown from the thriving flesh trade in other parts of the city. This led to calls for more policing in the quarter.

Much of the tong violence that flared up in San Francisco's Chinatown during the last decades of the nineteenth century involved women. In 1875, a "tong war" erupted over a prostitute, Xijiao, also known as the Golden Peach. It began near Ross Alley, where a tong member stabbed another man vying for Xijiao's attentions. The violence quickly escalated. After midnight on a spring evening, two dozen members of the Suey Sing Tong faced off against twenty-five members of an opposing criminal gang, the Kwong Dock Tong. Both sides carried knives, hatchets, and firearms. Soon after the fighting sparked by the rivalry for the woman began, the police arrived, but not before four tong members died and twelve others were wounded.

Such tong violence tore deep divisions in San Francisco's Chinese community. Leaders of the Six Companies sensed the rising tide of anti-Chinese feeling and sought to combat it by taking a public stand against trafficking and prostitution. Tens of thousands of white San Franciscans gathered during the 1870s to rally against the Chinese, whom they accused of stealing jobs and spreading immorality. The Six Companies wrote a letter to the newly elected president, Ulysses S. Grant, countering the many charges brought against them at the rallies and, at the same time, implicating white officials and customers in the Chinese sex slavery trade: "Quite a number of Chinese prostitutes have been brought to this country by unprincipled Chinamen, but these, at first, were brought from China at the instigation and for the gratification of white men. And, even at the present time, it is commonly reported that a part of the proceeds of this villainous traffic goes to enrich a certain class of men belonging to this Honorable nation."

The letter went on to describe how Chinese merchants had tried to send prostitutes back to China and succeeded to the extent of purchasing them tickets and boarding them on an outgoing steamer. But their plan was stymied by a white lawyer working for Chinese traffickers who, aided by police officers, blocked their departure by producing a writ of habeas corpus. "If officers would refuse bribes, then unprincipled Chinamen could no longer purchase immunity from the punishment of their crimes," the letter from the Six Companies stated.

Despite this impassioned and well-reasoned appeal, the Six Companies' letter to President Grant failed to halt either escalating anti-Chinese violence or the slave traffic. In California, where the vast majority of Chinese immigrants lived, the continuing economic downturn in the state led to long lines of unemployed men hoping to work for a dollar a day and a loaf of bread with a hunk of corned beef in it. Some of these workers began to turn their anger toward the Chinese, whom they accused of stealing their jobs. Tensions were building.

ONE NIGHT, in July 1877, a self-educated Irish immigrant named Denis Kearney called a meeting in a sandlot near what is now San Francisco's domed city hall. About six thousand men and women gathered in semidarkness as the new fuel-burning lamps at the speakers' stand sputtered and blew out unexpectedly. Someone pulled a fire alarm: rifle shots sounded, and the crowd exploded. A mob of about fifty men broke off from the crowd and rushed toward Chinatown, crying, "The Chinese must go!"

They stormed into a Chinese laundry, hurling a kerosene lamp against a wall and igniting a fire. Police tried to stop them but were beaten back. The mob then rampaged through the streets, targeting other Chinese businesses. At the intersection of California and Dupont Streets (now Grant Avenue), the mob reached a line of reserve police officers—the so-called specials that patrolled Chinatown. Wielding billy clubs, the officers cracked heads and spilled blood, dispersing the angry white agitators. Some flung stones at the Methodist Chinese mission house.

The next day, the city called for reinforcements. The navy dispatched two of its gunships from nearby Mare Island to the pier at the foot of Market Street. National Guardsmen arrived, as did a group of two hundred or so businessmen, who formed themselves into a so-called Committee of Safety. By nightfall, the rioting workingmen were pitted against militia and police. A fight erupted on Rincon Hill, with stones, pickaxes, and occasional gunfire. City officials and newspapers pleaded for federal help in restoring order to the city. Denis Kearney was arrested and charged with conspiracy to incite a riot. He soon got out of jail and helped form the Workingmen's Party, with an anti-Chinese platform, submitting a slate of candidates for city offices. His party played a role in electing a new mayor in 1878 who was sympathetic to its populist views, but Kearney himself soon faded from the city's political scene.

AMID THE GUNSHOTS, the stench of burning laundries, and the sounds of shattering glass, a few moments of grace occurred as the Presbyterian churchwomen continued to offer refuge to Chinese women. One was the first wedding to be held at the home, which took place on a Saturday in mid-April 1878. The bride was Ah Fah, one of the first residents of the Mission Home, and her groom was a Chinese Christian man named Ng Noy, who worked as a servant in a private residence. Ah Fah's owners had locked her in a dark room for six weeks after she'd tried to run away. When she learned she was about to be sold for $650, she tried to escape again, running to the missionaries because "they were Jesus people and do not sell girls."

About two years after her arrival at the home, the marriage ceremony was conducted in Chinese by a Presbyterian missionary and attended by the home's staffers and the couple's friends. In expressing the then widely held idea that civilizing values were best imparted through the family home, one of the white missionary guests wished the newly married couple well, trusting that their "future housekeeping" would "indeed be a home-keeping."

Overseeing the wedding was the Mission Home's new superintendent, Margaret Culbertson. Born in China and raised in rural New York state, Culbertson had traveled west to serve as governess to the children of a branch of the Mills family, the wealthy bankers who helped bankroll the mining industry during and after California's gold rush. She soon met the resolute Mary Ann Browne, an early supporter of the home, who spotted qualities in her that the home's other superintendents had lacked. Her instincts were correct, as it turned out, for Culbertson, with her kind eyes and her dark hair pulled back in a bun, was a good disciplinarian, an organized housekeeper, and someone who seemed to love her work.

When Culbertson first arrived, in May 1877, ten Chinese girls and women lived in the large brick house on Sacramento Street. It didn't take her long to transform it into a pleasant and orderly household, filled with fresh flowers and home baked cakes and cookies. As superintendent, she was responsible not only for deciding on duties and setting a schedule but also for bringing about the personal changes that the home's supporters hoped for: chief among which was to convert the home's residents, who'd often suffered terrible abuse, into pious Victorians.

A daily schedule was set to reinforce that goal. Known as "inmates" (as all residents of institutions including hospitals were referred to at that time), the Mission Home girls and women rose for 7:00 a.m. prayers, ate breakfast, spent the early morning hours doing housework, took classes in sewing and other subjects in the afternoon, ate dinner, prayed, and then turned the lights out.

Comings and goings from the home did interrupt the routine. Some of the residents left upon marrying; others returned to China.

Not all of them thrived. In one instance, Culbertson came downstairs an hour before morning prayers to find the body of a sixteen-year-old Chinese girl hanging by a rope from the banister. The teenager had lived in the home for three years after being rescued at the age of thirteen from a brothel in Chinatown. The girl had sometimes seemed melancholy, but that didn't seem to be unusual among the residents.

At the same time, "highbinders"—a nineteenth-century term used to describe first Irish and then also Chinese criminal gang members—regularly attempted to steal women back from the home. Occasional violence, constant pressure, and the intermittent threats Culbertson faced gradually undermined her health. But she had a natural aptitude for the legal wrangling her position required, and she frequently won custody from the courts of girls and women seeking shelter. It certainly helped that the Mission Home had strong ties to San Francisco's judiciary: the wife of Judge George Barstow, for example, was president of the Occidental Board from 1874 to 1877.

By the late 1880s, Culbertson was making regular courtroom appearances, sometimes accompanied by a young lawyer named Abraham Ruef (pronounced Roof), a San Francisco–born Jew of French ancestry who entered the University of California at Berkeley at the age of fourteen and graduated with honors after writing a senior thesis titled "Purity in Politics." He won admittance to the California bar in 1886, at the age of twenty-one. Abe, as he was widely known, was just starting his legal career when he began volunteering to represent the Mission Home in court.

In a typical case, Ruef successfully defended Culbertson's custody of an eleven-year-old girl who'd been purchased by a procurer for $500 and brought to San Francisco to be resold as chattel. Culbertson told the judge in the case that she had been offered a bribe for three times that amount—some $1,500—to give the girl back to the slave dealers. The young lawyer who wrote about "purity in politics," in this instance, prevailed.

7

The Celestial Quarter

In the decades following Culbertson's arrival at the Mission Home, small groups of white tourists, including middle-class women like herself, regularly visited the city's "celestial" quarter, a term used by Westerners during those years to refer to China, though the usage of the term "celestials" for the Chinese soon became pejorative.

After Commodore Perry sailed into Tokyo harbor in 1853, demanding that the formerly closed country open its ports to U.S. merchant ships, Western artists including Monet, Van Gogh, Cassatt, and Degas became transfixed by the Orient and depicted aspects of it on their canvases. Writers like Wilkie Collins and Rudyard Kipling soon followed suit, as did Arthur Sullivan and W. S. Gilbert in their famed comic opera *The Mikado*. Although Asian immigrants across the western United States were being violently persecuted and discriminated against, the culture of their home countries was a source of inspiration to many artists.

By the final decades of the century, the allure of Orientalism had also seized the imaginations of the American middle and upper-middle classes, influencing architecture, literature, music, and the visual arts. The resourceful women who ran the Mission Home unapologetically tapped this appeal to aid in their fund-raising efforts. Culbertson and the home's other staffers would usher dignitaries and other visitors into the home's "Oriental" room and surprise them with an unexpected juxtaposition of East and West as the Chinese girls and young women sang Christian hymns.

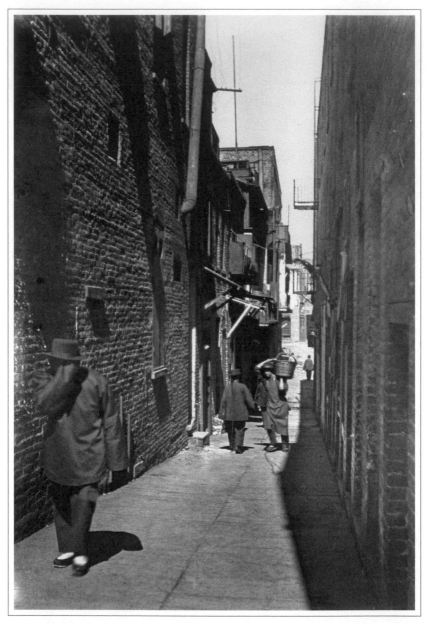

Chinatown residents were increasingly subject to tourists and photographers by the end of the century.

One such visitor was a young woman named Ellen G. Hodges, a devout Christian from Boston. Hodges's itinerary was typical for white tourists visiting Chinatown at that time. She started with a visit to a temple, then to a Chinese restaurant, followed by a stop at a Chinese theater and a trip to an opium den. Although San Francisco, in 1875, had been one of the first cities to ban the smoking of opium in dens, apparently the ban was not very successful. Sensational accounts of Chinatown aimed at tourists helped lure whites into a neighborhood where they'd normally never venture, in a nineteenth-century version of slumming.

Setting off on a May evening from San Francisco's luxurious Palace Hotel, Hodges was part of a large tour group of white visitors to Chinatown. A Chinese guide, Chin Jun, met them at a street corner in the quarter. He was tall with a long queue that hung down his back. To distinguish himself as a guide, his queue was braided with red silk.

The guide, who spoke English, led the group up a dark alley and then into a building where they climbed two flights of stairs to a temple. Hodges asked the tour guide about his own religious beliefs: the guide replied that he had been a Christian "for a month, but then gave it up." The group's next stop was a Chinese theater, where all the men seemed to be puffing on tobacco. To Hodges's unworldly ear, the fiddles, banjos, and other instruments in the orchestra seemed to "bang away," while the actors talked in falsetto voices. "After spending about twenty minutes here, we were glad to get out of the pandemonium," Hodges wrote.

The group's next stop was a Chinese restaurant that had beautiful rooms paneled with carved teak and tables inlaid with marble. Served tea and such treats as almond cookies, candied strips of coconut, and saucers of lychee nuts, Hodges was told that on different floors the prices varied. On the top, which was the most luxurious floor, a pot of tea served by a Chinese waiter in a spotless white uniform cost twenty-five cents. One floor down, the leaves used in the upper restaurant were dried and reused for fifteen cents a cup. At street level, the leaves were again dried and reused, with tea selling for a nickel a cup. It was a good story to tell the tourists, whether it was true or not.

The group lingered at the restaurant and then asked to see one of the opium dens, which by then had seized the popular imagination.

Chin declined, citing the group's size. Hodges was disappointed but made her way back to Chinatown on another day to explore it again. Unimpressed by the temple on her first visit, this time she was captivated by everything from the gong that worshippers struck upon entering, to the sumptuous silk curtains and gilded furniture, to the incense, or joss sticks, dropped to supposedly reveal how much money the tourists should pay to the gods on that visit. "I have given as much time as possible to Chinatown," she wrote. "I am fairly infatuated with the place."

On another day in May 1886, she joined a group of women on a classroom visit to the Chinese school run by the Presbyterian missionaries alongside the Mission Home. The girls, as was their custom, entertained their visitors by singing hymns. The most touching moment of her visit was when Chin Mooie, a blind resident of the home, sang the hymn "Light of the World" for the group.

The group's tour that day continued with a visit to the home of a former student who had married a Chinese Christian man. A young woman carrying a child in her arms greeted the group of white women at the door. The Chinese woman wore her hair in a formal style, with twisted "wings" on both sides of her head. Hodges asked her to turn around so she could see her hairstyle from the back. The Chinese woman agreed and then ran to get the small block of wood on which she rested her head at night, which helped preserve the elaborate hairstyle.

The point of that visit was to introduce potential donors, like Hodges, to one of the success stories of the Mission Home, which by then had been operating for a dozen years and had provided a home to hundreds of women. Hodges learned of the almost constant threats that the residents of the Mission Home faced from the larger Chinatown neighborhood. She was also told that the young women living at the Mission Home were in danger of being kidnapped, which explained why they were always escorted when they ventured beyond the safety of 920 Sacramento Street.

Hodges noticed the double bolts and bars on the home's windows and doors and was told that every Sunday two policemen were required to escort the girls and young women to and from the Presbyterian church, located about a block and a half away. "There is much difficulty in keeping away the Chinamen from the school," Hodges wrote, adding a "mob of a hundred or more Chinese . . . attempt to steal them on their way."

Determined to see an opium den before she left the city, Hodges took the advice of tourist brochures about the need for protection. She and four other visitors hired a police detective to lead them to the forbidden parts of the quarter. They arrived at a six-square-foot room in a cellar where several opium smokers lay and then descended two more stories underground. The detectives kicked open a door and led the group into another den. There, a Chinese man demonstrated for them how he warmed the dark, molasses-like opium over a small lamp, rolled it into a tiny hole in a pipe, and inhaled the fumes. "In our guilty hearts we thanked him," she wrote, "and still we wished to see worse dens. Our curiosity was at its height."

Their guide forced open yet another door, where the tourists were hit by a foul smell. "We merely peered in, and glad enough were we to

The original Presbyterian Mission Home where Margaret Culbertson served as superintendent, located on the edge of Chinatown.

get out of this hole, where lived twenty-four people and forty-six dogs and cats, all huddled together in a space six feet by eight! What is to be done with these Chinese is certainly a serious question."

Against this backdrop, Hodges was deeply impressed by what she had seen of the orderly household of the Chinese girls and missionary women, especially compared with the filth she'd witnessed on her tour of the opium dens. At the home, she wrote, the practice for years had been to teach the girls to wash and iron each week and to keep their rooms "scrupulously clean."

THE RHYTHM OF LIFE inside the Chinese Mission Home was experienced by Culbertson's nineteen-year-old niece, Margaret Belle Culbertson, who first came to live with her aunt for six months in mid-1887, about a year after Hodges's visit. Belle crossed the country from the family's hometown of Groveland, New York, in the Finger Lakes area. At the Oakland railroad station, her "aunt Maggie" stood waiting for her, carrying a bouquet of California poppies and wildflowers. They boarded a ferry to cross the bay to the city, disembarked, and rode a streetcar to the home.

Belle soon met the other members of the household at 933 Sacramento Street: the housekeeper, cook, and the Chinese girls themselves. The next morning, as Belle rose from her bed and prepared for the day ahead of her, the neighborhood around the Mission Home stirred to life. The rising sun illuminated the lanterns and banners that hung from brightly painted balconies. Chinese laborers emerged from small sheds on top of the neighborhood's buildings, where they had slept four or five to a tiny room. Others climbed from makeshift bunk rooms in cellars to the street level before setting off to roll cigars, make boots, and launder clothes. Chinatown at dawn seemed like a peaceful place.

Before long, the merchants on Sacramento and Dupont Streets slid their wooden display tables forward onto the sidewalks in front of their shops. They loaded them with baskets of foot-long green beans and other vegetables, which farmers grew on the outskirts of the city. Delicacies known as thousand-year eggs, imported from China, sat covered in a layer of clay, ash, and salt to keep them moist.

Some stalls specialized in seafood, such as whitebait-type fish and eight-inch-long squid, with their tangle of suction-cupped arms and feelers. Others carried dried foods: shriveled brown oysters skewered on bamboo, dried squid, dried pig livers, dried abalone, and dried seaweed for soups. Some shopkeepers decorated their windows with rows of red-skinned crispy ducks, which they hung by their feet after salting, drying, and pressing them in oil.

In the quarter's eighteen or so Chinese herb shops, proprietors would hang dried gourds above their counters each morning so that customers would know they were available to diagnose indigestion, constipation, and other complaints. To boost male potency, the herbalists might mix up a potion of ginseng, wolfberry, and the aptly named horny goat weed. Because many Chinese preferred Chinese medicine (and Asians were shunned at the city's hospitals for fear that their illnesses might contaminate other patients), Chinatown's herbalists had a thriving business.

From the Mission Home, which stood a few blocks uphill from the main commercial thoroughfares, the smells of the waking neighborhood were distinct. On fair days, undisturbed by rain or wind, the scent that drifted up the hill mixed freshly sawn wood from a nearby lumberyard, horse manure from a nearby stable, decaying vegetables, and incense from the nearby temples. This exotic blend of aromas led Western visitors to Chinatown to feel they had landed in Canton rather than a densely populated American city.

Belle joined her aunt that first Sunday in visiting the Chinese church, which was just down Sacramento Street from the Mission Home, walking past a series of brothels where white prostitutes worked. The religious services were conducted in Cantonese, which neither of the Culbertson women understood, and Belle found the experience strange, noting in her diary how many Chinese men were there on their own without women. Later that day, they attended a second service at the Congregational church, this time conducted in English. The following morning, they toured Chinatown. Belle expressed horror at the "dreadful" places that the Chinese had to live in and noted the clouds of blue tobacco smoke at the Chinese theater, as well as the odd sight of babies tied onto the backs of small children. That night, in her diary, she marveled at how she had been transported to China for a day.

In some respects, Belle's life in the Chinese Mission Home resembled the one she led growing up. While she wondered at the Chinese Moon Festival and was woken up by a minor earthquake—neither of which she was likely to have experienced in rural New York state—for the most part, she lived a quiet, domestic life. She baked, made quince marmalade, canned fruits, took embroidery lessons, and paid social calls. She also helped with the grocery shopping, cleaned the public rooms, and had enough time left over to enjoy the company of the home's residents, who once dressed her up in Chinese clothes for fun. For a sheltered and presumably virginal young woman, Belle didn't seem frightened or upset by the world that the young Chinese residents had fled to come to the home. Instead, she grew fiercely protective of them.

THE FIRST MONDAY of each month, the home hosted a luncheon meeting for the board and members of the auxiliary. The meetings were hardly mundane. On a June morning in 1876, Belle's aunt Margaret Culbertson told the women how she'd been served with five separate writs of habeas corpus on a single day. At twelve thirty, the women adjourned the meeting for lunch and afterward gathered in the parlor, where the Chinese residents performed short readings and songs. Holding antique lamps as props in their hands, they sang the hymn "Are You Ready?" with its verse suggesting Jesus as their groom: "Are your lamps all trimm'd and burning? Should the Bridegroom now appear?"

It was an apt choice to perform, for the Mission Home was serving as a de facto marriage bureau. Preparing for weddings between the home's residents and Chinese Christian men became one of Belle's jobs. She'd sometimes chaperone couples as they visited in the home's parlor. When she didn't have time for making her preferred delicacies such as custard layer cakes sprinkled with coconut, Belle would shop for cakes, candies, and nuts to serve at the wedding receptions. The celebrations themselves were influenced by Britain's queen, Victoria, who chose a white dress to wear on her wedding day in 1840, an unusual choice for that time.

Although traditional Chinese wedding gowns were red, brides from the Mission Home also were married in white, a color associated in China with death and funerals. Because most of the home's white staffers and supporters had only the most glancing familiarity with Chinese culture and lacked the skills to communicate directly with residents in their own language, they probably weren't aware of this cultural dissonance. Nor is there any evidence the Mission Home's Chinese brides objected to the color of their gowns.

For the most part, the wedding ceremonies were short and simple, though graced with freshly cut flowers and greenery. Couples would stand between the folding doors in the home's front parlor, and a minister would marry them. Afterward, they'd descend the steps to the street, into a waiting carriage. For good luck, the home's staffers, residents, and guests would fling rice.

Marriage was one of the best options for the girls and women fleeing slavery, because the opportunities for Chinese women in America to find paid work not involving sex were scarce. By marrying, they would gain their husband's protection. Yet until they married, they remained vulnerable. Belle witnessed what must have been frightening instances of Chinese men, accompanied by sheriffs and lawyers, searching the Mission Home looking for escaped prostitutes.

In one instance, a resident was sweeping outside the home when a man approached her and said something that frightened her. Belle heard and positioned herself on the home's worn and narrow wooden steps. Showing the same courage and practical streak that her aunt Maggie possessed, she refused to yield until the man left.

8

"To Have a Little Chinaman"

In rural Southern California, Dolly Cameron, now in her late teens, was living a quiet life. She had moved with her father and her siblings to a nineteen-thousand-acre ranch owned by Elias J. "Lucky" Baldwin, a pioneer speculator who'd earned his nickname from his extraordinary luck in a wide array of business deals across the state. Through foreclosures, Baldwin had acquired a large portion of what was originally known as the Rancho La Puente from two of Los Angeles's leading businessmen, who had hit hard times and were forced to sell. "By gad! This is Paradise," Baldwin was said to have exclaimed upon first seeing the oak-studded property in the San Gabriel valley.

Baldwin, who sported a pinkie ring on his left hand, had hired Dolly's father, Allan Cameron, as a ranch foreman in 1884, after the family had spent a few peripatetic years in Northern California. When Cameron became too ill to work, his son and namesake, who was known as Al, took over the job. La Puente was where Dolly and most of her sisters made their home in the mid- to late 1880s. Al's salary was small, but Baldwin provided a comfortable home for the family, with all the lamb they could eat from the ranch's sheep herds, as well as all the pheasant, geese, ducks, and quail they could hunt. Food was plentiful, but money was tight.

The lively social life of Los Angeles was half a day's ride from rural La Puente, so the Camerons sometimes socialized with the Baldwins at the nearby main ranch house. "Annie, Dolly & myself were over at the Millionaire Mr. Baldwin's house last week by invitation to

The Cameron family and friends picnicking at La Puente, the ranch in Southern California where they lived in the 1880s.

play whist where we spent a whole night after 10 o'clock and he told us to come any night we liked," Allan Cameron wrote to his daughter Jessie in 1884. He seemed pleased by the open-ended invitation from his boss, who spent most of his time at the new Baldwin Hotel in San Francisco and on his Santa Anita ranch.

The senior Cameron was apparently unaware of Lucky Baldwin's romantic and legal entanglements with young women who were not much older than his youngest daughter, Dolly. Just two years earlier, Baldwin had survived a murder attempt by a lover he had spurned. "He ruined me in body and mind," said the twenty-three-year-old brunette, one of Baldwin's distant cousins, after her arrest. Baldwin's exploits regularly landed him in the papers, where he was portrayed as a scoundrel.

Unlike his employer, infamous for his many wives and paramours, Dolly's father did not remarry after Isabella's death. Then in his seventies, the Cameron patriarch's life had been slowed down by his precarious health, particularly his vulnerability to colds and chest infections. He was not well enough to help his son with physically demanding tasks such as shearing the sheep. Yet his religious faith remained strong, and he urged his children to pray morning and night. God's "all seeing eye is upon you at all times," he told them.

The elder Allan Cameron moved his family often—from the San Joaquin valley to the outskirts of San Jose and then on to Oakland for various jobs—settling them in La Puente when Dolly was fifteen. They particularly enjoyed life at the ranch, which offered them rolling hills to roam, ponds to swim in, and the chance to ride retired racehorses owned by the Baldwins. (Later, "Lucky" Baldwin would build the Santa Anita racecourse.)

Their surroundings were bucolic, punctuated by the peak of Mount San Jacinto in the distance. But their troubles continued. The elder Allan Cameron died in 1887, and the family's money worries grew more pressing. By 1888, nineteen-year-old Dolly, a lovely young woman with clear skin, auburn curls, and a dry sense of humor, was on the verge of leaving La Puente.

For a young woman raised in a family where females would remain at home until they married, Dolly had daringly just started working in an office in a nearby village. She also became engaged to marry a friend of her brother's named George Sargent, a local land surveyor with an intense gaze. Her dream was to settle in a place of her own. "I think it's a shame to live on poor Al, and I want to begin before very long to lay up for my trousseau," she wrote to her sister Jessie, a teacher who had moved from California to Maui, to teach at a girls' school on the slopes of the dormant Haleakala volcano.

Having worked for only a week, Dolly, as well as nine other stenographers, was laid off because of a management change. That reversal meant she'd have to find some other form of paid employment. Sargent was working at one of the area's Spanish missions for a modest $65 a month (or just over $2 a day, which was less than a skilled laborer earned then), but he didn't plan to stay long in that job. His ambition was to go into partnership with Dolly's brother, Al. The two men hoped to buy a ranch of their own somewhere in Southern California.

Dolly shared their dream. "I wish awfully they could for I know it would pay very well indeed and stock ranches are so genteel. How I envy you living on a fine plantation," she admitted to her sister, who was living in Maui's up-country, with its large cattle ranches, Hawaiian cowboys (known as *paniolo*), and annual rodeos.

To gather enough for a down payment on their own family ranch, Dolly and her fiancé would need more money, because it was unlikely she would receive a dowry from her family. She hoped that George might make enough for them to visit Jessie in the Hawaiian Islands after they were married, but also admitted she would be grateful if they saved enough to keep themselves comfortable. A photograph of her taken around the time of her engagement to Sargent shows her with a steely gaze, her lips turned slightly downward. A pragmatic streak had already surfaced in her character.

Dolly confided to Jessie that her financial circumstances were tight and that she was unwilling to skimp on food. "I don't think it likely that we'll be married for nearly two years for I don't propose to live on love, and as both George and I have good appetites, I fear we couldn't even if we wanted to," she joked.

But her dreams of married life did include employing a house servant like the one she remembered her family having when they first moved to California. In passing, she mentioned the couple's plan "to have a little chinaman" who would help her entertain Jessie and her husband, Charles Alden Bailey, known as Charley, when they came to visit, using a racist expression ("a little chinaman") of the sort that was endemic at the time.

She signed the long letter to her sister using her family nickname, "With dearest love, Dodo."

TO "HAVE A LITTLE CHINAMAN" was then the ambition of many white householders in California, because the drudgery of laundry, cooking, and chores could otherwise fill entire days. Charles Nord-hoff, a journalist who wrote a series of articles about California for *Harper's* and *The New York Evening Post* in the 1870s, wrote one story titled "John," referring to the insultingly generic name that many white employers then used for their Chinese servants (as they used Bridget in referring to Irish maids and George for black Pullman porters):

> You ask his mistress, and she tells you that she has no disputes, no troubles, no worry; that John has made housekeeping a pleasure to her; if he is a cook, he does not object to help with the washing and ironing—in fact, does it better and quicker than any Bridget in the world. And John's master chimes in with an assertion that, since John has reigned below, the kitchen has been the delight of his eyes, so clean and sweet it is. Moreover, John markets for his mistress; he is economical; and he does not make a fuss.

In San Francisco, many middle- and upper-class families employed Chinese cooks and "houseboys," servants who performed household tasks such as sweeping, carrying cooking slops, and emptying ashes. William Randolph Hearst spent part of his childhood living in a large, elegant home on San Francisco's Chestnut Street, with a garden, piazza, and separate servants' quarters. George Hearst, who had parlayed his mining fortune into investments across the state and had recently been appointed a U.S. senator, employed a household staff that included a cook, a chauffeur, and what Phoebe Hearst described as a "neat and smart" Chinese houseboy. Young Willie amused his mother by learning some Chinese words from their Chinese servant and then imitating how he talked and behaved.

Mocking aside, the houseboys who lived on their employers' properties often had a better life than those who lived in Chinatown, where it was not unusual for two men to share a single bunk and for more than a dozen people to squeeze into a single room with no indoor plumbing. Living conditions in Chinatown were so bad that a San Francisco politician named William B. Farwell decided to investigate. Infectious diseases, such as tuberculosis, were real public health risks, linked to overcrowding, malnutrition, and poor sanitation. But Farwell was more concerned by the risk to white families than to the Chinese themselves, a perspective that much of the city's political establishment shared.

Farwell was elected to the city's Board of Supervisors in 1884 after serving in various government posts and as editor of the San Francisco–based *Daily Alta California*. As a supervisor, he launched an investigation of Chinatown. Leading a three-man committee, he mapped every single building in the heart of the district in 1885. He also color coded the buildings to designate the different varieties of activities in the quarter (Chinese gambling houses were shown in pink, Chinese brothels in green, sites of white prostitution in blue, and Chinese opium dens in yellow). This blocky rainbow map remains the now-obscure politician's legacy.

Farwell's investigators included lengthy and inflammatory details on crime, overcrowding, and squalid conditions in Chinatown. They counted 567 prostitutes among more than 30,000 Chinese living in the area. (About 4,000 of the estimated 30,000 Chinese in the city were women, so Farwell's report implies roughly one in seven Chinese women were prostitutes.) They also counted some 150 gambling dens and twenty-six opium "resorts," as these and other vice havens were sometimes called.

Farwell's background as a writer seeps into the report's overheated prose. Although the paper he had edited, the *Daily Alta California*, was well respected and powerful, the report resulting from the Board of Supervisors' investigation reads as if it came straight out of a dime novel.

Descend into the basement of almost any building in Chinatown at night; pick your way by the aid of the policeman's candle along the dark and narrow passageway, black and grimy with a quarter of a century's accumulation of filth; step with care lest you fall into a cesspool of sewerage abominations with which these subterranean depths abound. . . . It is from such pest-holes as these that the Chinese cooks and servants who are employed in our houses come.

Thousands of Chinese worked as domestic servants in San Francisco's white homes in the 1880s, and the report raised concerns about diseases such as leprosy (now more commonly known as Hansen's disease), tuberculosis, and elephantiasis, all of which periodically appeared in the Chinese quarter and sometimes in white areas as well. Farwell's report included a statement from a doctor at the city's smallpox hospital, noting that the city's first Hansen's disease patient, a Chinese man named Hong Tong, had died in 1875. Since then, there had been a total of seventy-nine cases admitted. Farwell compared San Francisco's situation with Hawaii's, where the number of Hansen's disease cases was far greater and authorities had banished the sufferers to the island of Moloka'i. He then went on to thunder that "if this evil of Chinese immigration is to go unchecked, we shall also have become a nation of lepers."

For years, immigration authorities at San Francisco's wharves had been putting visibly diseased passengers from China back on boats to be sent home. But because the city's thirty thousand Chinese con-

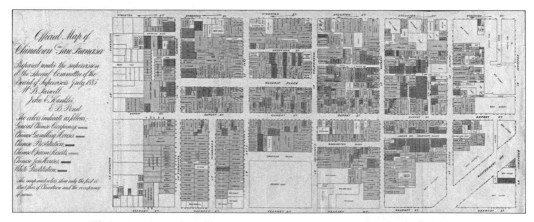

Farwell's committee produced a Chinatown "vice map" that purported to identify houses of prostitution, gambling dens, and opium "resorts" on a building-by- building basis.

tinued to toil as laundry operators, shoemakers, produce vendors, and servants—all occupations that put them in contact with whites—the health fears raised by Farwell's report were echoed in newspapers. Throughout the state, Chinese immigrants had built railways, labored in the mines, and planted and harvested crops in the agricultural fields that had created so much of the city's wealth. Yet because the Chinese were perceived as a threat not only to white labor but also to public health, efforts mounted throughout this time to clamp down further on Chinese immigration. It was a pattern that had repeated itself through the state's history, including with Irish laborers: import foreigners, work them hard, and then demonize them to drive them out.

The campaign was not just regional. In 1882, three years before Farwell's report, Congress had passed the first Chinese Exclusion Act, which banned Chinese laborers from entering the country for ten years and halted the Chinese from becoming U.S. citizens. Fueled by racism and the campaigning of populist labor movements, such as Denis Kearney's Workingmen's Party, this was the first law passed in the United States to specifically bar the immigration of a particular ethnic group. Other legislation followed, including the Geary Act of 1892, which extended the Chinese Exclusion Act another ten years and required all Chinese to register and carry residency papers.

These restrictions unintentionally gave rise to new methods and new players in the profitable enterprise of human smuggling.

9

Baiting the Hook

One boy from Guangdong province barely made it to California before Congress passed the 1882 Chinese Exclusion Act. Ng Poon Chew had just become a teen when he traveled by boat across the Pacific and landed in San Francisco. He headed south, to San Jose, to be someone's "little Chinaman," working as a houseboy on a ranch and pursuing his education. He eventually married a young woman from the Mission Home and became its lifelong friend and advocate.

Chew as a teenager made the trip to California to seek better economic opportunities abroad. Almost certainly he came legally, because there were no restrictions on Chinese males immigrating to the United States at that point (the exception was the 1875 Page Act, which restricted entry of prostitutes and other undesirables). As a boy in China, he had lived with his grandmother and been an assistant to a Taoist priest. But an uncle had immigrated to the United States, and at around the age of thirteen Chew and a cousin made the journey as well. In addition to working on a ranch, he enrolled in a mission school to learn English, where he was introduced to Christian teachings.

The young man arrived in California in the period of rising anti-Chinese violence, stoked by notions of white superiority and the fear that the Chinese were taking jobs that would otherwise go to white workers. Throughout the West, towns were forcing out the Chinese. Some held dances and fund-raisers to purchase train tickets and boat fares to transport them out of town. Others deployed armed guards to march them to depots or docks. Sometimes torchlight parades led

Ng Poon Chew led the Chinese Presbyterian Mission in Los Angeles between 1894 and 1898 and is pictured here in Western dress.

to arson attacks, beatings, and murders. Across the bay in Oakland, anti-Chinese agitators attempted to blow up Chinese laundries. Such agitation caused families like the wealthy Spreckelses of San Francisco to fire all the Chinese sailors from their Oceanic Steamship Co.

Chew adapted. He started wearing Western-style clothing, including stiff-collared shirts, and cut off the braid that hung down his back. He went to a local barber to have the rest of his hair cut in a Western style. "We don't cut hair for chinks!" the barber told him. He encountered the prejudice there that other Chinese were experiencing in far more virulent forms across the West.

Not all of Chew's encounters were hostile; his first teacher at the mission school in San Jose, a recently widowed woman named Mary S. Carey, treated him kindly. While his uncle had given him strict instructions to ignore the religious part of the teachings and focus instead on learning English, he absorbed both. Later he would recall his difficulties learning English, using the example of one time ending a letter to his teacher "I hope the Lord will bless and kipper you." He had understood the word "kipper" to mean "preserve."

Meanwhile, Carey and the other teachers who sought to educate the Chinese in San Jose faced harassment and threats. In 1887, their school, along with much of the city's Chinese quarter, burned to the ground, apparently torched by arsonists. Traumatized by what happened, Carey and Chew remained lifelong friends, perhaps bonded by the harrowing experience.

Chew moved to San Francisco, where his options to educate himself were limited. From 1871 to 1885, Chinese were banned from attending the city's public schools. This policy didn't change until the parents of Mamie Tape, an eight-year-old Chinese girl born in the United States, won a lawsuit in 1885 against the San Francisco Board of Education that allowed her to attend a public school. Her lawyer was William F. Gibson, the son of the prominent Methodist missionary Otis Gibson. To circumvent the possibility that she would attend class with white children as a result of the ruling, city officials forced Mamie to attend a separate school for Chinese and other Asian children opened shortly after the ruling.

In its *Tape v. Hurley* decision, the California Supreme Court ruled that Mamie Tape must be provided with a public education, although it largely disregarded Gibson's arguments citing the equal protection clause of the Fourteenth Amendment and focused instead on applying a state statute that said that schools were to be open to all children between the ages of six and twenty-one. This decision came more than half a century before the Supreme Court's landmark *Brown v. Board of Education* ruling, in which the Court found that state-sanctioned segregation of public schools was a violation of the Fourteenth Amendment and unconstitutional.

Yet the perverse result of *Tape v. Hurley* was decades of segregation of the Chinese in San Francisco's schools. If anything, the *Tape* decision seemed to heighten fears on the part of whites toward the Chinese as anti-Chinese violence continued. That same year, white hoodlums stoned the house of the Mission Home's Chinese organist.

Farwell's report on Chinatown, published about four months after the *Tape* decision, thunderously supported the school officials' decision to segregate Chinese schoolchildren based on the fear that they would spread disease to whites. His investigation had found that in a single house on Sullivan's Alley (now known as Jason Court, running between Pacific Avenue and Jackson Street), nineteen prostitutes were crowded in with sixteen children—a total of thirty-five people living in close quarters.

> We have shown that there is no distinct line of demarcation—here at least between domestic life and prostitution. We have shown that the painted harlots of the slums and alleys, the women who are bought and sold to the slavery of prostitution, are surrounded by children in some instances, and intermingle freely with the border class of family life where other children abound.... Speaking no language but the Chinese, born and nurtured in filth and degradation, it is scarcely probable that any serious attempt could be made to mingle them [Chinese children] with the other children of our public schools without kindling a blaze of revolution in our midst.

Such fearmongering was effective in keeping the schools segregated. Like thousands of other Chinese who had few other educational options, Chew turned to programs offered by missionaries. He enrolled in a "Ministry Program," a parallel project to the Mission Home, where he studied the Bible and continued to improve his spoken and written English. The Presbyterian church in San Francisco had housed the very first Chinese school in the city since 1854, when it opened its basement for classes. Its ministers continued to be among the few who advocated for the Chinese over the years despite intense hostility and a crescendo of race-baiting rhetoric.

The church's efforts were an expression of Christian compassion. But it also hoped to win converts. As a rival Protestant denomination explained about its similar strategy, "Desire to learn the English language is still our principal fulcrum in the effort to lift the Chinese into the light of Christian life. We could bait our hook with the bait of the English primer and make the primer speak to them of Christ."

TAKING THAT BAIT, Chew continued his education by enrolling in the San Francisco Theological Seminary with the goal of joining the clergy. He studied there at the height of anti-Chinese agitation, when boycotts, hiring bans, and other forms of harassment drastically cut San Francisco's Chinese population from nearly twenty-six thousand in 1890 to just under fourteen thousand in 1900. Yet Chew persevered and became the seminary's first Chinese graduate in 1892, earning high honors. He was ordained in front of a crowd of three hundred in San Francisco's Chinatown. So significant was the ordination of this charismatic young minister that the *San Francisco Call* reporter assigned to cover the event wrote that the crowd included some Chinese "unbelievers" who were there "to do their countryman honor."

Chew's resilience and achievement were remarkable, given the corrosive prejudice of the times. Fluent in Cantonese and English and a gifted orator, he was recognized by leaders of the Presbyterian Church for his talents. Chew became the assistant pastor to the influential reverend Ira Condit, based in San Francisco's Chinatown. Soon after, he won what seemed like a plum assignment: the church put him in charge of three missionary stations—in Los Angeles, Santa Barbara, and San Diego. A photograph from around that time shows him as a serious young man wearing a dark frock coat and white clerical collar. His hair is neatly trimmed and parted to the side, and he holds his head still for the photographer, gazing slightly upward.

Then in his mid-twenties and earning a small but steady income as an assistant pastor in San Francisco, Chew decided to marry before he moved south. Finding a suitable woman was not always easy for Chinese men in California: both the Chinese Exclusion Act and earlier measures to restrict the immigration of Chinese women to the United States continued to keep the gender ratio wildly lopsided in 1890, with about twenty-two Chinese men in the state for every single Chinese woman. Antimiscegenation laws banned Chinese men from marrying white women. So Chew looked for a wife at the Mission Home.

A BEAUTIFUL YOUNG CHINESE WOMAN named Chun Fah caught the young clergyman's eye. She had come to the home as a six-year-old, scarred and blackened, after suffering daily beatings from the Chinese woman who had purchased her as a household slave.

Chun was owned and mistreated by a notorious slaver on Jackson Street, where many Chinatown brothels were concentrated. Officers of the California Society for the Prevention of Cruelty to Children, a charity formed in 1876, had been tipped off about her. The society found her and brought her to the Mission Home in 1878 for her safety. Margaret Culbertson, the home's superintendent, recalled Chun's arrival:

> Well do we remember her as we first saw her, sitting by the fireside awaiting our return from church. As we drew near and spoke to her she shrank away frightened, while tears and sobs were her only response. An hour later we saw her quietly sleeping on her pillow, her hand tightly clasping a bit of candy, that sweet comforter of childhood's sorrows. As she grew up to womanhood, she learned English and became our interpreter.

In a standard ploy of irate slave owners who'd had their property seized, her owners filed a writ of habeas corpus—demanding that the child come before a judge as a way of challenging the home's right to hold her. Several court hearings later, a judge finally awarded Culbertson custody of the girl. Although she couldn't speak any English when she arrived, in just two years she had become more proficient in reading, writing, and speaking English than many of the home's older residents.

By her early teens, Chun was serving as secretary of the Light House Mission Band, a missionary society for young girls, and her gifts as a linguist allowed her to write reports for the group's monthly meetings, published annually by the Occidental Board. As a sixteen-year-old, Chun began working alongside Margaret Culbertson as an interpreter in court and on rescue attempts.

She became a favorite among the home's staffers, who nicknamed her Spring Flower. Her wedding to the young pastor drew so many people from Chinatown that the couple decided to move the ceremony from the quiet front parlor of the Mission Home to the much larger Chinese Presbyterian Church, a few blocks away. The altar was festooned with flowers, and the bride arranged her hair in a fan shape over her ears. Her groom had purchased her wedding gown of silk with gold embroidery from China. The Reverend Condit presided over the service, and a newly arrived resident of the home sang a Chinese song in celebration, accompanying herself on a traditional Chinese instrument.

Mission Home staffers did not disguise their sense of loss when, at age twenty, in 1892, she left the home to take up her life as a newly married woman. One of the Occidental School's teachers, Miss Baskin, described the home's "Spring Flower" as a luscious catch for the young minister:

> In this young Christian maiden he also secures the ideal of a Chinese beauty, which must consist of eyes of graceful almond shape, brows like the moon in its crescent, her face like the peach leaf, lips curved like the banana, wrists round and white as her ivory bracelet and fingers delicate and tapering, with all domestic graces included.

The marriage of the Reverend Ng Poon Chew and Chun Fah was one of the most notable of many matches that came out of the home. By 1888, just fourteen years after it was founded, the Mission Home could count fifty-five marriages. By 1901, in its annual report for the year, staffers took credit for 160 marriages. Ng and Chun went on to have a long union that produced five children. To honor the missionaries who changed their lives, they named their first child Mansie, the nickname of the Reverend Condit's wife, Samantha.

AS A YOUNG CLERGYMAN in Southern California, Chew remained motionless for a formal photograph in the mission that he headed between 1894 and 1898. The image that the photographer captured shows him wearing Western dress and holding a book that appears to be a Chinese-language Bible. Four men in Chinese dress accompany him, and Chinese translations of the Lord's Prayer and other Christian teachings hang on the wall.

He and other missionaries preached in their native tongue on the streets of Los Angeles on Sunday afternoons. But their efforts helped them recruit few new members to their church. Chew grew frustrated, admitting to his supervisor, "I feel so sad and discouraged on account of my own helplessness and inability to win more souls to Christ, while I see so many of my own countrymen on every side living in sin, with the mouth of hell open to receive them at any moment."

In 1898, a suspicious fire destroyed the Los Angeles Mission building. The church soon pulled its support from the missionary stations that Chew oversaw, despite his protests. Not long after, he decided to leave the ministry and find another way to use his gifts as an orator and leader. He apprenticed himself for two months to a Japanese-language publication in Los Angeles to learn the business and soon began printing his own small Chinese-language newspaper, employing two cousins to help run the press and edit it. After mailing copies of the paper to friends in San Francisco, he got an enthusiastic response and offers of financial support. He decided to move back from Southern California to San Francisco, the de facto capital of Chinese America, with an even more ambitious plan in mind.

Although Chew quit working as a pastor, he didn't give up on ministering to help his fellow Chinese immigrants. "The departure to San Francisco of Rev. Ng Poon Chew was a great loss," wrote Arthur Judson Brown, the administrative secretary of the Presbyterian Board of Foreign Missions, who visited the Los Angeles Mission shortly after

Chew left. "His return is still hoped for but he is now editor of the only Chinese daily paper on the Coast and with his family he needs a larger support than the Los Angeles work can give."

One of Chew's daughters later recalled that he decided to become a journalist because he believed he could reach more Chinese by starting a paper than by preaching. Chew himself told an interviewer in later years about the ministry, "I found the field too narrow." Instead of sharing his thoughts from the pulpit on Sunday, Chew would disseminate them every day, through the daily newspaper he founded and named *Chung Sai Yat Po,* or the Chinese-Western Daily. It soon became a leading advocate for Chinese American civil rights. Through his newspaper's pages, and in his personal life, Chew became an unflagging supporter of the Mission Home.

—===» 10 «===—

Life as a *Mui Tsai*

As Ng Poon Chew and his bride, Chun Fah, moved back to Chinatown from Southern California, many other Chinese were leaving the United States altogether. Between 1890 and 1900, the number of Chinese men in the country dropped by nearly 18 percent, to 85,341. The passage of the Chinese Exclusion Act sent the number of legal Chinese immigrants plummeting. The few Chinese who did arrive during those years came almost exclusively from the privileged classes.

Yet, in part because of the still glaring gender imbalance among the Chinese in America, demand for Chinese females as prostitutes and servants remained strong. One unintended consequence of the Chinese Exclusion Act was that it drove up prices for women and girls, because it was now far riskier and costlier to import them. Because the wives and daughters of Chinese merchants were exempted from the law, a common way to smuggle prostitutes in was to create false identities. Importers would fabricate papers purporting to show the women were merchants' wives and daughters and provide coaching on how to respond to questions from immigration officials.

As restrictions grew tighter, it also became more difficult for a single criminal entity to maintain control of the trafficking business. The Hip Yee tong soon lost its tight hold on importing women as other criminal groups moved in. One noteworthy entry into this nefarious trade was the criminal tong leader Fung Jing Toy, also known by the nickname Little Pete.

Some Chinese girls were smuggled to San Francisco to work as unpaid servants known as *mui tsai*.

Like Chew, he had been born in China and immigrated to California as a boy. He'd also learned to speak English by taking classes from missionaries, attending the Methodist Chinese Mission in San Francisco's Chinatown. As the new law forced importers to become more and more ingenious in how they smuggled women into the country, Little Pete proved especially adroit. Some of his ploys included cutting off their hair and passing them off as boys, concealing them in buckets of coal, and hiding them in padded crates billed as dishware.

He bribed customs officials and paid off both white and Chinese men for providing false information about the women he brought into the country. His knowledge of English and his familiarity with the white world proved invaluable. In a particularly devious move, he used expositions and fairs held in Chicago and Atlanta as a cover for his trafficking. During the Midwinter Fair, a world's fair that took place in Golden Gate Park in 1894, Little Pete was put in charge of preparations for the elaborate Chinese Exhibit, which was to feature a wooden pagoda adorned with carved dragons, a Chinese temple (known as a joss house, based on a corruption of the Portuguese word *deus,* or God), and a theater. He won government permission to import hundreds of Chinese workmen and performers, claiming that they would appear as actors, acrobats, and musicians in exhibits and parades. The women, though, spent very little time at the fair; they were soon working in the city's brothels.

San Francisco's newspapers ran outraged stories about Little Pete, whom they sometimes called Fong Ching. One reported that his smuggling scheme, in which he allegedly worked with the Six Companies, had earned him a total of $50,000—a fortune at a time when prime city lots could be purchased for $4,800. The headline of that story read, "How a Chinese Combine Managed to Clean Up over $50,000 in a Single Stroke."

Little Pete and other importers relied on a network of procurers inside China to supply them with girls and women. Sometimes these recruiters would lure the women with false stories of what their lives would be like in California, spinning fantasies about the bridegrooms or lucrative jobs waiting for them there. In other instances, they'd kidnap girls from cities and rural villages. Sometimes, desperate parents sold their daughters to procurers to help the rest of the family.

The practice of poor families selling girls was widespread in China during the late nineteenth and early twentieth centuries, exacerbated by famines, wars, natural disasters, and crushing poverty. Even though the British had by then condemned the practice of hawking humans for profit, the Chinese considered the sale of women within a patriarch's rights to decide how to meet his family's needs. Indeed, China did not outlaw the sale of children and women until 1928. Even then, the law was relatively toothless, because it did not challenge the Chinese patriarch's traditional prerogative to "transfer" daughters and wives if he felt it served the family.

GAMBLING DEBTS WERE the reason why a young girl named Tien found herself an unwitting passenger on a steamer from Shanghai bound for San Francisco. Tien Fuh Wu's family lived in a region about a hundred miles south of Shanghai. Their province, Zhejiang, experienced wrenching upheaval during the Taiping Rebellion, a war that raged for fourteen years and ended in 1864. For decades afterward, many of the province's villages remained abandoned, with buildings burned out and fields unclaimed.

Not only did Tien's parents survive a civil war in which an estimated twenty million people died; they also emerged with enough wealth to follow the custom begun by China's upper classes of binding the feet of their young daughters.

This practice had been afflicting Chinese women for close to a thousand years. First, a young girl's toes were broken and her feet were slowly and painfully bent into tiny, three-inch-long appendages—about half the length of a pencil or the size of a small clenched fist.

While many in China considered bound feet erotic, the custom effectively crippled generations of girls, because maimed feet made it difficult for them to walk or work. Yet throughout the nineteenth century, in wealthier families most girls between the ages of six and eight had their feet bound as a sign of gentility and to make them more marriageable.

Tien's feet were bound at the encouragement of her grandmother, who wore silk and satin gowns and brought delicacies for Tien's family to eat when she visited them. Even so, the grandmother's prosperity wasn't enough to offset Tien's father's financial troubles. His gambling debts had caused a crisis for the family.

One day, when she was still very young, Tien learned from her father that the two of them were going to visit her grandmother. As they stood on the wharf before boarding a boat to Ningbo, the large coastal city south of the Yangtze River delta near where her grandmother lived, her mother handed her a toothbrush and a new washrag in a blue bag. Then she began to sob.

"Don't cry, Mother," Tien said, trying to comfort her. "I'm just going to see Grandma and be right back."

Tien and her father climbed aboard and headed to their cabin, where he instructed the girl to eat her supper. He then locked her into the compartment and went back on deck. Tien didn't understand what was happening to her and grew anxious. Where was her father? She sensed that something was not right. Tears filled her eyes. She began to scream.

Her father had locked the compartment to prevent her from searching for him while he was gone. Then he sought out the woman with whom he would negotiate his daughter's sale. As her father and the woman discussed a price, Tien began to kick and shout, demanding to be let out. No one responded.

Strangers finally opened the door and Tien bolted out, hobbling up and down the boat on her tiny bound feet searching for her father. He had disappeared without saying good-bye, turning her over to someone she had never seen before. Until the end of her life, Tien never knew with any certainty her age when she was sold; she guessed she could have been anywhere from six to ten. Because she was so young, her father had dealt with a procurer of *mui tsai*, or children who would become household slaves.

The woman took her from Ningbo to Shanghai, where she walked through a set of red gates to a private home with a garden. There she met another woman who soaked off the tight cloth bindings around Tien's feet. Because the strips used to bind feet were seldom removed for foot washing, a terrible smell would have wafted up from Tien's squashed feet.

Several times a day, the woman instructed Tien to dangle her feet in a bucket of water to help them expand back to normal. Tien's most lasting memory of that time was not of having her feet released from their painful bindings but of the kindness of the woman in Shanghai, who hadn't asked her to work.

Tien's short period of relative leisure in Shanghai ended in 1892, when she traveled with yet a third woman to San Francisco aboard a steamer. She was probably smuggled in as a "paper daughter" who pretended to be a relative of a merchant to avoid the immigration restrictions of the Chinese Exclusion Act. While in transit, her experience as human chattel had been tolerable. Life as a *mui tsai* in San Francisco's Chinatown lay ahead.

WEALTHY CHINESE MERCHANT FAMILIES and brothel owners in San Francisco had adopted the *mui tsai* system from China. To formalize these arrangements, deeds of sale often accompanied the young girls. Some Chinese regarded importing girls to work as unpaid servants as a form of charity toward female children from poor families. Even the term itself suggests a benevolent intention: *mui tsai* means "little sister" in the Cantonese dialect.

While some *mui tsai* were mistreated or sexually abused, others were treated well and fed, clothed, and housed far better than they had been in their first homes. Yet the essential condition of powerlessness remained the same. After the girls turned eighteen, some owners would arrange marriages for them. Other girls were freed from their service to find their own paths. Some ended up making lasting friendships with the families they'd served.

This was the case for a young girl named Quan Laan Fan, who came to San Francisco as a seven-year-old in the 1880s after her parents fell into debt and were forced to sell her. She became a servant to a shopkeeper's family in Chinatown who generally treated her fairly. Sometimes, though, they lent her out to others, as when she was put to work for a family acquaintance rolling cigarettes. "I'd get sleepy . . . really tired. Then, they'd hit me. It was really tedious. I'd roll cigarettes all day long and there was no one to talk with," she said many years later. Still, by working as a *mui tsai* for a family who generally provided for her, she had helped her own family avoid possible starvation.

When Quan came of age in her late teens, the family arranged a marriage for her with a much older man whom she found repugnant. "He was too poor! Old and poor," she later recalled. "No money. Terrible!" Despite her disgust for him, Quan and her husband had eight children together. In later years, she found paid work as a telephone operator in Chinatown.

The *mui tsai* system was commonplace and legal in China. It was widely accepted that families had the right to sell their daughters and that filial piety, or the virtue of respect for one's parents, required daughters to accept their fate. Some late nineteenth-century Americans looked upon this practice with horror, seeing it as no less than another form of human slavery, which Congress had made illegal in 1865. By the 1890s, the newspapers regularly referred to the young victims of the *mui tsai* system as "slave girls" and, in what is today considered an ethnic slur, called the trade in Asian girls and women "yellow slavery."

Whether or not official papers accompanied the sale of the girls in China, and whether their parents sold them or traffickers kidnapped them, the *mui tsai* were nonetheless slaves before and after they reached the United States. If their owners mistreated them, they had few options and scant legal recourse. If they were very lucky, someone might report their existence to the California Society for the Prevention of Cruelty to Children or the Pacific Society for the Suppression of Vice, two of the leading children's charities operating in San Francisco in the 1890s. Because most *mui tsai* spoke only Chinese, these groups might bring them to one of the two Chinatown mission homes, which employed Chinese-speaking translators.

When Tien arrived in San Francisco in 1892, excitement was building for the Midwinter Fair. Dignitaries gathered for a groundbreaking ceremony in Golden Gate Park in August, and a stream of newcomers began heading into San Francisco to help construct the fairground buildings.

Instead of joining the performers in the green oasis of the city's 1,017-acre park, Tien ended up in Chinatown, where she was put to work as a servant in the Peking, a brothel. The young Tien watched the prostitutes get ready for work. At around 7:00 every evening, seven or eight girls, dolled up in silk or satin, would gather in the brothel's main ground-floor room and sit in front of a big window, facing the street. Like Tien, these older girls had probably been sold into slavery. Men would be lured into the brothel by the promise of what lay beneath their shiny frocks.

Tien, only ten years old or possibly even younger, didn't fully understand what was going on. But she knew that her owner wanted to keep her out of sight in the event of unwelcome visitors. When the police or any white people came, the brothel keeper would hide her under a bed and push a trunk in front of it to make sure no one saw her. The darkness, coupled with the uncertainty of when she might be allowed to come out, was terrifying, especially because she was forced to hide again and again. "Every time they were afraid I might be taken away, they hid me," Tien recalled.

Tien's experience with her first owner in Chinatown did not involve physical abuse or mistreatment. But she felt lonely. "I had no playmates, nothing," she said. As time passed, the brothel keeper found herself in debt, so she sold Tien to another woman who lived in a building that housed a lottery operation, a popular form of illegal gambling. Not only was Tien's second owner in San Francisco far less kind to her, but she spoke Cantonese rather than Tien's Wu dialect, making it difficult for Tien to follow instructions.

Physically small and probably malnourished, Tien found her new job overwhelming. She came to despise her new owners and their child—especially the baby's mother. "Oh, this woman was so awful!" she said. "They say she was a domestic servant before and was cruelly treated. She use to make me carry a big fat baby on my back and make me to [sic] wash his diapers. And you know, to wash you have to stoop over, and then he pulls you back, and cry and cry."

Tien grew desperate. Not only was she in pain from her work, but she was growing increasingly frustrated by her circumstances. In a position of almost complete powerlessness, she turned her anger on the one person who was smaller and more helpless than herself: the baby. At a particularly low moment, she reached behind her and pinched the infant's bottom as hard as she could. "I didn't care what happened to me," she said. She just wanted to inflict pain on the creature tormenting her.

The baby howled and its mother rushed to it. Soon, the mother realized what Tien had done. She retaliated by pinching and twisting her cheeks and arms. Then the mother grabbed red-hot tongs and pressed the iron tool into Tien's arm, filling the apartment with the smell of burning flesh.

"A Worse Slavery than Ever
Uncle Tom Knew Of"

On January 17, 1894, word of Tien's distress was delivered to the Mission House. Its supervisor, Margaret Culbertson, had taken an extended medical leave. Annie Houseworth, who had taught in the Chinese Presbyterian Church's mission school for many years, was temporarily serving in her place.

In the pouring rain, Houseworth, accompanied by two police officers and the home's translator, set off for a building on Jackson Street with a lottery operation on the ground floor and apartments, including the one where Tien lived. The front door was barricaded. But the officers entered a neighboring restaurant, climbed the rickety back stairs, crossed the roof, and then headed back down into the premises, where they unlocked and opened the front door. The group then searched the building, eventually reaching an apartment on the fourth floor.

Officers wiped tears from their eyes when they saw the burn marks on Tien's small body. One, who'd witnessed many horrifying instances of abuse, said he'd never seen anything so cruel. Tien's owner feigned affection for her to put off her would-be rescuers, but Houseworth and the officers were not deceived. "Much to our joy, we succeeded at last. We recognized the little thing by the wounds and bruises on her face, head and arms. Her owner took her in his arms and fondly pressed her to his heart. This embrace, however, greatly terrified the child as any tender show of regard was unusual," wrote Houseworth. "The next day

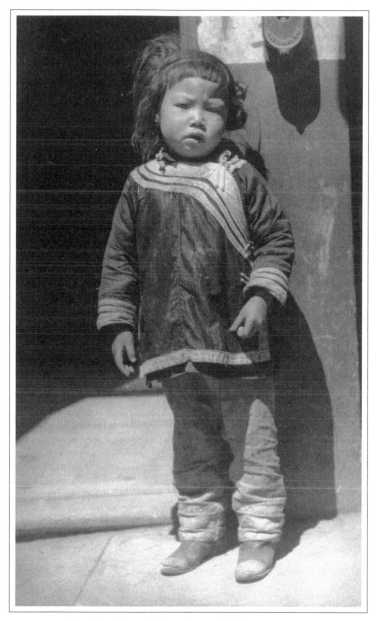

A young girl with unkempt hair and a troubled expression photographed in Chinatown.

I took out guardianship papers, and my little ward seems to think she is my special property."

Tien's fear was compounded by what had been a false start to her rescue. Houseworth had come to the apartment where she was kept but, to Tien's dismay, then left, because the only girl she saw seemed too tiny to be the twelve-year-old she was searching for. The woman who'd reported Tien's condition was distressed when she'd learned the mission workers hadn't recognized her. "Why didn't you take her?" she asked. "*She's* the girl." The group then returned, accompanied by two policemen.

By then, the home had been operating for almost two decades, and its staffers were experienced in entering brothels and tenements in Chinatown in search of abused girls and young women. But even on this second try, Houseworth and the policemen weren't sure Tien was the girl they were looking for. They undressed her and examined her for bruises and other marks. They found the burn scar on her arm where the woman had seared her with the metal tongs. They also found black-and-blue marks all over her small body, scarring on her face from severe pinching, and signs that her owner had tortured her by dripping hot wax from a burning candle on her arms.

The burns and bruising convinced them they'd found the right girl, and one of the large policemen lifted her up into his arms and carried her through the rain-drenched streets to the Mission Home. Tien was terrified. For all she knew, she was now being held captive by a group of white people, which could turn out to be a far worse fate.

"I was scared to death," she said. "All the strangers and I didn't know where I was going. Away from my own people and in the pouring rain."

But at the Mission Home, she found her refuge. "I got my freedom there," she said.

THE POLICEMAN CARRIED TIEN five blocks to 933 Sacramento Street, where some fifty girls were squeezed into the poorly ventilated, overcrowded former boardinghouse. They often slept three to a bed and a dozen to a room. Because the building lacked the space for a separate infirmary, girls who were sick with whooping cough, tonsillitis, measles, and influenza lived and slept next to girls who were healthy. While Tien would not be tortured in the Mission Home, she nonetheless faced significant immunological threats.

During the nearly two decades the home had existed, more than one of its residents had died from an infectious disease. One young physician then in her twenties, Dr. Minnie G. Worley, volunteered her time to take care of the sick or injured girls. Worley, a single woman who lived in the center of Chinatown, had specialized in gynecology and obstetrics at San Francisco's Cooper Medical College and was frequently called upon to attend difficult births. Her sister Florence was a missionary worker at the home, and their late father had been a prominent judge in San Francisco.

Once Houseworth got Tien settled and Dr. Worley had a chance to examine and treat Tien's burns and bruises, she retreated to the relative quiet of her office to enter a summary of the rescue into the home's eight-by-eleven-inch bound ledger. Ever since the home opened its doors in 1874, every time a new girl came to live there, the superintendent or another staff member would note her arrival and briefly describe the circumstances. In Tien's case, Houseworth wrote about the events of that rainy winter day in careful handwriting, using a different name from the one Tien would eventually adopt and referring to the cruelty of her owner. She took out the ledger and began writing:

> Tai Choie alias Teen Fook
> Was rescued by Miss Houseworth, Miss Florence Worley and some police officers from her inhuman mistress.

TIEN'S BURNS HEALED and her health returned. But the unhealthy conditions at 933 Sacramento Street, as well as the home's impressive record of sheltering hundreds of women—by one count, some 458 of them by 1893—convinced the women of the Occidental Board that they needed to find a larger residence for their project. Heeding the cries of the board's forceful president, Mary Ann Browne, the women collected donations of anywhere from a mere five cents to $100. Finally they succeeded in purchasing a new building right across the street, at 920 Sacramento Street.

In November 1893, staffers and residents led by Houseworth crossed the cobblestoned street carrying their belongings. They climbed the steps of the two-story Dutch Colonial building, passing beneath its brick, arched entryway, and stepped into its impressive foyer. The girls found thirty-five rooms in the large home, but the showpiece was what board members called "our Oriental room"—a parlor filled with Chinese furniture and objects. The Chinese vice-consul, who publicly opposed the criminal tongs and sex trafficking and supported the efforts of the Mission Home, along with various merchants, had helped furnish the room with gifts of tables inlaid with mother-of-pearl, porcelain vases, and green silk curtains.

Three months later, in February 1894, the board hosted a housewarming ceremony, attended by the Chinese vice-consul and his wife, local Chinese merchants, church officials, and a reporter for *The San Francisco Call*. The latter waxed wondrous at the mixing of cultures: "There was such an odd, picturesque blending of the far East and the far West ... that a stranger suddenly introduced to the scene would have been puzzled to say whether it was passing in Asia or America."

At that time, forty-five Chinese and a few Japanese girls were living at the home. During the party, they shyly peeked through the doorways at the guests and scurried out of the way as the dignitaries toured their dormitories and classrooms. Unlike the home's earlier superintendents, who had little sensitivity to what the young residents liked to eat or how they preferred to communicate, Culbertson—who had returned from her medical leave by the time of the party—realized the importance of embracing various aspects of Chinese culture. She made an effort to learn Cantonese, the language most of the residents spoke, to help in her rescues as well as in her attempts to convert the girls to Christianity, which was the key measure by which her supervisors and board members judged her success. She also taught them to sing hymns and quote Scripture, as they did for the guests that day.

The visiting dignitaries praised the work and the new Mission Home. "The better class of Chinese feel very kindly towards the home," said Vice-Consul King Owyang. "Considering the amount of good they have done, our work in furnishing this room has been very little."

But others in Chinatown resented the missionary women's rescues, which in recent years had started making dramatic headlines and becoming the subject of eye-catching newspaper sketches. The sheer doggedness of Culbertson and her lawyer was proving troublesome to Chinatown's brothel keepers, because the pair often won their legal battles to gain and retain custody of the young women.

The court cases drew attention to a business that the criminal tongs preferred to keep hidden. So did newspaper headlines. The same year Tien arrived, the *San Francisco Chronicle* assigned a reporter to investigate "Chinese slavery." His long, front-page exposé compared what was taking place in Chinatown in the 1890s to the world depicted in Harriet Beecher Stowe's 1852 antislavery novel, *Uncle Tom's Cabin*. Readers were horrified to learn that "slavery is not a thing of the past, but that human beings are to-day bought and sold into a worse slavery than ever Uncle Tom knew of." Focusing on the work of Culbertson and her colleagues, the reporter indirectly likened them to American abolitionists who had fought to end southern slavery forty years earlier.

Two months after that front-page story appeared, Culbertson woke to find a note left at the home's doorstep, alluding to the violence that had erupted through the years over "slave girls":

> To the respected teachers of the school: heretofore you have been taking too many of our prostitutes. . . . You are to let all these prostitutes go at once and you must make no further arrests from the brothels. If you heed this demand there will be no more lives taken, but if you continue to take away our income by taking our girls there will be more bloodshed. You Christian teachers, both men and women, be cautious in your goings and comings. We are the brothel-keepers.

The note ended with a dozen names of known operators of houses of prostitution, representing four different tongs. That alone was enough to raise the suspicions of the Chinese vice-consul. He doubted that it was actually written by the Chinese who were named and suspected that a white brothel keeper had penned the note. But whoever wrote it authored similar notes left under the doors of the nearby Methodist Mission and the home of the young minister Chew and his wife, Chun Fah.

The threats, real or not, came at a time when Culbertson and the other missionaries had started to disrupt the lucrative business of importing and selling women in Chinatown. The financial stakes were high. By then, the price for a prostitute had soared to $2,500 or even $3,000—more than double the price in effect before Congress had passed the Chinese Exclusion Act and nearly fifty times the monthly wage of a skilled laborer in the United States.

Pressures were building on the brothel keepers. The new law had made smuggling women into the country more difficult, and now the work of missionaries and other anti-vice crusaders was drawing more attention to the plight of trafficked Chinese women.

Dynamite

D olly Cameron, now twenty-five years old, climbed the steps of
the Mission Home. She passed beneath the brick archway and
lifted the heavy knocker on the front door. She wore her thick curls
piled on the top of her head in a style popularized by the "Gibson Girl"
illustrations that had just started appearing in American magazines.
She also topped off her thick cascade of hair with a hat that sprouted
silk hibiscus blossoms, trimmed with ribbons. Delicate white netting
covered her face as she stepped over the threshold.

Cameron's auburn hair now had strands of silver running through
it. In the almost seven years since she'd written to her sister about
her engagement and her plans for married life, Cameron had suffered a series of setbacks. Her father had died, and her enrollment in
a teacher-training course had come to an end, perhaps due to a lack
of funds. Her engagement to her brother's friend George Sargent also
had ended.

The breakup left her in an awkward position. At an age at which
many of her female contemporaries had married and already borne
four or five children, Cameron found herself single, childless, and without a job as she arrived at the home on April 20, 1895.

Evelyn Browne, a family friend from Oakland, suggested she take
a position in San Francisco. Evelyn's mother, Mary Ann Browne,
had been president of the Mission Home's board from its earliest
days, and from the Brownes Cameron learned that the health of the
home's superintendent was delicate. What's more, the superintendent's

A formal portrait of Donaldina Cameron when she was twenty-five.

second-in-command, Houseworth, had resigned a few months earlier. The home desperately needed help. With few other options available to her, Cameron left her quiet life with her family in Southern California to spend a year at the Mission Home in Chinatown teaching sewing.

A photograph of Cameron taken in 1895, the year she arrived in San Francisco, suggests she had matured a great deal in the years since her engagement. Her choice of clothing was sophisticated: a short-waisted jacket with a plush fur collar that had white lace spilling over it. A belt cinched in her waist, and white gloves covered her tiny hands, which gently clasped a pocketbook on her lap. Her long nose was aquiline and her skin as unblemished as a young girl's. Her determined expression suggests she is trying to stay motionless for the camera, as photographs of the time required.

Another longtime friend who volunteered at the home, Eleanor Olney, was there to greet Cameron when she reached the Mission Home in the afternoon—reflecting, perhaps, how understaffed it was. She led Cameron to a clean and sparsely furnished room, with a single mattress on an iron bed frame, a straight chair, and a small table. Like most of the windows at the home, hers were protected with metal grating.

Olney took Cameron on a tour, showing her the laundry room and kitchen and then upstairs to the schoolrooms and the home's resplendent Oriental parlor. Cameron and Tien probably saw each other for the first time that afternoon. From that day on, their lives would be closely intertwined.

Soon, another one of Culbertson's nieces, Anna, who had returned from New York to help her aunt Maggie, joined them in the small room. Introducing herself, she welcomed Cameron with a bouquet of white roses, a symbol of purity and new beginnings. Later that afternoon, the superintendent summoned Cameron to her office. There, the new sewing teacher saw a weary, middle-aged woman sitting behind a writing desk. She listened as Culbertson told her what had occurred earlier that day, before she'd walked up the steps to the home.

THAT MORNING, two boys were delivering newspapers to the homes and shops along the upper slope of San Francisco's Sacramento Street.

When one of the boys set down a paper on the doorstep of 920 Sacramento, he spotted a tube-shaped package wrapped in yellow paper marked "Hercules No. 2"—a popular pencil brand. A similar package, wrapped in the same kind of yellow paper, sat on a nearby windowsill.

The boy picked up one of the tubes and pretended to throw it at the other boy who was accompanying him on his rounds. His friend shouted, "Stop!" The threats against the Mission Home were well known in San Francisco; for several years, they had been regularly splashed across the papers. The boys who delivered the news must have absorbed at least some of it; they figured the tube contained dynamite.

Gingerly picking up the paper-wrapped sticks, they began searching the perimeter of the house for others. Another rested in the iron grating that covered the kitchen window. They bundled together the three wrapped sticks and brought them to one boy's father, a police officer. He notified Culbertson and his boss, San Francisco's police chief.

Culbertson was by then accustomed to the largely empty threats made against her by the home's enemies. She began her own search for additional dynamite sticks and found two more, placed in the basement window casements on the west side of the home, near the paved sidewalk on Prospect Place. Although she must have been shaken by the discovery, she underplayed the threat, telling a reporter for *The San Francisco Call* that because none of the dynamite sticks had fuses attached, it was impossible for them to have exploded.

She also speculated that the criminals who'd placed the dynamite around the Mission Home were hoping to intimidate its staffers because she'd helped their slaves escape. She had, after all, received a death threat earlier that spring warning her to leave the "slave girls" alone.

"She has often been threatened before," the *Call* reported, "and scoffs [at] the idea of there being anything more than bombast in the last discovery."

CAMERON NOW UNDERSTOOD the precautions she'd noticed as she climbed the steps to the Mission Home earlier. A policeman intermittently stood guard outside the home, and a full-time doorkeeper was stationed at the entrance to screen visitors. On Culbertson's orders, the doorkeeper made sure the front door was always bolted shut.

Knowing that Cameron had lived a protected life, surrounded by a loving family that had suffered some setbacks, Culbertson asked her newest hire whether she'd still like to work at the home after learning about the dynamite threat. The superintendent was giving the young teacher an excuse to change her mind and return to her family. But like Tien, Cameron didn't have many choices. Going home after her first day would involve a loss of face. What would she do if she returned to the ranch? Cameron assured her new employer that she wanted to stay.

At dinner that evening, Culbertson didn't have a chance to explain more about her work or the circumstances of the home's residents before she was called out on another rescue by a note asking for help. Middle-class white women rarely ventured out onto the streets unescorted by a man after dark: to do so would be to risk physical danger and being taken for a prostitute. Yet within half an hour, she'd returned with a frightened young woman wearing an elaborately embroidered blue satin dress. The Chinese interpreter who'd accompanied Culbertson on the mission took the woman to the kitchen, hoping to convince her to eat.

Culbertson was exhausted by her long day. Her hands were shaking as she asked Cameron to join her in her office. The two women sat together that night. Culbertson acknowledged that her new teacher's first day at the home had been a tumultuous one, between the dynamite threat and the request for help from another young woman in distress.

Confused by the newest arrival, Cameron asked the older woman to tell her more about the girl in the blue dress.

"A prostitute."

Cameron didn't speak.

Culbertson asked her if she had understood when she agreed to take the job that she would be living and working with girls and women who had been sex slaves.

"Oh yes. I have heard of rescued slaves. But I didn't know 'slaves' meant . . ." Cameron paused, reluctant to use a word rarely uttered in polite drawing rooms. "I thought the Home cared for orphaned and unprotected girls."

Culbertson, who'd been working in Chinatown for nearly eighteen years by then, began to explain how girls and women were sold—the younger ones as household servants and the older ones to gratify sexual appetites.

Was Cameron shocked by what she'd just learned? The Occidental Board's annual reports used euphemisms to refer to rescued former prostitutes. Only in recent years had Culbertson begun describing them in her reports somewhat more directly, referring to one recent resident as a former "slave girl" who had been forced to live in "dens of vice."

But Culbertson felt obliged to speak more frankly to Cameron. Some of the new sewing teacher's students had suffered unimaginable traumas, and Cameron would need to understand that if she were to be effective. As well, Culbertson might have assumed that Cameron, who was raised in a religious household in a rural setting, was herself sexually inexperienced, a common presumption made about women from middle- and upper-middle-class families during the Victorian era.

Cameron soon realized that she had signed on for her new start as more than just a teacher providing instruction in how to sew buttonholes and straight seams. She had enlisted to join the fight against slavery.

13

Devil's Playground

On the evening of July 3, 1895, a bullet from a .38-caliber gun shattered a bedroom window at the Methodist mission house on Washington Street, just two blocks away from where Dolly Cameron had been living since April. The bullet glanced off a sewing machine in the room and landed on the bedroom carpet. Two young girls were sleeping in the room at the time, but no one was injured. The only damage was broken glass.

At first, some speculated the shot might have come from an early Independence Day reveler. Shooting guns was traditional during some celebrations, and this shot was fired on the eve of San Francisco's annual Fourth of July parade, amid the exploding firecrackers of some celebrants. But others suspected the bullet was fired as a warning to Chinatown's do-gooders from brothel keepers and traffickers: stop taking our girls and women.

The English-language newspapers brimmed that year with sensational reports of violence and police corruption in the city's Chinese quarter. In 1895, headlines in *The San Francisco Call* included "Terror in Chinatown" and "Attacked by Highbinders." Indeed, at almost exactly the same time that Cameron arrived at the Mission Home, in the third week of April 1895, the city was jolted by the story of two teenage girls from San Francisco, both white, who were lured on a Sunday evening by a pair of Chinatown guides into a bordello, presumably to force them into prostitution.

The girls eluded their captors by screaming and running away. But

A scene of Chinatown after dark.

the policeman who heard their story arrested one of the two male guides, alerted the Society for the Prevention of Cruelty to Children, and ultimately sent the teenage girls to jail for their misadventure—much to the outrage of the younger girl's parents. (The older girl was a house servant, and no one advocated for her safety or rights.) Yet despite these stories, tourists continued to visit the quarter. If anything, the thrill of danger seemed to attract more outsiders to Chinatown.

While the number of violent deaths in Chinatown had halved since the early 1890s, the trend began reversing course in the second half of 1895 as unrest and violence in the quarter and in the city escalated. Violent crimes in the quarter spiked, while murders in the rest of the city also rose. The previous year, a shake-up in the San Francisco Police Department's Chinatown Squad had followed a grand jury investigation of its corruption. The graft system in Chinatown that Little Pete was intimately involved in was referred to as "the sack."

On a weekly basis, Chinese crime bosses would collect cash in a sack from operators of gambling houses and brothels. Those payoffs, totaling some $1,000 (or more than ten times the average police officer's weekly salary), would then be turned over to the Chinatown Squad's sergeant, who'd dole them out to the beat cops, the detectives, the department's chief clerk, and, according to rumor, one or more officials higher in the chain of command. The SFPD's longtime chief, Patrick Crowley, suddenly took ill and was unavailable when the grand jury called on him to testify about the alleged graft.

Because of the ongoing investigations, the police assigned a new team of patrolmen and detectives to work Chinatown. Determined to set themselves apart from their corrupt predecessors and demonstrate their willingness to crack down on crime, they'd use their axes to smash into the fortified doors of gambling dens, busting up furniture, belongings, and whatever else got in their way—without bothering with the legal pretext for their actions. Soon, outraged Chinese property owners filed multiple lawsuits against the squad, claiming tens of thousands of dollars in damage. The regrouped Chinatown Squad had embarked on seemingly indiscriminate busts, with little regard for injury to innocent bystanders.

Sometimes joined on its raids by a photographer, the newly reformed squad seemed to delight in causing mayhem in the quarter.

Prior to one raid, a squad sergeant ordered two patrolmen to go to a costume shop on Market Street. With the shopkeeper's help, they donned the slouchy hats and loose blouses of tong men and applied dye to their skin to look more "Asian." The disguises were apparently convincing enough to get them admitted to a fan-tan parlor, which the squad then broke up—arresting eighteen gamblers playing the ancient game.

Decades earlier, San Francisco's police department had started taking photographs of all people arrested in the city, pasting the head shots into albums and mounting them on the wall in what it called its "rogues' gallery." Starting in the 1860s, the department kept its "mug book" of Chinese suspected criminals separate from its collection of white suspects, to more easily identify criminal tong members.

The squad also documented itself. The Federal Bureau of Investigation hadn't been formed yet, so there was no national enforcement of gang activity—just local initiatives like San Francisco's Chinatown Squad, made up of plainclothes officers. A photograph taken that year

The San Francisco Police Department's Chinatown Squad.

shows a group of nine men, wearing top coats and bowlers, posing with an ax and sledgehammers in front of the police clerk August Pistolesi's grocery store, in the heart of Chinatown. Some of the men are grinning; others seem to relish their tough stances. The photograph might have been a bit of theater intended to raise the profile of the squad, or snapped as a bit of fun for the squad members themselves. Whatever the reason, the face of the only Chinese person in the photograph is blurred, while those of the white policemen are in sharp focus.

RELATIONS BETWEEN THE SQUAD and the surrounding Chinese community rapidly frayed. In one instance, a sergeant newly assigned to the squad, Jesse Brown Cook, threw a Chinese man down a set of stairs at a temple, breaking the man's ribs and leaving him severely injured. Cook claimed that the man had been acting as a lookout for a criminal tong and had "slipped" on the stairs.

Both the Chinese consul general and the Six Companies lodged complaints against Cook with the city. "This beating of Chinese in the street and in the stores has to be stopped," said the Six Companies' representative. "Beating a suspected Chinese because there is no evidence against him has to be stopped. I am free to confess that Sergeant Cook is the most brutal officer we have ever had in Chinatown."

The squad's supervisors took these complaints seriously; apparently, they had not authorized this level of violence, and Cook was improvising on his own initiative. They temporarily reassigned Cook away from the quarter (though he would return to the Chinatown Squad later). At the same time, the Six Companies (representing tongs, but publicly condemning the criminal activities of some tong members) and the consul's office decided to take matters into their own hands. They hired a squad of private guards and posted signs in the quarter demanding an end to the violence. The signs announced that in the future, the Six Companies and the consul's office would no longer bail out Chinese criminals. Those moves deepened growing divisions. Warring parties were soon posting their own flyers on the walls of buildings and telegraph poles.

On the morning of Sunday, April 28, just a week or so after Cameron arrived at the Mission Home, a throng of Chinese men gathered at the corners of Dupont and Jackson Streets, about six blocks away from the Mission Home. They jostled each other to read the eight-by-four-inch notices posted on the telegraph poles, mentioning "white devils" and "blackmail." So large were the crowds that morning that they blocked the cable cars that normally clattered through Chinatown.

If Cameron attended Sunday service at the Chinese Presbyterian church that day, she must have wondered at all the commotion. She wouldn't have been able to understand the messages on the posters themselves, because she didn't read Chinese, but translations of them appeared in the city's English-language newspapers the next day:

TAKE NOTICE

The white devils sent into Chinatown by Chief Crowley have lately been held in check. They do no more blackmailing. We are only relieved from one class of bloodsuckers to be afflicted with another. The captain and eight men appointed by the Six Companies to keep order are now worse than ever the white devils were. They are blackmailing the women, the opium sellers and the lottery games. None of us are safe from them and it is time they were done away with. We had to put up with the white devils, but we won't put up with the Six Companies' devils.

Officers from the SFPD ripped down the notices and began dispersing the crowd. The "shadow" guard hired by the Six Companies, made up of a captain, a sergeant, and seven private police patrolmen, remained in force, refusing to let the anonymous threats intimidate them. The violence in Chinatown continued. Soon afterward on Baker's Alley (also known as Murderers' Alley), things got so bad a Chinese gang member shot a man to death for merely kicking a dog.

ON SATURDAY NIGHT, January 23, 1897, shortly before the beginning of the Chinese Year of the Rooster, the crime boss Little Pete was relaxing in his home on the third floor of 819½ Washington Street. He lived there with his wife and three children above the large, thriving

A formal portrait of Little Pete with his family.

business they owned: a shoe factory called F. C. Peters & Co., where he, his uncle, and his brother employed about forty men.

Although F. C. Peters & Co. sold its shoes to Chinese and Caucasians alike, Little Pete's main occupation and source of funds came from his remarkably varied criminal enterprises, which allegedly included murder for hire in the escalating feuds between his tong, the Sam Yups, and the rival See Yups. After three trials, a jury in 1887 convicted him of bribing officials. A judge sentenced him to five years at Folsom Prison, but he was released after eighteen months. When he returned to San Francisco, he quickly got back into trafficking, again using the ruse of fairs and expositions to bring Chinese women into the United States. Some of those women had fled to the missions for safety, making both the Methodist and the Presbyterian homes into targets for angry traffickers.

That night in January 1897, Little Pete himself became a victim. He knew there was a price on his head of some $3,000 (more than three times what a teamster, at $3 a day, would earn in a year), yet he felt confident enough in his safety to send his bodyguards on errands while he walked down the stairs to the street and two doors down to a barbershop at 817 Washington Street. Sitting close to the door, facing Ross Alley, he eased into a chair, preparing to have his forehead shaved and his queue rebraided.

At about ten minutes past 9:00 p.m., just as he was relaxing into the barber's chair, two men rushed into the shop. They'd learned that the criminal tong boss was unprotected. As Little Pete lay in the chair, one of the men approached him with his gun drawn and fired four times. The first bullet struck the wall. The next entered just above Little Pete's right eye. The third entered his forehead, passing through his brain and killing him instantly.

Little Pete's assassins dropped their guns and fled. Smoke and the smell of cordite lingered in the air. More than a dozen police charged into the barbershop, recovering only one of the weapons. Crowds swelled that night outside the shop and on the street near the shoe factory. The news of Little Pete's murder dominated the front pages of the city's newspapers the next day. Despite many leads, several arrests, and a trial of a lower-level tong gunman, the police never solved the mystery of who was behind his assassination.

A rival criminal tong is believed to have ordered his death. The police rounded up a suspect who was tried before a jury, but prosecutors did not win a conviction. Little Pete's death detonated another round of violence in Chinatown as criminal tongs battled police forces for control of the quarter. Little Pete's funeral was one of the largest the city had ever witnessed. With firecrackers exploding and gongs clanging, police escorted a massive procession through San Francisco that included a resplendent hearse pulled by six black horses, a loud group of hired mourners, and an orchestra that played the funeral march from Handel's oratorio *Saul,* based on the biblical book of Samuel.

One of the people who attended the procession on January 26, 1897, was a handsome young writer named Frank Norris, who would later go on to fame as the author of *The Octopus,* a novel exploring the power of California's railroad monopolies. He wrote scathingly of the mob of about two thousand people, many of them white, who had arrived at the Chinese cemetery outside the city. He described how the crowd plundered the Chinese bowls, the tissue ornaments, the roast chickens and pork, and even the bottles of gin that were laid out on the platform where the funeral ceremonies for Chinatown's powerful tong boss were to be performed before the cortege even arrived.

Commenting more on his fellow Caucasians than on the Chinese, he wrote, "This was the last impression one received of Little Pete's funeral—a crowd of two thousand men and women, standing in a huge circle, stupidly staring at the remains of a roasted pig."

14

Chinatown in Tears

The death of Little Pete, who had been a linchpin of San Francisco's slave trade for many years, did not reduce the strain on
Margaret Culbertson, the Mission Home's long-serving superintendent. She'd fought against sex trafficking for almost two decades,
and over time her shoulders had grown increasingly hunched and her
slender frame ever more fragile. Not only had Culbertson responded
to rescue calls from Chinatown at all times of day and night, but she
managed an occasionally unruly household of forty to fifty girls and
young women. And she did this despite an internal injury that had
plagued her for years.

Sometime in 1892, during a rescue, a girl had delivered a painful
kick to Culbertson's midsection. The superintendent was reluctant to
talk about what had happened, because she didn't want the girl, who
lived at the home, to be blamed for harming her. But Culbertson suffered badly from what might have been organ damage and internal
bleeding. Her injury ultimately forced her to rest. Culbertson had
hoped that relinquishing many of her duties at the home would help
her recover. By the time Cameron arrived in 1895, it was clear that the
older woman was not regaining her strength.

Culbertson's legal battles compounded her health problems. To
gain custody of a single girl, she often had to make five or more court
appearances. Her opponents were relentless. In one case, an attorney
representing a brothel keeper attacked her integrity and the character
of the Mission Home. Because it was the home's policy to ask prospec-

Margaret Culbertson, the long-serving superintendent of the
Mission Home, holding one of its youngest residents.

tive bridegrooms to pay the $75 annual "back rent" of board and tuition for their brides-to-be as well as to pay for the dress, the cake, and the other wedding expenses (which were meticulously recorded so they could be reimbursed by the groom), the lawyer charged her with selling off girls—some of whom, he alleged, ended up working as prostitutes again.

Culbertson spent long hours on the witness stand being questioned about the hurtful and spurious charges. Despite the nearly forty women who came to support her in the courtroom (mostly friends and members of the Occidental Board), the experience of being attacked and, ironically, accused of selling girls was draining, even though she ultimately prevailed and eventually won custody of the so-called slave maiden at the center of the case. But that court victory didn't slow down the courtroom assaults against the Mission Home or its superintendent.

The stress of Culbertson's frequent courtroom appearances, along with mounting physical threats against the Mission Home and the risk of the residents' being kidnapped when they stepped outside, wore her down. So did living in a violent neighborhood, where hatchet-wielding rivals butchered each other in Chinatown's dense alleys. But what might have been most wearying was the inescapable fact that Culbertson and her colleagues were losing their battle against sex slavery.

In her annual report to the board in 1897, she recounted a particularly demoralizing episode that had taken place a month earlier. On March 22, authorities staged raids on nine separate brothels. They rounded up sixty girls and women from those houses and brought them to the Mission Home in a sweep of the kind that hadn't been seen in the quarter since Little Pete's death.

Pandemonium descended around noon when the police brought in the sixty women. Some shrieked and wailed. Others beat the floor with their shoes, "filling the air with their vile imprications [sic], denouncing the Home in no unmeasured terms," Culbertson wrote to her board.

The police were looking for a group of thirteen young women who'd recently arrived from China. The home's interpreter and lawyer interviewed all sixty and asked them if they would like to become residents of the Mission Home and take advantage of its protection. Amid the chaos of the roundup and the threats of deportation, most of the women rejected the offer. "No, no, no, Home no good," answered some, in a rebuff that Culbertson described as being delivered with scorn and derision. Perhaps they reacted that way because they'd heard the rumors planted by the brothel keepers. (One of these was that the superintendent was a white devil who drank the blood of captive girls to keep up her energy.)

The authorities detained the thirteen recent immigrants, hoping that they would provide evidence against corrupt customhouse officials, as well as against their traffickers and captors. (Prostitution was not against the law at that time: the authorities in this instance were hoping to find violators of the 1882 Exclusion Act.) *The San Francisco Call* ran a headline the next day describing the sobbing of the young women who'd been forced to spend the night at the Mission Home: "Chinatown in Tears."

Most of those detained were soon released to the brothels on writs of habeas corpus. Out of the thirteen, only three ended up becoming residents of the Mission Home. And they proved trying ones at that. Culbertson described them, whether out of condescension or sheer frustration, as "very rebellious subjects."

The experience was disheartening to Culbertson. She must have wondered, in her darker moments, whether the cause she'd devoted her life to was truly worth the cost. More troubling were the indications that some, if not many, of the subjects of her rescue efforts were not interested in her help. The invective hurled at her suggested that some—or perhaps many—of the "Chinese slave girls" that she and her supporters had hoped to save had no desire to become Christians.

In her report to the women of the Occidental Board about that episode, Culbertson seemed to be talking herself through a crisis of faith. Rhetorically, she posed the question: "Does rescue work pay?" She didn't define what she meant by "pay"; perhaps it was converting Chinese women to Christianity or, more broadly, the spiritual compensation she and other staffers received for engaging in Christian-inspired work to ease human suffering. But she answered emphatically, "Yes, it pays." For proof of this, she added, "We have a goodly number of Christian homes in this city and throughout the State." She then rebutted the notion that the Chinese were ungrateful for the missionaries' efforts. Since she'd become ill, she recounted, her Chinese friends had sent her many delicacies and tender notes wishing her a speedy recovery.

These were small yet meaningful signs of friendship. So was the joyful moment when one of the home's former residents, Ah Ching, gave birth to a baby girl. She was named Margaret, to honor the home's superintendent.

YET OTHER SMALL THINGS had started to grind away at Culbertson: the poor heating at the Mission Home, for example, which left the superintendent shivering during the cold winter months. For much of Cameron's first year, Culbertson lived as an invalid at the home, leaving responsibility for its forty-five residents largely to the newest and youngest staffer. The shadow of the superintendent's serious illness fell over the remaining staff, binding them together more tightly.

Although Culbertson returned to work for a time in 1896, she saw more clearly than ever the limits of her efforts and grew outspokenly frustrated by having been stymied in her decades-long battle against sex slavery. "The Occidental Board has done much in the twenty-two years of its existence in succoring and alleviating the sufferings of these enslaved ones, but has not been able to stop the traffic," she wrote in 1897. "There was a time when a check was put upon it, but it is now in full blast again."

She'd won many victories in court and helped hundreds of young women escape slavery. But the Mission Home's superintendent was clearly losing a private battle with her health. She scheduled a trip home to New York to rest. On a Monday morning in late July 1897, just two days after the birth of her namesake, Culbertson was too sick to manage the stairs for her departure. Staffers lifted her onto a stretcher and carried her to the railway station. The girls and young women living at the home wept as she left, fearing that they'd never see her again. Accompanied by her brother and sister, who had been attending a religious convention in San Francisco, as well as by her niece Anna, the superintendent was eased onto a train. Culbertson hoped to rest and recover at the family's home in Groveland.

But on July 31, just five days after her departure and before she reached home, Culbertson died. The news, which appeared in the San Francisco papers the next day, came as a profound shock to the residents of 920 Sacramento Street, as well as to the much larger circle of people whose lives she had touched. Over two decades, nearly seven hundred girls and women had found shelter under Miss Culbertson's care, first at 933 and then at 920 Sacramento Street. She had a profound impact on many lives.

She'd certainly affected Cameron, who'd found protection under Culbertson's guidance at a time when she was uncertain of her future. The older woman had been a mentor to Cameron, whose own parents were gone, and her death hit Cameron hard. Mary H. Field, who was brought in by the board as the acting superintendent after Culbertson's death, described Cameron as having suffered a "serious breakdown in September—brought on by incessant anxiety and care during Miss Culbertson's terrible illness."

Cameron's suffering was so deep that it prevented her from continuing her work. In the early autumn of 1898, she left 920 Sacramento Street and returned south to rest, leaving behind the quarter's scent of burning incense and returning instead to the comforting familiarity of La Puente's aromatic bay laurels and gnarled live oaks.

‹—◦ 15 ◦—›

Year of the Rat

Shortly before midnight on March 6, 1900, three men gathered at a coffin shop in Chinatown to examine the body of a forty-one-year-old Chinese man who had died earlier that day. The police surgeon, a city health official, and a young bacteriologist palpated the corpse's swollen lymph glands and found a small sore on his thigh. Piercing the skin, they drew blood and lymph fluids and placed drops of them under a microscope. With a stain that made the germs turn pink, they saw clusters of short, rod-shaped bacteria swimming under the lens. It looked like bubonic plague.

Confirming that suspicion would take days, but city officials leaped into action. That night, the Board of Health ordered a quarantine of Chinatown. Under the cover of darkness, some thirty-five police officers spread out around twelve square blocks. They strung ropes across key intersections and blocked foot traffic and wagons from coming in or out. Only police and health officials were permitted to cross the barriers; supplies to the quarter, at least at first, were passed under the ropes. Chinese who tried to leave the area were blocked by officers carrying nightsticks and pistols.

Most San Franciscans learned of the quarantine the next morning. Some read about it in the newspapers; others pieced together the story on their own after their servants, cooks, and porters failed to show up for work. The chef at the Palace Hotel struggled with the breakfast service, because a dozen or more of his Chinese employees couldn't get past the barricades to reach the kitchen. The Chinese who supplied

Crowded conditions in a tenement house in San Francisco's Chinatown.

hotels and restaurants from their gardens outside the city were unable to leave Chinatown to harvest their long beans and mustard greens. A story in the *San Francisco Chronicle* condemned the quarantine as having been too hastily imposed: "The central telephone in Chinatown was kept busy for hours making connections for angry citizens who were trying to get trace of missing servants."

A QUARANTINE ROPE STRUNG across Stockton Street prevented the Mission Home's residents and staffers from reaching Chinatown's main shopping area. The cable cars that normally rattled past Portsmouth Square on the Sacramento–Clay Street line were halted, and ships heading back to China left without passengers from Chinatown. Some people found their way in and out of the blockaded area by descending underground to pass through the connecting cellars of houses or by quietly traversing rooftops.

One of those interlopers was a nine-year-old girl named Leung Kum Ching, who slipped past the quarantine on March 8 to seek help for her gravely ill sister. The two girls were orphans who had been cared for by a Chinese family. When one of the girls had grown sick, the family grew anxious. They might have believed that her illness was an imbalance of yin forces or a possession by evil spirits. They certainly feared that she might die inside their home and release *sat hei*, or "killing airs." So they placed her outside, near the entryway to another building, and left her alone to die. Running for help and ignoring the shouts of a policeman stationed nearby, her sister found her way to the Mission Home and begged for assistance. There she met Cameron, whose spirits were restored after a period of rest at La Puente and who was even more determined to carry on the work of her late friend and mentor, Margaret Culbertson.

Cameron agreed to follow the young girl to her sister but first had to slip past the quarantine lines herself. A few years earlier, Cameron had cared for the wife of an herbalist who had a shop just outside the sequestered area. After hearing the story of the abandoned girl, the herbalist allowed Cameron to climb up onto the roof of his building through a skylight. She then crossed several roofs until she found another opening that allowed her to descend through a building and out onto the street, inside the quarantined area. Normally clothed in a high-necked shirtwaist and an ankle-length dark skirt, Cameron instead tried to blend in by disguising herself in dark Chinese clothing. The rainy weather cooperated: she hid her shiny clouds of reddish-brown hair beneath a black umbrella.

She found Leung's sister stretched out on three wooden chairs on the street. After making sure the girl was still alive, Cameron left her and reversed her route, making her way back to the Mission Home, where she telephoned the Board of Health. A doctor answered and helped arrange for an ambulance. Cameron and the home's Chinese translator, Yuen Qui, rode with it through the blockade. After examining the girl and diagnosing her with acute appendicitis, a condition that can be fatal if left untreated, the doctor allowed her to be taken outside the quarantine zone and into a bed at the Mission Home. Within hours of arriving, the girl died "among friends," as recorded in the Mission Home's logbook. Three days later, she was buried in the Chinese cemetery.

With loyalty born out of Cameron's quick efforts to try to save her sister, Leung (who became known as Ah Ching by residents and other staffers) moved to the Mission Home. As one of the home's staffers wrote in dense scrawl in the logbook, "Little Ah Ching wished to remain with us, so letters of guardianship were secured and she became a member of the Mission Family." Eventually, she joined Cameron on rescues as a translator, before returning to China as a kindergarten teacher, where she worked in a mission school in Shanghai.

AS FEARED, the forty-one-year-old man who perished on March 6 had indeed carried bubonic plague. The day after the existence of the bacteria was confirmed, the U.S. surgeon general in Washington, D.C., shipped almost two thousand doses of an antiplague vaccine to San Francisco. He promised to send thirteen thousand more soon after.

The surgeon general had prescribed a mass vaccination program in Chinatown, even though the vaccine itself—first introduced to the public only three years earlier, in 1897—was known to sometimes cause severe side effects. With risks of pain, high fevers, and even death from getting the shots, many Chinese vehemently opposed being vaccinated.

Some doubted its efficacy, while others mistrusted the white health-care workers who administered it.

Cameron, who by then had been appointed the Mission Home's superintendent, urged her girls to get the shot, which contained heat-killed plague bacteria. But some of them were terrified when the white doctors pulled out their syringes and asked them to roll up their sleeves. Immunizations such as these were novel, and it is unlikely any of the residents had received one before. One of the Chinese girls at the home grew so panic-stricken at the sight of the needle that she jumped through a second-floor window to avoid it, shattering her ankle. Brothel owners used such instances of girls fleeing the missionaries to instill fear: "See what they do to you at the Mission. They starve you and beat you until you are glad to get out."

Other Chinese hid from the health-care workers to avoid the dreaded vaccinations and circumvented their efforts by removing and hiding plague victims' bodies. They were hoping to avoid autopsies to confirm the cause of death, a practice that offended the Chinese, who believed that cutting into a corpse might prematurely release the soul before the proper funeral rites had been performed.

Some residents of San Francisco's Chinatown knew or had family members affected by an outbreak of bubonic plague in Honolulu's dense Chinatown a few months earlier. Health authorities established a quarantine, posting armed guards to keep people in and out, and con-troversially, in January 1900, set a planned fire that raced out of con-trol. Gusting wind blew embers from the controlled area to other parts of Chinatown: the fire burned for seventeen days and destroyed four thousand mostly Chinese and Japanese homes.

San Francisco's Chinatown was similarly under siege. Bubonic plague had arrived in the city on fleas feasting on the blood of rats, just as it had probably arrived in Honolulu. The outbreak began—in a dreadful irony—in the Chinese Year of the Rat. The quarter faced an onslaught from worried city and national health officials, some of whom suggested fire as a way to cleanse the neighborhood of the plague and prevent it from spreading to other parts of the city. Fortu-nately, they chose less drastic methods in San Francisco and avoided setting too many controlled fires, perhaps sobered by Honolulu's tragic experience.

·   ·   ·

IF THERE WAS any doubt that San Francisco's Chinatown was in crisis, the smell of bonfires and chemical disinfectants drove that home.
City workers burned refuse on the streets, scattered lime powder
against buildings in a kind of chemical snowstorm, and flushed sewer
lines with strong disinfectants. From their perch on the upper slopes
of Sacramento Street, the Mission Home's residents would have seen
white plumes of chloric smoke rising from the streets below them and
closed their windows to block the stench of the chemical vapors, along
with the quarter's burning garbage, from coming inside.

The *San Francisco Chronicle* and the *Call* covered the story extensively, and an enterprising reporter for the *Examiner* even went so far
as to get himself injected with the plague vaccine to catalog its side
effects. ("I was slightly dizzy, there was a ringing in my ears and I felt
I was drifting into a stupor from which I did not particularly care to
rouse myself," he wrote, adding that about eight hours later he began
feeling better.)

Chronicling the quarantine from inside Chinatown itself was
Ng Poon Chew, just starting his new life as a San Francisco newspaper
editor. After moving north from Los Angeles, Chew had struggled to
find a landlord outside Chinatown willing to rent an apartment to him
and his large family, which included four children and an infant by that
time. So he rented quarters on the outskirts of Chinatown, near other
Chinese Christian families.

He went to work in Chinatown and, at age thirty-three, founded
one of the first daily Chinese newspapers in the United States. Printed
in the lucky color of red, its first issue rolled off the presses on February
16, 1900, making its debut barely three weeks before city health officials
confirmed the first plague death.

From the paper's modest offices on Sacramento Street, Chew
placed a sign over its doorway: *Chung Sai Yat Po*, blazoned in red with
its translation, "The Chinese-American Daily Paper," in smaller letters below it. A set of narrow stairs led up to the offices, where Chew
served as editor in chief as well as translator (Chinese-language articles
appeared alongside some English versions). There was just enough
room for the press he'd bought from Japan, a composing room, and his

editorial office. The motto he'd learned from his grandmother: "If you will, you can."

The city's English-language papers expressed skepticism that the plague was real (their businessmen owners and advertisers, after all, stood to lose tourism dollars if news of a plague outbreak in San Francisco became known) and criticized the Board of Health for overreacting.

By contrast, Chew's urgent articles reflect the unnerving experience of working in an area ringed by police. The rumors of controversial mass inoculations had "plunged the town into disorder," reported *Chung Sai Yat Po*. From the start, the paper questioned the quarantine itself: "According to the epidemic prevention laws a yellow flag should be planted in front of an epidemic-afflicted house, or a house should be encircled by tapes to warn people off. But never have we heard of blockading a whole town." (Chew surely knew of the quarantine of Honolulu's Chinatown before its devastating fire, so perhaps he ignored that recent incident to make his point.)

Around noon on May 19, a team of city health-care workers climbed the stairs to Chew's office and found the bespectacled editor sitting at his desk. Crowds had been protesting the vaccine program outside the headquarters of the Six Companies. Neither the reassuring words of the Chinese consul nor the support of the Six Companies representative nor the pamphlets printed in Chinese and English explaining the program helped calm the situation. Hoping that his own successful vaccination might do the trick, Chew rolled up his sleeves and allowed a white doctor to inject him with the vaccine.

But as word spread of Chew's vaccination, an angry crowd gathered on the street outside his newspaper, threatening to attack him. The editor was forced to retreat to Oakland for a period while he waited for tempers to cool. In the meantime, furious readers canceled their subscriptions; Chew's young newspaper lost more than half of its subscriber base because of his decision to get inoculated.

While the swift public reaction to his decision must have been upsetting to him, Chew's comments to the *Examiner* reporter about the experience reveal his sly sense of humor. When asked whether he'd noticed any unpleasant side effects from the inoculation, he answered,

"I certainly did," in what the reporter described as his excellent English. "I haven't recovered yet."

The reporter remarked, "You don't seem to be ill."

"Ill? Oh no, it didn't affect me that way. I wasn't sick a minute. Someone told my subscribers what I had done and the news spread all through Chinatown. The following morning I awoke to find half my subscription list gone. I had hard work to explain matters and for a time it looked as if my paper would be boycotted. That inoculation may be all right as a sanitary measure, but it doesn't do to mix it with the newspaper business."

After he'd returned from Oakland and began hearing reports of other Chinese who'd submitted to the vaccination and then been incapacitated, Chew reversed his position and joined others who opposed the program. That might have been, in part, a calculated business decision following the swift drop in circulation his paper had suffered. Instead of urging readers to get the shot, his paper reversed itself and started referring to vaccination as "the torture of medicine." It also regularly alluded to the "wicked health officers" in its coverage.

A broad group of Protestant clergymen expressed solidarity with the Chinese, in opposition to city officials. It is not clear whether Cameron reversed her initial support of the vaccinations. But her memory of one of the Mission Home's residents, in a whoosh of black hair and clothing, plunging out of the window to avoid the needle would have been difficult to forget.

◦⟹ 16 ⟸◦

Instant Fame

C ity officials lifted the quarantine briefly, allowing shops to reopen and restock their shelves. They'd hoped the scattering of plague deaths in Chinatown would mark the outbreak's end. But following another spate of illness, the city reimposed the quarantine in May 1900, nearly doubling the number of police guarding the neighborhood's entry and exit points. Amid further mutterings that Chinatown should be burned down and all the Chinese living there removed to federal detention centers, city workers began erecting a high fence. They even got authorization to top it with barbed wire.

The quarantine zone zigzagged to avoid white residences, prompting a Chinese grocer whose business lay within the quarantined area to file a lawsuit against the city. He argued that the action was racially discriminatory because it was only enforced against the Chinese. A federal court judge agreed with the grocer's arguments and issued an injunction in mid-June ordering that the general quarantine be lifted (the Board of Health was still authorized to cordon off specific places infected with the disease). Although the city sent home the police guarding the perimeters of Chinatown, sanitation efforts continued. Inspectors continued to make house-to-house calls in Chinatown and to fumigate cellars with sulfur dioxide, as well as to spread chloride of lime on streets and sidewalks.

Despite these measures, the death toll mounted. It was the first known outbreak of plague in the continental United States, and by the epidemic's end in 1908 San Francisco had sustained 280 reported cases

A *Harper's Weekly* illustration from 1900 of the city's quarantine of Chinatown following an outbreak of bubonic plague.

of plague and 172 deaths—a number that may be vastly lower than the actual figure, because some of the deaths were misdiagnosed or covered up. In those eight years, the disease flared several more times. The epicenter was indeed in Chinatown, where crowded conditions and poor sanitation proved a breeding ground for rats, and most of the city's plague deaths occurred there. But the disease later spread outside the quarter to other parts of San Francisco as well: the extensive cleaning and decontamination that Chinatown underwent might have driven the rats, which carried the fleas that carried plague, to surrounding areas.

For Chinatown, the experience was a searing one. Many businesses were forced to close, and residents went hungry because of food shortages. The Protestant churches were among the few organizations in the city that supported the Chinese during the blockade by donating food and questioning the quarantine. Chew and his staff, in turn, played a crucial role in reporting on the crisis. Both the editor and his newspaper's fame spread from San Francisco, the center of Chinese America, to other cities and states with large Chinese communities, including New York, Seattle, and Los Angeles. Looking back on this traumatic period, he wrote,

> Western doctors quarantined Chinatown with the excuse of containing the plague. This was the first big event since the establishment of this newspaper. Bad omens appeared. The situation was volatile. Everybody felt insecure. People acted uneasily as if sitting on thorns. Everyone, inside and outside, used our paper as their ears and eyes. We became famous instantly.

It took a plague epidemic to solidify *Chung Sai Yat Po*'s role as a credible source of information for people living in America's largest Chinese community. But in coming years, Chew would play an even more crucial role in defending the civil rights of Chinese Americans. Though he would continue to take controversial stands, his decision at the very beginning of his career as a daily newspaper editor, when he decided to get an injection of plague vaccine as a human guinea pig, was one of his most dramatic.

.   .   .

CAMERON WAS Chew's contemporary. Thirty years old in the spring of 1900, she had returned from her rest at La Puente with renewed energy. And she was determined to take even more risks to help vulnerable girls and women. Climbing through skylights and skirting the quarantine lines had demonstrated her physical courage as the home's newly appointed head. But one of the most extraordinary instances of her daring also took place in the spring of 1900, when she went to jail to try to protect one of her charges. This took place in Palo Alto, south of San Francisco in the Santa Clara valley. Because it was best known then for its peach, cherry, and plum orchards, Cameron and the home's residents referred to it as "the country."

It began on March 29, 1900, three weeks after the city's first plague victim was discovered. At about 5:00 p.m., two Chinese men, accompanied by a policeman, climbed the stairs to 920 Sacramento Street and knocked at the door, which was always guarded. Ushered inside, the policeman pulled out a photograph and showed it to Cameron. The officer told her that the girl pictured, who was then around eighteen years old, was accused of stealing jewelry. He presented an arrest warrant for her.

"You have made a mistake," Cameron told them, glancing at the photograph. "We have no such girl here."

It had been nearly five years since Cameron had joined the staff of the Mission Home. She'd learned the ruses that traffickers and slave owners used to try to retrieve their human property. A standard one was accusing a runaway prostitute of theft—most often jewelry or other trinkets that had been given to them. That, along with writs of habeas corpus to challenge the right of the Mission Home to keep the young women in custody, was now almost routine and predictable to her. Like Culbertson before her, Cameron took unusual steps to outwit the slave owners.

Among them was to send the targets of such tactics belowground, to the Mission Home's basement. There a slender teenager could easily evade detection during searches by authorities armed with warrants. Dark corners behind sacks of rice, shelves near the gas meter, and folding double doors, where a girl could conceal herself, had been used as hiding places in the past. But this time, the appearance of the policeman took the staffers by surprise, and there wasn't time for the young woman, who came to be known as Kum Quai, to hide. Pulling out an arrest warrant, the police officer told Cameron, "Let us see for ourselves."

A staffer rang a brass gong, summoning the home's three dozen residents to the room that served as its chapel. Kum filed in with the rest. Cameron could tell from her frightened expression that she knew the Chinese men. They, in turn, recognized her and indicated this to the officer, a deputy constable from San Jose. He announced he was arresting her. They marched the teen to the door, without waiting for her to get a coat. Cameron, who stood at least a foot taller, hurried after her, with one of the home's Chinese aides bustling behind to hand them wraps. Refusing to leave Kum alone with the two men, Cameron joined the party on the thirty-five-mile train journey south.

They pulled in to the Palo Alto station at 8:00 p.m. and were met on the platform by a justice of the peace, Edgar G. Dyer. After returning with him to his office, Cameron requested that Justice Dyer hear the case against Kum right away, arguing that the Chinese men who'd accompanied them on the train were gangsters who would try to kidnap Kum and force her back into prostitution. But the justice refused, explaining that he couldn't try the case until the witnesses from San Jose had arrived. Then he left his office to attend a meeting at the local Elks Lodge.

Cameron and Kum remained in the office, where they ate dinner and waited. At around 11:00 p.m., a deputy constable arrived to lock the young woman up for the evening. Stubbornly vigilant, Cameron insisted on staying with Kum Quai. They were led to a primitive jail cell, lacking light, heat, or a bed. (The Mission Home's logbook described it as a "dark and filthy cabin that served as a jail.") The two Chinese men watched as the deputy shut and locked the door.

Sometime around 2:00 a.m., the women heard a key turn in the lock. Fearing for Kum's safety, Cameron had barricaded the door against intruders. The deputy demanded to be let in. As Cameron later recalled the late-night chaos in a first-person account published in *The Palo Alto Times*, "This I refused, saying that I feared the Chinese were around and would carry the girl off. I thought I heard Chinese voices, hence my fear."

As Cameron and Kum huddled in the dark, they heard the deputy stomp away, only to return soon after with another officer. Cameron refused to remove the barricade and demanded to know under what authority he was acting. "He replied that he was acting upon orders from Judge Dyer. I still declined to open." The two men went away briefly, only to return and begin hammering on the door of the cabin, possibly with an ax. She realized they would soon chop their way through and enter the cell. "Finding resistance useless, I removed the barricades."

One of the officers came toward the two women. Cameron grasped Kum by the hand and led her outside. Reaching for a police whistle tucked inside her clothing, she brought it to her lips and began blowing—hoping the high-pitched sound would summon help. At the same time, one of the constables grabbed at Kum and pulled her toward a waiting buggy, while the other untied the horse and jumped into the driver's seat, grasping the reins.

Kum clung to Cameron and pleaded in Chinese with the lawmen to allow the older woman to stay with her. One man pulled the women apart and then lifted the slender Chinese teen into the buggy. Cameron tried to climb in after her. The men pushed her out, and Cameron fell into weeds by the side of the road.

The constables then met up with Justice Dyer and convinced him—at 2:30 a.m. or so—to hold an impromptu trial by the side of El Camino Real, a dirt road that ran near the gates of Stanford University, founded fifteen years earlier. Alone with the men and terrified, Kum waived counsel and her right to a trial by jury. With one of her captors acting as her interpreter, she pleaded guilty to the charge of petty larceny and was fined $5, which one of the men paid.

Cameron, meanwhile, brushed the dirt and weeds off her clothes and made her way to a nearby drugstore, waking up the druggist, who then called the sheriff and asked him to organize a rescue party. He directed Cameron to a local hotel, which offered her a sofa and a blanket so she could try to get some sleep. But by the next morning, the story of the highly unorthodox middle-of-the-night trial had started to spread. Cameron's first-person account, which followed a news story, got extensive coverage in the Palo Alto paper. "In the name of law and public decency I protest against these proceedings and the treatment of a defenseless woman," she wrote.

Soon she had accumulated a group of local supporters for her cause. They included the influential reverend Dr. David Charles Gardner, rector of All Saints' Episcopal Church in Palo Alto (who would soon become Stanford University's first chaplain), a Stanford University Romance-language professor named S. J. Brun, and Emery E. Smith, a horticulturist at Stanford who helped plan San Francisco's Golden Gate Park and was one of Palo Alto's original five town trustees.

Within days, a mass meeting was held to hear testimony from Cameron and others about what happened that night. Hundreds of university students marched from campus to a public meeting hall on the unpaved thoroughfare of University Avenue. Even before the meeting began, people in the crowd started shouting angry denunciations of the officials involved in the kidnapping.

Fired up by the outrageous story of police and judicial complicity in what seemed to be a kidnapping for immoral purposes, the crowd then marched to the jail where Cameron and Kum had been held. Amid cries of "Tear it down!" some of the angry marchers ripped wood siding off the jailhouse shack. The crowd then marched down University Avenue to the center of town, carrying lanterns and torches. In the rising spirit of the Progressive Era, the protesters burned an effigy of the justice of the peace whose actions had so outraged them.

An even larger meeting took place in San Jose, where Bert A. Herrington, the lawyer who allegedly masterminded the kidnapping plot, had a robust practice representing Chinese clients. Thousands of people attended what was called the largest demonstration in the history of the city. Cameron, her lawyer, the Stanford professor, and a local judge all testified. What outraged them was not so much the fate of the Chinese girl as the apparent complicity of the local deputies and a seemingly corrupt justice of the peace. The key group of supporters, led by Stanford's Professor Brun, demanded the justice's resignation as well as prosecution of the officials. They also raised money to assist the district attorney in bringing corruption charges against the entire group.

With Cameron in charge at the Mission Home, a new era had arrived for their cause. Her measured testimony drew praise, and she captured the imagination of a *San Francisco Chronicle* reporter covering the meeting. Whether it was her clear complexion and reddish-brown curls or the fact that she was so calm and articulate, she clearly won him over. He wrote admiringly of how she "proved by her beauty and modest manner that she was a refined and cultured woman, and it seemed amazing how men could subject [her] to such vile indignities . . . as perpetrated in Palo Alto."

Kum Quai, of course, had acted courageously as well. She had left the brothel in Chinatown's Baker's Alley, a dark and narrow passage named for a nearby bakery. She took refuge in the Mission Home, despite intense pressure from gangsters not to do so. The meeting, which was attended by many Stanford students, ended with a motion to adopt resolutions supporting Cameron, a figure who might have struck them as a younger and more appealing version of the temperance crusader Carry Nation:

> We admire the fearless, heroic and womanly action of Miss Cameron in her efforts to prevent the abduction of her ward, which was accomplished under the guise of law. . . . [I]t is the duty of every man and woman within our county who has any regard for human rights and public decency to take such action as will not only secure the punishment of such offenders, but will in the future prevent recurrence of such gross outrages within our borders.

The public uproar led to criminal indictments of the deputy constable, the justice of the peace, and the two Chinese men on charges of kidnapping. A trial took place in the small town of Mayfield in Santa Clara County. In late June 1900, Kum (also known as Kim Quey) mounted the witness stand to tell her story.

Wearing American-style clothes and cloaked in a heavy veil that covered her face, she explained through an interpreter, John Endicott

Gardner, that she had come to the United States two years earlier to take part in the 1898 Omaha Exposition. That was one of the world's fairs used by Little Pete as a pretext to import many Chinese girls and women as prostitutes. A special act of Congress had permitted their entry, under the condition that they return to China a few months after the exhibit's closing. Few, if any, did. Kum Quai, for one, ended up in notorious Baker's Alley.

Kum testified in Cantonese, through Gardner, that she'd been pressured to lie on the stand, explaining that the lawyer Herrington had "threatened to put a bullet through my head" if she didn't perjure herself.

The interpreter asked her a follow-up question in Cantonese: "Have you a *Chuck-Jee*—a registration card?"

"No *Chuck-Jee*," she answered.

"Then, in the name of the Government of the United States, I place you under arrest!"

Kum Quai and Donaldina Cameron in 1910, a decade after the Palo Alto case.

The courtroom exploded, not only at the revelation that Herrington had threatened to shoot her, but at Kum's unexpected arrest. That meant the government would deport her, presumably keeping her out of the hands of the traffickers who'd fought so hard to get her. Cameron was relieved by the outcome, because it meant that for the time being Kum would remain with her at the Mission Home.

Herrington, however, panicked. Kum had accused him of threatening to murder her unless she perjured herself. He bolted from the courtroom, jumped into a buggy, and was chased down by the Reverend Gardner and another man, tailcoats flapping, in a lighter and swifter horse-drawn sulky. While Kum was placed into Cameron's custody and returned to the Mission Home, the court eventually dismissed the case against Herrington on the kidnapping charges for lack of evidence, because key witnesses had refused to testify against him. None of the indictments resulted in any convictions, and all five of the accused men went free. Kum Quai, after some time under Cameron's guardianship at the home, eventually found her freedom. She posed for a photograph alongside Cameron a decade later, wearing a triple strand of pearls, a formal Chinese gown, and a warm smile.

THE PALO ALTO KIDNAPPING CASE was a fiasco in legal terms. It failed to bring to justice any of the men who'd falsely accused Kum of a crime, abducted her, threatened her, and openly flouted the law in doing so. But the testimony in the case shed light on how unscrupulous white attorneys and officers of the law—most outrageously, the former district attorney Herrington and Justice of the Peace Dyer—had abetted traffickers. And it helped publicize the issue of sex slavery. The priest and the academics from Stanford who had protested the incident published an impassioned plea that focused attention on the trafficking of Chinese women in California.

The group's editorial ran in newspapers across the state and made Donaldina Cameron famous. "It is a matter of common knowledge that the State of California has long been disgraced by the slavery of Chinese-girls," they wrote. "The fact that this traffic is confined to Chinese subjects does not mitigate the offense against law and decency or lessen the moral responsibility of the citizens of the State."

Until that point, it had been clergymen who'd been the leading critics of human trafficking. Now the circle was expanding to include academics, students, and newspaper editors. Donaldina Cameron's name became associated with this crusade, and for the first time her fame began spreading beyond the city limits of San Francisco.

◦➾ 17 ⬅◦

Municipal Storm

On Friday, January 4, 1901, a gale roared through San Francisco toppling chimneys, downing telegraph poles, and tearing the roofs off buildings. Heavy rains muddied streets, flooded cellars, and, across the bay, forced the evacuation of a vagrant prisoner who had been sleeping on the floor of a jail cell, to prevent his drowning. Around dinnertime, the Weather Bureau clocked the winds at sixty-six miles per hour.

Two and a half blocks from the Mission Home, the howling storm blew the woodwork off a four-story building, making a clatter that Cameron and some of her young charges would have heard from their bedrooms on the home's upper floors. The flying wood plunged through a string of telegraph wires, leaving several strands, live with electrical current, dangling above the street.

Meanwhile, a different gale that would shake city hall and the police department was gaining momentum. On January 2, William Randolph Hearst's *San Francisco Examiner* unleashed a front-page exposé headlined "Chief Sullivan Carrying Out His Compact with the Gamblers in Defiance of Law." It alleged that San Francisco's chief of police was ignoring vice in Chinatown. Indeed, after a period of violent enforcement under a feared Chinatown squad, various police scandals had led to new leadership under Chief Sullivan, who took a decidedly more relaxed view towards vice. The police chief was "in alliance with criminals," the editorial page thundered.

Hearst pounded the subject for seven days. Exposés of vice in Chi-

A front-page exposé by the *San Francisco Examiner* helped prompt an investigation by state legislators into why the city's police department seemed to overlook vice.

natown dominated the front page of the *Examiner*, by then San Francisco's largest morning daily. The paper's cartoonists lampooned Chief William P. Sullivan—whom the mayor had picked for the job over Hearst's own candidate a year earlier. Sullivan was portrayed with his feet resting on his desk and hatchets and other weapons of enforcement mounted on the wall of his office, covered in thick cobwebs. On its front page, the paper charged that the police cracked down on brothel keepers who ran their businesses on Chinatown property owned by Mayor James D. Phelan's brother-in-law while ignoring illegal gambling and opium operations.

As the Victorian era officially drew to a close that month with the death of Britain's Queen Victoria, Hearst and other business leaders remained focused on extending the federal Chinese Exclusion Act, due to expire in 1902. Anxiety that the Chinese would take jobs away from white job seekers fueled the push to extend the law, and the populist *Examiner* favored extension. In the fourteen years since Hearst had been in charge, the paper's circulation had soared with his sensational approach to covering the news. He hired top journalists from across the country, published investigations by what the newspaper called its "*Examiner* Detective Corps," and ran reader contests offering tempting prizes. Consistent with its stance on the Exclusion Act, the paper regularly voiced America-first views that were blatantly xenophobic—particularly against the Chinese.

The paper's Chinatown coverage caught the attention of lawmakers in Sacramento, including a state senator named Arthur G. Fisk who called for an official state investigation into vice in San Francisco's Chinatown. The *Examiner* trumpeted its success and ran photographs of the assemblymen from across the state who'd been appointed to carry out the inquiry. For Cameron and the other crusaders in the fight against sex trafficking, the vice hearings would help them reach a broader audience.

THE ASSEMBLY COMMITTEE GOT right to work. On Monday, February 4, its members made their way to San Francisco's Hall of Justice, a newly built brick-and-terra-cotta edifice across from Portsmouth Square. In a courtroom, Chief Sullivan stepped onto a witness stand that the newsmen dubbed "the sweatbox" and testified that not only did the police know the location and financial scale of the gambling dens and other crimes in Chinatown, but they were doing nothing to suppress them. Indeed, the police chief had recently withdrawn the Chinatown Squad. Much to the amusement of the gathered crowd and to newspaper readers the next morning, Chief Sullivan admitted under oath that he'd never read the penal code.

Over the next week and a half, a parade of other witnesses testified, most notably the mayor. James D. Phelan, a dapper man who kept his mustache neatly curled at the tips and his beard closely trimmed, had campaigned as a reform candidate in 1896 on promises that he would clean up city hall. The mayor was hostile toward the city's Asian residents and, in 1900, had spoken at an anti-Japanese rally. He would later campaign for reelection to the U.S. Senate with the slogan "Keep California White."

In a courtroom packed with politicians, prominent citizens, and the mayor's supporters, the committee members wasted no time grilling Phelan to find out why he had not pushed for police enforcement in the quarter. Phelan acknowledged a long-standing tolerance of vice in Chinatown.

The most pointed questions focused on the mayor's brother-in-law, Frank J. Sullivan, who managed his family's extensive property holdings covering nearly two square blocks at the corner of Jackson and Pacific Streets, in the heart of Chinatown. Phelan argued that Sullivan had little to do with the properties: he just collected rents from the Chinese tenants. The mayor, quite improbably, claimed to have learned just a day earlier that a lottery operation was housed in one of those buildings. The committee was probing whether the lax enforcement in Chinatown was due to the financial interests of the mayor's extended family. That was the conclusion the *Examiner* drew as it mocked the diminutive mayor in a cartoon. It showed him squashed in terror by the police chief, tumbling back in his desk chair, as a lit bomb dubbed "investigation" threatened to blow them both to smithereens.

TWO OTHER PEOPLE TESTIFIED—Cameron and her counterpart at the nearby Methodist mission, Margarita J. Lake.

Lake, a single twenty-eight-year-old, had been hired five years earlier to work alongside her widowed mother in the Methodist Episcopal Church's rescue home on Washington Street. She was the first of the dozens of witnesses called to speak about a subject that seemed particularly fascinating to the out-of-town assemblymen: sex slavery in Chinatown.

Of keen interest to the committee was not so much the welfare of the girls and young women being trafficked as the ongoing concern over disease and moral degradation to the rest of the city. Indeed, it was that fear that fueled the next question: whether white boys and men were visiting the brothels and gambling dens of the quarter.

"I see a great many going in and out, especially on Bartlett Alley," answered Lake, a plain woman with deep-set eyes.

"And when you saw those white people going in and out, [the proprietors] refused to let you go in?"

Lake replied in the affirmative that she'd been barred from entering. But sometime afterward, she'd found a way in. "I disguised [myself] one night and went around with a Tourist party and we succeeded in getting into every house—that is, up to every window and we were not disturbed at all. I went there the next evening in a crowd and dressed as I always do and not one of us was allowed in." The floppy white deaconess collar that Lake wore might have tipped off the door guards as to her identity.

The committee then asked her if she would be willing to bring some of the young women to the courthouse to testify in front of the committee. Lake said no, explaining that any one of her charges would be in grave danger if they ventured out in public to testify.

"Do you feel that you would be jeopardizing the life of that girl if you brought her here to testify?"

"I'm afraid I might be," Lake said.

CAMERON, WHOSE FAME had soared after the wide-ranging coverage of the Kum Quai case in Palo Alto a year earlier, took the stand after her colleague.

She had dressed for warmth in a well-tailored overcoat with a stylish fur collar. Cameron's testimony revealed that like Lake, instead of calling on the San Francisco Police Department when it came to staging rescues, she relied heavily on the support of a man named Frank J. Kane, who worked for a Roman Catholic–based organization called the Pacific Society for the Suppression of Vice. Kane was willing to take girls and young women from brothels and Chinese homes on behalf of the missions without the legal documentation the police required.

On the witness stand, Cameron described her rescues with a level of detail and a matter-of-fact candor that she seldom provided in her annual reports to the Presbyterian board. Her written reports sometimes veered into sentimental accounts of how Chinese girls and women had come to the home and found safety, and perhaps religion or marriage. Like Lake, she described seeing parties of white tourists entering brothels in Chinatown, while the watchmen—sometimes white themselves and stationed outside—usually blocked her from entering. In fact, they warned the brothel owners when they saw her coming.

"They run upstairs ahead of us and tell the Chinese . . . through the wicket not to open the door for me."

Cameron, who did not reveal any doubt in the witness chair about her right to enter private premises to stage rescues, then told the committee that she sometimes received letters alerting her to the presence of very young girls in the brothels. One of the assemblymen asked her, "When you get such a letter, don't you as a rule give it to the Police?"

"No, I don't give those letters to the Police."

"Why not?"

"Well, I have been used to calling upon the Pacific Society for advice to assist me in these matters," she said, adding, "I have always found that Mr. Kane of the Pacific Society took a great interest in the matter, and he was more willing to devote his time in that regard and assist me I think. It was more in his line than in the line of the Police Department." Upon further probing, Cameron explained that Kane was more aggressive than the police themselves.

Asked whether the police gave her as much assistance as she required, she answered, "Well, I don't think they have shown the enthusiasm in the work that I should wish they would show."

"In what respect?"

"In forcing an entrance to those houses and in getting at the girls."

"Have they refused you to force an entrance, when you have asked them to do so?"

"Yes they have." The committee continued to explore what would now be considered the legally gray area of forced entry.

Asked whether Kane ever hesitated in prying open the door, she answered, "No he does not."

"He is always ready and willing to force the doors to get in at them?"

Cameron answered yes. The committee then asked whether a search warrant was legally required to force open doors. Cameron answered directly, without any hesitation over what we now call civil rights questions concerning lawful search and seizure.

"Well, the police authorities told me that they could not force the doors, that they could not demand an entrance without a search-warrant."

The committee then got to the heart of the matter: Cameron and Kane's use of possibly illegal means to enter private establishments to whisk away young girls and women. The question posed to her was this: "Has Mr. Kane forced the doors and demanded entrance without a search-warrant?"

Cameron answered, "I don't remember any occasion when he has had to break the door, but he demands an entrance in such a way that [the men] have always been able to get in."

"Do I understand you to say then that the Police are unable to get in and Mr. Kane is?"

Yes, Cameron told the committee. Kane could get into houses where she'd unsuccessfully tried to enter with the police.

Toward the end of her testimony, she mentioned one surprising anecdote of rescuing a girl from a brothel on Baker's Alley. Within a week or two of that rescue, someone—possibly the building's owners—had erected high gates barring public entrance to the alley. Cameron said she'd never been able to get into the notorious thoroughfare after that, although groups of tourists continued to be ushered in through the gates by the watchmen. When asked who controlled the alley, she answered, "I have been told that it belongs to the Sullivan estate."

.   .   .

READERS THE NEXT MORNING found a summary of the two wom-
en's testimony in a story headlined "Missionaries Describe to Investigators the Horrors of the Chinese Slave Trade." None of the papers
focused on the role of Frank Kane, who, as it turned out, had been
using an expired "specials" star—a badge issued by the police department to private individuals working as security guards or some other
form of law enforcement. The police department had apparently
revoked his star four years earlier, in 1897, but he continued using it
long afterward to force his way into Chinatown's brothels and homes.

Kane's combative rescue strategies, coupled with questionable
financial transactions, had also landed him in legal trouble over the
years—though it is unlikely that either Cameron or Lake knew this.
But after a contested custody battle between Lake and Kane over two
Chinese girls in March 1901, a month after the testimony, there is no
record of either of the mission homes using his services again.

18

"Forcing Me into the Life"

L ake and Cameron wouldn't allow their girls to come to the court-room to testify, fearing for their safety. So, on the afternoon of Monday, February 11, the committee took a field trip. The assembly-men made their way to the third-floor apartments of a mansard-roofed structure that stood on the corner of Washington and Stockton Streets in Chinatown. There, at the Methodist mission home, they began hearing the testimony of a seventeen-year-old resident. Newspaper reporters were excluded.

The seventeen-year-old, referred to by the pseudonym "Mary Doe," was the first to testify. She had been living in Chinatown with her mother, she said, but when she was eleven, her mother had died and her older brother, who planned to leave the city, put the girl in the care of a godmother. After being abused by her godmother, she was sold to a brothel for $1,980. How did she know that amount? asked a committee member. "I saw with my own eyes," she replied, "$300 paid down as a deposit for me. I heard the bargain and saw the deposit."

She escaped by fleeing to the rescue home. When the committee members pressed her on the brothel's location, Lake jumped in to explain that the street addresses and numbers on the buildings where prostitution took place were changed often—sometimes freshly painted over to make rescues more difficult, particularly when warrants had been issued for girls at specific addresses.

The next young woman to speak to the committee was Ah Gum, who apparently did not use a pseudonym. Also seventeen, she said that

A Chinese "slave girl" behind a metal grate.

she had been purchased for $2,200, a figure she'd seen on a red piece of paper with Chinese characters on it, her bill of sale. Ah Gum told the committee in detail what happened next as her new owners, two women, took her to the brothel where they planned to keep her.

"As soon as I got there I found many little rooms, and many men in them. I was taken around and shown to them. They said, 'Oh, yes, this is the new addition to the house, eh' and things like that. This woman said, 'You can do business here.'" When Ah Gum refused to prostitute herself, her owner pointedly asked, "What can you do? You are here, and if you want to go to [the Mission Home] it is like a prison, and the doors are always kept locked. They will starve you there, and you will soon die. If you do go there and try to get out they will put you in jail."

She wept "day and night" and initially refused to submit. But "they kept forcing me and kept on forcing me into the life," referring to her repeated rape. She initially had to make $10 every night for the brothel keeper from perhaps half a dozen or more customers. Girls and women who had been at the house longer and whom she described as "not so fresh" only had to make $8 a night and then $5. Ah Gum told the committee members she spent eight months in the brothel before escaping in October 1900 to the Methodist rescue home.

Not all the girls and women were slaves, Ah Gum said. The younger and more desirable girls and women were slaves, prevented from escaping by their owners. But there were some, usually older women, who'd bought their liberty and were working of their own free will. She also testified that the owners collected forty cents a week from each of the brothels to hire a white watchman "who lets them know the moment any of the Mission people are in sight."

LATE IN THE AFTERNOON, toward the very end of the committee's visit, the assemblymen met some of the youngest and most vulnerable residents of the rescue homes. In the dark, Lake led out a small group of children, ranging in age from a two-year-old just learning to talk to a six-year-old, and stood them before the five assemblymen and the translator.

"These girls have all been sold in Chinatown," Lake told them. "The price has been set on each one."

"Here is one," she said, pointing to a three-year-old Chinese girl who almost certainly wouldn't have understood what was being said, because it was in English, "that I took from its mother in a house of ill fame two weeks ago." It is unclear why Lake would have referred to the child so impersonally as an "it." Perhaps that was the court transcriber's mistake, which was soon repeated.

"This one," she said, pointing to another one of the little girls, "was sold for $100.

"This one," pointing to another, "$150.

"This one," motioning toward another child, "was sold when it was fifteen days old for $300. These have all been sold, and the bargain was made principally by their mothers, in Chinatown." Their mothers, in all likelihood, had themselves been sold, and the children they bore were probably the result of rape or unwanted pregnancies.

This was Lake's opportunity to drive home her cause to a group of elected officials who, if they were moved or even horrified by what they saw, might try to stop the trafficking of women and girls:

> We only rescue about one out of ten. We get word from girls that they want to escape, but the girls will not assist themselves in any way. They are afraid of the slave dealers. They are just hounded by the keepers and lawyers. When we go to a place after a girl, all the girls run. They have exits on back alleys and on the roofs of houses, and none will assist the others for fear of the slave dealers.

She continued,

> If there was ever slavery, this is slavery right here in our own City. Sometimes I feel like throwing up my hands and giving up, but if the Missions give up, there is no hope for them. It really seems as though something can be done, and we are hoping and praying.

THE COMMITTEE'S WIDE-RANGING EXAMINATION into the police department led to banner headlines and scathing newspaper caricatures. The stories made clear "that Chinese women and Chinese girls [mere infants, frequently] are bought and sold as chattels in said Chi-

natown in violation of a vital principle of our national life—a condition
of affairs that is a disgrace to the State of California."

The following month, the California legislature responded by adding a new section to the penal code, broadening the state's antislavery
law for the first time to include penalties against human trafficking. A
small but significant step forward, the girls' and young women's testimony had helped bring about this change. Later that year, Hearst's
paper helped block Phelan's reelection bid as mayor. The onetime
reformer was defeated. And Chief Sullivan, who admitted to legislators
that he hadn't read the penal code, let alone enforced it in Chinatown,
died of heart failure not long afterward.

19

"I May Go to Sleep Tonight
and Then Find Myself in Hell!"

T ien Fuh Wu never knew her age. She eventually used the date
of her rescue—January 17—as her birthday because it marked a
turning point in her life. If that burly police officer hadn't scooped her
up in 1894 and brought her to live in the Mission Home, she knew
there was a good chance that she would have ended up sitting in a
window in Chinatown, dressed in satin and silk, like the women she
saw as a very young girl when she worked as a servant in a brothel.

Compared with being an abused *mui tsai,* Tien lived an orderly and
protected life in the Mission Home. She attended the mission school,
where she learned to read and write in English and Chinese as well as
to sew and to help with the housekeeping. As one of the many children
in the home, she had little direct exposure to the violent world outside
its locked doors. The rhythm of her days was regulated by a schedule
set by the home's matron, which began with chores and ended with
bedtime prayers. The structure was a balm, and later in life she would
describe her childhood years in the home as "carefree."

Funds were scarce at the Mission Home. The children had no toys,
other than those they made themselves. Tien managed to scrounge
together small pieces of rope, which she tied together. She and the
other girls would venture down into the low-ceilinged basement to
play, where she used what she'd made as a jump rope and to create a

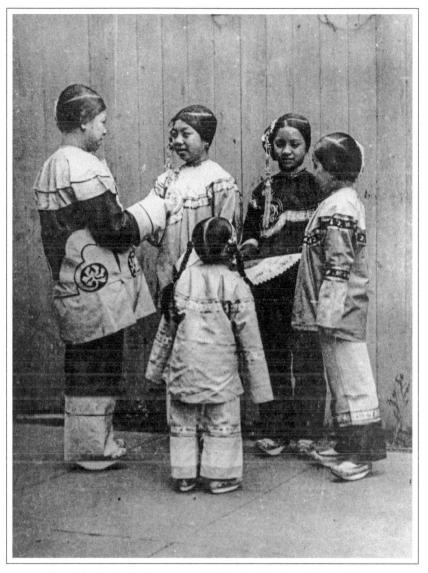

Five girls playing in the courtyard of the Presbyterian Mission Home.

swing. Her goal was to try to swing all the way up and touch the ceiling with her toes.

The older girls who worked in the kitchen wouldn't allow the younger ones underfoot. But Tien and some of the other girls discovered they could peek up into the kitchen through some latticework in the basement. One day, as she was looking through it, Tien spotted some sprouting potato seeds that had fallen through a crack. In an early sign of her resourcefulness, she decided to dig out the potatoes beneath the sprouts, but the other girls were too frightened to go farther into the dark basement because of ghosts.

"I was anxious to get those potatoes to eat," Tien told the others, who like her had suffered various forms of trauma before they arrived at the home. "Now, I'll be your captain." The girls found a large tin can and began beating on it with a stick to scare off any ghosts or demons that might be lurking—"bang, bang, bang to chase the spirits away." Tien led the way, and the noisy gang of girls made its way through the dark to claim the potatoes.

They lifted the dirty vegetables from the ground, set them aside where no one would find them, and waited until everyone had gone to bed. Slipping off their shoes to sneak past Cameron's room, they headed back down to the kitchen that night, washed the tubers, and popped them into the oven to bake. Apparently, it wasn't only toys and playthings the girls hungered for, but more food as well.

The girls also playacted characters from China. Even though Tien was very young when she left, she remembered some scenes from her time there. With no old clothing or rags to play dress-up in, Tien went down to the basement and found bricks to tie on each foot— pretending they were wooden shoes. She found a pole during a rainstorm and imagined she was a boat person, calling out her imaginary wares to customers in a Chinese dialect. The girls led imaginative lives that were separate from the adults in the home and learned as much from each other as from their classes.

Although much of the education provided by the Mission Home revolved around teachings from the Bible, the girls also created their own rituals based on Chinese folk beliefs. Once they discovered a dead bird. Instead of giving it a Christian burial by placing a cross at the creature's grave site, they decided to give it a "pagan burial," as Tien later described it, "like the Chinese ones we always saw, you know." Elaborate funeral processions of hundreds of people, accompanied by a Western brass band and the fragrant scent of burning incense, often wound their way through San Francisco's Chinatown, sometimes up Sacramento Street past the Mission Home.

The group of girls went to the home's backyard, off the narrow lane now known as Joice Street. To use the Chinese color of mourning for their ritual, the girls brought some white bedsheets into the garden and draped them around their shoulders. Taking the role of chief mourner for the little bird, one girl led the others in what Tien later described as "all kinds of incantations" and other Buddhist rituals. The girls crouched down on either side of the chief mourner in their white sheets, like a row of small ghosts, crying out, "Aiya! Aiya!"

On the cusp of becoming a teenager, Tien was warned by some of the older girls in the home that it was time for her to be baptized and take Communion. "The big girls, you know, always frightened us kids, and I used to take [everything they said] for the gospel truth." The older girls told her, "You better be baptized or else you will go to hell. Didn't know beans, you know, what it meant. I got scared, and I said I may go to sleep tonight and then find myself in hell!"

So Tien took the initiative and asked to be baptized—or immersed, in her words—into Christian life. When officials told her she was too young, Tien burst into tears. "I just cried and cried. I said, 'I may die tonight and I haven't been baptized and I will go to Hades, let the fire burn me.' And I was really scared."

But it wasn't just Tien's dread of the netherworld that led her to seek baptism: she also felt social pressure and a desire for acceptance. At first, she might have been described as a "rice Christian"—a term for someone who became a Christian to enjoy material benefits rather than having a true spiritual conversion. But by becoming a Christian, Tien found acceptance in the small and insular world of girls and young women living under the roof of 920 Sacramento Street.

The Mission Home reported intermittently to its board how many baptisms and Christian weddings it had performed, as a measure of whether it was achieving its goals. Tien's conversion would have been included in that tally and seen as a victory for the home. Her status and role as a leader among the girls undoubtedly rose once she got baptized. As time passed, Tien was no longer a "rice Christian." She became a true believer.

TIEN DESCRIBED HERSELF as "a happy-go-lucky tomboy." And she landed in trouble occasionally. An early confrontation with Cameron took place during an incident when she confessed to stealing food. Shortly after the young sewing teacher had arrived in the home in 1895, she visited a classroom where rows of wooden desks in graduated sizes faced the teacher's more substantial desk. The girls filed in and sat with solemn expressions on their faces. Someone, it seemed, had stolen several apples, a rare treat, from a case of the fruit that had been given as a gift to the home. Miss Culbertson asked the children who'd taken the fruit. After a long silence, Tien rose, tears rolling down her cheeks.

She admitted to the superintendent and the class that she had stolen them. The older girls had put her up to it, promising they'd shoulder the blame if she got caught. Cameron never forgot Tien's honesty and her courage in admitting she had stolen the apples, saying many years later, "She was born honest."

Even so, in their first years together at the home, the relatively privileged white staffer from the Scottish family had trouble with the former *mui tsai* from China who didn't always follow the rules and resented the newcomer.

One morning, Tien rose early to help another girl in the kitchen. Cameron scolded Tien for the racket she was making and ordered her to go back to her room at once. Tien was furious. "You don't need to tell me what to do," she spat back at the older woman. "I was here long before you came!" (In fact, she'd only arrived fifteen months before Cameron.) Tien was so angry she rushed to open the window of her room and pulled off her clothes, in an effort to catch pneumonia and die so that she could come back as a ghost to haunt Cameron.

BUT THEIR FRAUGHT RELATIONSHIP underwent a change in early 1901. Because Cameron and her predecessors as superintendent did not speak or read Chinese (despite Culbertson's effort to learn the language, she never became fluent in it), they relied on their Chinese aides to communicate with the girls and young women in the home and with those who hoped to move there. These aides were generally young Chinese women who'd grown up in the home and decided to stay on and work alongside the white staffers as translators. Cameron's primary aide at that time was a young woman named Leung Yuen Qui.

Leung had lived at the home for more than a decade. Under the alias Woon Tsun, she had been taken into custody on a Sunday afternoon in mid-November 1890, after leaving a house of prostitution on Waverly Place. An old woman named Kum Mah ran the brothel, which was in a new and large brick building adjoining the Baptist Mission Church in Chinatown. Leung's father had borrowed heavily from Kum Mah and gave the brothel keeper his daughter to repay his debts.

A formal portrait of Cameron's first Chinese aide, Leung Yuen Qui.

Word reached the Mission Home of Leung's plight, and an initial rescue attempt failed. One Sunday, workers at the Mission Home again heard that Leung would be visiting the brothel.

Staffers telephoned for a police officer, who picked her up and brought her to 920 Sacramento Street. To the police officer's and mission workers' surprise, the child was carrying $400 in gold coin, suggesting that the brothel keeper had employed her as a courier. The missionary workers returned the money to Kum Mah. They then embarked on a months-long series of court hearings against the brothel keeper to defend their guardianship of the girl. Between November 1890 and April 1891, Margaret Culbertson attended no fewer than seventeen court hearings to fight for custody of Leung, which the court ultimately granted to her. That legal battle attracted widespread press attention as well as donations to the Mission Home to fund its work.

Leung, meanwhile, repaid Culbertson by becoming a trusted translator and aide. The other girls at the home knew her as a quiet student, a good seamstress, and someone who loved to read. A photograph of her wearing formal Chinese robes shows a sweet-faced, contemplative young woman with Cupid's-bow lips. "She was different from me both in tastes and manners," Tien wrote about Leung many years later. "But I was strongly attracted to her" despite their differences. After Culbertson's death, gentle Leung became indispensable to Cameron as the newly named superintendent, especially during the Palo Alto case of 1900.

Leung first took ill in the spring of 1900. But in the fall, while aiding Cameron during a rescue in Fresno, Leung grew worse. She'd contracted tuberculosis, for which there was no cure at that time and which thrived in the crowded and unsanitary tenements where many of the Chinese lived. Her condition steadily deteriorated until she could no longer leave her bed in the Mission Home. In March 1901, Tien, who was then about fifteen years old, offered to help nurse the sick girl. Leung's condition worsened as she began coughing up blood and gasping for breath.

One morning, Tien was tidying up Leung's room. Shaking a dust mop out the window, she turned back to the sickbed. The tubercular girl's eyes stopped moving, and her frail chest no longer labored with each breath. "Something within me told me that she had just gone," Tien recalled. Stunned by the death—the first she had witnessed—the teenager made her way downstairs. It was breakfast time, and two of the girls who were eating broke out in laughter and ran to the front part of the house, where one of them dropped her bowl of rice. By the time Tien walked down the stairs, Cameron was lecturing the girls— ordering them to get a broom and dustpan and sweep up the mess. After reprimanding them, Cameron turned to the teenager walking down the stairs.

"Tien, you want me?" she asked.

"Yes, Lo Mo," Tien said. Like other girls in the home, she had started calling Cameron by that name, a Chinese endearment meaning "Old Mother." In private, some residents also called her Mama. Tien told her what she had seen, and Cameron climbed the stairs to the sickroom. When she realized her aide had died, Cameron threw herself beside the bed next to Leung's body, sobbing uncontrollably.

Stunned by Cameron's depth of feeling toward her Chinese aide, Tien struggled to find words to soothe or console her. "Don't cry, Mama," she said.

20

A Deathbed Promise

Death made regular appearances at the home. Tien had lived in the institution for five years when Culbertson left on a stretcher, only to die a few days later before reaching her family home in New York. Infants and girls also died during Tien's early years there, including Culbertson's namesake, Margaret, a baby born to a former resident two days before the late superintendent left 920 Sacramento Street for the last time.

Tien was around fifteen years old when Leung passed away, and this time Tien witnessed the new superintendent's profound grief for her aide, revealing the older woman's vulnerability and human side in a way the young teenager had never recognized or comprehended before. "I offered to help her in the work, because I felt very sorry for her, realizing how terribly crushed she was over her co-worker's death," Tien later said.

She often returned to this moment to explain, in later years, how she came to work as Cameron's aide in the Mission Home. Sold by her father and orphaned once she reached America, in her later years she reflected on her desperate need for love and attention. Until Leung's death, she'd felt she could never get close to Cameron, who doted on the younger children in the home and took them with her on outings to the grocery store, giving them five cents each to spend on treats. Tien, as a teenager, didn't get the physical affection or attention she craved from Cameron or anyone else. "I was hungry for love," she said.

So she promised on Leung's deathbed to help Cameron however

Pigtail Parade in Chinatown.

she could. Initially, most of Tien's time as Cameron's new aide was spent tending the two babies who lived at the home, Minnie and Yute Jo Ji, "watching over them as tenderly and conscientiously as though they were her own little daughters." But she soon began assuming some of the other responsibilities that Leung had long shouldered. She hadn't realized the full scope of the job when she began accompanying Cameron on rescues in Chinatown and translating for her in court. She earned $5 a month, a steady wage compared with the garment piece-work that was then the most common source of income for Chinese women in San Francisco.

Cameron, for her part, was deeply shaken by Leung's death. In that year's annual report of the Woman's Occidental Board of Foreign Missions, she expressed her sense of loss after the death of the young woman who'd been at her side since 1899, when she'd first become supervisor:

> The darkest shadow in many years was that which fell over our Home but a few months ago when dear [Leung] Yuen Qui, the lovely, wise and capable young interpreter of our Mission, began to fail in health. . . . We feel that no other will ever be quite what she was, and what shall we say of the deep, personal loss to us, of one whose every thought and act seemed to be for our help and comfort?

Cameron was, in fact, very much alone following Leung's death. Most of her contemporaries had married and started their own families. She had lost the woman she worked most closely with. Leung had been her sturdiest bridge to the home's Chinese speakers, as well as to China-town. The translator had been her ally in the courtroom and on rescues. At the time she wrote those words, she could not have known that the little girl who stole apples would become even more crucial to her.

AT THE COURTHOUSE, Tien soon realized that her limited vocabu-lary and schooling had not prepared her well enough for the complex job of translating for Cameron. She grew frustrated by the long and sometimes arcane legal terms used by the attorneys and wished she

Tien Fuh Wu in her traveling suit at the age of eighteen.

had had a better education to help her cope in court, where the cross-examinations were often hostile.

Yet Tien had a better education than many other Chinese women in San Francisco at the time. At the turn of the century, the city's system of educational segregation continued: officials directed Chinese children into public schools that were separate from those attended by white children. And by Chinese custom, educating boys took priority. For many Chinese girls and young women, the classes offered by the mission homes were often the only place they could learn to read and write at an elementary level. For older girls, like Tien, her options to continue her education in segregated San Francisco were few and far between.

Luckily, years earlier, Culbertson had helped arrange a "sponsor" for Tien—someone who would help financially support her by paying the cost of her monthly room and board at the home from afar. In Tien's case, the assistance came from a man at a Presbyterian church in Pennsylvania where Culbertson had spoken to the congregation about the rescue work she was doing in San Francisco. She described how Tien's slave owner had burned and tortured the little girl before she was rescued by a police officer and brought to the home. One member of the congregation, Horace C. Coleman, was so touched by Tien's story that he offered to fund a scholarship for her and another girl who had been rescued, even before meeting them in person.

When Tien learned of her good fortune, she was not only overjoyed; she used the existence of a sponsor as a weapon to hold over the other girls when they quarreled. She would tell them, "You better look out, my American papa will be here, he will give it to you!"

When she finally met Coleman in person (they exchanged letters after he became her sponsor), Tien recalled his striking appearance. He had traveled from Pennsylvania to attend a Sunday school convention in San Francisco and made a visit to the Mission Home's schoolroom as part of that trip. He was wearing a bright pink carnation in the buttonhole of his dark blue suit. Coleman had dark hair—"as black as any Chinese," she would later say—and a black, closely cropped mustache. As Tien recalled, "My American papa was the handsomest man!"

Tien, likewise, was a beautiful teenager. She had cheeks that were so rosy that sometimes people would tease her by asking if that was her natural color or if she rouged them. As part of their correspondence, she sent a photograph of herself to Coleman in which she was seated on a white wicker chair wearing a traditional Chinese gown. The black-and-white image doesn't show the blush in her cheeks, but it does show her sweet round face and full lips. Neither the scar on her jaw nor the burns on her arm are visible: instead, she holds an embroidered handkerchief in her lap, suggesting a peaceful domesticity that belied the violence of her early childhood.

The next day, Mr. Coleman paid her another visit. He hired a carriage to take them to the beach, the sound of horseshoes rhythmically striking the cobblestones as they made their way up past the mansions on Nob Hill, heading down again and past what had been an area of blowing sand and dunes known as the Outside Lands before its transformation into Golden Gate Park. From there they soon reached the wide expanses of Ocean Beach, San Francisco's westernmost boundary.

Tien, who craved love and attention, felt so comfortable with her sponsor that she was able to play with him, even tease him. With the Cliff House, a castle built by the city's former mayor Adolph Sutro, looming to the north, she found green strands of seaweed on the beach, picked them up, and began chasing him with them. She had fun with Coleman "just as if he were my father." There is no indication from Tien's accounts that her sponsor was anything but generous and kind to her.

Tien's playfulness reflected not only her comfort but also the reality that all the girls competed for sponsors and adults willing to adopt them. Usually, it was the younger girls who won the much-coveted adoptions—not older girls like Tien. So, while she later recalled that moment of chasing him on the beach as a sublimely playful one, it also must have been in the back of her mind that it was important for her future to bond with her "American papa."

Tien went to the train station the next day to say good-bye to Coleman, a quiet man who would later marry and have children of his own.

"Well, Tien, how would you like to come east someday?" he asked.

"Oh, Mr. Coleman, I would dearly love it."

He said he couldn't make her any definite promises, because he knew he'd have to first get permission for her to leave the home. But eventually, he helped arrange for Tien to attend the Stevens School, an elite girl's boarding school in the Germantown area of Philadelphia. (Grace Kelly, who became Princess Grace of Monaco, graduated from the school in 1947.) Mr. Coleman sent money for Tien's new clothes as she prepared to head east, and Tien and her "American papa" stayed in touch during her time at the school.

During her four years in Philadelphia, Tien didn't forget the Mission Home or Miss Cameron. She wrote letters "constantly from Philadelphia of her unshaken desire to return to the Home and take up her work where she laid it down to go East two years ago," Cameron reported in her annual review to the Occidental Board. But it would be a few more years before Tien chose to make good on her promise to Cameron at Leung's deathbed. Reflecting on the death of Cameron's former Chinese aide, she wrote, "I thank God for this grave experience, otherwise I might have led a selfish and worldly life."

21

Taking Public Stands

Cameron started thinking more deeply about the meaning of her work after her translator Leung's death. A few months after that sad incident, a profile of Cameron ran in the *San Francisco Chronicle*'s Sunday feature section. If the reporter had imagined the home's superintendent as being a battle-ax type, given her dangerous work of rescuing girls and women from sex slavery, he seemed genuinely surprised by Cameron's gentle demeanor, describing her as "young, well bred, and attractive . . . and probably the bravest woman in all San Francisco."

The profile wasn't entirely fluff. The reporter asked the superintendent a difficult question that might have offended some Christian missionaries: whether she thought the conversions among the Chinese young women were "permanent and sincere." Cameron answered the question tentatively and with introspection.

"I believe so. I believe it for the girls, at least," she answered. She went on to explain that while the Chinese had different customs, any doubts she might have had that a Chinese person could become a true Christian believer—a comment reflecting the widely held racism of the era—had ended with the death of Leung Yuen Qui. Leung not only professed but also practiced her Christian beliefs in the years before she died. "If she had been pretending she could not have kept it up to the end," Cameron explained, "she died in her faith, which makes me sure that it was more than pretense."

By then Cameron realized that not everyone believed in the effectiveness of rescue work; some questioned whether it led to genuine

Donaldina Cameron, superintendent of the Mission Home, with one of its younger residents.

conversions on the part of the rescued women. That year marked a change in how she described her mission to the women of the Occidental Board, whose leaders oversaw her work and paid her salary. Over the six previous years, she'd filled her annual reports with lengthy descriptions of rescues—perhaps believing the colorful details of Chinatown raids would enthrall her supporters and help convince them to reach more deeply into their pocketbooks. Now she delved into what the work meant.

On an overcast Friday afternoon in April 1902, Cameron stood before dozens of women seated in the parlor of the Mission Home. She had altered her usual message to tie the work of the Mission Home to the broader sweep of history. For the first time, she compared the work the home's staffers were doing to the work of abolitionists and other leaders who'd freed black slaves during the Civil War:

> It took only four years to set the negroes free throughout the whole of the South; for *twenty-five* years a few women have been wrestling with the Chinese slavery problem and it seems no nearer a solution now, than it did more than a quarter of a century ago when the rescue work was first organized. True, much has been done toward *lessening* the evil, but it does still exist in all its hideousness. To free the *negro* the entire forces of a great people were united, and no sacrifice either personal or political was considered too great toward that end. Could not the Christian people of our State, with the same consecrated effort and firmness of purpose, lift the stigma of slavery from the Chinese community and give to the Oriental women and girls in our midst, the privileges which we so richly enjoy?

The language Cameron used to frame the Mission Home's calling drew not only from people like herself who were opposed to slavery in whatever form it might take but also from the nascent women's movement, which had started in 1848 in Seneca Falls and was now taking hold in the United States and beyond. The newspaper headlines might have prompted her serious turn: on the very same day as Cameron's speech at the Occidental Board's annual meeting, Congress began debating an extension of the Chinese Exclusion Act, a law that, perversely, had increased the prevalence of human trafficking between China and the United States since Congress first passed it in 1882.

In a city where racism continued to be widespread and the press and politicians regularly disparaged the Chinese and Japanese as less than human, Cameron and other supporters of the Mission Home defied conventions of the time and reached out to offer help to a group of women who had almost no legal or political rights. She saw her mission as helping other women on their way to independence and hoped to give Asian women the same privileges that she enjoyed.

Cameron's awakening to the broader significance of her work took place in 1902, the same year that another crusader for women's rights— Elizabeth Cady Stanton—passed away. More than half a century earlier, while attending an antislavery convention in London, Stanton and her colleague Lucretia Mott had issued a call for a women's rights convention. At Stanton's home in Seneca Falls in 1848, that convention made the first formal demand for women's suffrage in the United States. Stanton died in the fall of 1902; it would take women across America almost two more decades to finally win the right to vote.

As Cameron matured and gained confidence, she had begun to look beyond her day-to-day responsibilities caring for women in the home. She began asking how she and the women supporting the Mis-

Donaldina Cameron and some of the residents of the Mission Home.

sion Home could help end the slavery in their midst, joining a growing number of women in the United States, Great Britain, and even China who were awakening to the possibilities of women moving beyond their domestic spheres to take public stands.

MARGARITA LAKE, at the Methodist mission home just a few blocks away, felt discouraged and isolated in her rescue work, despite the legislative success that grew out of the 1901 Chinatown vice hearings. Compounding her frustration might have been a recent struggle with Frank Kane, from the Pacific Society for the Suppression of Vice, over guardianship of two Chinese children. But whatever the reason, Lake felt thwarted in her rescue work at a time when Cameron was focusing on the underlying reasons for trafficking in Chinese girls and women.

"I am weary and discouraged in this single-hand fight for justice," Lake admitted in July 1902. "One great need I feel as the rescue worker among these slave girls is that of a Lawyer and Detective. For five years I have struggled with this awful traffic in slave girls in San Francisco, only rescuing one now and then, of the many who want to be saved. The older girls and especially those that are desirous of escaping are kept in dens barred and locked, watched by Chinese and white men. I am so well known that the minute I enter an alley, they are warned and it is impossible for me to get near them. I need a good detective to collect data for me, such as we can use in the courts." Kane, it seems, hadn't proved an effective or trustworthy ally for Lake.

Six months later, Lake and her mother were abruptly dismissed from their positions at the mission home. It is unclear why, but it might have been due in part to a bungled rescue attempt by Lake and Kane and their later, unrelated struggle over the guardianship of two Chinese girls. While it was Margarita Lake who had first asked California legislators to look into the issue of slavery in 1901, within two years she'd been forced to abandon her Chinese rescue work, taking a lower-profile job as a missionary at a nearby home for Japanese and Korean women. The Methodist Chinatown rescue work quietly continued under different leadership, on a much smaller scale than at the nearby Presbyterian home.

Thus, it was Donaldina Cameron who emerged in those years as the best-known and most outspoken leader in the campaign against Chinese slave trafficking in the West, as she began venturing into the political arena in a more open and forceful manner. While still overseeing a home sheltering as many as fifty girls and young women at any one time, she wrote letters not only to California's governor but also to his wife, testified before a congressional committee on immigration and education, entertained visiting Chinese dignitaries as well as the Scottish-born philanthropist Andrew Carnegie and his wife, and spread her message of compassion to an endless stream of visitors, some of whom she hoped could advance her cause.

In a single day, the home often entertained as many as twenty to thirty fellow missionaries, politicians, and society ladies. Over the Chinese New Year and other holidays, tourists came to Chinatown for the festivities, often stopping by the Mission Home for a visit. Occasionally, Cameron and her staff would receive up to a hundred people in a single day: often, the residents would sing, play, and recite poetry or verses from the Bible. Many times they'd be summoned from their beds, early in the day and late at night, for these performances.

Cameron and her staff realized that the children could serve as the home's most poignantly effective ambassadors. For example, once, after preparing and waiting much of the day for a VIP's arrival, a small group of residents decided instead to head up Sacramento Street to a grand mansion near Lafayette Park to bring a bouquet of flowers to the man they had hoped would be their guest but who was tending to his ailing wife. They returned home and retired for the evening—believing that he wouldn't come after all.

But at half past midnight, a messenger came to the locked doors of the Mission Home with news that their guest and his party would be arriving soon. Always frugal, the home's second-in-command, the matron, Frances P. Thompson, had turned off the gas that heated the home at night. She hurried to turn it back on again and roused the sleeping residents.

"Even the babies were brought down to sing their little songs and hymns and give verses of cheer and counsel from the Book of books," Thompson wrote. "The appreciation showered upon the wee trio quite repaid any effort that was made to entertain."

The guest they had been waiting for all day was the U.S. president,

William McKinley, who had canceled a packed day of engagements because of the sudden illness of his wife, Ida. Members of his presidential party made a late-night visit to the Mission Home, where they sat in the parlor as the young girls sang for them. To achieve her broader political aims, the Mission Home's capable supervisor was learning to use her rising influence, as well as her young wards' heartstring-plucking qualities.

22

Pink Curtain

By the turn of the century, the Mission Home was providing sanctuary not only to the Chinese but increasingly to Japanese, Korean, and even Syrian women. For some, the educations they received there helped them radically change their fortunes. That was true of a Japanese woman who lived at the home for a few years at the start of the twentieth century. Known by several different names during her time in America, she eventually became famous in her homeland as the writer and feminist pioneer Yamada Waka.

Like Tien's family, who sold her to pay off gambling debts, Yamada's family faced severe financial distress. Born in 1879, she was the fifth of eight children of a farming family that grew sugar beets. They lived near the mouth of Tokyo Bay, in a town not far from one of Japan's seven ports opened to foreign ships and traders in the nineteenth century. At sixteen, Yamada married a man a decade older than herself, probably hoping to help relieve her family's money woes. But the marriage was unhappy.

Desperate to help her family, she sought employment in Yokohama, the nearest big city. There, she met a jewel-bedecked woman, supposedly the wife of a successful businessman, who told her that if she went to America, she'd be able to fulfill her filial duties to her family by earning money, promising her she'd be rich in just a year or two. Yamada left Japan around 1897—two years after Donaldina Cameron first arrived at the Mission Home.

But Yamada's experience was devastatingly different from Cam-

Two Japanese prostitutes.

eron's. When the eighteen-year-old Japanese girl stepped off the boat in Vancouver, where it was easier to smuggle women than many U.S. ports, the supposed husband of the woman in Yokohama met her at the dock and took her to Seattle. She soon realized that like so many of the girls who'd made the same treacherous passage from Asia to North America, she'd been tricked by a procuress's convincing promises.

She ended up in a seven-story building in an area of Seattle known as the International District, which was lined with brothels catering to white and Asian men. Here, Yamada was distinguished by her exotic looks. With skin that was relatively dark for a Japanese woman and unconventional beauty by nineteenth-century standards, Yamada was recast by her owner as "Oyae of Arabia"—an unusual and memorable working moniker that echoed the name of her older sister, Yae.

There, she spent several horrific years in forced prostitution, working out of a spare room with a bed, a table, and a portable stove. Yamada had joined two hundred or so other Japanese women who'd been tricked or coerced into the sex trade in the International District at the turn of the century, offering sex to a stream of men from the late afternoon until the early hours of the morning. Most of the women left the more modest places, where they slept, to go behind the *pinku katen,* or "pink curtain," the misleadingly gentle Japanese term for a brothel.

The hotel where Yamada worked, which catered to non-Japanese, suggests she might have been a *hakujincho,* a "white man's bird," offering sex mainly to Caucasian customers. Her fame spread with the help of one of the many Japanese-language newspapers in Seattle. Because there were many more Japanese men than women living in the area, the Japanese newspapers regularly published readers' columns providing details on the reputations and looks of local prostitutes and barmaids.

In 1901, one of these newspapers published a column titled "Selection of Beautiful Women in Seattle," which singled out seven prostitutes working in Japanese brothels in the King Street area, where the International District was located. One of them was Oyae of Arabia, whose beauty and grace the columnist compared to Takao, a legendary courtesan who lived in Japan during the seventeenth century. While such ranking helped sell newspapers and direct trade to certain brothels, it also illustrates the way in which these women were regarded as objects that could be purchased. The newspaper ran a tanka, or poem, describing Yamada's popularity: "Yae cherry blossom is in full bloom; delighted men are crowding around her."

Yamada's beauty might have given her a more privileged life as a prostitute. But there is little doubt that she was brutally exploited and threatened during her time in the trade. To warn any women who might attempt to escape, pimps were said to have killed defiant prostitutes in a particularly savage way: they'd chop their bodies into many pieces, grind the flesh and internal organs, and liquefy what remained with a chemical—flushing the human sludge down the drain.

She endured years of suffering, forced to have sex with a succession of men, almost certainly under threat of death. The emotional and physical pain she felt eventually found expression in her writings. About the misery of her life as a human-trafficking victim in Seattle, she wrote many years later, "I lived in a corner of your country like a worm."

The man who eventually helped Yamada escape from prostitution was Tachii Nobusaburo, a Japanese journalist working as the Seattle correspondent for the San Francisco–based *Shin Sekai* newspaper, who might have met her through his work. The tall, outgoing reporter fell in love with Yamada. To help her escape, he fashioned her bedsheets into a makeshift rope that she used to climb out of her window.

Together, Yamada and Tachii headed south toward San Francisco, another city with a large community of Japanese immigrants. But Tachii's money ran out near Portland. He hid Yamada in an inn and returned to Seattle, where Yamada's furious owners demanded he pay off her debts or return her to them. Tachii managed to evade the pimps. He squeezed money from them by offering to bail out one of their thugs and then ran off instead.

Tachii returned to Yamada and purchased two boat tickets to San Francisco. They arrived safely, but Tachii had something different in mind from restarting their lives as a couple. In another crushing betrayal, he arranged for her to begin working again in a brothel, acting as her pimp and claiming a large portion of her earnings. The details of exactly what happened and why Tachii would turn on her like this are unclear. But within days, Yamada found a way to escape from her situation, leaving Tachii emotionally distraught and forced to wash dishes to support himself.

In the autumn of 1902, Yamada, like so many desperate girls and young women before her, found herself in the Presbyterian Mission Home. Indeed, according to the home's tally that year, some fifteen hundred women and children had taken shelter and lived there in the twenty-eight years since it first opened its doors. Some stayed for a few days or weeks, while others would spend decades there. The year Yamada arrived, there were already four other Japanese residents in the home, out of a total of thirty-eight girls and young women. The word had spread about the Mission Home beyond the Chinese and to the city's growing number of Japanese prostitutes.

The Mission Home's "Registry of Inmates" on November 1, 1902, suggests Yamada was brought there through a court order. It states that a man brought Yamada from Seattle and then tried to sell her to a "house of ill repute" on Pine Street (where many of the Japanese prostitutes in the city were located). According to the registry entry, both Yamada and Tachii were arrested, but the judge dismissed the case and notified workers at the Mission Home that Yamada wished to take refuge there.

As in Seattle, Yamada made an immediate and strong impression at the home, one that focused on her outward appearance as well as her intelligence. "She is a beautiful looking and very bright girl," the staffer wrote, noting that Yamada (who by then was known both as Hanna and Asaba) had refused to marry the man who brought her to San Francisco from Seattle and decided to live in the home instead. Yamada managed to disguise her true feelings from staffers and other residents of the home during this period: she was, in fact, obsessed with thoughts of revenge. She fantasized about burning alive the men who had abused her.

In the early days of Yamada's residence, Tachii made daily visits to the home—climbing up Sacramento Street and mounting its entry steps, then passing under the curved brick arch leading to the locked and guarded front door. The upcoming midterm elections dominated the headlines of the city's English-language papers, overshadowing a story that ran the same day that Yamada arrived on how San Francisco's society matrons turned out to hear a lecture on improving public schools.

Cameron told the distraught Japanese man that Yamada refused to see him. She then asked the emotionally unhinged man, now in his early thirties, to leave the house, explaining it was Yamada's decision to "never see the likes of you again."

Tachii had discovered that Yamada and some of the other residents visited a Japanese clergyman who lived about five blocks away on Sutter Street. Perhaps believing that a fellow countryman would be more sympathetic to his plight, Tachii showed up one day when the girls and the young women from the Mission Home were there and pleaded his case to the minister to allow him to speak to Yamada. The clergyman refused.

"This is the last time I'm going to beg you. Will you let me see her?" Tachii cried.

Turned down again, he reached into his pocket, pulled out a flask containing carbolic acid. He lifted it to his lips, gulped it down, and fell to the floor.

YAMADA, WHO HAD BEEN in another room in the building, rushed in, fell to her knees, and began crying. By the time a doctor arrived, Tachii was dead. In his pocket were several letters. One had burial instructions, addressed to Tachii's friend who was a fellow journalist. Another was addressed to the clergyman, asking him to "please take good care" of Yamada after his death and "be kind to her."

A Japanese American newspaper and the *San Francisco Chronicle* ran detailed stories on Tachii's dramatic suicide. Almost as an aside in a sentence added later, the home's registry entry on Yamada states that the man "committed suicide on her account."

The relatively young journalist's marker lies in the Japanese section of San Francisco's vast graveyard in Colma and reads "Tomb of Tachii Nobusaburo" on the front, with just three lines on the back: "Born March 2, 1871. Died December 5, 1903. Erected by Asaba Waka."

It was Yamada, then known as Asaba Waka, who erected the gravestone for the man who had helped her turn her bedsheets into a rope in Seattle and escape from her life behind "the pink curtain."

‹⁓◉ **23** ◉⁓›

Courage to Fight Evil

U nlike most women who found themselves forced into prostitution, Yamada left a large written record behind. Scholars believe
some of her short stories are lightly fictionalized versions of her own
experiences, including a passage that reflects the anger and revulsion
she felt toward men after her desperate years in Seattle.

In an essay she wrote long after her escape, she described the
intense loathing she felt:

> When I emerged from the underground, I was burning with hatred
> for people, especially for men. I kept wondering what I could do to
> get revenge on those devils who'd taken advantage of a poor woman
> and had sucked her blood. I thought of pouring gasoline on their
> heads and setting them afire. Fighting those men to avenge the poor
> suffering women—it was a fantasy that filled me with courage. Later,
> whenever I met a woman who cried because she was being abused by
> a man, I felt like fighting for her.

"Pouring gasoline on their heads" is the kind of revenge that Japanese women in the nineteenth and early twentieth centuries seldom,
if ever, expressed publicly. Such expressions of rage went against every
norm of women who put their own needs behind those of their husbands, fathers, and sons. Because she felt such red-hot anger, it's no
surprise that Yamada embraced the relatively cloistered life of the
Mission Home, living alongside other girls and young women who'd

Yamada Waka at the White House in 1937 after meeting with First Lady
Eleanor Roosevelt.

experienced similar horrors. In an essay she wrote titled "Love in Our Society," she compared her time at the Mission Home to entering a religious order, describing the spiritual transformation she underwent there:

> I fled into a sort of nunnery to escape the devouring male beasts. There I came into contact with a book I had always believed was reserved for a certain class: the Bible. When I read that there was a God ruling the universe and that under Him every creature was equal, I gazed up at the sky. Joy and yearning filled my heart. I forgot about the earth. The lamb that had been pushed around by cruel beasts suddenly felt protected by Almighty God. My thirst for direction and meaning was quenched. The stronger I grew, the more I drank out of the fountain of God's love. I began to feel an immense warmth towards all of Nature's creatures. I also acquired the courage to fight evil.

Like millions of downtrodden before her, Yamada remade herself through her belief in God. While she was by all accounts exceptionally intelligent, Yamada had received a limited education as a young girl in Japan. It is not clear that she'd been taught to read or write beyond an elementary level. Because she didn't have books as a child, the first book she ever read was the Bible. She learned quickly during school days, which ran from 9:30 in the morning to 3:00 in the afternoon and included lessons in writing, spelling, arithmetic, and geography. She soon found ways to make herself useful at the Mission Home by acting as a translator and teaching others to read.

Every morning in a sunny room with curtains on the windows and maps on the wall, she would invite some of the girls to sit by her side as she read the Bible out loud to them. Afterward, she and the English teacher gave them language lessons. As the home's newsletter enthused, "We had always hoped to produce a girl who could teach the newcomers. Asaba Waka is certainly one of the brightest and most dependable. Because of her unhappy experiences, she possesses a true sense of compassion for others."

She formally became a Christian in 1904, and her writings suggest her conversion was genuine. Describing how she'd lived in "chaotic darkness, without direction," her writings make clear that her biblical studies, with their emphasis on compassion for the downtrodden and forgiveness, changed her life. "The more I studied the Bible, the more the thick mist in front of me lifted. Finally, I saw the dawn."

IT WASN'T LONG before Yamada hit the limits of what the teachers at the mission school could offer to advance her education. Cameron decided to send Yamada to a well-respected English school run by a Japanese man on Bush Street. Largely self-taught, he offered coaching on spoken and written English, as well as instruction on economics, sociology, and other advanced subjects that were not commonly taught to women at that time. The teacher, Yamada Kakichi, was thirty-eight years old when the young woman from the mission school enrolled.

A seemingly confirmed bachelor, Kakichi quickly tumbled into love with his new student. He saw that she possessed a quick mind and an ability to grasp subtleties. Realizing that if he offered to pay her tuition people might gossip about them, he instead asked her to marry him. From Yamada's perspective, his respectful proposal gave her a new sense of herself.

"When I met him, I felt I was the worst kind of human being, an illiterate, nothing but a poor farmer's daughter. But Kakichi did not look at me as a lesser being. He treated me like a lady, which made me reexamine myself. Eventually, I gained self-respect," she wrote in an article published in 1934, shortly after his death.

The couple faced an initial hurdle in their effort to marry. Yamada had converted to Christianity while she was living at the Mission Home, but Kakichi, who read deeply in sociology, was an avowed atheist. Cameron and the other staffers had long denied permission to residents to marry unless the grooms were Christians. Yamada Kakichi's refusal to submit to baptism and conversion posed an obstacle to a church wedding for the couple.

Perhaps because Yamada had been such help as a translator and role model, Cameron granted Yamada her happiness and finally allowed the couple to marry in a church wedding. This might have reflected the changing nature of the Mission Home's work: initially focused on saving souls, its leaders were working in a climate influenced by other social movements of the day, including the progressive movement and the push for women's suffrage. To stay relevant and true to her commitment to protect vulnerable women, Cameron's perspective had evolved.

In a simple ceremony, the clergyman gave the couple his blessing. Staffers served a slice of wedding cake to everyone who attended. Yamada gathered her belongings from her room and left the Mission Home with her new husband, whose surname she took as her own. She and Yamada Kakichi returned to his lodgings on Bush Street, where a friend made coffee for the three of them.

Education proved the key to turning Yamada's potentially ruinous experience as a prostitute into her fierce resolve to help other women. It began with the education and care she received at the Mission Home and continued with Yamada Kakichi's determination that his promising student turned wife learn more. "My husband tried to pour all his knowledge and past experience into my brain. As for me, I sometimes would have preferred cooking. If I forgot where I put my book Kakichi became furious and pulled me out of the kitchen."

Her husband drove her hard, sometimes asking her why she would waste her time "being an ordinary housewife" when he saw qualities in her that suggested she could be more. This was at a time when there was a surge of volunteerism among middle-class women seeking to expand their influence beyond the home. The women's suffrage movement, which had gotten started in the United States by women fighting for the abolition of slavery, was now pushing for women's rights in general.

Yamada's education would allow her to advocate for powerless women and to write about her experience as a sex slave in a way few others could. She returned to Japan with her husband and became an outspoken and respected writer with a focus on women's issues, including setting up a refuge modeled on 920 Sacramento Street for Japanese women forced into prostitution. During a 1937 speaking tour that brought Yamada back to the United States, First Lady Eleanor Roosevelt welcomed the woman formerly famed as "Oyae of Arabia" to the White House.

24

The Chinese Mark Twain

While Cameron preferred to do her lobbying in front of boards, society matrons, and relatively small groups of officials, an eighteen-year-old female student from Shanghai was drawing attention for her powerful public oratory in front of thousands. In November 1902, a teen walked onto the stage of the Donn Quai Yuen, also known as the Grand Chinese Theater on Jackson Street, one of two large Chinese theaters in Chinatown, to deliver a powerful and fiery message to a packed house.

The speaker that afternoon was Sieh King King, who had recently enrolled as a student at the University of California at Berkeley. "She is petite but ambitious," wrote a reporter for *Chung Sai Yat Po* about her matriculation at Berkeley that fall. "Her goal, upon completion of her studies, is to return to China to advocate for women's education and to free Chinese women of thousand-year-old traditional bindings."

Sieh wore a fashionable silk robe and wide trousers and tied a ribbon to the end of the long braid she wore down her back. The daughter of a successful Shanghai merchant, she had already displayed a precocious talent for oratory. A year earlier, she'd delivered a rousing speech in Shanghai before thousands of people protesting a treaty forced upon the Chinese after the failed Boxer Rebellion that gave special rights to the Russians in Manchuria. (The Boxers, named for the martial arts exercise they practiced, were members of a nationalistic peasant movement that began in China's northern provinces. In 1900, they massa-

Interior of the Donn Quai Theater, where Cantonese opera and other events would draw audiences of several hundred people.

cred Western missionaries and Chinese Christians in a revolt against the spread of Western ideas and political domination.)

On this occasion, her message was unprecedented. To the citizens of the largest and most influential Chinese settlement in America, she proclaimed feminist ideas that were only then just beginning to spread in China—far ahead of those then being discussed among Chinese Americans.

On that cloudy, late autumn day, as a falling barometer threatened rain, hundreds of Chinese men squeezed against each other onto the theater's wooden benches just after noon. Chinese women sat in the gallery overlooking the stage. Sieh, who was expected at noon, was forty-five minutes late. When she finally did arrive, she was greeted with applause. She sat down briefly, sipped some tea, rose to face the audience, and then bowed before speaking in Cantonese.

She began modestly. Her purpose in the United States was "not to make speeches" but to study. She claimed to know little of current affairs, "being of the weaker sex and young in years." Then she launched into a forceful argument that China was weak as a nation because of "the crushing oppression suffered by women there."

The audience listened "like zealots," a reporter for the *San Francisco Chronicle* wrote, "when this girl . . . raged at the horrors of foot-binding, and, with all the vehemence of aroused youth, declared that men and women were equal and should enjoy the privileges of equals." Sieh's progressive views on women's rights, which might have grown out of her education by Christian missionaries, also had roots in China's 1898 Reform Movement, which held that China could only rid itself of foreign domination by modernizing itself first. She also boldly condemned the practice that the women at the Mission Home confronted daily: sexual slavery.

She preached to a receptive audience in San Francisco's Chinatown. Her messages about the importance of educating women and banishing slavery would certainly have resonated with Chew as well. His *Chung Sai Yat Po* ran an abbreviated version of her speech, in which she argued that China's problems were due to keeping its women ignorant, binding their feet, barring them from working outside the home, and excluding them from public affairs.

"It is imperative that schools for women be established all over the country so that all twenty million women in China can acquire reasoning and practice professions, thus allowing them to move forward on a complementary footing with men," she argued. "If we can accomplish that, then it would be impossible for our families not to thrive and our country not to be strong."

Sieh's message was one that Chew's newspaper had itself been spreading. By then, *Chung Sai Yat Po* was the largest of the quarter's four Chinese-language papers. It had a circulation of more than three thousand readers out of Chinatown's total population of around ten thousand. Through its news coverage, its editorials, and the speeches it printed by reformers, it had become Chinatown's leading advocate for Chinese American women's rights. Especially for those who didn't read English, the paper became their lens onto the wider world. And the old friend of the Mission Home, who by this time was known as Dr. Chew, became their spokesman.

WOMEN'S RIGHTS WAS just one of the issues that Chew's paper supported. The editor was particularly infuriated by the harsh treatment that his fellow educated Chinese faced as they attempted to enter the United States.

During a long and ugly period of xenophobia, lawmakers in 1904 extended Chinese exclusion indefinitely. The law and its enforcement became a pressing concern of Chinese Americans. Immigration officials had begun making it increasingly difficult for officials, teachers, and merchants—elite classes who were previously exempt under a long-standing treaty between the United States and China—to enter the United States. For the leaders of San Francisco's Chinatown—and therefore Chinese America—the situation became intolerable.

In San Francisco, Chinese dignitaries and scholars, alongside non-exempt immigrants such as laborers, were sometimes held for weeks at a time in heavily guarded converted offices known as the "detention shed." The two-story wooden building was located on the Pacific Mail dock at the end of Pier 40, at the foot of First and Brannan Streets. Inundated with nauseating sewage smells, it was chronically overcrowded and unsanitary. Illnesses spread through the facility, and sometimes inmates even died there. One prominent Chinese visitor

After leaving the clergy, Ng Poon Chew became a prominent journalist and speaker.

who was detained there for weeks in the spring of 1904 was Sun Yat-sen, a physician who would later become famous as the first president of the Republic of China.

Chew was also outraged by a new requirement for residence certificates—government-issued documents proving the immigrants' legal right to be in the United States—which he compared to making Chinese people wear animal tags:

> All Chinese, whether they are merchants or officials, teachers, students, or tourists, are reduced to the status of dogs in America. The dogs must have with them necklaces which attest to their legal status before they are allowed to go out. Otherwise they would be arrested as unregistered, unowned dogs and would be herded into a detention camp.

The rollback of what few protections were in place for the Chinese had continued in the first decade of the new century. In a 1905 Supreme Court decision, *United States v. Ju Toy*, the Court decided that all Chinese immigrants denied entry to the United States, even those claiming citizenship, could no longer appeal to the courts to hear their cases. Instead, the secretary of commerce and labor, who oversaw immigration cases, would have the final say—denying American-born Chinese their rights under the Fifth Amendment, and specifically its due process clause.

Chew teamed up with an Irish American journalist named Patrick Healy, who shared his anger over these and other issues. Together, they wrote *A Statement for Non-exclusion.* Published in 1905, the book began by tracing the very first ship to engage in Chinese trade—the *Empress,* which left New York for Canton in 1784 to purchase tea—and went on to rail against "the barbarism of the detention shed," decrying the unsanitary conditions and comparing the *Ju Toy* case to the *Dred Scott* decision, one of the catalysts for the U.S. Civil War. The book also implied that unscrupulous immigration officials had raped some female Chinese detainees.

A fluent English speaker, Chew had become a spokesman for his community. In 1905, Chinese firms had launched an economic boycott against doing business with America to protest the treatment of merchants and other members of the exempt class. Broadsides appeared on walls throughout San Francisco's Chinatown entreating local merchants to follow the boycott, which the Shanghai Chamber of Commerce had kicked off to protest the mistreatment of Chinese nationals at U.S. ports.

Chinese American leaders raised money and pushed for the act's repeal. *Chung Sai Yat Po* strongly supported the boycott, and Chew argued that the heightening of restrictions was a sign that the "U.S. government is attempting to expel all Chinese"—an idea which was not that far-fetched, given the dramatic drop in numbers of Chinese Americans in the first few years of the twentieth century. An outpouring of plays, novels, and folk songs from the Chinese American community during that time also depicted their racist treatment.

That spring, Chew agreed to a request from the Six Companies to go on a speaking tour across the United States to share his perspective on the boycott with mostly white audiences. With his trim Western-style haircut, his Teddy Roosevelt mustache, and his stylish suits, Ng Poon Chew cut a strikingly westernized figure on his cross-country tour. Not only did he address the U.S. House of Representatives in

Washington, but President Roosevelt granted him an audience. Chew helped convince the president to issue an executive order to the immigration service to halt its abusive treatment of Chinese merchants and travelers.

Later that year, the Chinese American community was invited to send a representative to New York to speak at a national conference on immigration. Chinese leaders chose Dr. Chew to speak for them.

Then thirty-nine years old, he traveled east in the cold, dark days of early December to the concert hall at Madison Square Garden, where he joined the American Federation of Labor's Samuel Gompers, Macy's co-owner Isidor Straus, and Terence V. Powderly, the powerful leader of the Knights of Labor. Scheduled to speak on the third and final day of the conference, Chew, with his witty remarks—which showed off his English fluency and his gift for navigating the tides of American political culture—delighted the five hundred delegates of the National Civic Federation. "I am here to plead the cause of the yellow people, not a yellow cause," he told them. "Some people have a great fashion of calling things they do not like yellow. You exclude the yellow man. You fear the yellow peril. I edit a white paper turned out by yellow men, and many white men turn out yellow papers."

The Chinese editor's verbal play on yellow people versus yellow papers (referring to the "yellow journalism" practiced by William Randolph Hearst and other American press barons) provoked laughter and applause. He used humor again to warm up the crowd, acknowledging some of the stereotypes of his people that had led to their exclusion in America:

> Of course, we have Chinese people of bad character, gamblers and opium eaters. If I were a woman I would rather my husband, if he insisted on taking something, took opium than whiskey. Whiskey transforms men into brutes. Opium transforms them into living corpses. The American, filled with whiskey, comes home and kicks his wife. The Chinaman comes home and his wife kicks him.

His demeaning remarks toward his own people and whites went over well. Chew then moved into his argument, which was not to repeal the Exclusion Act but to respect the long-standing treaty that allowed what he called the better classes—Chinese officials, merchants, teachers, students, and travelers—to enter the country. In a final and effective dig, he told them, "We want better men as inspectors of immigration—not the big-headed oyster-brained officials you have now."

Following Chew, one speaker made a personal attack on the Chinese editor. "The Mongolian race is opposed to the Caucasian. They corrupt our men and women," said Walter MacArthur. And Mr. Chew, "who addressed you, seems able to do more than most other editors. He can travel across the country to express his opinions when other editors in California are sticking to their business."

The audience booed and hissed in response. More troubling was Samuel Gompers, who disagreed with Chew's and President Roosevelt's position that the exempted classes be permitted easier entry, arguing that it would hurt the interests of the American workingman. Indeed, the problems at the ports continued, and the Chinese Exclusion Act—strongly supported by labor leaders like Gompers and Powderly and by politicians—remained in place until 1943.

Chew impressed the influential gathering. "He made the hit of the day," *The New York Times* reported, "even if his arguments failed of their purpose." Likewise, the boycott by the Chinese in America itself had all but fizzled out by early 1906. Yet the protests of Chew and other Chinese Americans to President Roosevelt did help curb some of the more egregious mistreatment of Chinese travelers. The protests also ended the talk of forcing Chinese Americans to register—the proposal that had prompted Chew's comparison to issuing tags to dogs.

As for Chew's own trajectory, the former minister's appearance at Madison Square Garden became one of the first of his hundreds of public addresses around the country. In later years, some called Ng Poon Chew the "Chinese Mark Twain."

25

" 'Ell of a Place!"

As Chew was traveling across the country using his unique blend of humor to raise whites' awareness of Chinese concerns, a nattily dressed German wearing a starched collar and a hat cocked to the side prowled through Chinatown's narrow alleys. A recent immigrant, the Berlin-born Arnold Genthe had arrived in San Francisco in 1895, the year Cameron first came to the Mission Home to teach sewing. To support himself, Genthe had taken a position as a tutor to the son of a prominent German family living in San Francisco, the Schroeders. His *Baedeker,* the popular tourist guide, warned, "It is not advisable to visit the Chinese quarter unless one is accompanied by a guide." Intrigued, Genthe headed straight to Chinatown to explore the famously dangerous neighborhood on his own.

He found painted balconies and girls in headdresses peering out from windows. He took in the pungent scent of sausages and heard the clang of cymbals and rings of temple gongs. What he called the "Canton of the West" was "something for me to write home about," he said. At first, he brought a sketchbook to illustrate Chinatown in his letters to his family in Germany, but he quickly realized that the act of pulling out his pencils and paper spooked his potential subjects. Instead, he began carrying a camera small enough to tuck into his pocket.

Genthe tried to be inconspicuous, but as a lanky, six-foot-two Caucasian, he couldn't help but stick out. A photograph of him when he was in his late twenties shows people on a Chinatown street gawk-

Arnold Genthe holding a camera in Chinatown.

ing at the strange, tall man as he looks down into his boxy camera's viewfinder.

By that time, Chinatown's residents were familiar with news photographers who would show up to document the quarter's crime scenes. They also feared the white immigration officials who had the power to upend their lives and who used photographs to identify both Chinese immigrants and criminals. But Genthe's intentions were different. He was a deeply educated man who'd earned his doctorate in philology, the study of languages. He sought truth in the street images he captured with his camera, preferring unposed street life to the stiff portraits of the day.

Genthe taught himself the relatively new art of street photography in Chinatown. "For my first experiment, I could scarcely have chosen a more difficult subject," he wrote. "The alleys and courtyards were so narrow that the light found its way through them for only an hour or two at midday. In order to get any pictures at all I had to hide in doorways or peer out from an angle of a building at some street corner."

He developed his first photographs under a dim red light in a closet darkroom on the top floor of the Schroeders' home. Underexposed or blurry, they were disappointing, but not so much so that he didn't go back, again and again, hoping to do better. He got to know some of the street characters who earned their living posing for tourists—a cadaverous opium smoker known as Jim, who collected nickels from the guides who brought visitors to see him puffing away, and San Lung, who sat on the corner of Stockton and Clay telling fortunes.

He soon met Donaldina Cameron and they became close friends. They were about the same age and had much in common as immigrants working in Chinatown and reliant on the grace of society patrons. (Genthe initially met some of the artistic and society people who also became subjects of his portraiture through the Schroeders and, later, through his fellow members of San Francisco's Bohemian Club.)

Like the reporter for the *Chronicle* who'd profiled Cameron in 1901, Genthe felt the superintendent was courageous in her work of rescuing victims of sex trafficking, and genuinely noble. Not only did he consider her as far removed from the stereotype of a rigid missionary as possible, but he believed she was culturally sensitive to the residents of the home.

"Miss Cameron was not a tight-lipped reformer who wished to make the world over into a monotone," he wrote. "She had respect and admiration for the art and literature of China and she saw that the girls she had taken under her wing were educated in its tradition." Genthe, with his own society connections, might have heard that Cameron's first cousin Sir Ewen Cameron held a powerful position in China as an executive at the Hongkong and Shanghai Banking Corporation and that another member of her extended family, William Robinson, had been honored as a commander of the Order of the British Empire for his service in Britain's Foreign Office. Although Cameron's father had struggled financially, she came from a large, well-connected, and worldly family.

Cameron, attuned to the ways in which her wards could help promote her cause, granted Genthe permission to photograph five of the rescued girls. He posed them in the Mission Home's courtyard, dressed in formal, embroidered robes and ornamental hairpieces. It is likely he snapped this photograph as they prepared for one of their many performances for visiting dignitaries. Genthe's presence behind the camera didn't make them stiffen into self-consciousness: to the contrary, he seemed to put them at ease. They look comfortable as they talk with each other.

In another image, young Minnie Tong, nicknamed Tea Rose, stands beside Genthe, smiling at the camera while he looks down on her paternally and holds her hand. It's not clear from the photograph whether he is looking at her fondly or with less pure intentions, but Genthe seems to have taken a particular interest in Minnie, who was perhaps seven or eight years old at the time. He also took a beautifully delicate second portrait of her in profile, looking downward, with a faint smile playing at her lips.

While Genthe eventually published and sold prints of his Chinatown photographs, including the ones of the Mission Home girls, he also sought to repay the friendship that Cameron had shown him. He noticed on his visits to the Mission Home that its walls were decorated with what he called "commonplace" lithographs and posters—no surprise, considering how parsimonious Cameron and her staff were forced to be by their limited budget.

Genthe was related to the renowned German realist artist Adolph

Minnie Tong, known as Tea Rose, with the photographer and friend of the Mission Home Arnold Genthe. He titled this photograph *Friends*.

Menzel and had grown up in a family that appreciated art. In his student days, he'd considered becoming a painter. He mentioned to Cameron that he felt it was unfortunate that the home's residents weren't being exposed to fine Chinese artwork instead. Cameron agreed but explained they didn't have the money to acquire it.

Genthe approached several San Francisco art dealers, who helped him obtain photographs and color reproductions of significant Chinese works that were then hung throughout the home. Genthe was so touched by the thank-you note the young Chinese resident Minnie wrote to him that he kept it "for the poetry of its style and sentiment," he wrote.

Little did he know that his own photographs would become some of the last remaining images of old Chinatown.

· · ·

ON THE WARM, STILL EVENING of April 17, 1906, Genthe attended a performance of the opera *Carmen* in which the famed tenor Enrico Caruso sang the role of the tragic lover, Don José. All four levels of the Grand Opera House on Mission Street were packed, and the gowns and gems worn by the society doyennes drew attention. Mrs. James Flood sparkled in her diamond-and-pearl-encrusted tiara, as did the wife and daughters of the publisher Michael de Young. It was surely one of the most extravagant displays of turn-of-the-century wealth that San Francisco had ever seen.

After ten minutes of lusty bravos and curtain calls, Genthe joined a small group of friends for supper. He then returned to his home on Sutter Street (he had left the Schroeders' house by then and found his own place) and went to bed.

Just after 5:12 the next morning, he woke to the sound of the Chinese porcelains he'd collected crashing to the floor. "The whole house was creaking and shaking, the chandelier was swinging like a pendulum, and I felt as if I were on a ship tossed about by a rough sea," he recalled. An ominous quiet followed. Just about to get out of bed, Genthe found his Japanese manservant standing beside him. He was asking permission to leave, which Genthe granted. The servant left with a basket of provisions, while Genthe made his way up to the top floor of the house to check on what had happened to his studio. The chimney had collapsed, and bookcases had toppled over. Deciding that his khaki riding clothes would be the most practical "earthquake attire," he headed for the street.

There he saw some improbable sights: an old woman carrying a birdcage with four kittens in it, a man wearing only his shirttails, having forgotten to put on trousers. He made his way to the home of some friends, and then the small party walked to the Palace Hotel. Even though there was no gas supply or electric power, the hotel—which had its own water supply and fire hoses—still managed to offer hot coffee, presumably by building a wood fire, to its distressed guests and others. Near the entrance to the dining room, Genthe spotted Enrico Caruso, wearing a fur coat over his pajamas. He was muttering to himself, "'Ell of a place! 'Ell of a place! I never come back here!"

Fortified with the bread, butter, fruit, and coffee that the hotel

provided for free in the glass-enclosed Palm Court, Genthe crossed
Market Street, where the stone cornices across from the *Call* building had crashed to the ground and the plate-glass windows had shattered from the earthquake's force. There was a powerful smell of gas
in the air coming from the ruptured mains. Smoke rose from fires
that had begun in the warehouse district along the eastern waterfront of the city. Dazed people were wandering the streets, some only
half-clothed.

Genthe returned to his studio. It didn't occur to him to pack up
his most precious belongings: he urgently wanted to photograph the
scenes on the street he'd just witnessed. Discovering upon returning
that his camera had been damaged by falling plaster, he headed to a
nearby camera dealer who told him to take whatever he'd like because
his place was "going to burn up anyway." Genthe picked a small 3A
Kodak Special, stuffed his pockets with film, and headed back out onto
the streets.

He made his way toward Nob Hill. The new Fairmont hotel, close
to being completed in April 1906, remained standing. With his borrowed Kodak, he snapped a photograph from Sacramento Street looking down onto Chinatown—at a spot about a half a block uphill from
the Mission Home. The image he captured that day remains one of
the iconic photographs of the devastation wrought by San Francisco's
earthquake and fire. Rubble strews the streets, building fronts have
crumpled, and stunned groups of people, with their backs turned to the
camera, stare east toward the financial district as billows of smoke rise
from below.

The Mission Home can be seen on the left, without apparent damage. Cameron and its residents are not in the frame. But within half
an hour of the earthquake's initial shock, dark plumes of smoke began
rising over the city. By that night, parts of San Francisco were fully
ablaze. From twelve miles across the bay in Berkeley, one observer
described "the flames shooting upward at particular centers with the
glowing discharge of a blast furnace . . . a pink glow and the occasional rumble of a dynamite explosion gave the picture a suggestion of
warfare."

In coming days, Genthe would snap a picture of an apartment

house on Sacramento Street near his own home. With its exterior gone and the furniture and decorations inside revealed, it resembled a dollhouse. With his borrowed Kodak, he'd also capture the shocking image of a blackened body lying in the middle of a street, incinerated by the flames, and a lone Chinese man looking over the stark landscape of the earthquake ruins.

⊷═ 26 ═⊷

The Lord Is My Shepherd

While Genthe and his society friends attended the opera the night before the earthquake, the girls and women of the Mission Home scoured sinks, swept floors, and dusted the woodwork from attic to basement. It was the eve of the Occidental Board of Foreign Missions' annual meeting. Under the direction of a new matron (Frances Thompson had resigned after six years), they hung curtains as well as a woven fishnet in honor of their expected guests. The net, which they draped in the chapel room, was a gift to the home from a former resident who'd become a Christian worker in China. And although the Christian symbolism of the net probably didn't escape them, they hung it because they found it beautiful.

The household was asleep when the first jolt hit. Like Genthe, Cameron compared the experience to being on rough seas:

> During the never-to-be-forgotten moments the solid earth took on the motions of an angry ocean, while chimneys crashed on to our roof, while plaster and ornaments strewed the floors, there was terror and consternation among the fifty Chinese and Japanese girls and children in the Home; but not one symptom of panic, or cowardice. Older girls forgot their own fears in anxiety to care for and soothe the little ones. Not one attempted to seek safety alone.

The five-story brick Mission Home remained standing after the quake, suffering only minor damage, while neighboring homes crum-

Arnold Genthe took this photograph looking down from Clay Street, just west of Chinatown, about a block away from the Mission Home, on the morning of the earthquake, April 18, 1906.

pled and deep cracks appeared in cobbled streets. It seemed safe enough that Cameron and the matron decided to serve breakfast that morning to the children and young women Cameron considered her daughters. Because the chimney had collapsed, they couldn't cook a warm meal. The matron slipped out onto the brick-strewn streets and managed to secure a large basket of bread from a nearby bakery.

Dressed and seated around little white tables in the dining room, the forty-seven residents sang a hymn together and then recited the words of the twenty-third Psalm: "The Lord is my shepherd; I shall not want." They then shared a meal of bread, apples, and tea brought over to the home by Chun Fah, the former resident who had married Chew. Apparently, the earthquake had not damaged the newspaper publisher's chimney, so they could still boil water.

As the girls ate breakfast, a strong aftershock hit. Cameron and some of the others, assuming it was safe, climbed the stairs to an upper floor. Peering east, past Chinatown and toward the docks of the Embarcadero, Cameron saw the small wreaths of smoke that she'd seen earlier that morning become dark clouds. Fires had ignited. She and the other women heard crackling noises, and the light took on an ominous hue. Cameron felt rising dread as she saw a cavalry force galloping through the streets below them. She soon learned that Brigadier General Frederick Funston, the acting commander of the army's Pacific Division, had ordered troops into the city without martial law having been formally declared. The situation was far graver than she'd first believed.

Several questions crossed her mind. Would another aftershock hit? Would the fires from the east approach the Mission Home? And most worryingly, how would she get her large household—which included a month-old infant, a three-month-old baby, and a one-and-a-half-year-old toddler—through the city to safety? To her relief, the home's family physician, Dr. Minora E. Kibbe, had skipped breakfast to walk about twenty minutes through the damaged city to check if anyone needed medical attention. The two women decided that Dr. Kibbe would bring the home's babies and youngest children back to her residence, which was to the west. Cameron watched as the doctor and a few of the older girls navigated their way past the heaps of fallen bricks and plaster up Nob Hill to bring the tiny ones to safety.

Cameron's close friend Evelyn Browne had spent the night at 920 Sacramento to attend the next morning's meeting. The women, joined by several of the home's board leaders, then decided the best course of action would be to move the residents west—away from the raging fires—to the First Presbyterian Church on Van Ness Avenue. Just as looters were using the disaster as an opportunity to steal, Cameron worried that traffickers could use the chaos to snatch back some of the girls.

THEY RUSHED TO GATHER their belongings before it got too dark. Cameron packed her small, leather bound Bible, the one she'd inscribed in April 1904: "Holiness is infinite compassion for others— Happiness is great love, and much serving." Then she tucked small mementos and precious photographs within its pages. The streets were beginning to fill with refugees seeking safety from the fires. Walking the mile or so together in a tight group, they carried bedding, clothing, and some food with them. At some point along the way, with Dr. Kibbe's help, they were reunited with the small children and babies.

After settling the girls in for the night at the church, Cameron realized she had forgotten something crucial: the home's documentation of its residents. Without it, she feared the slave owners would attempt to regain possession of her wards, arguing that there was no legal proof they'd ever sought refuge there. Sometime in the early hours of Thursday, April 19, she walked back to the home through the dark, pausing at the top of Nob Hill to look down at the shattered city below.

The streets were nearly empty, and soldiers stood guard in front of cordoned neighborhoods. After pleading to pass through to reach 920 Sacramento Street, she climbed the steps and passed through its doorway. The electricity was cut off, and the fires outside cast a red glare to the darkened interior.

Cameron lingered in Margaret Culbertson's old room, remembering the hours she'd spent with her late mentor. Almost as soon as she entered, a dynamite blast a block away set by city officials hoping to contain the fires jolted her into action. The soldier posted outside urged her to hurry.

Cameron gathered papers and valuables from her desk, most crucially the "Register of Inmates of Chinese Mission Home," a paper-bound volume containing details on every girl and young woman who'd entered the home since it first opened in 1874—829 of them by 1906. Taking a final look back at the place that had been her home for the past eleven years, Cameron walked down the stairs and out onto the dark streets to return to her sleeping charges.

By the time she reached First Presbyterian, the fire was approaching from three sides. As smoke obscured the rising sun, she decided her group should head toward the ferry. Realizing they had a long walk to the terminal and would not be able to carry everything they had brought with them, they improvised. Tying torn sheets to broom handles, the girls found a way to carry their possessions in two bundles over their shoulders—similar to how Chinese vegetable sellers carried their loads of bok choy and pea shoots. The girls laughed as they struggled for balance.

Some treasures were left behind, while others were saved. One young woman begged to be allowed to carry a large box containing love letters. In a softhearted moment, Cameron agreed, later writing, "Her look of genuine distress when advised to abandon the precious box was so appealing we had to save it." Young mothers carried their babies on their backs, and an old woman accompanying the group who'd recently lost sight in one eye dragged her bundle of possessions up and down the hills. A three-and-a-half-year-old named Hung Mooie was given the responsibility of carrying a package of eggs.

Skipping breakfast, the large group was forced to detour around the fires as it made its way down rubble-strewn Market Street to the ferry terminal.

Cameron, then thirty-six years old, felt intense anxiety as she led the band of more than sixty girls, women, and babies (along with at least one young boy) on foot through the heat and suffocating vapors. But she kept those feelings to herself and tried to buoy the group's spirits with humor. They could always stop and cook scrambled eggs if little Hung Mooie dropped the precious carton of eggs she was carrying. "Laughter was the tonic which stimulated that weary, unwashed and uncombed procession on the long tramp through stifling, crowded streets near where the fire raged," Cameron wrote.

They finally reached the ferry terminal, where thousands of other refugees were desperate to leave the city. It was an otherworldly scene. Cloaked in thick smoke, people had set folded mattresses, mirrors, chests of drawers, and bundles of clothing and linens on the ground, alongside wagons piled high with other household possessions. One man wearing a black bowler hat sat in a rocking chair as he waited for the next boat. Luckily for Cameron and her large party, a ferry was about to leave for Sausalito, a small fishing village in Marin County. They managed to talk their way on board and descend to the lower deck of the steamer, where they collapsed in relief.

THE GROUP CROSSED the bay, boarded a train at the Sausalito ferry terminal, and made their way north, probably first by train and then by wagon, up a hill to the new home of the Presbyterian San Francisco Theological Seminary, where Chew had graduated fourteen years earlier. In 1892, the school had moved from San Francisco to a fourteen-acre campus in the small town of San Anselmo. From a distance, its Romanesque-style stone halls and turreted clock towers looked like a Scottish hilltop castle transposed to California. But the earthquake had knocked over one of the towers, sending it crashing through the library and exposing books to the rain and elements. The earthquake also damaged faculty housing and dorm rooms.

So, while the campus might have looked grand from a distance, the group discovered that the only place available to shelter them was a barn—a biblical choice if ever there was one. Their refugee band had expanded to sixty-seven people, because a few more Chinese women and children fleeing San Francisco had joined them. Responsible for so many people, Cameron was dismayed by the accommodations. She wrote,

> Life in an empty barn, with very scanty bedding, insufficient food, one tin dipper [for water] and a dozen tea spoons and plates for a family of sixty is not comfortable; yet all made the best of the situation and share unselfishly the few necessities available.

They spent a week in the unheated structure, sleeping on the dusty floor with tattered bedding from a local orphanage. Hungry and shivering from cold, they survived mainly on boiled red beans, though some of the theological students helped scrounge additional food for them. More accustomed to books and prayers than sentry duty, the students also served as makeshift deputies, protecting the girls from the very real threat of slave owners hoping to recapture them. As one professor boasted in the racist vernacular of the day, the ministry students "kept the valley clean from rough characters and arrested a villainous Chinese who was prowling about the refuge of our Christian Chinese girls."

Cameron's burden of protecting, feeding, and caring for so many people weighed heavily on her. But in a letter she wrote soon after arriving in San Anselmo to her sister Jessie, brother-in-law Charley, and their daughter Caroline, she minimized her anxieties and discomfort: "Do not worry about me dears. Some of the people here are very kind to me and it is a great blessing to have a roof over our heads . . . the loft of this barn is clean & warm so [we] are really most fortunate."

It is clear from her letter that she was deeply shaken by what had happened: "I still feel sort of dazed and cannot realize that the experiences of last week are a reality. It seems more like a *dreadful dream*."

IT IS A TESTAMENT to Cameron's leadership that she and the other Mission Home residents escaped unharmed: more than three thousand people perished either directly or indirectly because of the disaster, and a quarter of a million people became homeless. Soon after Cameron and her charges left the city, fire swept through Chinatown, destroying most of its buildings, as well as the Fairmont hotel that loomed above it. The Mission Home's bricked entryway remained standing, with its stone letters bearing the legend "Occidental Board of Foreign Missions." But the disaster destroyed everything inside 920 Sacramento Street, including the Chinese prints recently donated through Genthe's efforts.

The German photographer, meanwhile, spent his first night after the earthquake camping in Golden Gate Park with thousands of others. The fire destroyed his home and studio on Sutter Street. He lost family papers, letters, photographs of his parents and brothers, and many of his negatives, which he later realized he could have saved by carrying them away in a suitcase. Returning to his studio afterward, he found thousands of negatives he'd made in San Francisco fused together into chunks of molten, iridescent glass. Luckily, though, by moving the most important negatives of his Chinatown photographs sometime before the disaster to the safekeeping of a friend's vault, he'd saved them.

For Cameron and her charges, one bright spot in the days after the disaster was the wedding of one of their own, Yuen Kum, to a man from Cleveland named Henry Lai, a match almost certainly arranged from afar by the home's staffers. The date for their nuptials had been set for April 21, 1906. The eager groom had arrived in San Francisco on the day of the earthquake and frantically sought his bride. He traced her to San Anselmo, and their wedding was performed three days after the group arrived. On the day originally planned, the couple took their vows in the seminary's ivy-covered chapel. The guests at the wedding showered the young couple with rose petals. And in a photograph that might have been taken around the time of the wedding, Cameron stands behind thirteen of the younger girls in the group on a bucolic hillside, their white clothing laundered and the younger girls' hair neatly plaited.

A few days later, Cameron's group moved to a house in the adjacent town of San Rafael. Cameron described it as a "Fairy Palace" shabby, old-fashioned, and situated at the end of a long drive hedged with rosebushes and acacias. While it was too small, the move from San Francisco had one positive effect: Cameron and the girls ended up spending the next few months in the sunshine of central Marin County, which was typically several degrees warmer throughout the year than San Francisco. A photographer captured a scene in front of the San Rafael house as more than fifty members of the household squeezed together onto its wide steps, the youngest at the bottom and staff members (one with a baby in her lap) at the top. The front door behind them is partially open, as if to signal its welcome.

27

"The Stress of Circumstances"

Like Cameron, Ng Poon Chew realized he'd left something crucial behind after the earthquake struck. As the fires raced toward Chinatown on the afternoon of April 18, he and his family gathered a few blocks from his newspaper office on Sacramento Street. Chew instructed Chun Fah to lead their children to safety in Golden Gate Park. The couple loaded their most precious belongings into their son's coaster wagon, and the children, led by their mother, pulled it by the handle as they walked west up Sacramento Street, away from Chinatown and the fires.

Meanwhile, Chew headed in the opposite direction, down the hill toward his iron-balconied three-story office. His witty remarks at the immigration conference in New York five months earlier had failed to sway many of the participants. Realizing this, he'd been working night after night for months on a manuscript about the contributions of Chinese immigrants to America. He was nearly finished with the book that he hoped would help ease entry to the United States for Chinese scholars, businessmen, and artists.

By that afternoon, water mains had broken and desperate firefighters had drained reservoirs. The Hall of Justice was smoldering. As the winds picked up, firefighters continued dynamiting buildings in hope of creating firebreaks. A firestorm had erupted.

Across the street from *Chung Sai Yat Po,* a building had already caught fire, and its timbers and bricks were crashing to the ground, sending dangerous sparks flying. The pages Chew had written were in

The home in San Rafael, California, where Donaldina Cameron and the girls and young women in her care took refuge after the 1906 earthquake. They dubbed it "the Fairy Palace."

Chung Sai Yat Po's offices. He was desperate to get there in time to save his manuscript. Chew tried to mount the stairs to his office, but a guardsman blocked him just as one had tried to block Cameron. When Chew tried to push past the guard, a second brandished a rifle at him. "Move on, move on," he growled. Cameron had been able to convince what were almost certainly a different set of white guards to let her in, but the Chinese publisher could not.

Reluctantly, Chew turned away from *Chung Sai Yat Po* and hurried up the hill to catch up with his wife and children. Officials had segregated the disaster's Chinese refugees into their own area, and the Chew family spent the next few nights camping in parkland nearly four miles away from Chinatown. Children were crying because there was nothing to eat, and one Chinese girl, nine at the time of the earthquake, recalled that in the Chinese encampment, the price of a five-cent loaf of bread had soared to $5.

Chew sent his wife and children to stay with friends in Berkeley, across the bay. He soon followed them and located a temporary home for his family and his newspaper in nearby Oakland, becoming part of a large exodus of Chinese out of San Francisco.

In the three days following the earthquake, fires destroyed 4.7 square miles, or roughly a tenth of the city, and more than twenty-eight thousand buildings. Flames consumed the office and printing press of Chew's *Chung Sai Yat Po*, as well as his unfinished book. Chinatown lay in smoldering ruins, leaving the entire population of San Francisco's Chinese quarter homeless, including Chew's family and Cameron's extended household of girls and women. By April 19, the day after the quake, all of Chinatown's residents were gone, some "brooding or weeping softly" as they realized they'd lost their homes and livelihoods.

The Chinese, overall, suffered more than many whites after the earthquake. Just as Chew was not able to convince the guards to let him retrieve his manuscript while Cameron, in contrast, managed to recover her logbook, many of San Francisco's Chinese residents had a far more difficult time rebuilding their lives in the city after the disaster than others. But one unexpected benefit to the Chinese was that many official documents went up in flames.

·   ·   ·

SOME OF SAN FRANCISCO'S LEADERS welcomed Chinatown's destruction as a way to rid the district of the Chinese and seize its twelve square blocks for redevelopment. "Fire has reclaimed to civilization and cleanliness the Chinese ghetto, and no Chinatown will be permitted in the borders of the city," intoned *The Overland Monthly,* a prestigious magazine based in San Francisco that had published the poem by Bret Harte that later became known as "The Heathen Chinee." Many of the city's Chinese residents—estimated at between fourteen thousand and twenty-five thousand at the time of the earthquake—fled in the days after the disaster. Some went to California's Central Valley, others to Los Angeles, and quite a few—with the help of Chinese government authorities—returned to their homeland.

But by far, the largest group went to Oakland, a busy port city with a small Chinatown of its own. By some counts, four thousand or so ended up in the town across the bay from San Francisco. Oakland officials did not welcome the Chinese with open arms. They segregated them into a tent city along Oakland's Lake Merritt called the Willows Camp. When it rained a few nights after the earthquake, officials offered shelter to white earthquake refugees first. At 3:00 a.m., the

Overlooking the destruction of Chinatown, April 1906, as photographed by Arnold Genthe.

shivering Chinese were finally marched, dragging their soggy belongings with them, to a garage.

Chew recognized that his newspaper could help mobilize the widely dispersed Chinatown community, so he and his team of journalists scrambled to resume publishing. On April 26, 1906—just eight days after disaster struck—the first issue of *Chung Sai Yat Po* appeared. Getting the paper out was no mean feat. An elder named Ng Yee Yin, who shared a surname as a member of Chew's clan, wrote out the entire paper by hand, and he even had to paint the characters backward so they could then be photographed and engraved for printing. Chew relied on this laborious process for months until the new printing press he ordered from Japan arrived.

In that first, post-earthquake edition of the paper, Chew predicted that San Francisco's leaders would seize on the disaster as an opportunity to move Chinatown. He exhorted his readers to rebuild the capital of Chinese America in its original location. He wrote,

> Everyone believes that the fire is an excellent excuse to move China-town, a plan that the Americans have long contemplated. Every Chinese believes that since they want us to move, we will not be able to rebuild it. We have not tried yet; how do we know we cannot do it?

At Chew's urging, Chinese leaders began resisting the city's efforts to displace Chinatown and instead decided to rebuild it in its original home. Chew and Cameron, meanwhile, were both determined to raise the money and deploy the political capital needed to continue their respective missions—one to serve as a voice for the Chinese in America, the other to help victims of human trafficking.

THE HOME IN SAN RAFAEL that Cameron had first described as a "fairy palace" soon became cramped and uncomfortable. Supporters had provided cases of clothing, warm bedding, and a new sewing machine, and Cameron and the sixty or so girls and their teachers expanded into every possible space, including the grounds around the home. They held classes beneath a donated tent they'd pitched on the grass and squeezed donated desks inside it. On warm days it got so hot inside that sometimes the teacher and her students would seek relief outdoors under a rose arbor.

Supporters sent money, including $10 from one Dr. Lapsley A. McAfee, treasurer of the Presbyterian Relief Fund. When Cameron did not promptly acknowledge the gift, Dr. McAfee made his displeasure known. Writing to him from San Rafael, Cameron made a flowery and somewhat acerbic apology that emphasized that she'd taken time on her day of rest to respond to him:

> Dear Dr. McAffee,
>
> Please cast the ample mantle of your charity on my failure to be business like! My intentions were of the best last Monday when I promised to promptly mail the script for ten dollars which you forwarded. I was ill that night Dr. McAfee and next day was travelling all over Robin Hoods farm the day following off to Carson City Nevada on a Chinese case and so forth and so on. Now at last comes the blessed day in seven when I must cease from some of my own labors. I was brought up to feel that one of the unpardonable sins was letter writing on the Lord's day and so I seldom permit myself to open my desk but there are necessary exceptions to all rules and this is one of them. I mean to thank you most heartily Dr. McAfee for the gracious interest you have shown toward our Chinese Home and the kind cordiality your letters have expressed. I regret exceedingly that stress of circumstances have caused me to appear unappreciative. Please do not consider me so but rather believe me to be most gratefully and faithfully yours in his blessed name. *Donaldina Cameron* Sabbath morning

Cameron had good reason for her delayed thanks. In the seven and a half weeks since the earthquake, she had moved a large group of vulnerable babies, children, and women across the bay, into a barn, and then into a nearby house—making sure they were fed, clothed, and bathed. Her constant duty of raising funds only accelerated, because now her goal was to rebuild the Mission Home in Chinatown. And because so many Chinese had resettled in Oakland, the superintendent increasingly found she was being called there for rescues or other reasons. Every venture was a four-hour round-trip ferry journey.

As the rainy season approached, which would make their outdoor space unusable, Cameron realized she needed to move her household once again. She began searching for a suitable house in July but encountered soaring rents and resistance among landlords to renting to such a large group of Chinese. With "much negotiating, urging, and pleading," in November 1906 she finally secured a house in Oakland's Chinatown. With gifts ranging from $5 to several chickens, the household could celebrate Thanksgiving together. At Christmastime, a supporter donated a tree, which Cameron placed in the new home's parlor, alongside gifts, candy, fruits, and nuts. Several of the Mission Home girls sang in that year's Christmas pageant at a nearby Chinese chapel.

THE NEW YEAR HAD barely begun when Cameron accompanied a group of uniformed and plainclothes Oakland police officers in an early morning raid on several Chinese brothels. A few officers carried axes in case they needed to break through barricaded doors. The city's leaders had grown increasingly concerned by the sudden surge in Chinese refugees. Before the earthquake, there were an estimated one thousand Chinese living in Oakland; by the summer of 1906, the Chinese population had swelled to some seven thousand. Fearing the newcomers would bring San Francisco's "slave girl traffic" to their East Bay city, which, until then, had mostly escaped it, the police decided to launch a preemptive strike.

Through the Mission Home's translator, the captain asked if any of the young women in the brothels wanted to leave under the protection of Miss Cameron. Only one, a seventeen-year-old girl who'd been sold in Bakersfield to work as a prostitute in Oakland several months earlier, took him up on the offer. Perhaps they were cowed by fear or determined to earn money for their families, but none of the others sought help or indicated they were under duress. To Cameron's joy, however, the raiding party did sweep up a four-year-old girl she'd been seeking for some months whose father had apparently sold her to a well-known trafficker.

"Police with Axes Are Out" read the headline in the evening edition of the January 11, 1907, *Oakland Enquirer*. As a show of force, the raids made for dramatic copy, even though Cameron and the police only retrieved the four-year-old and the teen. For Oakland authorities, that morning's raids had served their purpose: to demonstrate their decisive move against vice. "The police department is satisfied that there is none of the traffic in slave girls in the Oakland Chinatown such as the rumors led them to suspect . . . and not a present likelihood that there will ever be introduction of this feature of Orientalism which has been such a blot on the old San Francisco quarter," the paper concluded.

That same evening, shortly after the paper hit the newsstands, a tong leader named Lee Book Dong was murdered at his home in Oakland's Chinatown while eating supper—apparently in a dispute over a teenage girl. It's likely the girl, who fled the house before police arrived, was a victim of trafficking. Before the night was over, four other Chinese men were injured by gunfire on the streets of Chinatown.

The "blot," as crimes connected with tong violence and "Chinese slave girls" were called in the racist vernacular of the day, had made its way across the bay.

28

Homecomings

C hew found a way to overcome the racism and laws that restricted most of Oakland's Chinese to a crowded ghetto. In the months after the earthquake, he and Chun Fah discreetly strolled through Oakland's white neighborhoods, admiring the neat homes with their sunny gardens. They found a two-story house for sale about a mile away from the newly opened Claremont Country Club and instructed their real estate agent to submit a bid in the name of Dr. N. P. Chew, a name shared by a prominent white family. Chew signed the purchase papers for the home in the summer of 1906.

Very carefully, Chew's Americanized Chinese family, who wore Western-style clothing and spoke good English, moved in one at a time so as not to alarm the neighbors. First, Chew and Chun Fah moved in. Then their eldest daughter, followed by their second daughter, then their third daughter, and then their fourth daughter, and finally their son. As Chew later wrote, they quickly blended in:

> It wasn't long till I smoked my cigar harmoniously with the men in the block, my wife talked over the back fence with the ladies and my children played with the other children in the block, and so far as I have been able to learn, no one has ever been contaminated by association with the family.

.   .   .

Ng Poon Chew's newspaper, *Chung Sai Yat Po*, resumed publishing from Oakland shortly after the 1906 earthquake but soon moved its headquarters back to San Francisco.

THE CHEWS' SMALL VICTORY of integration took place at a time when some San Francisco officials were hoping to further segregate the estimated eight thousand Chinese who remained in the city. Abe Ruef, the lawyer who had volunteered his legal services to the Mission Home early in his career, was named to lead the city's Subcommittee for Permanent Location of Chinatown. What that meant, of course, was that Ruef would try to relocate the city's Chinese community to an area where the real estate was less valuable, far away from the eastern slopes of Nob Hill.

An early idea on the part of Mayor Eugene Schmitz and other city leaders was to move Chinatown to Hunters Point—a desolate area of mudflats and slaughterhouses on the city's southeastern border. As discussions got under way, officials ordered Chinese refugees to move from one segregated camp to another, while members of the National Guard and other citizens flagrantly picked through the smoldering ruins of Chinatown, looking for undamaged porcelain plates and other treasures. The disaster had also become the chaotic backdrop for racially motivated attacks: *Chung Sai Yat Po* reported that a Chinese man returning to the location of his destroyed home on Sacramento Street was stoned to death.

After hearing of forced segregation and maltreatment, the Chinese ambassador in Washington, D.C., lodged a formal protest. President Theodore Roosevelt also inquired about the city's treatment of the Chinese. Soon came a meeting between Ruef's subcommittee and local Chinese leaders, who made it known that they would not move to Hunters Point. Chinatown leaders instead threatened to move their sizable community, with all the economic benefits of trade and tourism that came with it, to a different city if San Francisco continued its threatening talk of relocating Chinatown.

As Ruef's subcommittee bogged down in internal disagreements, the few Chinese property owners began building rather than waiting for permits. (At the time of the disaster, the Chinese owned less than 10 percent of the land in Chinatown; an 1878 law forbade aliens excluded from citizenship, like the Chinese, to acquire title to property.) Rebuilding without permits was an effective blocking strategy— and possibly the turning point in the battle—because they knew whites wouldn't want to settle in a Chinese neighborhood. The Chinese also took the advice of Chew's paper to hire well-known legal counsel. They did, and those lawyers informed them they were under no legal compulsion to abandon their leases.

Surprisingly, they soon gained the crucial support of the mostly white property owners in the area, who recognized the value of the rents they'd been paid by Chinese tenants (and, by that time, might have realized the scheme to relocate Chinatown was dead). Together, white and Chinese landowners formed the Dupont Street Improvement Club, named after the main thoroughfare of Chinatown.

Out of the rubble and ashes rose a new "Oriental City," influenced by Look Tin Eli, a California born merchant who had founded one of Chinatown's largest tourist-oriented businesses, the Sing Chong Bazaar. Look, who was secretary of the Chinese Chamber of Commerce, helped convince other businessmen and property owners that they could attract more tourists by rebuilding in an "oriental style." The American architecture firm of Ross & Burgren designed Look's new building to resemble a multistory pagoda. While pagodas, or temples, in China are functioning buildings, the steel-framed top of the Sing Chong Bazaar was purely decorative. To create a sense of enchantment, this commercial temple was lit up at night by thousands of incandescent bulbs.

The city did its part by widening Chinatown's streets and alleyways, making it easier to navigate. Soon, others followed, building in what the late historian Philip P. Choy called a "pseudo-Oriental style," taking Chinese elements, such as the curved eaves of a pagoda and wrought-iron balconies decorated with the traditional Chinese "double happiness" motif, and transforming new structures into something unique using Western materials and methods. The San Francisco Real Estate Board applauded the rebuilt Chinatown, which had renamed its main thoroughfare Grant Avenue, as picturesque and tourist-friendly. Tiny lights and the exuberant use of the Chinese colors of red, yellow, and green helped turn a dark and crowded ghetto into what one contemporary architectural journal called "the fantasy of the Far East."

·   ·   ·

SOME REFORMERS HOPED the 1906 earthquake and fire would rid the city of prostitution and human trafficking. But the city's brothels reappeared almost immediately, and the lucrative business of trafficking resumed.

From their temporary base in Oakland, Cameron and her staff continued rescuing young girls and women throughout California. She also kept up the steady pace of her fund-raising appeals, usually accompanied by several young Chinese girl singers. Supporters from across the country rallied to her side, moved by the thought of Cameron's large household lacking a permanent home. To help rebuild the Mission Home, many prominent donors such as the New York philanthropist Grace Dodge and the Chicago inventor Cyrus McCormick together gave more than $50,000.

Those funds produced a practical, though somewhat inelegant, new house for Cameron, staff, and residents. The new Mission Home was a stocky, square structure made of dark, irregularly shaped "clinker bricks" reclaimed from the fire. It rose in the same spot where the old Mission Home had stood: the steep slope of 920 Sacramento Street, retaining some of its original walls. Around it, the neighborhood was only "sparsely rebuilt," as one Mission Home staffer wrote, and dismayingly bleak compared with the "teeming" Chinatown of Oakland, where they had come from. In 1907, the new home's cornerstone was laid by Mrs. Muriel Wing, or Ah Tsun, who entered the home as a sixteen-year-old in 1877 and had worked as a teacher and home visitor for the mission ever since.

On April 14, 1908, San Francisco's mayor along with many other dignitaries arrived on an overcast Tuesday afternoon to formally dedicate the rebuilt Mission Home. Chew, whose destroyed newspaper office had been just down the street, displayed his loyalty to the Mission Home and its feminist mission by speaking at the ceremony. "In Peking, we have a daily newspaper published by women, for women exclusively," he told them, making a point about China's advances in female empowerment. "Have you anything like that in the United States?"

Chew knew firsthand the power of women helping other women. He also knew intimately the bitter racial divides that had led to segregation and violence against the Chinese. This ongoing racial antagonism, which had led to the founding of the Mission Home three decades earlier, remained just as pervasive in 1908 as it had been in 1874. And for that reason, in his view, the Mission Home was a much-needed refuge. Chun Fah, Chew's own wife, was an example of how a "woman's work for women" organization could change lives.

⊷═ 29 ═⊶

Municipal Crib

The fight against human trafficking was a battle against entrenched corruption at the highest levels of San Francisco's government, including Mayor Schmitz's office itself. And the woes of Abe Ruef, the former legal counselor to the Mission Home, kept piling up. The home had found an irreproachable champion in Henry E. Monroe, who replaced Ruef as its lawyer, but it was becoming increasingly clear to Cameron and her allies that they were fighting city hall.

Ruef's primary nemesis was the crusading newspaper editor Fremont Older. Lean, balding, and six feet two, Older lived in the luxurious Palace Hotel with his wife, Cora, a novelist and nonfiction writer. Older had become convinced that the Schmitz administration was corrupt and that curly-headed Ruef was negotiating and accepting payoffs on the mayor's behalf. His paper, *The Bulletin,* reported that when the mayor instructed supplicants to go "see Ruef," he expected them to pay handsomely for whatever city permit or license they were seeking. Ruef—who had no official title in the administration—served as Schmitz's fixer and bribe collector.

Starting about sixteen months before the earthquake, in November 1904, Older's *Bulletin* ran a sensational series of stories on a Chinatown establishment it dubbed the "municipal crib." Three partners connected to the Schmitz administration bought a decrepit opium den at 620 Jackson Street in Chinatown, just five blocks northeast of the Mission Home and a place undoubtedly known to Cameron. Soon after, the Board of Health condemned the building as unsanitary and ordered it

Dance halls in the red-light district of the city, known as the Barbary Coast, which bordered Chinatown.

torn down at city expense. City officials then issued a permit for construction of a three-story building in that same spot.

The building contractors, it turned out, had ties to the mayor. When construction was nearly completed, a city inspector found that the building, officially called the Standard Lodging House, contained about a hundred small cubicles, a common layout for large houses of prostitution. Clearly, it was being built as a "crib." The inspector reported this, but the mayor's brother Herbert Schmitz, who was president of the Board of Public Works, reprimanded the inspector and buried the report.

The brothel opened in May 1904 as a high-turnover operation, offering sex for twenty-five cents in the basement cubicles where the Mexican prostitutes worked and a dollar for the services of the French prostitutes on the top floor. Women of various nationalities worked on the other floors. Older was convinced that prostitutes were being forced to make payments to Schmitz and his cronies. And although the newspaper editor had been gathering evidence of the Schmitz administration's corruption since it took power in 1902, this time Older was gunning for more than just breaking news: he wanted indictments.

Prostitution was only loosely regulated in most parts of the country in 1904. In some red-light districts, such as New Orleans's Storyville, it operated openly and with the encouragement of city leaders, who hoped to restrict vice to a roughly nineteen-block area near the French Quarter. But bribery and graft on the part of city officials were illegal, and that's where Older and other city reformers saw their opportunity. Six months after the brothel at 620 Jackson Street opened, his paper began running stories with such sensational headlines on mayoral corruption as "Gang Given Brothel Corner!" (The "gang" in this case referred to Mayor Schmitz and his cronies.)

A grand jury began investigating. Members of the jury even took a field trip to Chinatown, where they visited 620 Jackson Street and witnessed city police officers posted outside the building as streams of men headed in and out. When he was called before the grand jury, Mayor Schmitz staunchly denied the charges that he and Ruef were profiting from the brothel. But support of the Standard Lodging House from police and city officials was a sign of how Cameron was, quite literally, fighting city hall in her efforts to free sex slaves and disrupt trafficking.

It wasn't until a young Chinese woman calling herself Lily came to Older's office at *The Bulletin* that he thought he might have enough evidence to bring the mayor and Ruef to trial. The editor agreed to offer her protection. That evening, Lily brought along another young woman, presumably also a prostitute working in the "municipal crib," who had information about payoffs to officials. She, too, agreed to testify before the grand jury. The next morning, Lily told the jurors what she knew. But the other woman changed her mind and refused to talk. To Older's dismay, the jury decided there wasn't enough evidence to indict the mayor or the bagman. (A "bagman," which first came into use in the nineteenth century, is someone who collects or distributes illicitly gained money.)

Older refused to back down. With the 1905 city elections approaching, he decided to go to Washington, D.C., and meet with Francis J. Heney, a federal prosecutor working in the Roosevelt administration. The editor met Heney over lunch at the Willard Hotel hoping to convince him to lead a corruption case against Schmitz and his lawyer, who had gained the nickname Boss Ruef. Still stinging from the grand jury's decision not to bring charges in the "municipal crib" case, Older presented another possibility he hoped might stand up in court.

That case began in 1904, when Mayor Schmitz ordered the police to investigate the city's so-called French restaurants—prominent establishments such as Marchand's, Delmonico's, and the Poodle Dog that had dining rooms on the ground floor and private chambers upstairs for sexual trysts. Ruef made one of these restaurants, the Pup, his headquarters—dining there most nights and conducting his affairs (presumably involving business deals, not sex) in one of its private rooms above Stockton Street. After the city threatened to close the French restaurants, its operators learned that Ruef would argue their case before the San Francisco Police Commission if they gave him $10,000 annually for two years. After they paid him, the city reissued their licenses. Once a grand jury heard evidence of what had transpired from the restaurant owners, it indicted both Ruef and Schmitz on five counts of extortion.

Heney agreed the case sounded promising and suggested that his colleague William J. Burns, a former Secret Service agent he'd worked with, would be just the man to gather the evidence to bring Schmitz and Ruef to trial. Heney also suggested a whopping budget to begin with: $100,000 (or the equivalent of about $2.7 million in today's dollars). Older's job would be to raise these funds privately from some of the wealthy businessmen in San Francisco who wanted to rid the city of Mayor Schmitz and his cronies.

The next morning, Older was ushered into a meeting at the White House with Theodore Roosevelt. The twenty-sixth president, who wore round, rimless spectacles, seemed sympathetic to the editor's argument for a federal corruption probe. Heartened to have brought his crusade to the president's attention, Older returned to San Francisco. In late 1905, Heney arrived in the city to pursue the case. But on the morning of April 18, 1906, the earthquake and subsequent fire that destroyed much of San Francisco also gave the mayor and his lawyer a temporary reprieve.

OLDER'S MISSION TO TOPPLE the Schmitz administration had been a lonely one: before the earthquake, few newspapers followed the *Bulletin*'s investigative stories. But that changed after 1906, when evidence mounted that Schmitz and his cronies were exploiting the disaster to generate profits for themselves. A group of city leaders, including the industrialist Rudolph Spreckels, agreed to help fund the federal investigation against the Schmitz administration. The Spreckels's newspaper, the *Call*, began running dramatic stories on the graft probe, as did the *San Francisco Chronicle*, then owned by the de Young family. The city was divided into bitter political factions, with many business leaders and current and former officials pitted against each other.

One such story, headlined "Secret Service Enmeshes Ruef in Chinese Slave Traffic," reported detailed testimony from a slave dealer about how Chinese girls and women were smuggled into the United States. Officials would acquire fraudulent affidavits of marriage from a notary, employ an attorney with influence in the immigration service, bribe a Chinese interpreter, and, crucially, make a friend of the inspector or higher official who would signify that the exclusion law had been complied with. The slaver's testimony suggested that Ruef and the Schmitz administration were intimately involved in these payoffs.

Another article, describing Ruef as the "arch grafter," reported that Secret Service agents were gathering evidence that would prove the lawyer had been closely involved in trafficking Chinese girls and women into the city. Spreckels's paper alleged that Schmitz's bagman was involved in "the sale of human beings into slavery, a graft that put pretty, innocent Chinese girls upon the auction block and delivered them, mere chattels of the market, into the immoral dens."

What the story didn't mention was that the "municipal crib" at 620 Jackson Street, which had been destroyed like the rest of Chinatown in 1906, had been quickly rebuilt and expanded by a third. Now it was a four-story building with some 133 cubicles inside. On occasions when a trolley had no female passengers, conductors would shout, "All out for the whorehouse!" when it stopped near the building on Jackson near Kearny. Rival brothels located near it had either closed or never reopened after the earthquake.

White city officials and policemen had long profited from Chinatown vice, with little consequence. The graft trials, led by the San Francisco city attorney William H. Langdon and assisted by Heney, spotlighted the institutional forces that Cameron and the Mission Home were up against in fighting sex slavery.

In late 1906, a grand jury handed down a flurry of additional indictments against Ruef, the police chief, and Mayor Schmitz. Prosecutors were not able to make a case against Ruef for human trafficking in Chinatown, so they focused instead on bringing a wide array of graft charges against him. After a byzantine series of events, including the apparent murder of a witness, an assassination attempt in court on the prosecutor Heney, and an escape attempt by Ruef, the lawyer eventually agreed to testify against his former boss Schmitz. After hearing the testimony, a jury found the former mayor guilty of extortion. Sentenced to five years in San Quentin, he spent only a few months in the county jail while his sentence was on appeal. The district court of appeals nullified his conviction and Schmitz went free.

More than two years later, on December 10, 1908, Ruef was sentenced to fourteen years in San Quentin prison for bribery. Older cheered in the courtroom when the jury foreman read the verdict. Yet it soon became clear that Ruef would be the sole defendant of the graft trials to serve time in prison. Not long after Ruef entered San Quentin, Older came to visit him. Concluding that the disgraced lawyer had been a victim of the prosecution, which had reneged on its promise of immunity, and possibly anti-Semitism as well, the editor, in a shocking reversal, asked Ruef to forgive him.

Older began campaigning for Ruef's early release. To drum up public sympathy, Older encouraged Ruef to write about his experiences. He agreed, and *The Bulletin* ran his confessions as a series titled "The Road I Traveled: An Autobiographic Account of My Career from University to Prison, with an Intimate Recital of the Corrupt Alliance Between Big Business and Politics in San Francisco."

Ruef, who had titled his college thesis at Berkeley "Purity in Politics," found an occupation he could pursue from his prison cell: writing for *The Bulletin*. After spending four years and seven months in San Quentin, he was finally released early with the help of Older, his former sworn enemy.

Abe Ruef (right) on his way to San Quentin prison.

⤙⟹ 30 ⟸⤙

Paper Son

On the morning of Tuesday, November 17, 1908, a few weeks before Ruef's sentencing, the usual fog settled over San Francisco, muffling the raucous banter of longshoremen. An elderly immigration inspector, nicknamed "the Professor," made his way along the waterfront, past cargo and passengers, to Pier 40. He climbed a set of stairs and entered a long wooden warehouse perched on piles over the bay. The Chinese called the place *muk uk*, or "wooden house." Others called it "the detention shed."

The seventy-six-year-old inspector, Joseph Burwell McChesney, came to interview a passenger who'd docked three days earlier aboard the SS *Asia*, a steamer that had arrived from China and Japan. His paperwork indicated he was a merchant's son from Guangdong province distinguished by two features: his unusually short stature—he stood five feet one and a half inches tall—and the long, vertical scar that ran down his forehead.

Traveling under the name of Leung Foo, the passenger was facing a crucial test for permission to set foot on U.S. soil as a legal immigrant. He had brought a set of documents to prove his age—twenty-one—and his identity as the son of a legal Chinese American resident. At the turn of the century, immigration authorities denied entry to as many as a third of all Chinese immigrants to the United States, but mostly to less educated laborers and people they suspected of being criminals. It was by no means certain Leung's paperwork would pass muster.

McChesney, the elder statesman among half a dozen inspectors for

A photograph from the immigration records of Leung Foo,
a.k.a. Wong See Duck.

the U.S. Immigration Service's Chinese Division, had drawn this case. He'd spent three decades as a high school principal, and his academic background had earned him the honorific "Professor." Aiding him were an interpreter, translating between English and Chinese, and a stenographer, writing down and later typing the answers to McChesney's questions.

Speaking Sze Yup, a dialect from the Pearl River delta, Leung pledged to the inspector that he would answer his questions truthfully.

"What is your name and age?" asked McChesney, whose words were then repeated back to Leung in Chinese.

"Leung Foo; age 21 . . ."
　"Where were you born?"
　"Lew Long village . . ."
　"How large is that village?"
　"About 70 houses."
　"Where is your house located?"
　"First house on the fifth alley."

The interview, which was typical in the types of questions it posed, headed toward the crucial issue of Leung's family.

"What is your father's name?"
　"Leung Bing Chung, member in the firm of Yee Chong & Co., number 156 Waverly Street, San Francisco, California."
　"Did you ever see your father?"
　"I have not seen him since he left China for this country."

McChesney then spread a series of black-and-white head shots on the table in front of the young man. The inspector asked Leung to point out the photographs of his father and of one of the witnesses who had attested to his identity, as well as to his own photo. Leung pointed to the correct images. Indicating that he'd understood the interpreter and had nothing further to state, Leung signed his name at the bottom of the document in Chinese characters. The young man had passed this first, critical test.

· · ·

THE REAL NAME of the young man calling himself Leung was Wong Hee (a.k.a. Wong See Duck), and his effort to immigrate to America had begun the previous summer, after his father purchased false identity papers for him. An older man calling himself Leung Bing Chung had sworn before a notary public on August 11, 1908, that he was a "lawfully domiciled merchant" in San Francisco. For more than a year, the man claimed, he had been a partner at Yee Chung & Co., a company on "Waverley Street" (now known as Waverly Place) in Chinatown that sold cigars and other merchandise.

As required under the 1882 Chinese Exclusion Act, the elder Leung swore that he had "not engaged in the performance of any manual labor, except as is necessary in the conduct of my business as a merchant." He also stated he had a minor son living in China who wished to join him in the United States. Attached to the notarized form were black-and-white head shots of Leung and his alleged son (in fact, Wong See Duck), both with shaved foreheads and wearing similar black *changshan*. These were formal Chinese tunics that members of the elite merchant class wore: Chinese laborers wore loose-fitting shirts and trousers. The men looked similar, with broad foreheads, thin lips, and serious expressions.

A notarized statement was necessary because the earthquake and fire of 1906 had destroyed the immigration records of most of the Chinese who'd landed in San Francisco. Although the outer walls of the city's Hall of Records had withstood the disaster, flames had consumed the documents inside. This destruction created a loophole that those who had entered the country illegally soon found a way to exploit.

The Exclusion Act allowed those with established merchant status to bring in family members from China as part of the "exempt class" of immigrants that also included diplomats, students, and travelers. With the slate wiped clean by the fire, there was no way to prove—or disprove—that an immigrant had been born in the United States or had entered legally, so documents could be fabricated to claim American birth and legal residency and, by extension, help others back in China to enter the country.

Merchants such as Leung Bing Chung soon recognized they could sell off "slots" of fictional family members, offering a "paper son" such as Leung Foo the opportunity to enter the country and circumvent the law. The system worked like this: an immigrant (usually male) would purchase falsified documents in China attesting that he was the son or grandson of someone who was already legally in the United States. He would memorize the invented family details so that when asked by U.S. immigration authorities about what village he'd come from, the paper son could offer a story that lined up with the father's. This practice became widespread in the years after the 1906 calamity. Hundreds, perhaps thousands, of Chinese immigrants entered the United States using this risky and costly system, which involved the creation of false papers and a trail of graft to pay off officials along the way.

In 1908, the year that Leung applied to enter the United States, these methods of skirting the Exclusion Act were still new. Eventually, immigration authorities caught on to "paper sons" and the sudden appearance of many more American-born Chinese under the so-called earthquake exemption. It is unclear whether McChesney was suspicious of the young man he'd interviewed on the SS *Asia* that November day in 1908, although he did note his prominent scar on the forms he submitted to his superiors, a possible sign of membership in a criminal tong.

Before allowing Leung to leave the ship, McChesney headed to Chinatown, where the sound of pounding hammers signaled the rapid rebuilding of the quarter, with five-story buildings rising where there had once been rubble. At the corner of Waverly and Washington Street, he paid a visit to Yee Chong & Co., to confirm the cigar shop did, indeed, exist and that the young man's ostensible father, Leung Bing Chung, worked there. McChesney asked the forty-three-year-old man almost exactly the same questions he'd asked the twenty-one-year-old.

"Where were you born?" he asked.
"Lew Long . . . a village of 70 houses."
"Where is your house located?"
"First house on the fifth alley."

McChesney then asked,

"On what papers did you land?"

"Section 6; my papers were destroyed by fire."

He was referring to a section of the Exclusion Act that stipulated that all Chinese people (other than laborers who were entitled to come to the United States under the law's provisions) be issued a certificate by the Chinese government. It listed their name, title or official rank, age, height, physical peculiarities, occupation or profession, and place of residence in China. Leung Bing Chung told the inspector that his certificate had burned in the fires that razed Chinatown in 1906. He also said he was the father of eight children—seven sons and one daughter—and that his wife, who had bound feet, still lived in China.

The elder Leung's answers echoed what the younger man had told him. McChesney circled back to the white character witnesses listed on Leung's notarized statement: Isidor Rinaldo, who worked in a cigar shop, and Newton E. Cohn, a real estate man. Both swore to Leung's status as a merchant. McChesney also checked with the clerk of the city's rebuilt records bureau. His conclusion? In a memo dated November 23, 1908, he wrote, "There are no material discrepancies. . . . I recommend the applicant be landed."

McChesney, perhaps unwittingly, had allowed an immigrant into the country on the basis of forged papers. He wasn't the first, or the last, immigration official to do this at a time when the Exclusion Act required all would-be immigrants from China to go through an often-protracted process to gain entry. Whether McChesney did so intentionally is unclear. But in the years before he joined the immigration service, a series of Chinese inspectors had been arrested and found guilty of schemes to extract bribes from Chinese immigrants in exchange for permitting them into the United States. (One con man, Arthur Spencer, pleaded guilty in 1901 to impersonating a Chinese inspector in Spokane, Seattle, and Victoria and selling fake certificates to Chinese immigrants.)

A Treasury Department appointee, McChesney earned a good salary of around $1,400 per year, which was twice as much as the average annual wage of a Bay Area teacher. There is no evidence that he accepted a bribe to allow Leung entry. But by 1909, a year after he examined Leung, "Professor" McChesney left his government appointment and retired to the "fine residence" he'd built ten years earlier in the bucolic village of Mill Valley, north of San Francisco.

For Leung Foo, who entered the United States in late 1908 with forged documents as a "paper son," the story of his interrogation in the detention shed was just the beginning of a long, sordid criminal career in the United States. Later, the diminutive man with a scar would leave for China and return to San Francisco several times under his exempt status as a merchant. His paperwork was always in order, and he encountered no significant difficulties or delays entering or leaving the United States. But all the while he was transforming himself into the notorious slave dealer Wong See Duck, and soon he would cross paths with the women and girls of the Mission Home.

Dragon Stories

Around the same time that Wong See Duck entered the country, Tien Fuh Wu, the former household slave, gained some fame of her own. Under the pseudonym Teen Fook, she appeared in *Dragon Stories*, a booklet intended to draw attention and donations to the Mission Home. Released in the fall of 1908 by a Presbyterian publisher in Oakland, it was bound with cord and a Chinese coin for decoration. Included were some of the pre-earthquake photographs that Genthe had captured of Chinatown. The publisher printed two thousand copies just in time for Christmas.

Wu was in Philadelphia when the booklet came out, attending the Stevens School, a well-regarded college preparatory academy. Wu's benefactor, Horace C. Coleman, paid her train ticket and tuition, and she lived with the family of a Presbyterian clergyman, the Reverend Henry W. Frost, the North American director of the China Inland Mission. Wu joined a large, busy household: the minister and his wife had seven children, including a two-year-old boy.

Not only were the winters in Philadelphia much colder than San Francisco's, but the summers felt "so sultry" to Wu that she never really got used to them. She had to make other adjustments as well. As a former Chinese *mui tsai*, she couldn't have been more different from her classmates, most of whom came from wealthy American families. It was "not easy for a poor orphan girl," Wu later explained to the historian Him Mark Lai. But she lacked for little while she was there, and like her more privileged classmates she proudly wore a white dress at

Tien Fuh Wu was educated in Philadelphia and Toronto before returning to the Mission Home as a staffer.

graduation. "It's a wonder I wasn't spoiled with all the luxuries back east," she said.

Wu features heroically as an interpreter in *Dragon Stories*, even more so than Cameron herself, who is referred to only as "the missionary" or the "Mother-teacher." One of its stories describes how the interpreter pushes her way into a brothel, reassures a fearful girl, and convinces her to enter the Mission Home. As Wu's leading role in *Dragon Stories* shows, her work was crucial to the white missionaries because it allowed them to communicate with traumatized girls and women who often spoke only Chinese.

No writer is named, but one of Cameron's supporters might have penned the booklet (and referred to the Mission Home's residents as "excited little maidens," which was far more sugary than the annual reports Cameron wrote each year to her board). *Dragon Stories* is notable for showing how some of the rescued girls doubted the missionaries' benign intentions, fearing they would murder them, and for underscoring the crucial role of Chinese interpreters in rescue work. Indeed, it is unlikely that Cameron could even have convinced the doorkeepers at the brothels to let her inside without the tenacity and language skills of Wu and her aides.

Dragon Stories begins by recounting how, at 7:00 one morning, the missionary and Wu, who would have been a teenager at the time of these events, set off from the home—"Teen Fook excited, as usual, and eager for the fray." When they reached the tenement, the missionary and a white policeman hid themselves while Wu rang the bell and stood before the small peephole in the doorway.

After some time, the shutter covering the peephole slid open. A Chinese woman peered out at Wu and asked, in Cantonese, "Who is it?"

"A friend," Wu answered.

"What do you want so early in the morning?"

"Open the door and let me in," Wu said. "I have something to tell you which I cannot out here on the stairs."

Cautiously, the woman opened the door. When she caught sight of the missionary and the policeman, she tried to slam it shut. By then, Wu had slipped in, followed by the others.

"Shut your doors, shut your doors!" the woman shouted to the occupants. Inside the building, doors slammed and the sounds of scurrying could be heard. The policeman guarded the exit while the missionary and Wu went from room to room, searching for the girl they'd been alerted to. (*Dragon Stories* does not explain whether the girl wished to be rescued or how they had learned of her.) Down a long, dark passage, they saw a curtain flutter. A haggard face peered out for a moment.

They rushed forward and pulled back the curtain. The girl's hair was matted and, although she was thin, she kicked and screamed, believing she'd been captured by the White Devil.

The other girls and women in the brothel shrieked as the missionary and Wu dragged the girl away. A police officer had also rushed up the stairs. He hoisted the girl over his shoulder and carried her out of the house. The small party marched to the nearby Hall of Justice, where they planned to petition a judge for custody of the girl. As they made their way through the streets, Wu ran by the policeman's side, speaking to the girl in her own language and trying to soothe her by telling her they were taking her to a beautiful home where there would be plenty to eat and everyone would love her.

"No, no, you are going to kill me! Let me go!" the girl cried, perhaps influenced by her owner's warnings against the missionaries, and grew more distressed as they passed through the tall doors and into the Hall of Justice. They waited several hours for a judge, and during that time Wu struggled to calm the girl down. She finally resorted to rolling up her sleeves to reveal her own bare forearms. Wu explained that she, too, had been a *mui tsai* and that her owner had seared her, pointing out the still visible burn scars. That evidence seemed to quiet the girl once she realized Wu understood what it was like to be enslaved. Without a fight, she accompanied them later that day to the Mission Home.

One of the older girls took the newcomer upstairs for a bath. After combing out her hair and dressing her in clean clothes, she led her to a room and showed her the small bed covered with white sheets that had been assigned to her. Before the older girl left, the rescued slave, called Ying Leen in the story, asked her, "Why do you do it? What puts it into your head to do all this for me when you never saw me before?" The older girl doesn't answer, but the narrator of the story reflected that newcomers to the home "invariably ask the same question, puzzled to know what prompts the strange kindness."

·   ·   ·

THE TEEN FOOK CHARACTER in *Dragon Stories* might not have been entirely based on Tien Fuh Wu: it could have been based on a composite of Cameron's various Chinese aides. The booklet also does not mention any of the discomforts of serving in the role of interpreter. Later in life, Wu recalled that hunger was one of her strong memories of working alongside Cameron on rescues. "We were, always short of money, and you know a growing girl of teen age was always hungry. 'Never mind, Tien, when we're home I'll get you a nice beefsteak,'" she recalled the superintendent telling her. "They only cost 30 cents."

Wu might have sometimes been hungry, but she demonstrated heroic levels of resourcefulness and focus in pursuing her own education. After receiving a diploma from the Stevens School in 1909, Wu headed north, to the Toronto Bible College, for two more years of study. Her sponsor remained Coleman, who by then had started a family of his own. Of the more than a thousand girls and young women who had passed through the Mission Home between that time and its founding in 1874, Wu was one of only a dozen or so whose tuitions were paid through individuals. She had become one of the home's most promising "native helpers"—a condescending term used by many missionaries for their non-Caucasian aides.

Not only were these helpers among the most enthusiastic of the Mission Home's converts: they were also living proof of how it could transform lives. But their jobs were not without risks. The Mission Home's aides sometimes faced criticism and even threats from other Chinese. Over the years, Wu and the other aides received frightening letters and spoken taunts railing against them for cooperating with whites against their own people. One particularly alarming letter to Wu called her a prostitute:

Tien Fook, stinking sow, now you are interpreter in the Mission House & have the backing of the House so you even dare to arrest a family girl. Are you not afraid that God will punish you?

A notation on the letter states one part is "too vile to translate—accuses Miss Wu of being a prostitute." Then it continues,

If God has eyes He will certainly punish you. You have overreached yourself & in so doing negroes, dogs & thunder will come after you.

Cameron recognized the danger that Chinese staffers faced by going on raids, Wu explained many years later, and took special measures to try to protect them from vengeful slave owners. "Miss Cameron was more fearful about us who helped her. They [*sic*] feel they take advantage of their own people. After a raid, Miss Cameron won't let me out again for a month or two just for protection," she recalled. Indeed, over the years, Wu would receive even more violent threats because of her mission work.

Wu was well out of harm's way during her relatively cloistered studies in Philadelphia and Toronto. When she completed her two years of study at the Bible college in 1911, she was then in her twenties, well educated, fluent in two languages, and culturally conversant in both Chinese and Western ways. A photograph from around that time shows her in a light-colored Western-style traveling suit. She's wearing an embroidered or crocheted collar at her neck. Black gloves cover her hands, and a stylishly large black hat accentuates her round face and full lips. Standing in front of an elegant Chinese screen, Wu looks feisty, perhaps even defiant.

Uninterested in becoming a wife and mother, Wu had turned down multiple suitors. She didn't, it seems, have much use for the opposite sex, joking that "men are very useful when it comes to moving furniture."

She clearly had ambitions beyond becoming a wife. In an article titled "Chinese Slave Girls: A Bit of History," published by *The Overland Monthly* while Wu was in Philadelphia, one of the home's early supporters wrote of Wu and other college-educated former Mission Home residents: "Some of them become ambitious for a higher education. Two are in a college, tuition free, and two are in Eastern seminaries supported by Eastern friends. They refuse to listen to any offer of marriage, however flattering, in their desire to teach their own people."

Indeed, after Wu's formal education ended, she decided to return to the household she knew best: the Mission Home in San Francisco. Cameron needed Wu to come back because one of the home's other interpreters, Tye Leung, had recently left to take a new job. By choosing to return, Wu joined a movement of social workers, reformers, and labor and women's rights advocates whose tireless efforts helped form what would eventually become known as the Progressive Era.

In June 1911, Wu returned to San Francisco to work alongside Cameron on rescues, as her interpreter, and to help supervise the home. Her sense of obligation surely played a part in her decision, as did her emotions. The Mission Home was the place where Wu had spent more years than any other and had the deepest ties. Because she could barely remember her own mother, father, or grandmother in China, throughout her life Wu would consider Cameron and the other residents of the home the closest thing she had to a family.

Tiny

Working as a Chinese aide at the mission brought privileges as well as perils. Another resident who became an interpreter for the home was Wu's predecessor, Tye Leung, whose story illustrates how difficult it could be to associate closely with white people, both on a professional and on a personal level. As a nine-year-old, Leung was sold by her family to be a *mui tsai* in Chinatown. Three years later, at the age of twelve, she fled to the Mission Home. She soon became one of Cameron's "native helpers." Because she was just four feet tall, Cameron nicknamed her Tiny.

Unlike many at the home, Leung was born in San Francisco and never experienced sex slavery. Her father earned $20 a month working in a shoe shop in San Francisco's Chinatown, and her mother helped run a boardinghouse on Jackson Street. From an early age, she learned English at the Presbyterian mission school in the neighborhood. Her teacher taught her to sing and brought her to church meetings.

A marital crisis drove her to the Mission Home. By the first decade of the twentieth century, many more residents had begun coming to the home to escape bad domestic situations. To avoid an arranged marriage with an older man in Butte, Montana, Leung moved to 920 Sacramento Street. "I stayed there and learned Christianity and became a Christian woman," she wrote. Because she was bilingual, she could help interpret for Cameron and the other white staffers, as well as order Chinese foodstuffs for the Mission Home's large household. (All the

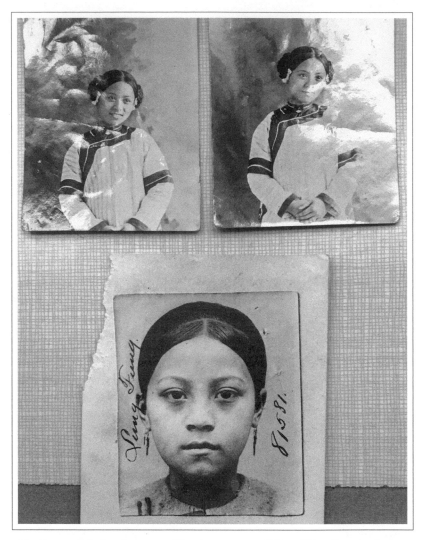

Tye Leung Schulze, known as Tiny, became one of Donaldina Cameron's most trusted aides.

residents were required to perform household chores, and some of the older ones became paid staffers.)

Leung was one of the sixty or so girls who followed Cameron through the burning city to safety in the hours after the 1906 earthquake, amid the raging fires. Years afterward, Leung recalled how Cameron had offered her parents shelter in San Rafael following the disaster, even though they were not Christians. By 1909, when Wu was away at school, the superintendent was working closely with Leung, who served as her interpreter in court hearings and at the notorious detention shed at the wharves. Leung proved herself such a valuable aide at the mission over the years that when a new immigration station at Angel Island opened in 1910, Cameron recommended her for a newly created position as assistant matron there, earning $720 a year, the equivalent of about $18,000 today.

"Tiny" thus became the first Chinese woman to hold an official role in the U.S. Immigration Service, functioning as an interpreter and cultural go-between for Chinese immigrant women and immigration officials. In its annual report that year, the Woman's Occidental Board proudly noted that this "capable young interpreter of the Mission Home" had been appointed to the job of matron in charge of the Chinese women's ward. The monthly newsletter for the women of the Occidental Board patronizingly gloried: "How splendid it is to know we shall have a dear Christian girl to do this work among heathen women!"

Leung commuted about an hour each way by boat to the small island in the middle of the bay that would soon become known as the Ellis Island of the West. Despite her long hours at work, she remained close to her friends at the Mission Home. Indeed, that spring, Leung traveled with Cameron and another Chinese aide, Margaret Woo, to Los Angeles to appear at an executive meeting of the Board of Foreign Missions, which oversaw missionaries around the world.

Leung and Woo changed out of the shirtwaists and ankle-length skirts they normally wore and put on Chinese costumes of "oriental splendor" that caught the attention of a local newspaper reporter and were surely meant to impress the supporters of the home. So did Leung's new job, which "distinguished her as the only Chinese woman employed by the United States government as an interpreter."

When Leung stepped forward at the meeting to offer her thanks, tears came to people's eyes. One of the ministers remarked that if her accomplishment "were the only result of the work of the Board, it was enough."

In 1912, the newspapers featured Leung as an example of a progressive Chinese American woman. Accompanying one article about her was a photograph of Leung behind the wheel of a Studebaker-Flanders, smiling at the camera. The previous year, in 1911, California women had won the right to vote—well ahead of most of the nation. The caption describes Leung as "the first Chinese woman in the world to exercise the electoral franchise."

She remained in her job at Angel Island until 1913. Her departure was not voluntary. During that time, Leung fell in love with a white immigration inspector named Charles Frederick Schulze, a man of German and Scottish descent. Defying their parents' wishes and the state's antimiscegenation laws, which made it illegal for white people to marry a "Negro, Mulatto, or Mongolian," the couple traveled to Washington state, which did not have such a law, to marry.

A newspaper ran this photograph of Tye Leung behind the wheel of a car as an example of a progressive Chinese American woman.

Both lost their civil service jobs as a result: Schulze as a white man with a Chinese wife, and Leung, who lost her job at Angel Island.

Leung, who by then was known as Mrs. Schulze, returned to school to learn bookkeeping and eventually found work as a night-shift operator at the Chinese Telephone Exchange. It took her husband longer to get a job, but he finally found a position servicing Dictaphones and typewriters for the Southern Pacific Railroad. Despite their struggles, Leung ended the six-page account of her life by thanking the woman who had helped her so much over the years.

"I owed a lot to Miss Cameron who was so tender and good," she wrote. Over their ten years together, the missionary who was both friend and mentor taught her "to know what's right and wrong." Leung ended her life story with what may be interpreted as a final reflection on her longtime friend and former boss, writing, "Still we are all human." It is not clear what Leung meant by this. Cameron's vulnerabilities, as Leung only hinted at, were deeper than the newspapers and the Mission Home's supporters understood.

◆══ 33 ══◆

Missionaries of the Home

C ameron's diary from 1909 captures the genteel and often quiet reality of her day-to-day life. Except for brief mentions of daring rescues, her terse, handwritten account shares some similarities with a typical turn-of-the-century lady's journal. Intentionally or not, Cameron's diary underplays what must have been her often overwhelming and chaotic experience of running a large group home and acting as a mother to dozens of girls and young women. It imposes order on a domestic situation that often veered away from her period's tranquil ideal of the comforts of home and hearth.

She often started her entries with a notation on the weather: "very wet today" or "very warm, lovely day." Most of Cameron's entries record the traditional duties of a middle-class mother: writing letters, taking the girls to doctor's appointments, buying them new shoes, paying bills, going to church on Sunday mornings, and decorating the Mission Home for weddings. That year, the home took in the largest number of girls and young women in its history, with well over fifty residents at most times throughout the year. More than half were teenagers or younger. Cameron oversaw their feeding, housing, and many legal challenges.

To escape the chaos of the crowded conditions, she occasionally took ferry trips across the bay to Livermore or other cities with one or more of the residents she referred to as her "daughters"—returning late in the evening laden with blossoms they'd picked in the East Bay hills. Other times she spent the night with her friend Eleanor Olney or

A view of the rebuilt Mission Home as a cable car passes by.

a few nights away with one of her sisters, who now lived in Northern California. As always, she hosted many visitors. Her brother-in-law, Charley Bailey, came to see her several times that year in the Mission Home. She once had a visit from her former fiancé, George Sargent, whom she barely mentioned in her diary except to say that he "took luncheon." The photographer Genthe also came calling on her with a group of friends in tow.

To maintain order amid the many comings and goings, Cameron relied on her matron to train and organize the residents in their domestic duties as housekeepers: the girls and young women did much of the cooking, washing, ironing, scrubbing, and sewing for the large household. As Cameron wrote that year in her annual report, "Some of us are old fashioned enough to believe that the best mission workers begin by being 'missionaries of the home first.' So we endeavor to urge upon our Chinese girls the importance of being good housekeepers. And then we encourage them to marry Christian Chinese." The idea was to train the residents to leave the Mission Home, ideally as brides, and to form their own Christian households.

There were six weddings that year; some residents left the home to teach or become missionaries. But because of steady turnover at the home and frequent visitors, residents and staffers often sickened, adding another layer of complexity to running a group home. In late September 1909, several residents came down with a mysterious ailment. Cameron herself struggled through it. "I felt quite ill today but was able to keep up and work," she wrote. The next day, one of her aides grew ill, and by that evening a doctor ordered Cameron to bed. "I could not speak and felt very wretched. Did not sleep one moment all night. Children doing quite nicely."

The next morning, she felt too weak to get out of bed. A doctor visited her, and she slept most of the day while parts of the Mission Home were fumigated, apparently to rid it of disease. Cameron was incapacitated for three more days, until she managed to rouse herself to dress, but then felt too weak and returned to the comfort of her bed. By the following day, she made it downstairs for breakfast.

Cameron's condition continued to improve over the next few weeks, but some of the younger residents of the home developed rashes. She took two of them to a doctor, who couldn't diagnose the problem so promised to send a prominent San Francisco pediatrician, R. Langley Porter, instead. On Friday, September 17, Cameron noted that she'd spent the day waiting for Dr. Porter. He arrived the following day and diagnosed the children with scarlet fever.

More girls got sick, and staffers notified the Board of Health about the situation. (Scarlet fever was then still a public health concern, sometimes causing clusters of deaths.) In her diary entries over the next few days, Cameron expresses anger at not being able to reach or get clear answers from the medical authorities, possibly reflecting their racism toward the Chinese. She spent a whole day on the telephone trying to get some help from both private and city doctors. (The Mission Home had five doctors listed on its staff that year, including its longtime volunteer physician, Minnie Worley, but Chinese patients continued to face discrimination and limited access to local hospitals and doctors.) She was determined to find help.

A team of doctors eventually arrived at the Mission Home and decided to quarantine it, based on the outbreak of scarlet fever. The girls began to improve, but that autumn held other unfortunate surprises, reflecting just how accustomed Cameron and her charges had become to violence in Chinatown.

On a pleasant Sunday morning, November 14, Cameron and several of the residents attended church in Chinatown. Walking the few blocks back to the home, several of the girls saw a shooting on Stockton Street. The man wielding the gun apparently belonged to a criminal tong. Because they were eyewitnesses to the crime, their safety must have been one of Cameron's primary concerns. The next day, a newspaper reported that "a number of Chinese children playing nearby saw the tragedy and gave chase to the murderer" as he fled up Sacramento Street and through an alley that bordered the Mission Home.

Cameron barely mentioned this incident in her diary, perhaps because violence still erupted regularly on the streets of Chinatown. She noted only in passing that "Alice and Ida saw the man who did the murder." She doesn't note whether they were among the children who chased the murderer.

If anything, her fourteen years at the home had inured her to tong battles. Observers noted that she would get a look of stern determination on her face at tense moments. Cameron's grit was clear by that time. Not only was it evident by her unconventional choice to live and work for many years in the ethnic ghetto of Chinatown. But in defying her era's domestic expectations for women to exert influence mainly within the close confines of home, she instead chose to be a public figure who ran a large institution and spoke out and acted in defense of Chinese women. After she had lived through an outbreak of bubonic plague, a devastating earthquake and fire, and repeated threats from slave owners, a Sunday shooting probably seemed a relatively unimportant brush with violence.

⊷⊶═ 34 ═⊶⊷

Matchmaking

W u's first job when she returned to the Mission Home in 1911 was overseeing the housework: she quickly proved herself adept at assigning tasks and making sure they were done well. She was so organized that she kept what some residents called her "Book of Lamentations"—a list of what needed to be done each day and who was assigned to do it. An immaculate housekeeper herself, Wu would pull on her white gloves to check if they'd done the dusting properly, residents joked. As one former staffer recalled years later, Wu was "a stern taskmaster and would keep them to it. But she was very kind and fair in her judgments so the girls trusted her."

Wu won Cameron's trust as well. Not long after returning to San Francisco, Wu began traveling on Mission Home business across the country. An unusual privilege for a single Chinese woman living in America at that time, it was one that Wu enjoyed because of her role as Cameron's primary aide. By the second decade of the twentieth century, much of her and Cameron's time was spent arranging marriages and checking up on former Mission Home residents to make sure they were safe and content. Some of Wu's many duties were to judge the characters and intentions of prospective grooms and accompany former residents as they married men from out of town.

In May 1915, Wu traveled to the East Coast to escort two Mission Home brides to their weddings. The three women stayed at the Philadelphia home of a former resident, Qui Ngun, and her husband, Wong

Potential grooms were carefully vetted by Mission Home staffers, and weddings frequently took place in the home's parlor. Donaldina Cameron is standing behind the wedding party.

John, who had married in the 1890s. On a Sunday morning, she wrote to her mentor,

> Dear Lo Mo:—
>
> Here we are all at Qui Ngun's lovely home. She has repaired and enlarged the house and everything is very comfortably furnished. My brides feel very much at home here. . . . Jean [one of the two brides Wu is accompanying] wants me to tell you that she likes Mr. Won Fore, and I like his face very much. He looks to me that he is a kind and a good man and I am glad to think that Jean will have a nice husband, and a good home. . . .
>
> Jean says that she is very sorry that you cannot be here for her wedding, and wants to send you special love. Also she sends love to all the teachers and girls, and hopes that you are all well in the Home.
>
> Jean and her future husband are going to have their wedding feasts on the 6th and 7th of June. How I wish that you could be here for the banquet. John thinks that she is going to get lots of presents.
>
> Qui Ngun & John & the family also us three send you much love. Do take care of yourself. From Tien.

While Wu is warmly affectionate in her letter toward Cameron, there is a hint of worry in the final line. Wu, after all, had witnessed Cameron's emotional breakdown in 1901 after the death of her aide. She must have noticed, even with all her traveling, that Cameron was growing wearier. She was more likely to succumb to down periods as she assumed more burdens.

Cameron had recently expanded the home's remit to include caring for more babies and young children, some of whom had been abandoned or were the offspring of residents. The home at 920 Sacramento Street, built on a narrow lot that was 80 feet wide and 137½ feet deep, was jam-packed, swelling to as many as seventy residents at one point—an all-time high. The crowded conditions forced staffers to give up their quarters for nurseries and dormitories and forced girls to occasionally sleep on cots or on the couch beside Cameron's own bed.

Cameron, in turn, fretted about the influence the older residents were having on the younger ones—especially after discovering that one of the toddlers at the Mission Home was uttering Cantonese profanities. As Cameron struggled to raise funds to establish a separate home for the youngest and more innocent children in her care, her slender, athletic frame began to change under the strain, growing thinner and even more angular.

Cameron also experienced personal losses during those years. Then in her forties, she had become engaged in 1911 to marry a man almost twice her age, a fellow Presbyterian named Nathaniel Tooker, who had made his fortune in sugar. Cameron had become good friends with Tooker's two daughters and had been invited to spend time at their estate in New Jersey as their houseguest. Nathaniel Tooker asked Cameron to marry him on one of her trips, and she warmly accepted his proposal, even though he was old enough to be her grandfather.

Perhaps she craved security or a place in a comfortable household alongside Tooker's daughters or hoped that the quiet and orderly life of a married woman would offer her relief from the pressures and constant change of life in a group home. She must have realized that it would probably have been a chaste marriage and that she might have ended up caring for him as his health declined. She kept her reasons for accepting his marriage proposal private, but she'd agreed to marry the elderly man, and Cameron returned to San Francisco apparently having decided to hand over her duties at the mission.

Once again, Cameron did not make it to the altar. In 1911, she received a telegram from one of his daughters, Mary Tooker, that read, "Lean hard and take courage. Father died today." Nathaniel Tooker had passed away suddenly at age eighty, before he and Cameron could be wed. She'd shared her plans with almost no one, and tried to hide her bereavement, but became worrisomely thin. Her board granted her a six-month leave.

The Tooker sisters bonded even more deeply in their grief with the woman who would have been their stepmother. They agreed to help fund a new home in Oakland for the younger members of the mission household. Named the Tooker Memorial Home, it opened in 1915 in East Oakland. (It later moved into a building designed by the architect Julia Morgan on the campus of Mills College.) While the Tookers' gift solved the problem of how to house the younger children, Cameron now had two homes to oversee, separated by several miles of San Francisco Bay's cold, treacherous waters, which could only be crossed by ferry (the San Francisco–Oakland Bay Bridge wouldn't open until 1936).

Adding to her troubles, Cameron's brother, Allan, died suddenly five years later, in 1916. It meant that the care and financial support of Cameron's unmarried sisters shifted to the superintendent's shoulders as the principal wage earner among the surviving Cameron siblings. Wu had been wise to urge Lo Mo to take care of herself, given the heavy emotional and financial load her mentor was carrying.

CAMERON AND WU REMAINED single yet spent much of their time arranging and supervising Mission Home marriages. It's not clear whether either one of them saw the irony in this. They and many of the other staffers at the home were single women devoted to professional careers in missionary work who personally "had encountered in their own lives few of the daily restraints of Victorian marriage," as one historian noted.

They were "old maids and widows" who were leading "a manless existence," according to one staffer.

Nonetheless, they held strong opinions about what constituted a proper marriage and grappled with details small and large. Cameron had befriended a fellow San Franciscan with Scottish ancestry, John Hays McLaren, the long-serving superintendent of Golden Gate Park, who provided clipped greenery for wedding ceremonies at the home, with Cameron and others purchasing blooms from the city's flower mart. Wu, in turn, made sure the children taking part in the weddings didn't embarrass themselves. She'd check with the couple's young ring bearer just before the wedding to make sure that he had gone to the toilet in order to avoid an accident marring the ceremony.

Between the home's founding in 1874 and 1928, as many as 266 of the Chinese women living there were married. Cameron relied heavily on Wu and other staffers to scrutinize young suitors to determine whether they had good characters. Cameron would oversee the process: she'd ask Wu and the other aides to write letters in Chinese to try to determine the men's marital and family circumstances. Handicapped by her own linguistic shortcomings, she relied on her Chinese staffers' detective skills and intuitions.

There was no shortage of willing suitors for the Mission Home's residents. With exclusion laws still in place, Chinatowns across the state and country continued to have dramatically skewed sex ratios. In California, there was one Chinese woman for every twenty-two Chinese men in 1890 and only one for every five Chinese men by 1920. That helps explain why Wu and other Mission Home staffers found themselves immensely popular with potential grooms.

"Everybody is after me for girls," Wu wrote to Cameron on a trip to Boston in 1915, jokingly adding, "I might as well open a Matrimony Bureau here in the east."

Humor aside, Cameron and her staff faced a real challenge in determining which suitors were sincere and which ones hoped to use marriage as a pretext for capturing women for prostitution. This concern explains why the Mission Home's doors remained guarded, visitors were screened, and staffers reviewed all incoming and outgoing mail, confiscating letters they considered inappropriate. Potential grooms were vetted for their religious beliefs and their finances, as well as whether they had wives or concubines (women who lived and had sex with them, but were lower in status than wives). The ideal husband was a financially secure Christian man who had no other wives and would be able to support his bride and any children. After marriage, it is unclear how many of the couples remained practicing Christians.

As patronizing as the missionaries' actions seem, they were considered to be justified. Cameron had been appointed the legal guardian of many of the residents, some of whom had been violently abused before entering the home. And there was little doubt that some abusers sought to regain a hold on their former captives. With no other parental or legal guardian to help arrange marriages for them, and with restrictions imposed by the home that barred them from meeting men on their own, Cameron assumed the role of parent herself.

As she explained her role as a matchmaker to one journalist, "I am their mother, under the law, they look to me, and so I have made dozens of matches and have dozens of sons-in-laws scattered throughout the country. And so far, I have not had to regret the choices I have made for them." Cameron visited her married "daughters" in Minneapolis, Philadelphia, Boston, and other cities where they'd settled. They offered her hospitality and, in some instances, named their children Donaldina or Donald after their beloved Lo Mo.

TO HELP FORMER RESIDENTS become effective "missionaries of the home," Cameron and Wu stayed in touch with many newly married brides. Wu used her language skills and determination to check up on them. In some instances, she offered them counsel. "You will be glad to hear that my little advice to Ah Young's husband has been a success," she wrote to Cameron. "He told his wife that he will never scold her nor [be] unkind to her again. How I wish that I could see our married girls often for I do believe it makes some difference with their husbands."

While some former residents, like Qui Ngun in Philadelphia, enjoyed happy marriages, others did not. Wu's matchmaking failures became a source of shame to her. She admitted to Cameron that she was "greatly humiliated" while she was in Boston that one of the home's former residents, Sieu Cum, had been badly treated by her husband. "It is well known in Chinatown how very cruel he was to Sieu Cum," Wu wrote. "People have told poor Sieu Cum that her husband is out of his mind (little bit simpleminded or crazy) and she is somewhat afraid of him."

Wu's suspicions toward men intensified as she got involved in more complex trafficking cases. As the Mission Home's fame spread through newspaper stories and Cameron's public speaking, she and her staff were increasingly called upon to help in other cities. One such case involved the attempted rescue of a young teenager in New York City. About fourteen years old, Ah Ying had been spotted weeping on her way to the train station, accompanied by a much older man known to be a criminal tong boss. The Chinese woman who saw the crying girl wrote a letter to a missionary describing how the teen "had to be led like a dog" on her way to being sold into prostitution. The missionary who received the letter was Mary E. Banta, who ran the Chinese department of a Methodist mission on the Lower East Side of New York.

In the steaming depths of summer from the Bowery, Banta asked Wu for help and passed along an address in San Francisco's Chinatown where Ah Ying had apparently ended up—ironically, in a store just one block down from the Mission Home on Sacramento Street. "I shall send you this letter on the wings of prayer and faith hoping God will direct your movement in an effort to recover this helpless child," Banta wrote. "And if you get her it will lift a great burden from my heart as well as yours."

Unlike the breathless and successful rescues related in *Dragon Stories* and Cameron's annual reports, the effort to gain custody of Ah Ying was an exercise in legal maneuvering and frustration. Wu reported to Cameron that the teen had been transported to San Francisco and sold for the astronomical sum of $3,400—an unusually high amount for a sex slave. While Ah Ying's plight was known to many in New York's Chinese community, few were willing to come forward. (An outside matchmaker who had apparently helped facilitate the faux marriage was one target of Wu's wrath: she wrote to Cameron that the matchmaker knew all about the case but was "such a coward and won't make any statement.")

Wu and Banta could not convince an Immigration Bureau inspector to try to force the trafficker to hand over Ah Ying. The teenager was shuttled from Seattle to New York, then on to Boston, south to Florida, and finally to San Francisco in a nine-month odyssey. Wu's anger rose. "You know mother, that these men don't know how to handle Chinese cases and I am afraid from their blunders which led Leung Kai Ming [the alleged trafficker] to take the girl out west. I am in doubt that they will ever get the girl at all," Wu wrote to Cameron in a letter from New Jersey. Wu also feared Ah Ying's captor would slip out of the country: "I hear that he is a very cunning sly man and presents himself very well."

But Ah Ying's case ended well. One Sunday evening, someone phoned the Mission Home, which now had a "phone closet" off its wood-paneled foyer, to alert Cameron and Wu that Ah Ying had been seen at a brothel in San Francisco. With the aid of a detective, Wu helped bring her to the Mission Home. Soon, Ah Ying told Cameron about another girl being held captive. The home convinced a judge in juvenile court to issue a warrant for her. Then Ah Ying and Wu used their experience and contacts to guess that the girl might be headed to a Chinese theater where a popular play had just opened.

Wearing Western clothing that made them stand out from the many theatergoers clad in traditional Chinese garb, Wu and Ah Ying brashly took seats in the middle of the house and scanned the crowd. About half an hour later, the girl arrived—escorted by a guard hired by her slave owner. Ah Ying sprang up, alerting the officers waiting near the rear entrance. The two former slaves, working together, had correctly predicted the third slave's whereabouts.

35

The "Joy Zone"

To show the world how far it had come from the 1906 disaster that had left it in smoldering ruins, in 1915 the city of San Francisco hosted what might have been the most gorgeous world's fair ever conceived. The Panama-Pacific International Exposition was a fantasy of minarets, pale green domes, and twinkling gems that celebrated the recent completion of the Panama Canal and promoted San Francisco as a gateway for Pacific trade.

On its opening day, Saturday morning, February 20, as a light rain gave way to sunshine, more than a quarter of a million visitors pushed their way through the fair's entrances. Inside, they discovered that the marshy area near the city's northern shoreline, between the Presidio and Fort Mason, had been transformed into an audacious display of technological and cultural wonders. The fair's centerpiece was a forty-story tower covered with more than 100,000 pieces of colored glass "gems."

In the sunlight, the Tower of Jewels sparkled. At night, colored searchlights illuminated it. Concealed ruby lights helped create the illusion that the entire 435-foot structure had burst into flames. The effect was meant to demonstrate advances in materials science and lighting, as well as to symbolize San Francisco's miraculous recovery from the earthquake and fire nine years earlier.

But behind the fair's dazzling effects were darker displays, most notably an attraction depicting the most vicious and persistent stereotypes of Chinatown vice, which sparked outrage among Chinese lead-

The "Underground Slumming" exhibition at the 1915 Panama-Pacific International Exposition, featuring promises of "opium dens" and "slave girls."

ers. Located in the entertainment section of the fair known as the "Joy Zone," the walk-through exhibit was conceived by the theater impresario Sidney Grauman. It exploited a long-standing myth about San Francisco's Chinatown: the existence of underground chambers that were the setting for unspeakable sins.

This urban legend probably began with the tour guides who flourished in Chinatown in the latter half of the nineteenth century. Frank Norris, a popular writer of that era, set one of his stories, "The Third Circle," in this mythical underground Chinatown. Published in 1909, it told of a white tourist who disappears while having tea with her fiancé at a restaurant in Chinatown and is discovered many years later in a squalid opium den, four floors below. It begins, "There are more things in San Francisco's Chinatown than are dreamed of in Heaven and earth. In reality there are three parts of Chinatown—the part the guides show you, the part the guides don't show you, and the part that no one ever hears of."

Tour guides reinforced this myth by leading visitors down stairways and into cellars, creating the impression they were descending four or five floors into secret spaces and slave quarters. In fact, they were just following the slope of the hill through existing basements. They'd also pay opium smokers to become tourist attractions; Genthe recalled befriending a Chinese man who had collected nickels from tour guides for years for letting tourists peek into his shack to see him smoking. (Years after the 1906 disaster, Genthe took a tour of rebuilt Chinatown and unexpectedly met his old friend, still lying on a heap of rags puffing on his opium pipe. "Hello, Doc," the man said when he recognized him. "Long time no see, how you been?")

GRAUMAN TAPPED INTO the same noirish fascination that fueled Norris's imagination in "The Third Circle"—much to the dismay of the young Republic of China. The outbreak of war in Europe the previous summer had forced Britain and Germany to withdraw from San Francisco's world's fair, but the Republic of China, founded just three years earlier, decided to participate as a way of parading its progress. It re-created a miniature "Forbidden City" on two and a half acres to show its wonders to the world and demonstrate its modernizing republic. With buildings shipped from Shanghai, the Chinese Pavilion had eight palaces, a pagoda, an elaborate entrance gate, and a replica Tai-ho Tien (Hall of Supreme Harmony), modeled on the one in Beijing.

Grauman's "Underground Chinatown" exhibit, which was part of the fair's entertainment "Joy Zone" rather than the official Chinese exhibition, was a glaring contrast to the sedate and dignified Chinese Pavilion. Visitors would enter the reconstruction of nearly a mile of the supposed subterranean tunnels and dens of pre-earthquake Chinatown. Signs beckoned them, promising salacious spectacles such as "Opium Den in Full Operation" and "The White Slave Girl."

Cameron and Wu both saw the controversial "Underground China-town" exhibit. Nearly nineteen million people visited the fair during its 288-day run, even though World War I severely curtailed foreign attendance. The fair dominated the life of the city that year, and its fifty-cent admission ticket was a relatively small price to pay for the chance of catching sight of such luminary fellow visitors as Helen Keller, Buffalo Bill Cody, and former president Theodore Roosevelt.

On their way to see "Underground Chinatown," Wu and Cameron would have passed many other entertainments, including the "Streets of Seville," where "bloodless bullfights" were staged; "Dixieland," with leering African American caricatures looming over a giant watermelon slice; and the notorious "'49 Camp," where liquor flowed and actual gambling and prostitution took place.

When they reached the seven fluted roofs of the Chinese pagoda, visitors would have walked past relatively innocuous Chinese curio shops and restaurants, descending to Grauman's belowground fantasy. There, they would have seen a distorted and sensationalized version of the world they, and others who were enslaved, had worked and lived in for decades. While "Dixieland" and the "'49 Camp" were controversial, Grauman's shameful depiction of the Chinese, in particular, became a flash point for blatant racism.

Like other paying visitors, Cameron and Wu would have encountered actors pretending to threaten them with hatchets, wax figures of bleary-eyed addicts in an opium den, and actresses pretending to be prostitutes "imported" from China calling out to them from behind bars. They might even have seen a scene of a white woman forced into sex slavery by a Chinese drug lord, though that particularly offensive scenario was only enacted when no Chinese visitors were present, so only Cameron might have seen it.

Witnessing their life's work reduced to titillating entertainment must have been upsetting for Cameron and Wu. But they knew, perhaps more acutely than most of the fair's visitors, that Grauman's exhibit came at a time when concerns over human trafficking and sex slavery were reaching a fever pitch.

In 1913, California voters had passed the Red Light Abatement and Injunction Act, which aimed to shut down brothels by punishing the property owners. It went into effect just a few months before the fair opened, but San Francisco's leaders did little to enforce it, and the law remained in limbo amid legal challenges. Eventually it would become one of the reasons why the Mission Home began handling fewer sex-slavery cases. But the heightened public awareness surrounding the new law might help explain why Grauman's exhibit featuring prostitution and the capture of a sex slave proved wildly popular with visitors—much more so than the official Chinese exhibit's sedate landscape paintings on silk and black lacquered furniture.

GRAUMAN, A NATTY DRESSER and gifted showman, was pointedly capitalizing on the rising national anxiety surrounding "white slavery." Lurid stories abounded of young country girls arriving at city train stations to be befriended by "cadets" who'd drug and rape them. The next morning, the girls would wake to find themselves prisoners in a brothel. So alarming were these stories that muckraking journalists published exposés documenting instances of forced prostitution and Congress appointed a commission to undertake a two-year investigation. Its findings helped Congress pass the White Slave Traffic Act of 1910, called, ironically, the Mann Act—not after the clientele of prostitutes, but after the Illinois congressman who pushed for the law.

White slavery did, in fact, exist and was a term used to convey the idea of women held in bondage against their will, regardless of color or race. In England's early industrial era, factory workers first used the term to describe their low salaries and poor work conditions, but the expression soon took on a more specific meaning. In 1905, a conference of fifteen European nations used the term "white slavery" to discuss the problem of trafficking in women and children.

By the time of the 1915 world's fair, journalistic accounts had fueled a full-blown panic in the United States that hundreds of thousands of women and girls were being captured and sold into prostitution. And indeed, from June 1910 to January 1915, 1,057 persons were convicted of white slavery in the United States, with abundant affidavits and court records attesting to the actual existence of this crime. It was not a myth, as some historians have argued, although some accounts of it were surely sensationalized.

"Underground Chinatown" gave it a blatantly racist spin—showing Chinese men as the slavers and both white and Chinese women as the victims. Protests poured into exposition headquarters about Grauman's offensive fantasy. "Underground Chinatown is a disgrace to the Exposition and a slander upon the Chinese people," wrote the Republic of China's commissioner to the fair, calling it a "daily insult both to my Government, my people, and its civilization, promoted by a theatrical establishment maintained for profit."

The Chinese Chamber of Commerce condemned the exhibit for its "indecency and horror." The Chinese Six Companies called it "repulsive and disgraceful" and demanded that it be closed immediately.

Notably, the editors of the major Chinese newspapers in San Francisco wrote a joint letter protesting the exhibit and its exploitation of the myth of an underground Chinatown in the strongest of terms. As founder and editor of the city's most influential Chinese daily, Chew might himself have penned this fiery and deeply frustrated letter to the fair's president, referring to what the 1906 disaster had revealed about Chinatown. "When the debris was removed from the Chinatown ruins, no underground passages were visible or evident; nothing but ordinary basements as are common in quarters occupied by American people," he wrote. "This fact should brand as false all attempts to create the impression in the public mind that there is or ever has been an 'underground Chinatown.'" Chinese church leaders from Chinatown also weighed in. Among the two dozen or so pastors, church elders, and missionaries who signed their names was the former slave Tien Fuh Wu, whose title was then assistant supervisor of the Presbyterian Mission Home.

There was a single protest letter about "Underground Chinatown" from a group of white people: Protestant pastors, church officers, superintendents, and teachers working in Chinatown. Complaining that the exhibit's portrayals of the Chinese were false and unfair, they also objected to what they considered a "slur upon the Christian religion." Apparently, in one of the acted-out scenarios, the Chinese "criminals" grabbed hymnals after being surprised by the police. To pretend they were engaged in worship, rather than wrongdoing, the actors began singing a hymn "held in sacred veneration by almost all the devout people of the world."

Among the nearly two dozen signatures to the church leaders' protest letter, one stands out for its large, flowing script: Donaldina Cameron's. She joined the others in taking the unpopular stand of defending the Chinese, who would continue to be harassed and discriminated against in America well into the middle of the twentieth century.

THE FAIR'S PRESIDENT, Charles Moore, largely ignored the first round of letters voicing the Chinese community's objections to "Underground Chinatown." After all, there were more than eighty thousand exhibits at the fair, and letters of complaint poured into his office on everything from drinking alcohol to visitors tumbling out of rides to bawdy shows and prostitution on the fairgrounds. To the second round of protest letters, which arrived in mid-March, his secretary eventually issued a curt, one-sentence response stating, "I assume you are aware that the objectionable features of 'Underground Chinatown' have now been suppressed."

Indeed, on the evening of March 26, a group of guards employed by the fair shut down Grauman's exhibit. But that was only temporary. By June 1915, it had reopened with very much the same themes—this time stripped of any Chinatown reference, with over a hundred figures now intended to show the evils of opium, morphine, and cocaine use. Renamed "Underground Slumming," it replaced the actors who'd played opium smokers with wax figures and used white women to play the roles of the imprisoned prostitutes.

In its rapid remake, no Asian actors were used. But indirect references to Chinatown remained, including a large sign that read, "Go slumming through Old San Francisco. A guide takes each party through opium dens—slave girls." And although the fair was intended to celebrate the closing of the East-West divide, the exhibit's ugly stereotypes of Chinese sinfulness persisted. The fair's directors continued to refer to Grauman's exhibit as "Underground Chinatown" long after its official renaming and the fair's closing at the end of the year. Grauman was obviously inspired by Chinese design, for a dozen years later he opened his Chinese Theatre on Hollywood Boulevard.

≈≋ 36 ≋≈

Fruit Tramps

Cameron, who lived in a region famous for its seismic instability, had long provided a stable home to vulnerable girls and women. But by the second decade of the twentieth century, the institutional foundations that were supporting her mission were starting to crack. As superintendent of two group homes, she was often responsible for more than a hundred residents. Faced with continual staff turnover, new board members, and mounting financial pressures, she needed help.

One person who understood her challenges was the Reverend John H. Laughlin, who had supervised the Presbyterians' work with the Chinese on the West Coast for more than a decade. Based at the nearby Presbyterian church in San Francisco's Chinatown, the oldest Asian church in North America, he was the lead signatory of the church leaders' letter protesting "Underground Chinatown." The clergyman frequently walked a short block east on Stockton Street and half a block up the hill on Sacramento to visit the Mission Home. He knew how overburdened Cameron was as he watched her struggling to manage both 920 Sacramento Street and the Tooker Home in Oakland. With that in mind, he decided to find her another assistant.

On one of Laughlin's many trips to Los Angeles, he attended a Sunday evening vespers service. A dark-haired woman in her early thirties rose to sing. Her name was Ethel Higgins, and he learned she had graduated from Mount Holyoke College before moving to Los Angeles to become the superintendent of the church's Chinese mis-

Residents of the Mission Home earned money through seasonal work as fruit pickers in the Santa Clara valley.

sion in that city. Perhaps it was her unassuming appearance with spectacles perched on her nose, her self-deprecating humor, or her strong religious convictions, but something about the transplanted New Englander made him think she might be a good aide to Cameron.

Laughlin introduced the women, and they soon arranged to meet each other in Los Angeles. Missionary work had once been one of the few professional jobs open to women, but in recent years it had become increasingly hard for church organizations to find candidates willing to take on such stressful work at such low pay. By the first decades of the twentieth century, ambitious women were turning instead to social work, academia, medicine, business, or architecture. At the same time, mainline Protestantism was starting to lose some of its sway in the face of growing religious skepticism.

Cameron and Higgins hit it off. The younger woman made a short trip north with some friends in July 1915 to visit the Panama-Pacific International Exposition. While there's no record of whether she went to the Joy Zone or to Grauman's by-then-renamed "Underground Slumming" exhibit, Higgins did climb the steps and ring the bell at 920 Sacramento Street to see the Mission Home for herself.

Ushered into the foyer, she was met by the mingled scents of warm vanilla, spices, and butter. Out came Cameron, balancing a plate of freshly baked cookies in one hand and holding the hand of a small Chinese girl in her other. The Mission Home's welcoming, maternal feel—very different from the cold institution she might have expected—and Cameron's effective salesmanship helped persuade Higgins to move to San Francisco and join the staff the following year as assistant superintendent.

Higgins's hiring meant that Wu could take a leave of absence from the home to pursue her dream of tracking down her family. By the fall of 1916, Wu had saved enough of her $25-a-month salary to return to China with one of the home's teachers, Mrs. Yeung. She hoped to locate the family she remembered: her mother, father, older brother, younger sister, and the beloved grandmother she had thought she was going to visit when she left her home the last time with her father.

"Mrs. Young's [sic] mission was to provide for an aged mother," Higgins wrote, "and Miss Wu's to search for her parents, from whom she has received no word since she was parted from them as a tiny child." By the time Wu returned to China in the fall of 1916, it had been more than two decades since her father had sold her on board ship to pay his gambling debts. In the meantime, a revolution had toppled the Qing dynasty. China had ended thousands of years of rule by emperors and dynasties and was now a republic. Its president, Sun Yat-sen, was educated in the United States. China had become a different place, and Chinese women had made significant strides toward equality, particularly in education since the new Chinese government had set up a broad range of schools for girls and women.

To her sorrow, Wu's search for her family in Zhejiang province south of Shanghai was fruitless. "I never found any of them. I couldn't find the place," she told a historian many years later. In the area where she came from, there had been intermittent uprisings and fighting for decades. Given how precarious her family's financial situation had been, it is likely that Wu's family had been forced to leave their home, like so many others during those tumultuous years. Without any remaining blood ties to the country of her birth, she returned to San Francisco, to the only home she had. She felt an obligation to return because the women at the home, especially Cameron, "had helped to rear me."

WU'S RETURN to 920 Sacramento Street meant that Cameron now had two trusted assistants capable of running the home. Higgins immediately rose to a higher position than Wu based on her race, even though she, like Cameron, did not speak or read Chinese and thus was forced to rely heavily on Wu and other Chinese aides. The presumption at that time on the part of the Woman's Occidental Board was that a white woman would be taken more seriously in the courts and by authorities. Wu, who had been born in China, faced racism and the threat of deportation at any time.

Having Higgins and Wu in place allowed Cameron to take some much-needed time off for herself. In early 1917, she traveled to balmy Florida to visit the Tooker sisters. The Mission Home's housekeeper, an African American woman named Alice, wrote to Cameron to tell her how things were going and to urge her to focus on her own well-being. "Now don't think you are to answer my letters for I would rather you would spend that time, for gathering the roses for your *health*. Miss Higgins is filling her place fine as a step Mother in the house, tries to do everything she thinks you would want done for your little brood of chicks. Lovingly yours. Alice."

While Cameron was gone, an extraordinary event took place on Valentine's Day in San Francisco. A so-called Morals Squad of police officers went door-to-door among the many brothels of Chinatown and the Barbary Coast, evicting prostitutes. Some fourteen hundred women were forced out onto the streets. The city's police chief ordered the brothels closed before evening and set up a blockade to enforce the order. The era of "the gentleman's agreement" to tolerate vice within bounds had ended, at least temporarily. Although Higgins did not mention the raids in her report to the board that year, the Mission Home experienced an influx of Chinese women seeking shelter after that raid.

Cameron remained in Florida for at least two more months, missing that year's annual meeting in April. Friends wrote to her with news of board and staff changes. One letter came from a concerned friend who, like the housekeeper Alice, urged her to take care of herself. "I hope you are being very good and resting your tired self," wrote the friend. "We miss you terribly but we want you to remain with Miss Tooker and allow her to 'mother' you until you are entirely well again."

Soon after receiving that letter, though, Cameron decided she should return to San Francisco. After spending the first few months of 1917 with the Tookers, she wrote to her board, informing them that she was "made over" by her vacation and expressing her desire to return to her job. She might have decided to go back to work sooner than she'd anticipated because, when she was in Florida, the United States joined the Allies and entered the war against Germany.

THE BOARD AGREED to her request to return to work, and Cameron came home to 920 Sacramento Street. It wasn't long before Cameron, Higgins, Wu, and some of the home's older residents found a way to contribute to the war effort and earn some money. With so many men shipping out to Europe and President Woodrow Wilson urging the nation to conserve food, farmers needed help to harvest their ripening fruits and vegetables. A group of about twenty of the older residents, wearing overalls and carrying their own bedding for sleeping out-doors, went to a ranch south of Stanford University. It rained the first night, leaving them soggy and poorly rested, but the small crew spent the next day picking apricots.

They tried again at a ranch near Los Gatos. It rained for three days, but this time the young women from the Mission Home could take shelter in packing sheds, where canvas cots to sleep on had been pro-vided. It was hard, uncomfortable work, particularly as temperatures climbed, but it earned the Mission Home some badly needed money and helped the ranchers. They became "fruit tramps," a derogatory term used at the time for migrant workers. Their earnings were put toward a year's supply of each girl's clothing and shoes, as well as a gift for the home. Any leftover funds were kept for each resident to use as she wished—"starting a wee bank account for each, if possible," one board member wrote, to safeguard the residents' savings.

The fruit picking continued for several more seasons, with thirty residents participating at one time. After covering the camp's expenses, the young women who volunteered as fruit pickers donated $100 of their combined earnings to the home. Such a sizable gift reflected their gratitude for having been offered a safe and secure refuge by Cameron and her staff.

In addition, some family members of the residents paid small amounts toward the girls' and young women's upkeep—often $5 or $10 a month, supplemented by the residents' own earnings from their labor in the home. The contributions from the Chinese community had risen over the years as the number of children arriving at the homes whose own families could not take care of them climbed. Slowly, the Mission Home was starting to resemble an orphanage, and its financial obliga-tions kept mounting.

⊶⟾ 37 ⟽⊷

"Are You Wearing a Mask and Taking Precautions?"

Despite the supplementary income earned from fruit picking and the girls' families, the organization's finances grew even tighter. In 1919, it cost about $20,000 a year to operate the two homes. To raise funds, Cameron crisscrossed the state, sipping tea and making her pitch to wealthy women. In the drawing room of Mrs. H. J. Crocker, the wife of one of the state's Big Four railroad barons, she raised $22.50 in an afternoon, while in Pasadena it was Mrs. J. A. Freeman who hosted a get-together attended by Mrs. Gamble and family, who made a very large donation of $602. Cameron raised nearly $4,500 on that single trip—or roughly a quarter of the two homes' 1919 expenses.

Cameron's charisma and her ability to convince supporters to open their pocketbooks undoubtedly boosted her clout in dealing with her local board and its overseers in New York, where it had moved from Philadelphia. Her fund-raising skills were crucial as the ground continued to shift beneath her. The generation of women who'd founded the Woman's Occidental Board nearly half a century earlier was passing away, and her longtime champion on the West Coast, Laughlin, had died in November 1918. Months later, Cameron had to adjust to a new, less pliant board president, Mrs. Rawlins Cadwallader, who would usher in major changes in the organization in the years ahead. They were not ones that Cameron welcomed.

Fund-raising remained a constant worry, and it was one that Cam-

Residents of the Mission Home also earned money through their sewing. This is a photograph of the home's Industrial Department, where they received training in how to use a sewing machine.

eron, her staff, and the board shared. After Higgins's mother died in 1918, Ethel and her sister made a gift of $500 in her name to the Mission Home, allowing it to expand its Industrial Department, which taught residents such practical skills as weaving and how to operate a sewing machine. The gift covered a teacher's salary for a year. The woven blankets that the residents made on looms were sold at the home's annual fund-raising bazaar. The industrial training also provided residents with an alternative to marriage— offering them marketable skills.

Gifts to the homes were sometimes financial. Ng Poon Chew made a sizable $50 donation, and the Tooker sisters continued their generosity with a gift to the children's home of $250. Others donated food or clothing—everything from shellfish, dried fruits, and jellies to crib quilts and undergarments. Although she surely appreciated even the humblest of gifts, the board's new president soon began pushing for larger donations, another responsibility—raising more money—for the home's already overburdened superintendent to shoulder.

Cameron did achieve at least one major fund-raising coup that year: a gift from Robert Dollar, the Scottish Presbyterian founder of a sprawling lumber and shipping empire. Shortly after the 1906 earthquake, Dollar and his wife, Margaret, hosted the Mission Home's residents at Falkirk, their country estate in San Rafael. They'd remained strong supporters of Cameron and her work through the war years. Indeed, Margaret Dollar would eventually become a vice president of the Woman's Occidental Board.

The Dollars' gift came amid the flu pandemic of 1918, the deadliest in history, which killed an estimated twenty to fifty million people worldwide. (One victim was Phoebe Apperson Hearst, an early supporter of the Mission Home who gave Christmas gifts to the girls and young women for many years. Cameron's longtime supporter Laughlin might also have died from the flu.)

Faced with increasingly crowded conditions for the young children in the Tooker Home and the small annex nearby that the board had rented as an overflow location, Cameron realized a larger building was needed. Her concerns about overcrowding had grown more urgent after influenza swept through the Mission Home, sickening nearly all its residents and staffers. "Not one death out of almost fifty cases!" Cameron wrote to her board that year, praising the "tireless and faithful nursing of Miss Higgins and Miss Wu." At the Tooker Home, although thirty of its fifty or so residents fell ill, none died. The board's fear of contagion led it to cancel its meetings for several months. A worried former teacher wrote to Cameron that year, asking, "Are you wearing a mask and taking precautions?"

To address the overcrowding, Cameron approached Robert Dollar for help. The white-bearded shipping magnate, widely known as Captain Dollar, spent a morning touring the cramped, three-story frame home in East Oakland, where some children slept in the hallways and bed linens were hung in the closets during the day to make room for study. There were unpleasant smells inside the home from poor plumbing, and outside it from a nearby slough where old ships were abandoned. After a close inspection, he concluded it was not a healthy environment for children.

"Tell your board to go out and find any piece of property they think adaptable and I'll buy it for you," he told Cameron, adding that his offer included constructing a new building as well. Elated, they found what they believed was an ideal parcel of land near the campus of Mills College in Oakland. Wooded, on nearly four acres, and overlooking San Francisco Bay, its serene setting was a vast improvement over the current Tooker Home's malodorous and cramped quarters.

IN A SIGN of how women had begun entering professions from which they'd once been barred, the Woman's Occidental Board chose the female architect Julia Morgan to design and oversee its new Oakland home's construction. Born in San Francisco in 1872, the year before the founding of the Woman's Occidental Board, Morgan became the first woman licensed to practice architecture in California. Not yet famous, she would gain celebrity for a project she began around that same time, in 1919: William Randolph Hearst's massive "castle" at San Simeon.

Morgan was undoubtedly familiar with the Chinese Mission Home in San Francisco. After the 1906 earthquake and fire, she'd won the assignment to help restore the Fairmont hotel, which loomed over 920 Sacramento Street and Chinatown. Morgan worked out of a nearby construction shack, located just below the hotel and close to the shell of the destroyed Mission Home. When she was working late at night, rats would jump over her feet.

She also designed buildings for women's organizations across California and in Hawaii, including ten YWCA buildings. At the 1915 Panama-Pacific International Exposition, she worked on the interior spaces for the YWCA Building on the fairgrounds, where mothers could leave their babies while visiting the fair, rest if they got tired, and enjoy an inexpensive meal at its cafeteria. The fair's YWCA became a safe place for the estimated three thousand women who worked at the exposition.

Morgan also designed several buildings on the Mills College campus, including its mission-style bell tower, or campanile, and library; she then won the assignment of designing the mission home for Chinese children, which would be located close to campus. Cameron dealt with Morgan directly, bringing someone new into her orbit at a time when she was losing some of her longtime allies, such as Laughlin, and influential supporters, such as Phoebe Hearst.

Mary Tooker was involved in the plans and had strong opinions on what the new home should look like. She suggested that the house have a large, sunny living room with a fireplace, books, and plants—avoiding the mistakes of the hastily built and poorly insulated 920 Sacramento Street, which she described as having always been "like an icebox in winter. I know for I lived there and just escaped pneumonia," referring to one of her periodic stays with Cameron and her charges.

Morgan, as a pioneering female architect, had much in common with Cameron, Wu, and Higgins. They were independent-minded professionals who had chosen to work full-time rather than to marry. In different ways, they had devoted themselves to creating safe and stable places for vulnerable women.

Quiet Defiance

By 1920, Cameron had lived in the group home on Sacramento
Street for a quarter of a century. Because she often housed around
fifty girls and women at any one time, the only place she had to herself
was a cramped bedroom up a set of stairs that hadn't changed much
since the home was rebuilt after the 1906 earthquake. Her private space
was a drab room with scuffed pine floors, secondhand furniture, and
much-laundered bed linens. Her closet was so small it could fit only
two pairs of shoes. It was not the kind of refuge she might have hoped
for in her fifties.

If anyone understood how depressing her surroundings were, it was
Wu. As Cameron's assistant and the staffer who had been with her the
longest, Wu decided to take steps to rectify that. She wrote to many of
the home's former residents who'd left to start families, attend school,
or work, asking them to contribute money toward a gift for Lo Mo.
Many responded.

When Wu asked Cameron what kind of gift she would like, the
superintendent insisted she didn't want anything for herself. She
instead asked Wu to use the money to set up a scholarship in her
name at a school for the blind in Canton. Wu, always strong-minded,
ignored her boss's suggestion and waited until Cameron left town for
a few days to attend a conference in San Diego. With Higgins's help,
she embarked on a bold plan: she emptied Cameron's room, moving
her furniture into the hallway, and began transforming it into a cheer-
ful refuge.

Donaldina Cameron in a Chinese robe.

Over scratched boards, a workman laid new hardwood flooring. A painter began patching cracked windowsills and woodwork and covered them with a coat of fresh white paint. For the walls, workmen hung a delicate floral paper. The Chinese rug that had been given as a gift to Culbertson decades earlier and then handed down to Cameron suddenly looked less threadbare and more elegant against the new floorboards.

Cameron arrived back at the home just before her anniversary dinner. She was accompanied by a deeply troubled young woman who had just been released from a hospital after attempting suicide. Wu insisted Cameron leave the young woman with her and go up to her room to unpack and change her clothes before the gathering. Wu stayed with Cameron long enough to see her reaction to her redecorated room: Cameron took a deep breath, absorbing the smells of the fresh paint and the newly laid floors and admiring the flower-patterned walls.

Wu had also purchased a bolt of silk brocade fabric, hoping that Cameron would be back in time for a dressmaker to stitch a special gown for her. She arrived too late. Still, her friends found a way to celebrate her: when Cameron pulled open the door of her narrow closet, she was surprised to find a rose-colored dress and a pair of silver shoes. Eleanor Olney Babcock, the now-married friend who had welcomed her on her first day at work in the home in 1895, had written her a note: "Dolly, will you wear this tonight for your girls, who are disappointed that time will not allow the brocade to be made up? I hope the slippers won't pinch your toes."

Other gifts followed: The board gave her a silver basket filled with roses. Her "daughters" gave her an inscribed watch that read, "From the girls—April 15, 1895 to April 15, 1920." Cameron was presented with a mysterious package wrapped in silver paper and tied with a red ribbon. It contained a large photo album, dedicated to Cameron in silver Chinese characters. Another gift was a delicate fan displaying scenes of violence and calm in Chinatown.

Meanwhile, the young woman whom Cameron had brought to the home that day could be heard from a third-floor bedroom moaning from the pain of opium withdrawal. Wu asked her to try to muffle her cries because of the party. From Wu's perspective, months of planning had gone into the celebration, and many of the home's most important supporters were downstairs. Instead of being angered by Wu's demand, the young woman slipped an opal ring off her finger. She then asked Wu to give it to Cameron as her gift to Lo Mo.

WOMEN'S GROUPS OF the Presbyterian Church chose 1920 as their jubilee year, marking half a century of their worship and service throughout the United States. (The Presbyterian Church dates its establishment in the United States to the 1630s.) As the Occidental Board's new president, Cadwallader oversaw the Mission Home's own celebrations that year, which would take place during its three-day annual meeting in April. Just a few months after the start of Prohibition, it was a bittersweet gathering for the organization as its old guard made way for the new.

To help bring to life the history of the Occidental Board's founding in the early 1870s, some of its members dressed in old-fashioned clothing and staged dramatic reenactments of scenes from the Mission Home's history, including rooftop rescues, fleeing the city after the 1906 earthquake, picking fruit, and a former resident in a cap and gown marching to receive a university degree.

Four of the board's original supporters attended the festivities— including the indomitable leader Pauline Robbins, then ninety-two, who'd been spat upon all those years ago as she tried to secure lodgings on Sacramento Street for former Chinese sex slaves. Ethel Higgins recounted Cameron's history with the home, describing her as an "altogether inexperienced and frightened young person" when she arrived in 1895 who, three years later, had taken on "the whole burden of the work . . . with misgivings."

She fulsomely praised Cameron but also acknowledged, with a humorous reference to her freshly painted bedroom, how private her boss was: "We have a feeling that if we pass too often this way we will come to a door marked 'Strictly Private,' and with fresh paint. So we withdraw."

On the surface, these celebrations united the Mission Home with its supporters and gave them a chance to reflect on the accomplishments of nearly half a century (at the time of the jubilee celebrations in 1920, the Woman's Occidental Board was in its forty-seventh year) and a reminder of the vast—and, in some instances, seismic—changes that had swept the state and the nation since the founding of the home. Women had won the right to vote in California nearly a decade earlier, in 1911; in August 1920, the Nineteenth Amendment, granting suffrage nationwide to women, would be ratified. With Prohibition and the Red Light Abatement and Injunction Act, San Francisco had become a tamer city than the one the pioneering members of the Occidental Board had fought against.

Now the organization faced internal threats. These played out through a rift developing between Cameron and her bespectacled board president, Cadwallader, over its shaky finances. "The high cost of living, as well as added numbers in the Homes, almost doubled the expense of running the Chinese rescue work, the responsibility of which had to be borne wholly by the Occidental Board," warned Cadwallader.

In the months leading up to the annual meeting, Cadwallader had corresponded with Presbyterian officials in New York over how to meet operating expenses, admitting that "we have these children and are faced with the problem of giving them the actual necessities and when I think of the meals that we give them, I am ashamed." The residents mostly ate rice and vegetables; they were served small amounts of eggs and meat when the homes' monthly budget could afford them. The food shortages of the war years had exacerbated the skimpy rations.

Even before Cadwallader became president, there were signs the Occidental Board was unhappy with Cameron's management. It ordered a reorganization of the Tooker Home in 1918, including a directive that Cameron would visit it at least once a week and submit a "monthly *written* report" and that the home would not be allowed to employ unlicensed teachers.

By 1919, the first year of Cadwallader's presidency, the board ordered a series of belt-tightening measures that Cameron couldn't have interpreted as anything but criticisms of her. They included requiring bids from at least three different suppliers, in consultation with a board committee, and a rule that "none of the girls in the Home be permitted to get supplies on credit unless accompanied by Miss Wu or an American Teacher."

·   ·   ·

ANOTHER THREAT CAME from rival churches aiming to expand in Chinatown. One of the missionaries who pointed this out was Dr. Charles R. Shepherd, an Englishman who'd been posted to San Francisco in 1919 after four years of teaching in China. Shepherd counted nine Protestant groups and one Catholic group working in Chinatown shortly after he arrived, all offering classes in English and religious services, though few offered shelter for vulnerable women. "There seemed to be an appalling amount of duplication, and, I regret to say, far too much competition," he wrote.

The problem? Too many rescuers and too few rescued.

An interdenominational group began discussing the feasibility of mergers. Shepherd, a newcomer willing to speak his mind and a fluent Chinese speaker, wrote vividly of first meeting Cameron at a gathering of all the religious and social workers of Chinatown. "She regarded me appraisingly with eyes that were gray, flecked with gold, clear and steady. Unquestionably sympathetic were those eyes, and yet within their depths shone a gleam of quiet defiance," wrote Shepherd, who judged her a determined and resolute woman.

Cameron soon invited Shepherd for a private chat at 920 Sacramento Street. They sat together in the formal reception room on the ground floor of the house, presumably behind closed doors. "I asked you to come," she said, "because I want to speak with you about something that has been on my heart these many years." She then spoke quietly, but intensely, about the need for a home to house the small boys in the community who were without parents.

"There are so many of them," she continued, "orphans, half-orphans, foundlings, and children from broken homes. Already we have five of them right here in this house which is intended only for young women." She explained they couldn't keep caring for the boys much longer. "It is no place for them. And then, too, they need a man's influence. They need a father." She told him that the Presbyterians and Methodists had long cared for "needy girls; but no one has ever seemed to think about the boys."

After mulling it over, Shepherd agreed. Cameron had succeeded in defusing the well-justified concern that there was too much duplication of efforts in Chinatown. She'd also recruited a new ally to take responsibility for some of the young boys who had previously been under her care. Ultimately, Cameron's homes remained independent, and Shepherd, in 1923, opened a Chinese boys' home in the East Bay called the Chung Mei Home for Chinese Boys.

AS SKILLFUL AS CAMERON PROVED in winning Shepherd over to her side, it soon became clear to officials at the Presbyterian Church's head office that they needed to make some changes. By the end of the jubilee year, they'd dissolved the old Woman's Occidental Board, the volunteer organization in San Francisco that Cameron had long reported to, and moved oversight for the homes to New York. Cadwallader instead ran a "District" operation separate from the mission homes under Cameron's leadership.

The residents of 920 Sacramento Street rang in the New Year of 1921 with good cheer: Cameron helped two of the older residents pluck the feathers off turkeys for a feast that evening alongside her friend Evelyn Bancroft, then took a large group from the home to the beach for "a really happy time."

The next few weeks were busier than ever. The next afternoon, Cameron and Wu boarded a train for Seattle on an urgent case. A book that the residents of the home had given Cameron as a Christmas gift kept her engaged in reading during the journey. The following weeks were filled with calls and visits to district attorneys' offices and judges and telegrams in Washington state, Idaho, and California.

Cadwallader kept trying to undercut Cameron, reporting to their bosses in New York that "the real number of cases rescued from immoral slavery is comparatively small. Not ten per cent." While Cadwallader revealed this fact as part of a struggle for power, she was correct that the number of rescues had been steadily falling in recent years. Most of the girls and young women who ended up at the homes arrived because of difficult domestic situations, rape, or immigration problems rather than because they were victims of sexual slavery.

Out of dozens of new residents entering the homes each year, only a handful came after being "rescued" by Mission Home staffers. Yet rescue stories had proven highly effective for fund-raising and were the source of much of Cameron's clout with her New York supervisors. So were the funds raised "off the books" by Cameron personally rather than through the board's efforts.

Ultimately, the powers that be sided with Cameron, whom they'd worked with for decades and who was a celebrity and effective fundraiser in her own right. Both the Occidental Board and the troublesome Cadwallader soon disappeared into the organization's history.

39

"Sargy"

One surprising aspect of the 1920 jubilee celebration was the appearance of officers from San Francisco's Chinatown Squad. Acting out scenarios alongside board members dressed in period costumes, the officers helped dramatize some of the raids they'd assisted in over the years, taking them over rooftops and into dank cellars. One even waved a torn white handkerchief, like the one that he and Cameron had used to identify themselves to an enslaved girl during a rescue.

A recent addition to the Chinatown Squad, rejoining it the year after the jubilee celebrations, was John J. "Jack" Manion. He'd been reassigned in March 1921 to head up the squad, with orders to reduce crime in Chinatown following another spate of tong killings. Cameron and Manion had worked on their first rescue together in 1916, when he was first on the squad, and his return was welcomed by the superintendent, coming at a time when her older friends and defenders were starting to dwindle.

Manion, born in 1876 in the bucolic hamlet of Ross, California, had joined the San Francisco Police Department at the age of thirty-one, just after the earthquake. A close and trusted friend of San Francisco's police chief, he reluctantly agreed to take over as head of the long-troubled Chinatown Squad amid a flare-up of tong violence.

He soon began enforcing vagrancy laws against people in Chinatown with no visible means of support, repeatedly rearresting them until they left. (This policing method would later be found uncon-

Sergeant John J. "Jack" Manion, known as "Sargy," became head of the Chinatown Squad in 1921.

stitutional.) He also attended a meeting in February 1921 of criminal
tongs in which their leaders reached a peace agreement. A photograph
from that meeting shows Manion and several Chinese men, all wearing
black Western-style suits, in a room where the blinds are drawn. Buns
and plates of other delectables sit on a table in front of the men. None
of them, including Manion, are smiling.

The story goes that after the leaders signed the document, Manion snatched it from the table, folded it, and put it in his coat pocket,
announcing that because he now had the names of all the leaders, any
of them who broke the law would be deported. Whether that is a true
account or apocryphal, the murder rate in Chinatown did drop dramatically under Manion's watch, according to city records.

Yet one criminal tong member who continued to elude the Chinatown Squad's close watch was Wong See Duck, now a member of the
powerful Suey Sing tong. After immigrating to the United States as a
"paper son," he had established roots in Chinatown working for several
companies before opening his own business on Grant Avenue, a hard-

A peace meeting between rival tong leaders in San Francisco's Chinatown, February
1921. Jack Manion is seated at the right-hand corner of the table, at the end.

ware store. As a merchant, Wong See Duck was permitted to travel freely between China and the United States.

Over the years, the ostensible merchant had accumulated enough wealth to help finance a sophisticated trafficking ring that operated undetected for years, bringing dozens and perhaps even hundreds of women to Chinatown as sex slaves. Whether Wong was one of the somber, dark-suited men photographed alongside Manion after the 1921 "peace talks" is unclear, but Manion and Wong would confront each other in the future.

THE SQUAD, MEANWHILE, focused on cleaning itself up under Manion's leadership. For many years, Cameron hadn't always called on police officers for help, in part because she knew some took bribes to alert brothel keepers of impending raids. That changed soon after Manion arrived. Indeed, one of the largest rescues they worked on together took place three years after he took over as head of the squad, in the early morning hours of St. Patrick's Day 1924. It was a rainy March dawn. Manion and two plainclothes officers stood on the corner of Grant Avenue.

"Good morning, gentlemen," said Cameron, sheltered beneath an umbrella, accompanied by Wu and Higgins. "Are we ready?"

Manion nodded and the six of them walked north up Grant Avenue, under the streetlamps still glowing at 5:00 a.m., to Jackson Street. "You stay across the street," Manion told her. "All right, boys, follow me," he ordered.

A big man, standing well over six feet and famed for his ability to deliver an accurate punch from either hand without appearing to look at the person he was hitting, Manion headed to 654 Jackson Street, armed with a vagrancy warrant for a teenager believed to be in the brothel keeper's custody. Manion had scouted the building and knew it had a skylight that was sometimes left open.

Manion grabbed onto an overhanging balcony and hauled himself up. His men followed. When they reached the narrow roof, he opened his overcoat and pulled out a length of rope, which he had wrapped around his waist. Despite the slick surfaces and continuing rain, he inched his way to the skylight, which had been left ajar.

Placing a piece of wood across the open skylight, he tied the rope to it. Slowly, he lowered himself down some twenty-five feet. The second officer also descended safely. But the third caught his foot in the rope and crashed to the floor, waking up the house's occupants. Pandemonium ensued: whistles blew and a shot was fired. Women and their clients emerged into the hallway. One young woman demanded to know why they hadn't been warned of the raid, because they had paid a bribe to an intermediary. Manion swung open the door, carrying a small, frightened girl in one arm. He whistled, beckoning Cameron, Wu, and Higgins over to the front door of the still-darkened house.

"Congratulations," Cameron told him. That was one of the last of the large "slave houses," as Manion called them, to be raided in those years: most of the Chinese slaves were rounded up and soon deported. A single teen involved in the raid, Yum Gue, chose to enter the Mission Home under the care of the woman who was still known in Chinatown as *Fahn Quai*, Foreign Devil, or *Bái Mógǔi*, White Devil.

Manion, who came to be known by the nickname "Sargy" in the neighborhood and who was honored by being named the godfather to several Chinese children, considered Cameron "one brave woman." They also shared a deep faith in God, even though they worshipped at different churches. Manion, for one, made time each day to attend Mass at Old St. Mary's Cathedral on Grant Avenue and California Street, founded in 1894, the year before Cameron arrived in Chinatown.

Years later, Manion admitted that when he first met Cameron, "I feared that we might not get along so well together because she is, of course, Protestant, while I am a Catholic. But, I soon found out, a difference in religious viewpoint made little difference in our personal contacts. We came to be very good friends." Cameron, it seems, had a gift for friendship, especially with those who could advance her cause.

40

Bessie

In a garbage-strewn alley in Chinatown around the turn of the century, a photographer captured a striking tableau. Cameron, wearing a full black skirt that fell just above her ankles and a dowdy, small-brimmed hat, gazes toward the camera. Standing next to her is a similarly garbed Chinese woman, possibly Wu. A man in a suit stands partway up a ladder propped against a brick building. On a balcony above him, a man who appears to be a plainclothes police officer holds in his arms a girl with a long black braid hanging down her back. She's the "slave girl" being rescued.

Almost certainly staged for the camera, the resulting photograph remains the best-known image of Cameron at work. Probably a photogravure, a high-quality printmaking process intended for publication, the photograph shows all four figures in sharp focus, suggesting it might have been shot to accompany an article about the Chinese Mission Home, aided by the San Francisco Police Department's Chinatown Squad. Yet during the second and third decades of the twentieth century, rescues of that nature tapered off, in part because of the general crackdown on brothels following the Red Light Abatement and Injunction Act.

More and more, the women who sought shelter at the Mission Home were there for other reasons, including to escape domestic abuse and to fight deportation threats by immigration authorities. As the instances when Cameron and her staff forcibly entered brothels

Donaldina Cameron (far left) and police officers stage a rescue of a Chinese girl.

became more infrequent, there were still large numbers of girls and women entering the homes—some through their own volition.

One of those was a young woman named Bessie Jeong, who defied her family and sought out Cameron's help. She wasn't rescued; she saved herself from an arranged marriage, eventually parlaying the relationships she formed at 920 Sacramento Street to obtain a remarkable education. Despite receiving little or no financial or emotional support from her relatives after the age of fifteen, she became a pioneering Chinese professional woman. A source of great pride to Cameron, Jeong's story illustrates the lengths to which staffers went to help this unusually focused and talented member of the Mission Home household.

WHEN SHE WAS FIFTEEN, Bessie Jeong's father told her he planned to take her to China with him, possibly to fulfill his paternal duties by arranging her marriage. Jeong, who had witnessed the desperation of her older sister when pressured by her family to marry a man the age of her grandfather, saw this plan as a threat to her independence. "Oh, I'm ready for the auction block. I better not go if I know what's good for me," she told a pair of oral historians many years later. "Prized Jersey— the name 'Bessie' always made me think of some nice fat cow!"

Before the Chinese Revolution in 1911, it was not unusual for poor, working-class parents to marry off their daughters at a young age to help provide for the rest of the family. Typically, a matchmaker would present prospective grooms to the parents: the bride would have little say and often wouldn't meet her husband until the wedding day, when, dressed in red silk, she was carried into his home.

But Jeong's family was not poor. Her father was a merchant in San Francisco who frequently traveled between China and the United States. Her mother, a second wife to him, had once had bound feet. The family had survived the 1906 earthquake and fire, and eventually Jeong's father decided he wanted to return to his homeland. Instead of facing an arranged marriage in China, Jeong's American-born older sister settled on a groom who would keep her in the United States. Her parents gave her two to choose from—one in his twenties with a large family of siblings and the other more than twice as old and, presumably, wealthier. Her parents presented the choice to her: Because of the younger man's large family, "you would be a sort of slave to all of them. This other man is fifty years old, but he can give you everything, he has no family. Better to be an old man's darling than a young man's slave."

Taking her parents' advice, Jeong's sister married the older man. She soon realized her mistake. She became wretchedly unhappy in the marriage. Jeong witnessed her sister's misery, because their parents allowed the new bride to take Bessie along with her to the new household in Weed, California, near the Oregon border, as a companion and helpmate. The elderly groom, who first worked as a cook in a lumber camp and then became a manager, would begin shouting at them at the crack of dawn and continue his abuse until well after nightfall.

"He had a horrible disposition, suspicious and jealous, and my sister's life was one long tragedy with him," Jeong recalled. Violence—or the threat of it—was part of her daily life as well as subjugation, because her sister's husband also did not believe in educating girls.

Only through her own and her sister's perseverance did Bessie begin attending classes in a one-room schoolhouse at age ten. Bessie was a fast learner, ignoring those who called her "a little Chink" or flung playground taunts like "Ching, ching Chinaman, sitting on a rail. . . . On came the train and off went his tail." When asked about this in later years, she chose not to see it as racial prejudice: "I wasn't insulted by it 'cause I didn't realize I was Chinese, really. And the children didn't mean anything by it. They didn't mean to be insulting or anything like that. So I just grew up like any average American child."

IN 1915, when she was about fourteen years old, Jeong traveled from Weed to San Francisco to visit the world's fair. Like so many others, she was captivated by the fair's centerpiece, the sparkling Tower of Jewels. It might have been during that visit, while staying in her brother's boardinghouse, that she first learned about how Cameron was helping Chinese women and girls who "were being sold on the commercial market."

Jeong, whose Chinese name was Jeong Yoke Ying, also came to learn more about Cameron from her sister, who had begun writing heart-wrenching letters to the missionary describing her violent husband. In a letter from June 1916, she described how she'd decided to give her husband in Weed one more chance, but if he threatened "to kill me again I will come right down to you by myself so you don't have to come up for me now."

Born and raised in San Francisco, Jeong had never visited China. In late 1916, when she was fifteen years old, her father purchased a ticket for her and two of her brothers to accompany him to his homeland. The night before their planned departure, Jeong announced she wouldn't go. By then she'd been separated from her father for several years. Living with her sister in Weed, she'd clearly learned how to stand up for herself.

Jeong told him that if he insisted she board the boat the next morning, she would run away to the Mission Home and throw herself on its protection. Her father couldn't believe his daughter would disobey him in that way.

"The home will not keep you for life," he warned her.

"I don't want it to keep me for life," Jeong said. "I want a chance to learn, so that I can take care of myself!"

"There is no use in talking," he told her. "Get ready for the boat tomorrow."

The relatives Jeong was staying with agreed with her father: they thought the sooner the rather homely teen, with her round, moonlike face, became a bride, the better. But Jeong was determined not to be forced into matrimony. She wanted to focus on her education instead.

Neither her father nor any of her family members in San Francisco believed that Jeong would carry out her threat to run away. So when she told the relatives she was staying with in San Francisco that her sister in Weed had asked her to visit Cameron to relay the news of her marital troubles, they permitted her to visit the Mission Home. She left the boardinghouse where she was staying first thing on the morning of the planned departure and found her way to 920 Sacramento Street, arriving at its doorstep on the shortest day of the year—December 21, 1916.

Cameron was there when Jeong climbed the steps of the stocky brick Mission Home. Because Jeong wasn't fleeing physical abuse or slavery, she was unsure at first about how to handle the situation. Cameron initially offered to write a letter on her behalf to the U.S. consul in Canton so that if she got into trouble, she could use that. But Jeong realized that such a letter would be of little value to her: "I knew that if I went to one of these little interior villages [in China] I would have no say whatsoever about anything. If I once consented to go, I would be lost." Jeong knew that the American consul would not be able to rescue her if she ended up in an abusive marriage.

Cameron told her that she could stay at the Mission Home and attend school if they could convince a judge to allow it. Meanwhile, her father and brothers were frantically searching for her before their steamer left. From Cameron's bedroom window, which looked down on Sacramento Street, Jeong remembered seeing one of her brothers riding the streetcar up the hill, looking for the rescue mission. She panicked. "He couldn't see me, of course, but I was so guilty and frightened, I hid under the bed." Later that morning, her father and brothers boarded the ship without her.

◺ 41 ⬖

Heavens for Courage

The California Superior Court judge Frank Murasky issued an order naming Cameron as Jeong's legal guardian in mid-January 1917. Because Jeong's father was in China at the time, the juvenile probation officer noted that her father retained the right to present his side of the case to the court at any time. In fact, once Jeong's father and brothers arrived in China, they were kidnapped by bandits hoping for a sizable ransom.

Jeong's sister was overjoyed when she learned of her younger sibling's escape to the Mission House. She wrote to Cameron a few weeks after the judge's ruling to thank her. "You have no idea how proud I was to hear that you are helping my sister get a good education," she wrote. "All I care is [*sic*] give her a good education so she can make good use of herself without getting married."

Jeong, in turn, dove headfirst into her new life at the Mission Home, attending school and embracing its religious teachings. It wasn't long before she asked to be baptized at the nearby Presbyterian church. "God had a hand in my life, because how would a little girl be able to say to her parents, 'I'm not going' and get away with it?" she later reflected. Jeong found support and encouragement in some unlikely places, including from a cousin who told her in the Chinese dialect they spoke, "*Nga ega tin ne do ahma,*" which roughly translated means "I give you the heavens for courage."

With encouragement and tutoring, Jeong quickly passed through grammar school. Insisting she attend an endowed school in San Fran-

Dr. Bessie Jeong, with two of her charges in 1937, when she ran the home's "baby cottage."

cisco that offered college preparation as well as practical skills such as laundering, housekeeping, sewing, and millinery, Cameron paid a personal visit to its trustees. At first, Jeong was not admitted to the largely white school because she was Chinese. But Cameron persisted, recognizing that Jeong had an unusually strong drive for learning. Eventually, they enrolled her.

Soon, Jeong became a leader among her peers: "I was the first girl to say, 'Hey, we're not going to be homemakers, we're going to be career girls.'" She recalled that hers was the first class to balk at spending their time making tailored suits and infants' layettes. "We're not having babies, we're going out in the world and contribute," she recalled she'd said, many years later. Her outspokenness earned her respect; although she was Chinese, she was elected class president by her mostly white fellow students.

Jeong already had several advantages over the other girls and young women living in the Mission Home. She could come and go as she liked, because she had no angry former owners or enemies looking for her, unlike others, who were escorted when they left the house for fear that slavers might snatch them back. Because she spoke the Sze Yup dialect, she would sometimes be called upon at Angel Island or the nearby San Quentin prison to serve as a translator.

In June 1917, Jeong learned that her sister had become ill. Before Jeong left the Mission Home to see her sister, Cameron presented her with a special gift: a dainty amethyst heart. After spending about two months in Weed that summer, Jeong returned to San Francisco in mid-August. But her sister's plight was growing more urgent, and she headed north again in October 1918—at the time when influenza had swept through both 920 Sacramento Street and the Tooker Home in Oakland, sickening many of the residents. Cameron didn't have a spare moment during that frightening autumn, and Jeong worried when she didn't hear from her. To her guardian, she penned a short, plaintive note on October 16 that read,

> Dearest Lo Mo:—I have been waiting to hear from you but you have not written so I have given up hopes of hearing from you. I have been expecting to have the pleasure of your visit but I presume you have been very busy.

Will you please let me know when you would like to have me come down? I am ready to come at any time.

I hope that I am still welcome at "920."

With much love and kisses,
Lovingly, Bessie Jeong

Less than two weeks later, Cameron received a Western Union telegram. On its distinctive yellow paper, she read the words "SISTER PASSED AWAY—SUNDAY MY FUTURE VERY INDEFINITE WILL ADVISE YOU LATER BESSIE." Jeong's sister, like so many others, had died in the influenza epidemic, leaving behind an eight-year-old daughter named May Louis Wong. Although Jeong tried to convince her brother-in-law to allow her to bring May with her to the Mission Home, he refused. Jeong returned to San Francisco alone.

CAMERON VIGOROUSLY ADVOCATED over the years for Jeong, more so than for many of the other residents of the home, perhaps because she sensed Jeong's academic potential. With few resources of her own, Jeong chose to attend San Mateo Junior College after high school in 1924, in part because it cost very little. Around that time, Cameron introduced Jeong to Mrs. Gilchrist, a fellow Presbyterian Scotswoman and the wife of an officer of the Standard Oil Company, who hired her for $20 a month to cook, iron, and wash dishes in their San Mateo home. Cameron also connected her with several of the home's longtime board members, making the case that Jeong had the academic potential to attend a four-year college. They agreed to help pay her tuition, if she was accepted.

Cameron used all her influence to make sure that happened—aiming for Jeong's admission to Stanford University, which in the 1920s accepted very few women to its Palo Alto campus. On July 8, 1925, Cameron wrote a heartfelt recommendation letter, urging the college to accept her, describing how Jeong had worked for two years in the Gilchrists' home while earning good grades at the junior college. Cameron urged the university to admit her so "she may continue the higher education she has so courageously struggled for during the past eight years."

Around the time that Cameron was penning her recommendation letter, Jeong accompanied Higgins on the annual fruit-picking trip, which in the summer of 1925 was a particularly uncomfortable and challenging one. As Higgins noted, many of the home's residents had never been outside the city and were not used to the outdoors. They arrived at the camp on the first day, only to find bare ground, rather than the more comfortable accommodations they'd been promised. Seven miles from the nearest place to buy groceries, they found the primitive camp's larder bare when they arrived.

Jeong took charge of the cooking and planning of the meals and quickly got to work. Within a few hours, she had supervised the stove setup, built the fire, unpacked the utensils, and rustled up enough supplies from the food they'd brought to make dinner that night for everyone. "In all this time, amid the utter confusion, she had not once become disconcerted or impatient, and she had succeeded in keeping up the spirits of the girls," wrote Higgins, in a letter of recommendation she wrote for Jeong to a board member who she'd hoped would help support her. It was during those difficult weeks in the country that Jeong got the good news that she'd been admitted to Stanford, where the student body was overwhelmingly white and male.

That fall, Jeong embarked on challenging premed studies, hoping to become a medical missionary. She also took on paid jobs to help foot her tuition bill and expenses—including babysitting for the grandchildren of Stanford's first president, David Starr Jordan, who had retired from the university but remained a prominent figure.

With her heavy course load and outside jobs, Jeong faltered in her math and chemistry classes that first fall. Cameron, alarmed by what she called her protégée's "unnerved and discouraged" state, asked the board members who were already paying her tuition to fund a private tutor for her: "I believe that she will get through all right if we can find someone who will coach her, even once a week."

Cameron's entreaties were successful. Jeong worked with a tutor and turned her academic situation around. In June 1927, she became the first Chinese woman to graduate from Stanford. Slightly older than most of the others in the graduating class, Jeong had majored in biology and found time to serve as corresponding secretary for the Cosmopolitan Club, a group dedicated to promoting international understanding. As Cameron proudly wrote of Jeong's graduation, "It was a happy reward [to see her] lead the long procession of black gown graduates through the beautiful 'Quad' of Stanford University on Commencement Day."

Jeong headed east to Pennsylvania, spending a year at a Bible college as a step toward becoming a medical missionary. She then enrolled in the Woman's Medical College of Philadelphia, where she continued to receive emotional and financial support from the staffers of the Mission Home. Graduating as an M.D. in 1932, she returned to California, hoping to serve her residency at the Los Angeles County Hospital. It was there that she had her most brutal run-in with racism: the hospital, it seemed, had a policy of automatically rejecting Asian applicants. Upon learning of this, Cameron wrote to congressmen, senators, judges, and the state Civil Service Administration. With Cameron's help, Dr. Jeong served her residency at the hospital.

Jeong persuaded the hospital to begin an outreach program to poor Chinese in Los Angeles. After completing her residency and being offered a job at the UCLA hospital, she instead decided to return to the Mission Home to help care for the youngest children living at the Ming Quong Home (the renamed Tooker Home) before entering private practice.

As a pioneering Chinese woman physician, she encountered some resistance from potential patients who were reluctant to be treated by a female doctor. She listed herself as "B. Jeong" in public directories to try to avoid this. "If they see 'Bessie,' they hesitate, even women sometimes, to go to a woman doctor," she said. "So I put 'B. Jeong' and before they know it—it's kind of embarrassing to turn and run, you know—they sit down and I try to make them feel at home with me."

BECAUSE OF JEONG'S EDUCATION, she understood the slave trade in a way that other residents of the Mission Home did not—as a business that lured investors by the temptation of easy profits and relatively low risk. "I hate to say this about my own people, but it's like this. It's like stocks, like an investment, all kinds of people get mixed up in it," she said. "I don't believe they will ever get rid of that till they get a generation that couldn't stand for that sort of thing, and respectable people couldn't get mixed up in it. It'll take a good long while. I'd like to help get rid of that!"

Dr. Bessie Jeong helped bring about change by becoming a notable member of her generation of Chinese American women who not only refused to "stand for" the enslavement of women but devoted their lives to caring for the young, sick, and vulnerable. Her astute analysis of the economic underpinnings of sex slavery would prove all too true in a trial that would shake Chinatown.

42

The Thwack of Bouncing Balls

On the afternoon of December 2, 1932, a group of nine Chinese women left the Mission Home and headed toward San Francisco's waterfront, where at four o'clock that afternoon one of the largest luxury liners ever built was scheduled to depart. Carrying most of their worldly possessions, the women couldn't have missed the bright red dollar signs highlighted on the ship's white funnels.

Leading them was Wu. Round and even more outspoken and opinionated in her middle age, Tien Fuh Wu was known and sometimes feared as "Auntie Wu" by the residents of the Mission Home. Immigration officials and court officers who crossed her path over the years addressed her formally as "Miss Wu." To Cameron, who had known her as a brave and relentless champion for girls and women for more than thirty-five years, she was "dear Tien."

The ship that Wu and her charges boarded that December afternoon, the SS *President Coolidge,* was owned by the Dollar Steamship Co. It boasted two saltwater swimming pools, a gymnasium, a beauty salon, and unusually spacious accommodations. These were for the pleasure of its first-class guests, not for passengers like Wu's small band, which was traveling in steerage.

In the depths of the Great Depression, ticket sales were weak for passage on the art deco ocean liner. The 654-foot-long ship could carry nearly a thousand passengers, but it often sailed only half full. That wasn't surprising, considering that the jobless rate in some American cities was approaching 25 percent. An estimated two million people

Children playing in a sandlot in San Francisco's Chinatown.

wandered the country, homeless. A month earlier, the Republican president Herbert Hoover, who had promised "a chicken in every pot," had lost the election to the Democrat Franklin D. Roosevelt.

For the most part, Chinatown's residents hadn't suffered as much from the downturn as many others. There weren't Hoovervilles in Chinatown. The past discrimination that had prevented many Chinese from taking jobs in other parts of the city helped shelter many of them from the nation's widespread economic catastrophe. The violent scapegoating of the Chinese in the 1870s didn't repeat itself in the early 1930s. Tourists continued to visit Chinatown's "chop suey" restaurants, sampling salted plums and dried abalone, and to wander through its curio emporiums and shops, which sold everything from firecrackers to porcelain "foo dogs."

But Chinatown, too, was changing rapidly. Its "bachelor society" of the early days was giving way to families. At the start of the 1930s, the dramatic gender imbalance of the late nineteenth century had begun to even out. Immigration officials began allowing more marriageable women into the country in 1924, boosting the birthrate. In 1900, Chinatown had about 14,000 residents. By the time of the 1930 census, Chinatown's population had grown to 16,303. The sounds of children playing on the sidewalks and in the narrow alleys could be heard throughout the neighborhood.

The thwack of bouncing balls and gleeful shouting became familiar to the residents at 920 Sacramento Street after 1927, when Chinatown's first playground was constructed on an empty lot below the Mission Home on Waverly Place. Built into the hillside, the small, two-level playground held the neighborhood's first swing sets and slides, as well as a small basketball court. Throughout Chinatown, former brothels with their iron-barred windows were converted into much-needed family housing. Oddly shaped signs hung from doors and windows that stated, "This Is a Private Family: No Admittance!"

To serve the growing number of young working women in Chinatown, the architect Julia Morgan designed a new YWCA on Clay Street, a block away from the Mission Home. The Mission Home's longtime board member Mrs. P. D. Browne helped bring it about, as did Chun Fah, the former Mission Home resident and wife of the *Chun Sai Yat Po* editor. Yet despite the involvement of these progressive women, open segregation continued: the Chinese women who boarded at the new YWCA were required to stay in a separate side building, away from white staffers and residents.

For families and individuals in trouble, Chinatown's churches and charitable organizations offered a safety net. Still, some problems seemed intractable. Wu was one of a panel of ten prominent Chinese residents tapped to put together a survey of social work needs of the Chinese population of San Francisco for the city's Community Chest in 1930. Their report highlighted some of the harsher realities facing Chinatown, including the fact that the neighborhood's death rate was almost three times as high as the rest of San Francisco's.

This was due not to tong violence—there were only two gang-related killings in Chinatown in 1930, according to the report—but to infectious diseases such as tuberculosis and pneumonia, exacerbated by the crowded conditions. The Chinese community, supported by the longtime Mission Home board member Browne and other church leaders, had responded to the city hospital's refusal to treat Chinese patients by building a Chinese hospital of their own. Next door to it on Jackson Street was a free herb dispensary, housed in a modest one-story brick building, where the poor could consult with a traditional herbalist.

The report also revealed the changing nature of the girls and young women seeking refuge at 920 Sacramento Street. In 1930, the Mission Home housed forty-seven Chinese residents, including eleven children and babies. Slipped into the report was the fact that the largest category of residents were boarders, many of whom had been awarded the privilege of living in the home while awaiting the resolution of their immigration cases, rather than staying in the detention facilities of Angel Island. Only nine of the forty-seven residents were categorized as "rescued girls," indicating the long-term trend away from the home's traditional calling. Yet to all of them, the home offered education, vocational training, and counseling.

"In recent years, this traffic in Chinese women and children has in large measure been suppressed," the report noted. "There is now very little call for rescue work of this type." It went on to argue that there remained a strong demand for other kinds of "protective work," including instances of child and family protection, referring to instances of domestic abuse.

As the world around them changed, Cameron and Wu had to adapt. But how to do that? As Cameron wrote to one of her superiors in New York, "You will see Tien Wu and she will tell you better than we can write about the present status of our Chinese work here in San Francisco, and some of the difficulties we face as we try to make adjustments, and reorganize our work in the Mission Home to meet changeing [*sic*] conditions. . . . I have longed with all my heart for your clear vision and constructive mind to help those of us who live too near the problem to have a true perspective."

Although sex trafficking continued, Cameron and Wu spent much of their time grappling with thorny immigration issues. Together, they came up with a plan to try to foil traffickers who preyed on vulnerable women deported back to China. They hoped to cut the snake off at its head.

AS THE WORLD HURTLED toward a second world war, Cameron grew closer to Wu, now sturdy in middle age and wearing eyeglasses. Approaching retirement, Cameron increasingly relied on Wu for translating, meting out discipline, and traveling with Chinese-speaking residents. Wu also began doing more of the public appearances and speaking engagements that Cameron no longer cared to do herself. Cameron trusted Wu completely and believed that she was fully capable of carrying on their work on her own when the time came.

One example of Cameron's confidence in her protégée came when she assigned Wu to lead the eight women on their journey aboard the SS *President Coolidge*. All of them had lived at the Mission Home for long periods, waiting for final decisions about whether they could stay in the United States or would have to return to China. As U.S. immigration officials continued to deport the Chinese under the Exclusion Act, the Mission Home agreed to care for them as their immigration cases wound their way through the court system, offering a better alternative than the prison-like conditions of Angel Island and its sometimes corrupt officials. When long, official-looking letters arrived at the

Mission Home's front desk from Angel Island, Cameron and the other staffers sometimes felt afraid to open them, knowing that they could be deportation orders.

Letters bearing bad news had arrived for each of the Mission Home residents boarding the steamer that December afternoon. They would have to return to China, and it was "far better to go back on your own than be deported," one staffer explained.

Their situations also reflected a problem that Cameron and Wu had long struggled with. How could they, in good conscience, put vulnerable young girls and women onto ships bound for China without accompanying them and arranging for someone to meet them when they arrived? The risk was that slavers, who continued trafficking women from Asia during those years, would snatch them back.

As Cameron argued, "The fate of these helpless girls is dreadful to contemplate if sent back to China, because they have incurred the bitter enmity of the entire slave importing ring and will inevitably fall into its hands if returned alone to China. Death or return to slavery here or in the Straits Settlements [British settlements in Southeast Asia that included Singapore] are the only alternatives, unless Christian friends provide protection."

Cameron learned of the risks of recapture in a letter from a missionary couple accompanying one of the home's residents back to China. A price of $1,000 had been set on the girl's head. When the ship reached Honolulu, an immigration officer came to the missionaries' cabin and assured them she would be safe out on the ship's back deck. They took her there, and soon the ship's Chinese interpreter brought two Chinese men to see her. A spy watched the girl from stairwells and elsewhere for the rest of the journey, apparently hoping to recapture her.

The missionary couple managed to elude the traffickers on that journey and guide their charge to safety in China. During the trip, they grew fond of the young woman, who had absorbed the teachings of the Mission Home. "The thought of Miss Cameron seems to have gripped her. Who knows, the Lord may be preparing another Tien Fuh!" one of the missionaries exulted.

· · ·

CAMERON, MEANWHILE, had reached the conclusion that it was ineffective to attempt to solve the problem of trafficking only from San Francisco. It required a coordinated effort between rescue workers in China and in the United States. Referring to a trip east that Wu had made earlier that year to reinforce the same point, she wrote, "I am sure Miss Wu has helped to make clear to you and the other members of our Board in New York . . . only through the cooperating organization doing protective and rescue work in South China can we hope to entirely suppress the slave traffic."

Cameron had initially contacted a Shanghai-based organization called Doors of Hope, a rescue mission for women who had been sold or tricked into prostitution. However, it soon became apparent that this would not be a feasible place to send residents from the Mission Home. Not only was it hugely overcrowded, caring for some six hundred girls and women already, but most of the residents were from central and northern China, where the dialects, cuisine, and customs were very different from those of Canton, where most of the home's residents came from.

Cameron and Wu hoped, instead, to deepen ties with a Chinese woman who had received her medical training in the United States: Shi Meiyu, also known as Dr. Mary Stone. Working alongside an American missionary, Jennie Hughes, Stone had founded the Bethel Mission in Shanghai, a self-supporting hospital, church, and Bible training institute. In the spring of 1931, Stone and Hughes had stayed at 920 Sacramento Street as guests. They then headed east to New York to meet with fellow missionaries and discuss the possibility of opening a rescue home for women in southern China where deportees from San Francisco could be sent.

Dr. Stone urged Cameron and the Presbyterian board to allow Wu to accompany the group of eight to Shanghai. The Cantonese dialect that the girls and women spoke was different from the one spoken in Shanghai. And three of the young women on the trip had testified against slave dealers, making them particularly vulnerable. Wu's competence and her long experience with traffickers made her an ideal guardian for them.

Dr. Stone also hoped that once Wu arrived in China, she would help them set up the new home called Bethel South. Convinced by Dr.

Stone's arguments, the board granted Wu a six-month leave to pursue that project. Cameron, through her friendship with the Dollars, arranged discounted steamship fares for her longtime assistant and five of the girls, in part by tapping into a small bequest from a former staffer, a member of the Mills family. The U.S. government paid the steamship fare for the others.

But while "Auntie Wu" and the group in her care might have passed through the ship's air-conditioned staterooms or glimpsed its onboard theater where silent movies were projected, the group of Chinese girls and women eventually descended on that December day to their austere accommodations on the lowest levels of the ship.

43

Little General

The SS *President Coolidge* was a fast steamer, traveling at just over twenty-one knots an hour. It reached its first stop, the port of Honolulu, in a little over four days, gliding past coral reefs and the jutting brow of Diamond Head to reach the harbor. On land, the long tradition of the Royal Hawaiian Band serenading the disembarking passengers continued, as well as the custom of placing fragrant plumeria blossom garlands around the necks of passengers from the first-class cabins.

Wu wrote to Cameron throughout the trip, describing two new acquaintances aboard as "some very pleasant gentlemen"—one the newly appointed head of the tourist bureau at Peking (now known as Beijing) and the other a scholar at the University of Southern California. Whether Wu had any romantic interest in these men is unclear: she was approaching fifty and had turned down several suitors over the years. But she wrote humorously to her mentor about the men's struggle with seasickness: "They are congenial and gentlemanly, but both are feeling the motion of the boat so I gave them some of our salted olives and ginger!!"

Once the ship left Honolulu, heading east toward Shanghai, the group faced long stretches of time with little to do. On Sunday morning, December 11, they climbed three floors to the ship's deck to get some fresh air and to attend an outdoor religious service. They were joined by some of the Chinese men on board (perhaps the two gentlemen Wu mentioned who'd suffered from seasickness).

Tien Fuh Wu (standing in the back, on the left) and Donaldina Cameron (seated, center), with a group of women who may have been Mission Home staffers.

A missionary on board told the Bible story of the prodigal son, a fitting choice, perhaps, for a group returning to their homeland after painful experiences. He spoke in English, and Wu translated his words into Cantonese. The group's religious studies continued throughout the journey, with daily readings from the book of Acts each morning from ten to eleven. "We have a godly group of men, women and children; and I hope God spoke to the hearts who were there," Wu wrote to Cameron.

Heading into an unfamiliar part of China where she would face many new challenges, Wu sought out the counsel of the missionary couple. She found their stories interesting and took from them the lesson of "how God supplied all their needs and the remarkable way He gave them their passage to America and England; I had to tell them how God answered [the] prayer for my passage to China." As it turned out, Wu would need her faith, because the trip would not go as planned.

THE SMALL GROUP REACHED Shanghai and made its way to the impressive compound of the Bethel Mission, with its iron-balconied Gospel Hall and its towering Bible Seminary. There they were met by Dr. Mary Stone, who was known for her radiant smile and independent thinking. As one of the first Chinese women to obtain a medical degree in the United States, she was also the first Chinese woman to become an ordained minister in central China, spreading Christianity to whole villages through her work.

In the 1920s, she and the flame haired American Jennie Hughes, with whom she adopted five orphans, had quit the Methodist Woman's Foreign Missionary Society in protest, because they felt it was offering the "rice Christianity" of social action without faith. The two women, who shared a bed and were apparently lovers, then went on to found the Bethel Mission as a nondenominational organization: Hughes ran the church and Bible college, and Stone ran the hospital, China's largest nursing school, and a medical clinic for poor migrant workers in Shanghai. They were a powerful pair of allies for Wu to have in a country she'd left long ago.

Wu spent a happy day with the women in Shanghai, and soon she and her charges were off on the next leg of their journey, to the British colony of Hong Kong. On New Year's Day 1933, Wu wrote to Cameron that she felt great anxiety upon learning that the apartment that Hughes had rented for the group in less expensive Kowloon had fallen through. Where would they go? Money was tight, and it is not clear whom she could turn to for help.

"I cast it upon the Lord," wrote Wu, and soon she learned that a nearby mission had agreed to take the group in. The Chinese minister in charge instructed his students to carry the group's luggage from their cabin to the pier and assigned someone to keep an eye on it there, because the scene was "strictly pandemonium," Wu wrote. "The coolies snatch baggage to get work." The group arrived late in the afternoon and didn't get off the pier until ten that night after all the luggage had been located.

But the group's fortunes soon improved. It turned out that the Mission Home's former Bible teacher Mrs. Chu King had recently vacated a comfortable third-floor apartment on one of Hong Kong's steep "Ladder Streets" after buying a house nearby. The group negotiated a monthly rent even lower than King had paid and discovered that it was just a block away from a police station, which added to their sense of security. Dr. Stone and Hughes joined them there, occupying the parlor while Wu and one of the girls slept on the veranda. Dr. Stone vaccinated the entire group for smallpox, and Wu started hunting for a rental property to establish Bethel South.

Dr. Stone wrote to Cameron praising her protégée: "Miss Wu is like a little general having secured a flat and made all the arrangements before we arrived from Shanghai." Wu's forceful personality, honed over the years as the disciplinarian of the mission household, apparently served her well in the early days of her new assignment. Dr. Stone also hoped Cameron would extend an invitation to Bessie Jeong, who had recently earned her medical degree, to consider joining their small band in Kowloon and help establish a hospital and nurses' training school like the one they had in Shanghai. "Please tell your Dr. Bessie Jeong that the opportunity is waiting for her," Dr. Stone wrote.

Dr. Stone and Hughes planned to divide their time between Shanghai and Hong Kong until they found the right person to take Wu's place in running the new rescue home. What happened next is not clear, but they apparently didn't find that person or find the right location. It might have been that fast-moving political events in China forced them to cancel the project: Japan had seized Manchuria from China the previous year, and tensions between the two countries were rising. As war began to seem imminent, they abandoned the plan altogether. Stone and Hughes returned to Shanghai and spent the next four decades together. Wu headed back to her adopted homeland.

Wu's trip had not been a complete failure: she had found situations for each of the young women she'd escorted to China. On May 3, 1933, after six months away, she disembarked from the SS *President McKinley* in San Francisco. Officially designated an illegal alien herself (the immigration service had searched but could not find a landing record for her when she first arrived in San Francisco as a child in 1893), Wu was granted an exemption after two white witnesses, Cameron and another staffer at the Mission Home, testified for her. She was readmitted into the United States based on an official recommendation stating that her "loyalty and integrity have been of the highest character."

Wu knew she was highly regarded by her missionary colleagues and immigration officials. Her permit to reenter the United States noted that she was just four feet eleven and a half inches tall and bore a small scar on her forehead, possibly a mark left by her abuse as a slave when she was a child. To Cameron and the home's residents, the short-statured Wu was a much larger presence whose absence they'd keenly felt.

Receiving a warm welcome when she returned to 920 Sacramento Street, Wu nonetheless felt disappointed that she had not been able to establish a home in southern China. Offering refuge on both sides of the Pacific was a goal the two women shared, but circumstances beyond their control forced Cameron and Wu to abandon their dream of establishing an outpost in China to help combat the slave trade.

44

Shangri-La

By the 1930s, most vestiges of pre-earthquake Chinatown had disappeared. Construction crews had paved over the district's quaint cobblestoned lanes. Where street vendors had once set up their awning-covered stalls to sell sacks of rice and boxes of perishable produce, drivers of cars with out-of-state license plates now parked. Shopkeepers had replaced the red curtains and wooden planks they once pulled across their entrances with pane glass windows and locked doors.

Grant Avenue, approached from the south, marked the end of the city's financial district and the beginning of the steep ascent into Chinatown. After Prohibition ended in late 1933, the neighborhood transformed itself into a glamorous nightspot. Chinese cocktail bars and lounges began appearing, followed by nightclubs such as Forbidden City, the Kubla Khan, and Shangri-La (a fictional land described by James Hilton in his 1933 novel *Lost Horizon*). Blaring neon signs replaced delicate paper lanterns.

Small cigar factories, such as the one that Cameron saw on her first trip to San Francisco as a child, gave way to larger import-export businesses. The perfume of hand-carved camphor chests and exotic teas imported from China drifted out from these storefronts and onto Grant Avenue, mingling with the tantalizing smell of moon cakes and warm custard tarts from the new Eastern Bakery.

Gone were the days when the few Chinese women who ventured out onto the streets demurely hid their faces behind fans. As the

Grant Avenue, the central thoroughfare of Chinatown, had
been transformed by neon lights and paved streets by the time this
photograph was taken in October 1933.

elderly Ng Poon Chew wrote, the "Chinese lady is no longer dressed in the full regulation of real Chinese fashion" but is "suddenly transformed into a vivacious, independent, self-assertive" woman wearing high heels, bobbed hair, and a beauty spot on her cheek and carrying lipstick and face powder in her pocketbook. Courtship took place directly between young people, he noted, while arranged marriages faded into the past.

Chew, whose walrus mustache had whitened with age, now spent most of his time at his Oakland home, on doctor's orders. His newspaper, *Chung Sai Yat Po*, continued to publish daily and had moved back to offices on Sacramento Street in Chinatown. On March 12, 1931, Chew's eldest daughter Mansie, named after the missionary Samantha Condit, drove her father to sit in on one of the paper's editorial meetings. Chew joked with his employees and quoted them one of his favorite sayings: "The newspaper is the people's tongue."

The next day, Chew sat down for supper at his home, surrounded by his wife of many years, Chun Fah, and their five grown offspring. The patriarch bowed his head to say grace: "Lord, bless this bread to our use and we to thy service." After the prayer was done, his family members raised their heads and saw their famous father and husband wrinkle his brow. "I have a little pain," he said. His hands, which had been joined in prayer, parted. His head fell forward, hitting the table.

Shortly before his sixty-fifth birthday, the former crusading editor Ng Poon Chew passed away, marking the end of an era.

ONE OF THE EVILS that Chew's newspaper had long condemned remained in Chinatown, however. The Wing Lee Co., located at 900 Grant Avenue near Washington Street, had become one of the neighborhood's larger businesses. It was the hardware store owned by an investment group led by Wong See Duck, by then a well-fed man who slicked back his hair with pomade. Although he traveled back and forth between China and the United States ostensibly buying hammers, nails, and other products for his store, his real trade was still in human flesh.

The Wing Lee Co., of course, was just a front. As a member of the powerful Suey Sing tong (one of the tongs involved in the 1921

"peace talks" brokered by the Chinatown Squad's Jack Manion), Wong
See Duck for many years had been arranging the transport of young
women from China to the United States by claiming they were blood
relatives of legal Chinese American residents. To smuggle them in, he
took advantage of the same loophole he'd used when he had arrived in
San Francisco in 1908 as a local merchant's "paper son."

By the 1930s, Wong had not only developed a sophisticated system
for importing women but also organized a syndicate of investors to
help finance his trafficking operation. Funds from the investors helped
pay for a procurer, the person who obtained the girls in China bound
for prostitution or servitude in the United States and paid steamship
fares for the women and their escorts. Chinese men in America willing to falsely claim to immigration authorities that they were related
to the young women added another layer of deniability between the
criminal activity and its investors. The traffickers also covered transportation from the port where the women landed (often Seattle) to San
Francisco. These up-front costs could be sizable.

Photo from case files of *U.S. vs. Wong See Duck*. Prosecutors argued that Wong
See Duck was involved in a large West Coast trafficking ring. One of Jeung Gwai
Ying's owners, Yee Mar, stands to the right of the woman in the fur-collared coat.

One of the young women the syndicate imported in 1933 was nineteen-year-old Jeung Gwai Ying, the young woman who'd fled from the Jackson Street beauty parlor to the Mission Home at dusk on December 14, 1933. The syndicate's investment in her helps explain why her decision to flee while getting her hair done was so courageous and risky. Jeung's investors and the people who subsequently purchased her services had paid heavily for the petite teen. If she escaped, her owners not only stood to lose her potential earnings—perhaps as much as $9,000 that year alone (more than the price of the average new house)—but also risked her identifying her captors to law enforcement officers. She knew enough about their business to expose it as a criminal enterprise.

Jeung's journey had begun in July 1933 aboard the SS *Cleveland*. Traveling under the pseudonym of Lee Long Ying, she landed in Seattle after about a two-week trip from Hong Kong. With her was a young man named Wing Quong Hing, whom Wong See Duck had given the job of accompanying her from China. It was probably during that passage across the Pacific that Jeung and the man began a sexual relationship. He stayed with her when she arrived in San Francisco, guarding her before she entered the underworld of forced prostitution.

At the time the syndicate sold Jeung that fall in San Francisco for $4,500, her pregnancy was not yet evident. But by mid-December 1933, when she fled to the Mission Home, her belly had begun to swell, which may be why she didn't button her overcoat at the beauty parlor. She must have feared for herself, because her earning potential for her owners as a prostitute would decline as her pregnancy progressed. But more likely, she feared for the future of her unborn child.

RATHER THAN RISK being spotted along a more open street, Jeung could have chosen to take a safer route to the Mission Home through some of Chinatown's alleyways. Chinatown's side streets and narrow passages were where prostitution, gambling, and other disreputable activities continued to take place. "Smoking rooms," masked at their entrances by wet blankets to disguise the sweet smell of opium, could still be found there in the 1930s. These backstreets were also home to some of the neighborhood's many sweatshops, where Chinese women operated whirring sewing machines for twelve or more hours a day.

The barred and guarded Mission Home offered Jeung safety. By becoming a resident, she entered a community of women who understood the trauma she had experienced. Cameron and Wu listened to her story after she arrived and then settled her down for the night. Over the next few days, they telephoned the Chinatown Squad's Sergeant Manion, who came to the Mission Home to hear her account of how she'd escaped her captors. The home's staffers and the police braced themselves for an effort by Jeung's owners or by the syndicate that had brought her to the United States to retrieve what they considered their valuable property.

Despite the possible threat, holiday spirits remained high at 920 Sacramento. As the Christmas holiday approached, friends donated a spruce tree, which filled its main hall with the tang of evergreen. On Christmas Eve, staffers filled stockings with candy, nuts, and small gifts and hung them by the fireplace. A portly friend of the home, dressed up as Santa Claus, distributed presents to the children and bags of food to nearby impoverished families. Residents reenacted the birth of Jesus

Jeung Gwai Ying and her son, David.

in a manger and, for their Christmas dinner, feasted on their favorite Chinese foods; later, the staff and guests, including the new Chinese consul K. L. Kwong, a Harvard Business School graduate, joined Cameron and Wu to eat a turkey dinner.

That spring, as she moved into the final term of her pregnancy, Jeung repeated her story to Arthur J. Phelan, head of the Immigration and Naturalization Service's legal department in San Francisco. He, in turn, contacted A. J. Zirpoli, an assistant U.S. attorney who worked in an adjoining office at the Federal Building. At her side was Wu, who translated her words from Cantonese into English and helped protect the heavily pregnant woman. In the early morning hours of Friday, May 18, as the rest of the household at 920 Sacramento Street slept, Jeung gave birth in a hospital to a baby boy she named David.

ZIRPOLI, PROSECUTOR of the case against the infamous bank robber "Baby Face" Nelson around that time, was intrigued by Jeung's story. He knew it had been years since a trafficker of Chinese slaves had been convicted in California and talked the possibility of prosecuting over with Phelan. A key question was whether Jeung would hold up under the pressure of public scrutiny and cross-examination. Thinking back to Jeung's courageous flight to safety, Zirpoli concluded she would.

Months of investigation ensued, with the combined San Francisco legal and immigration team reaching out to contacts in Seattle and China. They searched through hundreds of immigration photographs; a first big breakthrough came when they saw a photograph of a square-jawed man named Leong Chong Po.

Phelan, who initially found the photo, exclaimed out loud as he read the record card. It revealed that another name the man used was Wong See Duck, one of the most powerful merchants and tong members in Chinatown. Zirpoli let out a whistle as he realized what the team would be up against.

"Are you sure?" Zirpoli asked him.

"No, but I'm going to have Jeung Ying look at the picture," replied Phelan.

Phelan headed to the Mission Home and showed Jeung the black-and-white photo. She identified him as the man who had trafficked her—the same man whom Cameron and Wu had heard rumors about as a criminal tong member involved in trafficking over the years.

The team soon issued deportation warrants for Wong See Duck and seven others. The men denied knowing Jeung and retained a team of San Francisco lawyers. Meanwhile, investigators were working to piece together the details of Jeung's journey from Hong Kong to the United States. But they were struggling to find evidence linking Wong See Duck and Jeung's sale.

Their next breakthrough came in the form of a yellowed, single-page account statement from what Bank of America called its "Oriental Branch" in San Francisco. The team had searched the branch's records until it found the account of the Wing Lee Co.: on November 17, 1933—the day after a $500 down payment had been made on Jeung's sale—that same amount was deposited into Wong See Duck's business account. Although he had eleven supposed active partners in the business (in addition to thirty-three passive partners who provided only capital), none of them could account for this transaction. The only person authorized to sign checks and move funds into and out of the account was Wong See Duck.

The investigators soon began to suspect that the merchant and his syndicate of investors had successfully followed the same formula for trafficking many other women besides Jeung into the United States—hiring a procurer in China, providing coaching papers, forging identity papers, and sometimes arranging an escort to meet the women in Seattle and accompany them to San Francisco. Ultimately, they would either sell the women in San Francisco or oversee their forced prostitution themselves. Theoretically, the women could purchase their freedom from the money they saved from their earnings. But the reality was that sexually transmitted diseases, abuse, and dependence on opium or alcohol often made that impossible.

Over the years, Wong See Duck and other traffickers had generally eluded prosecution. Early in 1934, police had arrested Wong and other members of the Suey Sing tong in Oakland, although ultimately no charges were brought against him or the men. The arrests were a response to a threatened tong war, rather than prostitution or human trafficking. Cameron, Wu, and the other women of the Mission Home were keenly aware of the legal system's inability to successfully prosecute slavers. As one supporter wrote in 1921 about the rare conviction of a slave owner who received a scant one-year sentence, "In the course of the 47 years of their rescue work, the convictions have been negligible."

Yet with Jeung's testimony, the prosecutors believed they could build a strong enough case to convict Wong See Duck and his wife, who they suspected ran the racket together, and the pair of women who purchased Jeung in an apartment at 826 Jackson Street. They brought their evidence to a grand jury, which handed down indictments against eight men and women. In December 1934, twelve months after Jeung first fled to the Mission Home, the police issued arrest warrants against them. After New Year's, they were rounded up and jailed.

Wong See Duck's lawyers posted a mere $3,000 as bail for his release—about the same price as a single one of the many "slave girls" he was alleged to have bought and sold over the years. Walking out of jail, Wong See Duck's good fortune seemed to hold.

$\leadsto\!\!\Longrightarrow$ 45 $\Longleftarrow\!\!\leadsto$

Broken Blossoms

Their jury trial began on March 5, 1935, in the gray stone U.S. Court and Post Office, one of the few buildings south of Market Street to have survived the 1906 disaster. Four of the defendants had fled the country, but the ringleaders, who owned property in San Francisco and whose children attended schools in the city, remained. They hired a powerful team of lawyers, most of whom were white, to defend them. For Jeung, a new mother without any resources or family network of her own and whose only support came from the Mission Home, Wong See Duck must have been an intimidating force to confront.

Jeung wore Western-style clothes and no makeup as she rode the elevator up to the courtroom, surrounded by Cameron, Wu, and other staffers, who feared she might be snatched away at the last moment by criminal tong members. The young woman stepped into the wood-paneled courtroom to testify. She had little or no formal education and did not speak English, yet the case rested almost entirely on her as the prosecution's star witness.

The defense team subjected her to intense questioning. Surely, she must have realized that the prosecution's case rested on her performance on the stand. If she proved an unconvincing witness, he might be acquitted—putting her own life at risk, as the tong members' phalanx of lawyers seated on the defendant's side of the courtroom made clear. His lawyers were ready to pounce, and they did. After she made a

LEONG CHONG PO
.I. 17888

City of _____ San Francisco _____ (Date) _____ Oct. 14, 1932

To Officer in Charge, Port of _____ San Francisco

Sir: It being my intention to leave the United States on a temporary visit abroad, and to depart and return through the Chinese port of entry of _____ Seattle, Washington _____, I submit herewith evidence of my lawful residence within the United States and apply, under the provisions of the laws of the United States (specifically Section 7, Act approved September 13, 1888) and Rules 13 to 15 of the Regulations of the Department of Labor drawn in conformity therewith, for pre-investigation of my claimed status as a lawfully domiciled laborer. I am prepared to personally appear before you, at such time and place as you may designate, and produce the following-named witnesses to prove my statutory qualifications for this return certificate:

Name _____ Address _____

Name _____ Address _____

Description of Property or Debts (aggregating at least $1,000), or wife, child or parent resident in the United States. **wife, KUNG SHEE, living in U.S., also children living in U.S.**

I hereby agree that the above-described claims shall remain as they now exist until my return.

I am 44 years of age; my height is 5 2½ ft. in.

and my physical marks are **line scar on forehead, pit scar in front of right ear**

My address is **900 Grant Ave.**

Signature in Chinese 梁昌善

Signature in English Leong Chong Po

Subscribed and sworn to before me this 24th day

of October 1932

G. G. Heckert,
Chinese and Immigrant Inspector.

(Triplicate)

Port of _____
Seattle, Wash.
Date _____ OCT 31 1932

LEONG CHONG PO

Seattle 7032/2098

Returned to Officer in Charge, with recommendation that on the basis of the evidence submitted herewith this application _____ approved.

Approved and returned to _____

X W Lynch

Chinese and Immigration Inspector.

Officer in Charge.

Immigration records for Leong Chong Po, a.k.a. Wong See Duck, from October 1932.

seemingly small misstatement about being sold to Wong See Duck in Hong Kong, they claimed that she'd perjured all her testimony.

The young woman crumbled under the pressure. As one account described it, she grew silent under the questioning, "covering her face with trembling hands." The judge asked her if she'd like to add anything more on her own behalf. Unable to speak, she shook her head no. After deliberating for twenty-four hours, the jury of twelve concluded it was deadlocked, with ten casting a guilty vote and the other two remaining unconvinced. The holdouts, Zirpoli believed, doubted Jeung's testimony because they dismissed her as a prostitute rather than someone who'd had the courage to speak out in public after surviving the experience of being trafficked and sold into sex slavery.

The mistrial was disheartening for the women of the Mission Home. On the drive home from the courthouse, Jeung clung to Cameron, hoping to avoid news cameras and the public gaze. In a letter to the home's supporters, Wu described the experience as "beastly" and explained that "the importers and slave owners hired the best attorneys to contest the case, since they had the money." This time, Wong See Duck's lawyers had convinced the judge to block Cameron and Wu from being in the courtroom during the woman's testimony. As Wu wrote, "During the trial, Miss Cameron and I were forbidden to be present in the Court Room, lest we might give her moral support. But God gave us wisdom, and we sent in other Mission workers to the Court Room. Only God knows fully what it cost her to testify, morally and physically."

Jeung's son, David, was not yet a year old at the time his mother took the stand. The Mission Home's newsletter for March 1935, the month of the trial, noted that "920's beloved baby" had two teeth already, with more coming through. Although many ten-month-olds become cranky from teething pain, David, it seems, had not: "Even this trying experience hasn't spoiled his very good disposition!" The newsletter, understandably, did not mention the painful public humiliation that David's mother had just gone through, focusing instead on the positive.

THE PROSECUTORS PRESSED ON. Jeung told authorities that she'd met another enslaved woman at Wong See Duck's apartment: Wong

Prosecutors located a second woman, Wong
So, who agreed to testify against her traffickers.

So, a parentless girl who had worked in a firecracker factory in Macao
before coming to the United States. It turned out that the man who
had accompanied Jeung on the steamship had continued to work for
Wong See Duck in China. He convinced Wong So to come to the
United States under a false pretense, telling her she would be married,
and also gave her a thick coaching book—like the one that Jeung had
used—and spent a month in China tutoring her on the details that
would help convince immigration authorities in Seattle that she really
was the daughter of a legal Chinese American citizen.

Like Jeung, Wong So was met in Seattle by Wong See Duck, his
wife, and a young woman who was supposedly the girl's sister. Her
journey was similar, but when she arrived in San Francisco, the price
Wong See Duck sold her for was even higher than Jeung's: $5,400.
Afterward, Wong So disappeared: despite efforts by Zirpoli to locate
her in time to testify, she had apparently been hidden away by the traf-

fickers. Perhaps it was a coincidence or, more likely, a sign of Wong See Duck's confidence after his trial ended with a hung jury, but three days after the judge's decision to declare a mistrial, the prosecution's team found Wong So and arrested her in the small agricultural town of Salinas, where the plight of migrant workers would later be brought to life by the novelist John Steinbeck. At three in the morning, immigration officers brought her to the Mission Home.

The story she told investigators matched Jeung's. What's more, Wong seemed tougher and more confident as a potential witness than Jeung had turned out to be. The prosecutors realized that putting her on the witness stand could dramatically bolster their case against Wong See Duck and his alleged co-conspirators. They convinced a judge to order a second trial and called a press conference to lay out their findings. The *San Francisco Examiner* reported the development in a banner headline on its front page of April 18, 1935: "S.F. Slave Girl Names High Ups." The prosecutors claimed the ring led by Wong See Duck was smuggling more than fifty young women a year from China into the United States, selling them for $3,000 to $6,500 apiece.

The second trial began less than two weeks later. Wong So, whose dark hair was bobbed in the style of the Chinese American movie star who shared her surname, Anna May Wong, was unshakable on the witness stand. She spoke with vigor and defended her statements forcefully during cross-examination. So convincing was her testimony that the jury only needed an hour to confer before returning with their verdict. They unanimously found Wong See Duck and the three other defendants guilty. All four were jailed and deported.

BECAUSE CAMERON HAD BEEN barred from the courtroom during the retrial, she had resumed her heavy travel schedule and was in Chicago at the time of the jury's decision: staffers sent her a telegram with the good news. After reading about the guilty verdict, she might have turned to the sleeve of her well-worn Bible, which she carried with her on her frequent travels across the country. There, she had pasted a yellowed newspaper clipping of the first half of a verse written by the abolitionist Julia Ward Howe:

Such a heart I'd bear in my bosom, that, threading the crowded streets,
My face should shed joy unlooked for on every poor soul one meets;

The second half of the verse, which related more directly to the news of the guilty verdict, expresses an optimism in obtaining justice:

And such wisdom should crown my forehead, that, coming where counsels stand,
I should carry the thoughts of justice, and stablish the weal of the land.

Wu and the other staffers in the home rejoiced at the guilty verdict—hoping that the successful prosecution of the slave ring would discourage other traffickers and would encourage other captives to run away. The trial also underscored the gaping holes in the immigration service's efforts to halt the flow of immigrants entering the country using false identities. As one staffer wrote, "We feel quite limp now. We've been so tense, following the case day by day in court. There hasn't been much time to do much else."

The newspapers and true-crime magazines such as *Real Detective* and *True* magazine heralded the case as being pivotal in ending the slave trade in Chinatown. Another magazine, *Famous Detective Cases*, reported extensively on the investigation and the trial, and based its account on the perspective of one of the assistant U.S. district attorneys working on the case. The Chinese papers themselves, including *Chung Sai Yat Po*, provided daily coverage of the two back-to-back trials of a Chinatown merchant and his trafficking ring, providing daily transcripts of the court proceedings with headlines such as "Sex-Trafficking Witness . . . Is Recaptured."

It took enormous courage on the part of Jeung and Wong, as former "slave girls," to step into the witness stand and testify against people who were far more powerful than themselves. In Jeung's case, she did it twice: testifying in the first trial and experiencing a painful cross-examination, and then again, during a second. Yet despite their courage, white newspaper headline writers underscored the damage they'd experienced as women who'd been trafficked, rather than their bravery, by dubbing them "Broken" or "Trampled Blossoms."

THE PATHS OF THE WOMEN who'd been captured by the slave ring veered off in sharply different directions after the verdict. Jeung, Wong, and a third woman named Leung Louie Gin, who had also been trafficked by Wong See Duck and his associates, were all living in the Mission Home after the trials. (Leung was discovered in New York and sent to live in the home in June 1935, two months after the convictions. When she arrived, she was six months pregnant. She delivered a healthy baby girl that September and named her Alice.)

The home, which tried to keep very young babies with their mothers rather than sending them to the Ming Quong children's home, the "baby cottage" now run on a volunteer basis by Dr. Bessie Jeong, embraced its two youngest residents: Jeung's child, David, and Leung's baby, Alice. Cameron kept a black-and-white photograph of a group of nine Chinese children from the baby cottage in her Bible: David and Alice might have been among them.

"Auntie Wu," who never had children of her own, delighted in the youngest members of the household: "Now little David and Alice are our great joy and comfort at '920,'" she wrote in a newsletter to home supporters. "They are safe here—but what about their future? Poor things, [the women] are to be deported, and the poor babies, what will become of them? God certainly has given us great responsibility for these lives entrusted to us."

Because all three women had entered the country using false identity papers, they were each subject to deportation. But only Wong, the confident woman with the bobbed hair whose testimony in the second trial swayed the jury to convict, ended up being deported. She left San Francisco in September 1936 aboard the SS *President Coolidge*, the same steamer that Wu had traveled in on her journey to China four years earlier. Meanwhile, the rumblings of war between China and Japan were growing louder.

Immigration officials allowed the women with babies to remain in the United States, and both married. Leung converted to Christianity and entered into a marriage blessed by the Mission Home. Jeung's story was more unusual. Shortly after she fled to the Mission Home in 1933, the man who had accompanied her to the United States, Wing Quong Hing, returned to China. Eight years later, he returned to the United States and contacted Jeung at the Mission Home, where she was still living.

In May 1941, with Cameron's help, the couple was married in Santa Cruz, California. Jeung's new husband sorted out his immigration problems, and the couple set up their own household in San Francisco with seven-year-old David. Jeung took the name of Lois Qui Wong and gave birth to a daughter named Donna and another son, Franklin. She had used a fictitious name on the birth certificate for herself and David's father, but it is likely that David's father was the man who accompanied her to the United States and later married her.

Jeung spent the rest of her life living quietly, as a mother and homemaker. Before she died in 1999, few ever discovered her crucial role in freeing herself and fighting the slave trade. As for Cameron and Wu, the "Broken Blossoms" trial became not only the first major conviction of a slave ring operating between China and the West Coast but also a resounding validation of their life's work.

Epilogue: "Blessed Tien"

For more than four decades, Wu and Cameron called the old brick house at 920 Sacramento Street their home, living and working together amid a large community of women and children. Neither woman ever married or gave birth: the home's residents became their extended families. Cameron regularly referred to Wu and the others who came through the home as her "daughters," and, indeed, she'd become the legal guardian to hundreds of them over the years. Cameron listed "my Chinese family," including Tien Fuh Wu, in the back of her Bible. Many of the home's residents, in turn, called her Mama, Mother, or Lo Mo for the rest of her long life. For years, her "daughters" sent her letters, gifts, and Mother's Day cards.

Cameron reached her employer's mandatory retirement age of sixty-five in 1934, amid the Broken Blossoms trials. For several years after that, she remained attached to the home as special director of Chinese casework. In one instance, Cameron became alarmed by what she considered the Sacramento district attorney's mishandling of a case involving a teenager who alleged she'd been raped and impregnated by her former Chinese School teacher. After the Sacramento court dismissed her case, Cameron was asked by the girl's widowed and illiterate mother to advocate for her fifteen-year-old.

When Cameron failed in her effort to convince California's attorney general to take up the case, she and Wu made several train trips to Sacramento on behalf of the girl to negotiate with the Chinese elders representing the thirty-four-year-old teacher accused of rape. The girl

Donaldina Cameron and Tien Fuh Wu with an unidentified woman between them on the steps of the Mission Home.

was a member of a powerful tong family, as was the teacher, resulting in rising tensions between the two tongs over the allegations.

One evening in April 1937, about a month after the girl gave birth to a baby boy with a healthy thatch of black hair, Cameron and Wu walked a few blocks to Waverly Place in San Francisco to appear before the Chinese Peace Association, an organization established by the tongs two decades earlier to settle disputes within the wider Chinese American community. Their goal: to avert violence and achieve justice for the young mother and her newborn.

Cameron had received an alarming handwritten letter before the meeting from someone describing himself as a "neutral" member of the Chinese community warning her that "guns will begin to fire" unless she backed off. The newspapers, too, reported that tong gunmen were on alert, awaiting the outcome of the talks. Cameron and Wu stood before the group of Chinese men that night, using their joint knowledge of Chinese culture and Cameron's diplomacy to try to avert a tong war over the case.

Understanding the threat of statewide violence in this dispute, Cameron typed out her remarks to the Chinese leaders, handwriting her last-minute corrections and additions, and read them to the gathering of Chinese leaders, as Wu translated her words:

> Surely no man of the Chinese race could repudiate his own baby boy, and I rejoice   that your [clan] member has proved himself to be a true man by accepting responsibility for this little baby boy whom he has brought into the world.
>
> I have lived among the Chinese people for forty two years. You are MY PEOPLE and I have deep respect and sincere affection for you my friends, so I hope that you will trust me in this case and unite with me to bring both families into a truly happy agreement.

With Wu and Cameron's intervention, the Chinese Peace Association reached a settlement that night and averted a tong war, demonstrating that Cameron not only understood and respected the culture of Chinese Americans but, in this instance, successfully navigated her way through it with her Chinese colleague's help. Cameron was widely credited for her successful efforts to bring about peace in the Chinese

American community. "Praise was on every side for a very kind and influential American lady, one who has always championed the cause of justice and befriended those who are oppressed, a Miss Cameron," concluded an investigation into the State of California's case against the teacher. "She heard of the case of Lily and the shameful treatment [sic] it was handled in court and has taken up the girl's cause to obtain justice for her."

HAVING KNOWN AND WORKED closely with Wu for decades, Cameron had absolute faith in her Chinese aide, who she hoped would become her successor as superintendent of the home. (Higgins had been promoted to director of the Ming Quong Home in Oakland in 1930.) But Wu demurred, explaining that she did not feel qualified to take on the role and preferred to continue working alongside her lifelong friend Cameron, who was then taking on special cases. As Wu wrote to Edna Voss, her supervisor in New York, she had three reasons for turning down the job:

> First, owing to the fact that I am Chinese, which sometimes causes prejudice. . . . Secondly, I feel most inadequate for the position as I have not sufficient education to meet present demands. . . . Thirdly, I have been working with Miss Cameron for almost thirty years and trying to help the unfortunate class of Chinese women and girls, although, in my inmost heart, I have always longed to help the children. Yet, God seemed to choose me for this other class when so few seemed to care for them. Miss Cameron has not many more years left to work with me. If I should direct affairs in the Home, I could not do the outside work with her. Only a few more years or even less I [would] rather finish this task with her.

She thanked Voss for the "great privilege" of being offered the job and reiterated her belief "that an American person should be head of this work."

Voss replied to Wu a week later that her letter was "one of the sweetest I have had for a long time and just the kind I would have expected from you, self-effacing, humble, with no thought whatever except the Christian cause to your people . . . our confidence in you is unbounded and that we are sure that had you felt you could accept the leadership at '920' you would have made a success at it."

Not long afterward, a young white woman, Lorna Logan, accepted the job as superintendent. By then, Cameron's reputation for fearless daring had been burnished by a local writer named Carol Green Wilson. Stanford University Press had published Wilson's biography of Cameron, *Chinatown Quest,* in 1931. With the days of rooftop rescues long gone, Logan's primary role was to ease the transition of the Mission Home toward providing education and social services to Chinese immigrants.

Cameron's successor did not have a warm relationship with Wu like the one Cameron enjoyed. She described what she considered Wu's shortcomings, including her need to "rebuke and advise everyone who comes near her [that] drives everyone away," in a confidential report to her supervisors in New York. Initially Logan also spoke very little Chinese, so she, too, was forced to rely on Wu and other Chinese speakers' help to do her job. But after a year's sabbatical in Hong Kong to study Cantonese, she returned with enough language skills to counsel Chinese speakers.

Cameron's principal regret, as she told her successor not long after Logan took over the job, was that she'd never learned to speak or read Chinese herself, lacking the time and the natural ability for languages. She had requested time off to study Chinese, which her supervisors did not grant her. (Cameron couldn't carry a tune while singing hymns, and so it was not surprising that she was unable to acquire a tonal language like Cantonese.) She wrote to her successor, "It is almost a tragedy that neither of my Boards, nor I, fully comprehended the vital importance of acquiring the language, and a better knowledge of the people, through residence in their own country."

By the late 1930s, Cameron had moved out of the home and was caring for her elderly sisters and sister-in-law. To honor her, the Presbyterians renamed it the Donaldina Cameron House in 1942, although Cameron objected to having the home named after her. By 1951, Wu had retired too. Cameron settled in a tidy home in Palo Alto, where rosebushes graced the front garden and photographs of her far-flung friends and "daughters" filled her living room. She invited Wu to join her and arranged for her to live in a small cottage next door. They entertained visitors with tea and cake, "Auntie Wu" pouring for Cameron as her hands grew shaky.

"Auntie Wu" adopted Cameron's many nieces and nephews as her own. She brought them Chinese food on their birthdays, presented them with ivory chopsticks as gifts, and made sure to arrange window seats for them to see the annual New Year's parade in Chinatown. Cameron's family remembers her fondly as being as warm and loving as their aunt Dolly was stern and forbidding in her old age. After Cameron died on January 4, 1968, at her home at the age of ninety-eight, ministers conducted her memorial service in both Chinese and English.

Cameron left the little cottage to Wu, which provided her with financial security before she died in 1975. In one of the oldest cemeteries in Los Angeles, where Cameron's father, mother, and siblings are all buried, Cameron and Wu were also laid to rest.

I MADE THE JOURNEY to Evergreen Cemetery in East Los Angeles a few years ago to visit Cameron's and Wu's graves and pay my respects. Evergreen, which was established in 1877, just three years after the Mission Home, like most other cemeteries in California, barred Chinese from being buried there until well into the twentieth century, instead relegating their remains to a nearby potter's field.

That small detail—that a woman from a Scottish American family and her Chinese friend and colleague were buried together in the same family plot—had lingered with me. I thought about the life journeys that each of these very different women had taken. One started in New Zealand and the other in China, but they ended up interred close to each other in one of the city's oldest graveyards, their plain markers surrounded by dying grass and bare earth.

After five years researching their lives, I remain fascinated by how these two immigrants from distant continents leaped barriers of race, class, and culture to unite in a shared mission: to offer refuge for vulnerable women. Was it a coincidence that both Cameron and Wu were themselves motherless when they first met in the mid-1890s? Was it a surprise that they both chose to forgo the traditional path of matrimony and homemaking and instead devoted themselves to running and providing a safe home to other women? Perhaps it was their shared faith. Or, it might have been that running the home together offered a better opportunity for them to take charge of their lives than being wives might have done.

As I worked on this book, a few people asked me whether I thought Cameron and Wu were lovers. It's impossible to know because Wu's private correspondence disappeared after her death, as did much of Cameron's. The most telling indication of what their relationship was came from a letter I found written by Cameron in 1941, shortly before she moved to Palo Alto, describing how she felt about the long-time colleague and friend she called "Blessed Tien":

> It is going to be VERY hard for me to move further away from my beloved Chinese people; but they are wonderful about seeking me, so I trust they will find their way even to Palo Alto if we are able to move there . . . no daughter could be more faithful and devoted, she is a great solace to my heart since I left San Francisco, and the community where I had lived so long.

There is no doubt that Wu, in turn, was deeply devoted to her adopted mother. On January 4, 1968, then in her early eighties, Wu peered through her wire-rimmed spectacles to read passages from the Bible as her oldest and dearest friend lay dying. Cameron might not have been conscious that her most devoted Chinese "daughter" was beside her. Yet it was "Blessed Tien," the former slave girl, who bore witness to the final breath of 白魔鬼, the woman once known as the White Devil of Chinatown.

Acknowledgments

Over the five years that I worked on this book, I met many times with the Cameron House archivist, Doreen Der-McLeod, the former executive director of the home, to review materials related to the "Broken Blossoms" case and other files. More than a decade ago, Ms. Der-McLeod organized Cameron House's historical files, which have remained largely closed to the public for more than a century to protect the confidentiality of former residents and their families. Over tea and many Chinese lunches, I had the privilege of getting to know Doreen, and I am deeply grateful to her for her generosity in sharing her time and offering guidance on these papers, as well as for making many introductions.

I should also note that Doreen and Cameron House Board President the Reverend Gregory L. Chan led the courageous effort to publicly acknowledge sexual abuse allegations against the Reverend F. S. Dick Wichman, who led Cameron House's youth ministries from the late 1940s until his retirement in 1977. Wichman denied the charges and resigned before Presbyterian authorities could bring them against him; statute-of-limitations provisions prevented the San Francisco District Attorney's Office from prosecuting him. About fifteen years ago, Der-McLeod helped lead a reconciliation and healing process for the Cameron House community, acknowledging the truth of the allegations of abuse and offering a public apology to the survivors in June 2004. Wichman died three years later.

Judy Yung, professor emerita of history at UC Santa Cruz, kindly shared material from her decades of groundbreaking work into Chinese American women's history with me. I am also deeply grateful to Professor Yung and to the late Chinese American historians Him Mark Lai and Philip P. Choy. Him Mark Lai's immense collection housed at UC Berkeley's Ethnic Studies Library, in particular, was helpful, as was his taped interview with Tien Fuh Wu, which I believe was the last interview she ever gave before her death.

I was helped by many librarians and archivists around the world and wish to offer my deepest gratitude to Sine Hwang Jensen, the Asian American studies librarian at UC Berkeley's Ethnic Studies Library, who kindly allowed me and my research intern Chung Hoon "Jeremy" Rhee from Brown University to examine the unprocessed papers donated by Tye Schulze's family. Likewise, I am grateful to Tim Noakes and Everardo Rodriguez at Stanford University's Department of Special Collections for their help in plowing through the sizable Mildred Martin Papers, as well as the staff at the Hoover Institution at Stanford. In the Special Collections of the Yale Divinity School Library, I appreciate all the help provided by Martha Smalley, Joan Duffy, and Kevin Crawford. Thank you to UCLA Special Collections librarian Molly Haigh for her help. At the San Francisco Public Library's Daniel E. Koshland San Francisco History Center, I am particularly indebted to Thomas Carey, the city archivist Susan Goldstein, and "history detective" Christina Moretta.

The magnificent Bancroft Library at UC Berkeley holds a special place in my heart. I spent many happy hours in its stately Heller Reading Room poring over its massive Chinese in California collection. I am grateful to Theresa Salazar, the curator for its Western Americana collection, as well as the Bancroft's director, Elaine Tennant, its deputy director, Peter Hanff, and its curator of pictorial collections, Jack von Euw. The independent historian Roland Hui, whom I first met at the Bancroft, offered help with key Chinese American translations, as did Patrick Chew, and I appreciate the historical perspective offered by my fellow Bancroft Library Council of Friends members David Lei and Bruce Quan. Through David Lei, I was fortunate to meet the scholar Dr. Jeffrey L. Staley, who answered countless questions from me about Methodist missionaries in Chinatown and generously shared primary materials with me. I am grateful for his help. The staff of the San Francisco Theological Seminary's branch librarian, Stephanie Miller, was most helpful, as was her predecessor, Mary Moore.

In search of Cameron's Scottish roots, I visited the Highland Archive Centre in Inverness and was assisted by Jan McDonald, Fiona Mackenzie, and Debbie Potter. Accompanying me to Inverness was Carole Clarkson, my beloved and intrepid aunt, who did all of the driving and kept her good spirits throughout. I wish I could also have traced Wu's Chinese ancestral home, but because she herself, to her great sorrow, was unable to locate any members of her family on her trip back to China in 1916, I did not attempt to try so many years later. Rebecca Jennison at Kyoto Seika University kindly reviewed my characterization of Yamada Waka for accuracy. Robert S. Wells, a retired navy captain and historian, kindly shared materials on Margaret Culbertson with me.

I've been fortunate to receive generous support for this project from the National Endowment for the Humanities, which provided me with a Public Scholar Fellowship for 2016–2017, and from the Carey Institute for Global Good in Rensselaerville, New York, as a member of its fall 2017 class of Logan Nonfiction Fellows. Thank you to the program heads, Tom Jennings and Carly Willsie, and especially to the Carey Institute's vice chairman, Josh Friedman, whom I first met through Columbia University's Graduate School of Journalism and who encouraged me to apply. I was also the 2017–2018 Mayborn Fellow in Biography. I am particularly grateful to the biographer James McGrath Morris for his astute comments on my manuscript and for his and his wife Patty's generous hospitality in New Mexico.

Special thanks go to my friend Dr. Dora Wang, also a resident of New Mexico, who brought her deep sensitivity as a reader and her kindness and compassion as a psychiatrist to reading the manuscript and offering me comments, as well as her boundless hospitality. For more than a decade, I have had the privilege of being a member of a San Francisco writers' group, North 24th Writers, which has profoundly shaped this book. My gratitude is endless for these brilliant women: Allison Hoover Bartlett, Leslie Berlin, Jeanne Carstensen, Leslie Crawford, Frances Dinkelspiel, Katherine Ellison, Sharon Epel, Susan Freinkel, Dr. Katherine Neilan, Lisa Wallgren Okuhn, Gabrielle Selz, and Jill Storey. The Berlin/Dodd family kindly shared their home with me while I was working in Stanford's Special Collections. Likewise, my friends Marjorie Sun and Cora Yang generously read later versions of the manuscript and offered their wise suggestions. Catherine Thorpe, who worked with me on my two previous books, also brought her sharp intelligence to this one, for which I'm grateful. The poet Rebecca Foust offered her inspiration and solidarity. Liz Epstein, founder of Literary Masters and my treasured, decades-long friend, offered her thoughts on the idea for this book in its earliest stages, and I thank her with all my heart.

My editor at Knopf, Ann Close, was a delight to work with from start to finish. I'm deeply grateful for having had the opportunity to bring this book to life with her. Her assistant, Todd Portnowitz, helped wrangle the historical photos from archives all over the country as well as taking on many other tasks behind the scenes. With grace and good humor, Gabrielle Brooks embraced the challenge of helping this book find its audience. Michael Carlisle, my longtime literary agent at Inkwell Management, played a crucial role in shaping the proposal and finding it a wonderful home with Alfred A. Knopf. My friend Constance Hale also kindly helped me with the proposal. Most of all, I could not have undertaken this project without the love and support of my family—literally, this project was a family affair. My siblings and their spouses, Jennifer and Sandy Israel and Greg and Julie Flynn, were unflagging sources of moral support and cheer. My husband of three decades, Charlie Siler, read and edited many drafts of the manuscript and even videotaped events at Cameron House that I could not attend. Charles Cody Siler transcribed the often hard-to-understand decades-old audiotapes from the Mildred Martin Papers. Andrew J. Siler accompanied me to Stanford to work in the archives.

With my deepest love and gratitude, I dedicate this book to Charlie, Cody, and Andrew.

Cast of Characters

DONALDINA CAMERON Longtime superintendent of the Mission Home, born to a Scottish American family. The home's residents called her Lo Mo, or "Old Mother," while her enemies called her *Fahn Quai*, Foreign Devil, or *Bái Móguǐ*, White Devil.

NG POON CHEW An immigrant, he became the first Chinese graduate of the San Francisco Theological Seminary but quickly realized he could have more impact as a newspaper editor. He married a former Mission Home resident, Chun Fah.

MARGARET CULBERTSON The Mission Home's superintendent before Cameron. She brought order to the home when she arrived to take over in the 1870s and hired Cameron as a sewing teacher.

ROBERT DOLLAR Known by the honorific "Captain Dollar," he owned a steamship line that operated between China and the United States and became a major benefactor of the Mission Home.

ARNOLD GENTHE A German immigrant who settled in San Francisco and taught himself photography. He befriended Cameron and residents of the Mission Home and documented Chinatown with his camera.

ETHEL HIGGINS A New Englander who became one of Cameron's assistants shortly after the Panama-Pacific International Exposition of 1915. She worked alongside Cameron and Wu for years.

DR. BESSIE JEONG The first Chinese woman to graduate from Stanford University, she fled to the home at age fifteen when her father tried to force her to marry.

JEUNG GWAI YING A teen who escaped her owners and made her way to the Mission Home. She twice testified against her captors in a lengthy trial that resulted in the conviction of a major criminal ring.

LITTLE PETE The nickname for the criminal tong leader Fung Jing Toy, who was a skilled trafficker of Chinese women to the United States, using world's fairs and other events as a cover. He lived in San Francisco's Chinatown.

JACK MANION An Irish American inspector appointed to the San Francisco Police Department's Chinatown Squad in 1921 who became an ally of Cameron's in her fight against the criminal tongs that controlled trafficking and prostitution in San Francisco.

FREMONT OLDER A crusading journalist and editor of *The Bulletin* who exposed the white-owned "municipal crib" in Chinatown and widespread municipal corruption, leading to the city's graft trials after the 1906 earthquake.

PAULINE FOWLER ROBBINS Also known as Mrs. E. V. Robbins, she was a forceful early supporter of the Mission Home who was spat in the face and suffered other indignities in her efforts to find it a home and then stabilize it.

ABRAHAM RUEF A French Jewish attorney who offered legal advice to the Mission Home early in his career. He later became the corrupt mayor's chief bagman.

EUGENE SCHMITZ Nicknamed Handsome Gene, he was San Francisco's mayor during the earthquake, convicted of extortion during the graft trials that followed, and ended up in San Quentin prison. He was widely considered Ruef's puppet.

TYE "TINY" SCHULZE A former resident of the home who went on to fame as one of the first Chinese American women to cast a vote in America. She worked at the immigration station at Angel Island as a translator and defied the era's antimiscegenation laws by marrying a white colleague.

WONG SO A former sex slave who testified in the second of the "Broken Blossoms" trials.

WONG SEE DUCK A Chinatown merchant at the center of the "Broken Blossoms" case who for years had helped smuggle in women from China to San Francisco.

TIEN FUH WU A former *mui tsai,* or household slave, who came to the Mission Home as a child, she joined the effort to free other women from slavery and other forms of oppression.

AH TOY The most famous Chinese prostitute and madam in nineteenth-century San Francisco, who frequently took to the courts seeking justice.

YAMADA WAKA A Japanese woman forced into prostitution who originally worked in Seattle, made her way to San Francisco, and found refuge at the Mission Home before returning to Japan.

Timeline

1865   Congress passes the Thirteenth Amendment, formally
        abolishing slavery in the United States.

1869   Donaldina Cameron is born in New Zealand on July 26 to
        a Scottish family.

1871   Eighteen Chinese men are killed by a mob in Los Angeles.
        Fifteen of them were lynched.

1872   Cameron, accompanied by her mother and five of her six
        siblings, arrives in San Francisco on Christmas Eve aboard
        a steamer from New Zealand.

1873   A group of women form the California Branch of the Woman's
        Foreign Missionary Society.

1874   The Occidental Board rents a small apartment as a house of
        refuge for Chinese women.

1874   Cameron's mother dies when Cameron is five years old and
        living on a sheep ranch in the San Joaquin valley.

1875   Congress passes the Page Act, prohibiting Asian prostitutes
        and forced laborers from entering the country.

1875   A tong war in San Francisco's Chinatown erupts over "Golden
        Peach," a Chinese prostitute. That same year, San Francisco's
        board of supervisors passes a "queue" ordinance requiring every
        Chinese prisoner in jail to have hair clipped within an inch of
        the scalp.

1876   *Chy Lung v. Freeman,* U.S. Supreme Court case known as the case of "22 Lewd Chinese Women."

1876   Congressional committee conducts month-long investigation of Chinese prostitution in San Francisco. Police abuses committed by "specials" come to light, and legislators abolish special officer beats in Chinatown.

1876   Amid violence in the streets of Chinatown, the Chinese Six Companies appeal to the board of supervisors for protection.

1877   "Sandlot" riots in San Francisco as mobs clash with police and wreak havoc in Chinatown.

1878   Ah Fah marries Ng Noy at the Mission Home.

1882   First Chinese Exclusion Act passed by U.S. Congress, prohibiting Chinese laborers from entering the country and prohibiting naturalization of Chinese immigrants.

1882   Attorney Abe Ruef begins handling cases for the Mission.

1884   Cameron and her family move to La Puente, where her father, Allan, is hired to manage the sheep operation on Lucky Baldwin's ranch.

1888   Cameron becomes engaged to George Sargent.

1892   Ng Poon Chew graduates from the San Francisco Theological Seminary and marries a former resident of the Mission Home, Chun Fah.

1892   Congress passes the Geary Act, requiring all Chinese to register and carry photo identifications, a law opposed by the Six Companies.

1894   The Mission Home moves to its newly built building at 920 Sacramento Street.

1894   Tien Fuh Wu rescued as a *mui tsai,* or household slave, and brought to live at 920 Sacramento Street.

1895   Five sticks of dynamite are found at the Mission Home.

1895   Donaldina Cameron arrives at the Mission Home at 920 Sacramento Street in San Francisco to teach sewing. Margaret Culbertson is then superintendent.

1895 Sergeant Jesse Cook assigned to head the Chinatown Squad.

1897 Assassination of Fong Ching, a.k.a. Little Pete.

1897 Margaret Culbertson dies. Mary H. Field becomes superintendent, and Cameron suffers a nervous breakdown.

1899 Late this year, Donaldina Cameron is appointed superintendent of the Mission Home.

1900 Bubonic plague scare in San Francisco; Chinatown is quarantined.

1900 Cameron is jailed overnight in Palo Alto, followed by protests and a legal battle.

1900 The *San Francisco Examiner* begins its graft investigation of Chinatown, alleging the police took bribes to overlook vice. Fremont Older is the editor in charge of the paper.

1901 Fisk Commission inquiry, led by California state legislator Arthur Fisk, begins hearings prompted by the *San Francisco Examiner*'s investigation into Chinatown graft.

1903 The president is expected to visit the Mission Home. Cameron writes to California's governor, George Pardee.

1905 Japanese children in California ordered to attend segregated schools.

1905 Andrew Carnegie and his wife visit the Mission Home and make a donation.

1906 On April 18, the day planned for the Mission Home's annual meeting, a powerful earthquake shakes San Francisco. Fires rage across the city. Cameron leads her charges to safety.

1906 San Francisco's mayor, Eugene Schmitz, and Abe Ruef are indicted following the "French restaurant" scandal.

1907 Abe Ruef flees and is captured. SFPD police chief also indicted.

1907 Abe Ruef pleads guilty to an extortion charge; less than a month later, Schmitz is found guilty.

1908 Cameron and the Mission Home residents move from Oakland back into newly rebuilt 920 Sacramento Street.

1910   Angel Island Immigration Station opens.

1911   Wu returns from college in the East to the Mission Home and joins the staff. Around this same time, Cameron's brother, Allan, dies.

1912   Women vote for the first time in San Francisco.

1913   Statewide Red Light Abatement and Injunction Act takes effect.

1913   California state law aimed at Asians bars aliens from owning land.

1915   Panama-Pacific International Exposition opens in San Francisco.

1918   Great flu epidemic.

1920   Cameron marks twenty-five years at Mission Home. Wu and the residents plan a celebration.

1921   Jack Manion assigned to Chinatown Squad of SFPD amid a statewide tong war.

1923   The Reverend Charles Shepherd publishes his novel about a Chinese girl sold into slavery, *The Ways of Ah Sin*.

1932   Wu accompanies eight deportees to China for six-month stay. Lives with Dr. Mary Stone/Shi Meiyu in Canton.

1933   Groundbreaking ceremony for construction of the Golden Gate Bridge.

1933   Prohibition (Eighteenth Amendment) repealed.

1933   Jeung Gwai Ying flees from beauty parlor to Mission Home, setting off the "Broken Blossoms" case.

1935   Trial begins in "Broken Blossoms" case. Deadlocked jury.

1935   Second trial begins in "Broken Blossoms" case, with additional testimony from a trafficked woman, Wong So.

1952   Wu retires. Cameron gives her the cottage adjoining her own home in Palo Alto.

1968   Cameron dies, with Wu by her side.

1975   Wu dies.

A Note on Names and Language

In the Chinese system of naming, the family name precedes the given name. Jeung Gwai Ying's family name is Jeung, and her given names are Gwai Ying. In this book, I have used surnames for all adult characters and given names when characters are children. Because Jeung was an eighteen-year-old when she first appears in the book, I refer to her by her last name. When I introduce Cameron for the first time as a toddler arriving aboard a steamship in San Francisco, I refer to her as Donaldina, or her nickname Dolly, in part to distinguish her from other members of the Cameron family. In adulthood, I refer to her as Cameron, though she was generally referred to with the honorific "Miss Cameron" at the time.

Tien Fuh Wu, who was smuggled to the United States as a child, has an unusual name. Her surname was probably Wu, and in China she would have been known as Wu Tien Fuh, but because she spent most of her childhood in San Francisco, her name on official documents became Americanized, with the surname placed at the end. I refer to her as a child as Tien, a word that in the Wade-Giles Romanization of the Chinese refers to heaven or sky, and then as an adult as Wu. The Reverend Ng Poon Chew is another example of a name that became Americanized. While his given surname was Ng, he and others called him the Reverend Chew or Dr. Chew as an adult. For this reason, I call him Chew throughout the book.

The Japanese writer who came to be known as Yamada Waka posed a different set of problems. Yamada was the surname of the man she married in San Francisco, but during most of the period when she lived in the United States, she was known by various names, including Asaba Waka and Arabian Oyae. I've chosen to call her by her married surname Yamada, following the example of her biographer Tomoko Yamazaki.

One final note on language: the title of this book refers to the term that Cameron's enemies used to call her at the time—*Fahn Quai*. In colloquial Cantonese, *Fahn* means foreign or white, and *Quai* means ghost, monster, demon, or devil, so the phrase can be translated variously as "Foreign Ghost" or "White Devil." It was a sensational epithet that headline writers in the early twentieth century seized upon and helped spread. Donaldina Cameron worked for decades in a world where racism was endemic. This term reflects that. There is no doubt she was a target of racial hatred as a white woman who waged a fight against slavery in Chinatown for decades. Yet, at the same time, the Chinese press in San Francisco, representing the community rather than the criminal tongs, referred to Cameron respectfully in its coverage as 女師, or "female teacher."

Some scholars, in turn, have rightly noted that the language Cameron used in her reports to her supervisors and supporters was patronizing or demeaning toward the home's residents. There is no doubt it was, as was so much of the language used by social service agencies toward young women and girls at the time.

But in Cameron's private writings about Wu, it is clear to me that she held her Chinese colleague in the highest esteem and knew she couldn't have done her job without her. Indeed, what makes her and Wu's relationship so fascinating is that they both overcame the widely held prejudices of their time to fight slavery and other forms of oppression side by side.

A Note on Sources

I was privileged to visit many great archives, libraries, and private collections to research this book. The National Archives and Records Administration in San Bruno, California, has a rich repository of court files and transcripts of Immigration and Naturalization Service interviews on the "Broken Blossoms" case. I located and examined these files, which total hundreds of pages of mostly single-spaced notes on the case. I also examined immigration files on Wong See Duck, Jeung Gwai Ying, Donaldina Cameron, Tien Fuh Wu, and others, as well as the partnership investigation case file for the Wing Lee Co.

Cameron wrote annual reports describing her work at the house for four decades. The reports from 1874 to 1919 are housed at the San Francisco Theological Seminary, and reports from 1920 to 1940 are housed at the Presbyterian Historical Society's archives in Philadelphia. Cameron kept personal diaries, but only fragments of these remain from much of 1909 and the first three weeks in January 1921. Some of her papers and letters are archived at Cameron House's archives in San Francisco, and there is additional material on her and Wu at the Presbyterian Office of History in Philadelphia. Although letters between Cameron and Wu exist in the Cameron House files as well as the Presbyterian Historical Society, they were primarily related to cases and generally were not personal.

The Cameron family kindly provided me with its family papers, which included some materials from Donaldina, including her Bible dating from 1904, some personal letters and photographs, and the portions of her diary from 1921. I am grateful, in particular, to Cameron's grandnieces, Ann F. Cameron and Catherine M. Cameron, a professor of anthropology at the University of Colorado, Boulder, who dedicated her recent book, *Captives: How Stolen People Changed the World,* to her childhood "aunt," Tien Fuh Wu. Both women generously shared their memories of "Auntie Wu" and their great-aunt Dolly with me and read portions of the manuscript concerning the Cameron family history. Despite my efforts to locate any papers Wu might have left after her death in 1975, I was unsuccessful. It is possible that both women, to protect their privacy, decided to destroy any private papers before their deaths.

The biographer Mildred Crowl Martin interviewed Cameron late in her life and made recordings of those interviews, which I and my research assistants transcribed. These recordings reveal very distinct voices of Cameron and Wu, which are somewhat muffled in Ms. Martin's biography, *Chinatown's Angry Angel.* The author donated these tapes as well as a large cache of the research materials and correspondence related to Cameron to Stanford University. After I reviewed these papers, it became clear that her book was authorized, edited, and financially supported by the Presbyterian Church and Ms. Martin did not look at her subject as critically as one might have liked. But she was able to interview a number of women who worked with or passed through Cameron House before they died, and so, in this respect, the collection she left to Stanford is an invaluable resource. The sixteen audiotapes of interviews with Cameron, Wu, and others are a particularly rich resource, offering insight into the characters in their own words.

Likewise, I transcribed what appear to be long-forgotten audiotapes of interviews done by the independent scholar Sarah Refo Mason in the course of her research into missionaries. Housed at the Yale Divinity School, her interviews with Cameron and Wu's colleague Lorna Logan were particularly helpful in offering insight into their working relationship. That said, none of Cameron's biographers focused on the partnership between Cameron and her longtime aide and friend, Wu, with the exception of the late scholar Peggy Pascoe. I am indebted to Pascoe's meticulous scholarship in her book, *Relations of Rescue,* and her various articles, in detailing the often-complex relationships between missionaries and so-called native helpers.

There are other key sources that offer insights into Cameron and Wu's friendship and working relationship as well as detailing the many challenges they faced together. Many of their letters are located at Cameron House, and the biographical files from the Presbyterian Historical Society on both Cameron and Wu provide additional primary source material on these two women.

In contrast to the lack of information about so many of the residents of the Mission Home, there is a rich record of the life of Wu, including a biographical file with an untitled manuscript from 1934 that contains her childhood memories and some of her most poignant reminiscences of working at the home, including her witnessing Cameron's breakdown at the deathbed of her first Chinese interpreter. Perhaps even more so than Cameron, she told her own story of being rescued as a child slave many times over the years as a way to drum up support for the home's work. Her letters to Cameron reveal her sly sense of humor, according to Doreen Der-McLeod, who has read many of them. Because very few Chinese slaves left behind personal accounts of any sort, Wu's writings are extraordinarily rich material.

The Hoover Institution at Stanford's Survey of Race Relations contains material on the Chinatown police inspector Manion as well as notable first-person accounts of some of the Chinese American immigrants who passed through what is now known as Cameron House. In addition to material contained in archives and libraries, I had the opportunity to interview a number of people who personally knew Cameron and Wu. They include Cameron's extended family members and former board members and staffers of Cameron House, including the son and the grandson of Kwang Lim Kwong, the Chinese consul in San Francisco. My thanks and friendship to the late Robert Kwong, Cameron's godson, who gave his only son the name Joseph Cameron Kwong, in honor of the friend they still refer to as Miss Cameron.

Notes

Organizations and Abbreviations

The women's organization that came to be known as the Occidental Board existed under several different names over its long history. For most years from 1874 through 1920, it published annual reports, variously under the auspices of the Woman's Foreign Missionary Society, California Branch, Occidental Board, and Occidental Branch. After 1920, supervision of the Mission Home moved to a national board, based out of New York. In general, I refer to these reports as coming from the Occidental Board of Foreign Missions of the Presbyterian Church.

Repositories

Bancroft Library	University of California at Berkeley, California
Cameron House Files	Case files, records, and photographs of Cameron House, San Francisco, California
Ethnic Studies Library	University of California at Berkeley, California
Hoover Institution Archives	Stanford University, Palo Alto, California
NARA	National Archives and Research Administration, San Bruno, Seattle, and Washington, D.C., branches
PHS	Presbyterian Historical Society, National Archives of the Presbyterian Church (USA), Philadelphia, Pennsylvania
SFTS	San Francisco Theological Seminary, San Anselmo, California
Stanford	Special Collections of Stanford University Libraries, Palo Alto, California
SFPL	Daniel E. Koshland San Francisco History Center of the San Francisco Public Library, San Francisco, California
University of Oregon	Special Collections and University Archives, University of Oregon, Eugene, Oregon

Yale Divinity Library   Special Collections of Yale University Divinity School Library, New Haven, Connecticut

Preface

xi **thousands of mostly Chinese girls:** Donaldina Cameron is often credited with aiding as many as three thousand women from the time she began working at the Mission Home in 1895 until her retirement in 1934. The home has case files and other forms of documentation for nearly two thousand women who passed through over its entire history (it opened in 1874), though some files cover more than one person, according to Doreen Der-McLeod, the retired executive director of Cameron House who organized its records. Because many of these files cover more than one person (particularly in instances where babies were born or children accompanied their mothers), an estimate of the total number of residents is between twenty-one hundred and three thousand.

Prologue

3 **It was nearly dusk:** This narrative account of Jeung Gwai Ying's escape to the Mission Home is based on case files housed in the National Archives and Records Administration's San Bruno and Seattle offices, as well as Cameron House files. NARA holds the files for the U.S. District Court's Criminal Cases 25293, 25294, and 25295, *U.S. v. Wong See Duck,* as well as various Deportation Investigation Case Files and Immigration Arrival Investigation Case Files. The portrait of the surrounding neighborhood of Chinatown in the early 1930s is drawn from photographs of Jackson Street and other parts of Chinatown from the San Francisco History Center at the San Francisco Public Library and contemporaneous accounts of Chinatown during that period. Laundry still hangs into the evening hours from the metal balconies of buildings that haven't changed much since the 1930s.

3 **Jeung's journey to the United States:** Statement of Applicant (Lee Lon Ying a.k.a. Jeung Ying) Taken at Presbyterian Mission Home, March 6, 1934, National Archives and Records Administration. Jeung states she was born on February 17, 1915, so she would have been eighteen years old at the time she landed in Seattle and, five months later, in December 1933, when she fled from the beauty parlor to the Mission Home.

5 **"a very dark place":** Ibid. Jeung stated that Wong See Duck told her, "If you don't go, either you or I would die, for I have spent so much money on you. You would have to go live in a very dark place." See also the transcript of testimony dated March 13, 1934, from the U.S. Department of Labor Immigration and Naturalization Service, Case 12016/5916, NARA.

7 **They led Jeung to an adjoining parlor:** Carol Green Wilson, *Chinatown Quest: One Hundred Years of Donaldina Cameron House, 1874–1974,* rev. ed. (San Francisco: California Historical Society, 1974), 181.

7 *tell us your story:* Details of Jeung Gwai Ying's arrival at the home in December 1933 are drawn from several biographies of Donaldina Cameron, including the earliest by Carol Green Wilson, *Chinatown Quest,* which was first published before this incident occurred and then reissued in 1950 and again in 1974, as well

as many contemporaneous newspaper and magazine articles. The most helpful secondary source on what became known as the "Broken Blossoms" trial is by Edward Wong, former executive director of the Angel Island Immigration Station Foundation, in his article "Broken Blossoms: A Struggle from Servitude to Freedom," *Prologue* (Spring 2016).

1. Queen's Room

8   **On February 23, 1869:** Malcolm E. Barker, ed., *More San Francisco Memoirs, 1852–1899: The Ripening Years* (San Francisco: Londonborn, 1996), 208–10.

8   **"the united strength":** Kevin J. Mullen, *Chinatown Squad* (Novato, Calif.: Noir, 2008), 33.

8   **later advertised for sale:** *Daily Alta California*, April 22, 1869, 3. Opium was not illegal in the United States at that time, but it was subject to duty, so smugglers would try to bring it into the country without paying those taxes on it.

8   **brothels, which operated openly:** San Francisco's brothels were allowed to operate openly until 1917, when California's 1913 Red Light Abatement and Injunction law took effect, according to Yong Chen, *Chinese San Francisco, 1850–1943: A Trans-Pacific Community* (Stanford, Calif.: Stanford University Press, 2000), 76.

10   **drawn by job opportunities:** Iris Chang, *The Chinese in America: A Narrative History* (New York: Viking, 2003), 66.

10   **largest city west of the Mississippi:** Philip J. Ethington, *Public City: The Political Construction of Urban Life in San Francisco, 1850–1900* (Berkeley: University of California Press, 2001), 2.

10   *dai fou*, **or "big city":** Chen, *Chinese San Francisco*, 2.

10   **most Chinese men joined a** *huiguan:* Scott Zesch, *The Chinatown War: Chinese Los Angeles and the Massacre of 1871* (New York: Oxford University Press, 2012), 36–38.

11   **men without women or children:** Judy Yung, *Unbound Feet: A Social History of Chinese Women in San Francisco* (Berkeley: University of California Press, 1995), 18.

11   **census workers tallied:** Lucie Cheng Hirata, "Free, Indentured, Enslaved: Chinese Prostitutes in Nineteenth-Century America," *Signs* 5, no. 1 (1979): 24.

12   **They could buy a girl from Canton:** Otis Gibson, *The Chinese in America* (Cincinnati: Hitchcock & Walden, 1877), 136.

12   **the term "involuntary servitude":** Andrés Reséndez, *The Other Slavery: The Uncovered Story of Indian Enslavement in America* (Boston: Houghton Mifflin Harcourt, 2016), 301.

12   **the scope of the Thirteenth Amendment:** Ibid., 304–5.

12   **the Six Companies:** There are numerous accounts in the press of the Six Companies' efforts to halt the trafficking of women in the 1860s, including "The Imported Chinese Females in Court on Habeas Corpus," *Daily Alta California*, June 28, 1868.

13   **the business thrived:** Jacqueline Baker Barnhart, *The Fair but Frail: Prostitution in San Francisco, 1849–1900* (Reno: University of Nevada Press, 1986), 48–50.

13   **auctions of Chinese women:** Chang, *Chinese in America*, 83; Barnhart, *Fair but Frail*, 47.

13   **the Queen's Room:** Gibson, *Chinese in America*, 138.

13   **"The girls and women were critically examined":** Ibid.

13   **Potential buyers would closely:** The most detailed description of what took place at these auctions comes from the Reverend Otis Gibson, who expressed disgust at the practice but did not state specifically what happened during the examinations. During this same time in Great Britain, however, widespread medical examinations of women believed to be prostitutes were taking place and are detailed in a biography of Josephine Butler, the Victorian-era women's rights campaigner. See Helen Mathers, *Patron Saint of Prostitutes: Josephine Butler and a Victorian Scandal* (Stroud, U.K.: History Press, 2014).

13   **The men saw a group of Chinese women:** This description of Chinese prostitutes descending from a steamship in San Francisco comes from Albert S. Evans, *À la California: Sketches of Life in the Golden State* (San Francisco: A. L. Bancroft, 1873), 319, as cited in Barker's *More San Francisco Memoirs*.

14   **"new story of slavery":** "The Late Celestial Arrivals," *Daily Examiner,* Oct. 22, 1869, 1.

14   **"loathsome in the extreme":** Herbert Asbury, *The Barbary Coast: An Informal History of the San Francisco Underworld* (New York: Basic Books, 2002), 182–83, citing *San Francisco Chronicle* article of Dec. 5, 1869.

14   **in 1870 passed a law:** John Soennichsen, *The Chinese Exclusion Act of 1882* (Santa Barbara, Calif.: Greenwood, 2011), 61.

2. "The Cussedest Place for Women"

16   **"elevate and save the souls":** Gibson, *Chinese in America,* 203.

18   **She was baptized:** Ibid., 204–5.

18   **published by Gibson:** Although Gibson had worked in China for a decade, he spoke Cantonese at that time so poorly he must have relied on a translator to help him understand and then write down Sing Kum's story. The scholar Dr. Jeffrey L. Staley believes Gibson taught himself the Cantonese dialect in later years. For more details on Gibson, see Mae Ngai, *The Lucky Ones: One Family and the Extraordinary Invention of Chinese America* (Princeton, N.J.: Princeton University Press, 2012), 61.

18   **"I thank God":** Gibson, *Chinese in America,* 220.

18   **The steamer arrived:** "Arrival of the Nebraska," *Daily Alta California,* Dec. 25, 1872.

19   **The younger Cameron children:** One of the Camerons' fellow passengers was William Greer Harrison, an Irish-born thirty-six-year-old who would become famous during his lifetime as a member of San Francisco's Bohemian Club, formed earlier that same year by journalists, artists, and musicians. Harrison was one of the first presidents of the city's Olympic Club, which was devoted to sports. He first met Dolly aboard the *Nebraska* and, as family legend had it, held the toddler in his arms aboard ship.

19   **The *Nebraska* was uncomfortable:** Just a week after the Camerons' ship left Port Chalmers, the Webb line, the struggling mail venture undertaken by the New Zealand government that owned the steamer, sold off most of its stake in the business, which included the *Nebraska,* the *Nevada,* and a third sister ship, the *Dakota.*

20   **Construction in San Francisco:** Ben Tarnoff, *The Bohemians: Mark Twain and the San Francisco Writers Who Reinvented American Literature* (New York: Penguin Press, 2014), 160–61.

20 **"practically blinded the eye"**: "Christmas Goods," *Daily Examiner,* Oct. 22, 1869, 1.

21 **the hotel had slashed its prices**: Barker, *More San Francisco Memoirs,* 221.

21 **"a town of men and taverns"**: Ibid., 178. Excerpted from Samuel Bowles, *Our New West,* published in 1869.

21 **"I realized then"**: Donaldina Cameron, taped interview by Mildred Martin, 1967, Mildred Martin Papers, M0780, Department of Special Collections and University Archives, Stanford University Libraries.

22 **more than twelve thousand Chinese people**: U.S. Census Office, *A Compendium of the Ninth Census, 1870* (Washington, D.C.: Government Printing Office, 1872), 29.

22 **the death rate**: 1872–1873 Municipal Report for the city of San Francisco, SFPL.

22 **"free white labor"**: Frederick H. Hackett, *The Industries of San Francisco: Her Rank, Resources, Advantages, Trade, Commerce & Manufactures; Conditions of the Past, Present, and Future, Representative Industrial Institutions, Historical, Descriptive, and Statistical* (San Francisco: Payot, Upham, 1884).

3. Reveille Cry

23 **"Our hearts too are cheered"**: The Reverend Ira Condit to the Reverend John C. Lowrie, June 13, 1873, Condit Family Papers, Presbyterian Historical Society (hereafter cited as PHS).

23 **to teach himself Cantonese**: Annual Report of the American Bible Society (1871), 778. Gibson spoke a northern Chinese dialect and, as of 1871, was unable to speak Cantonese. But according to the scholar Dr. Jeffrey L. Staley, Gibson did eventually become fluent in Cantonese as well.

23 **Gibson rose to prominence**: Elizabeth Lee Abbott, *Inward Fire: Chinese, Scottish, American Origins, Legends, and Truths of the Early Chinese American Christian Experience* (San Francisco: Moy's Daughter, 2012), 296–97.

25 **"Chinese women are brought here"**: "Chinaman or White Man, Which? Reply to Father Buchard," 14, accessed Sept. 25, 2014, www.oac.cdlib.org.

25 **By March 25, 1873**: Mrs. I. M. Condit, "The Occidental Board: An Historic Sketch," *Woman's Occidental Board of Foreign Missions* (1893): 8.

25 **The skies were clear**: U.S. Army Signal Corps, *Daily Bulletin of Simultaneous Weather Reports, Signal Service, United States Army, with the Synopses, Indications, and Facts* (1875).

25 **paths and palms**: Gregory J. Nuno, *Union Square: A History and a Redesign* (University of California, Department of Landscape Architecture, 1985). "A History of Union Square," *Argonaut* 4, no. 1 (Summer 1993), 24.

25 **a meeting at the Calvary Presbyterian Church**: "Woman's Missionary Society," *Daily Alta California,* March 26, 1873.

26 **a missionary named Emily Gulick**: Maria Jaschok and Suzanne Miers, *Women and Chinese Patriarchy: Submission, Servitude, and Escape* (London: Zed Books, 1994), 10–13.

26 **"silently stole away"**: Mrs. I. M. Condit, *A Quarter of a Century* (pamphlet printed to accompany the board's 25th Annual Report, 1898), 5.

26 **a popular poem:** Robert L. Gale, *A Henry Wadsworth Longfellow Companion* (Westport, Conn.: Greenwood Press, 2003), 59–60. The last two lines of the poem are "Shall fold their tents, like the Arabs, / And as silently steal away."

26 **the Woman's Foreign Missionary Society:** "Woman's Missionary Society," *Daily Alta California,* March 26, 1873.

27 **sprouted up throughout America:** Peggy Pascoe, *Relations of Rescue: The Search for Female Moral Authority in the American West, 1874–1939* (New York: Oxford University Press, 1990), 5.

27 **"heathen Chinee":** Bret Harte, *That Heathen Chinee, and Other Poems Mostly Humorous* (London: J. C. Hotten, 1871), 15–18.

27 **Defying convention, Condit:** *Presbyterian Magazine,* 1920, 137.

27 **"The bitterness not shown":** The Reverend Ira Condit to the Reverend John C. Lowrie, June 13, 1873, Condit Family Papers.

27 **"So Christianity gathered":** Gibson, *Chinese in America,* 200–201.

27 **an article in the influential California magazine:** A. W. Loomis, "Chinese Women in America," *Overland Monthly,* April 14, 1869, 344–51.

27 **She moved to the city:** Abbott, *Inward Fire,* 307.

28 **Cole reported to Gibson:** Gibson, *Chinese in America,* 201–2.

28 **Samantha Condit, Emily Gulick, and Caroline Cole met:** Condit, *Quarter of a Century,* 5.

28 **It was an offshoot:** Pauline Fowler Robbins, "The Occidental Board of Foreign Missions of the Presbyterian Church, 1873–1911," 1912, PHS. The women met again on April 14, 1873, this time at San Francisco's First Presbyterian Church, according to a 1920 organizational history of the Occidental Board.

28 **passed the motion:** Condit, *Quarter of a Century,* 8.

28 **"A *Home* is the reveille cry":** Woman's Foreign Missionary Society of the Presbyterian Church (Presbyterian Church in the U.S.A.) et al., *Annual Report of the Occidental Branch of the Woman's Foreign Missionary Society of the Presbyterian Church* (San Francisco: C. W. Gordon, 1874), 7.

29 **"woman's work for women":** Pascoe, *Relations of Rescue,* 5–7.

4. "No Ordinary Person"

30 **"woman always holding":** Jeremy Agnew, *Alcohol and Opium in the Old West: Use, Abuse, and Influence* (Jefferson, N.C.: McFarland, 2013), 87.

30 **one of the few Chinese women:** Charles P. Duane, "Pioneer Days," *Daily Examiner,* Jan. 23, 1881. Also see Curt Gentry, *The Madams of San Francisco: An Irreverent History of the City by the Golden Gate* (Garden City, N.Y.: Doubleday, 1964), 58–59.

32 **"to gaze upon the countenance":** JoAnn Levy, *They Saw the Elephant: Women in the California Gold Rush* (Norman: University of Oklahoma Press, 2013), 167. There are numerous accounts of this, including Mullen, *Chinatown Squad,* 29.

32 **The judge ruled against her:** Duane, "Pioneer Days."

32 **"every body knew that famous":** Frank Soulé, John H. Gihon, and Jim Nisbet, *The Annals of San Francisco: Containing a Summary of the History of . . . California, and a Complete History of . . . Its Great City: To Which Are Added, Biographical Memoirs of Some Prominent Citizens* (New York: D. Appleton, 1855), 384.

32 **"Atoy" had "immigrated":** "Law Courts," *Daily Alta California,* March 8, 1851.

32 **"blooming with youth"**: "Law Courts," *Daily Alta California,* Dec. 14, 1851.

33 **"Miss Atoy appeared to be"**: Ibid.

33 **Ah Toy recovered her pin**: "City Intelligence," *Daily Alta California,* Dec. 16, 1851.

33 **By one tally**: "Local Matters," *Daily Alta California,* Aug. 15, 1852.

33 **she attempted suicide**: "Tag-Rag and Bob-Tail," *Sacramento Daily Union,* Nov. 19, 1855. This newspaper reported in 1855 that the "celebrated Chinese courtezan [*sic*] tried to destroy her own life on Thursday night, in San Francisco, by swallowing poison."

33 **"the most indecent"**: Soulé, Gihon, and Nisbet, *Annals of San Francisco,* 384.

33 **later renamed Grant Avenue**: Philip Choy, *San Francisco Chinatown: A Guide to Its History and Architecture* (San Francisco: City Lights, 2012), 109.

33 **Eventually, she became**: Gentry, *Madams of San Francisco,* 61.

34 **She joined eighteen other women**: Chen, *Chinese San Francisco,* 79, 290–91.

34 **The census for 1870**: Like the vast majority of nineteenth-century Chinese immigrants to the United States, Ah Toy left no diaries or letters describing her experience. But because she proved an irresistible subject to the city's many journalists, Ah Toy's life commanded attention in a way that few other lives of Chinese women had.

34 **two-sentence newspaper item**: "San Jose Items," *Daily Alta California,* Oct. 14, 1871.

34 **she lived a long life**: "San Jose Buries China Mary," *San Francisco Examiner,* Feb. 2, 1928.

34 **Allan used to tease Isabella**: Catherine M. Cameron, "Cameron Family Background," Nov. 28, 2014, 3.

34 **a wealthy man**: 1861 Scotland Census, www.ancestry.com.

34 **A financial crisis struck**: Kenneth N. Cameron, "Cameron Family History," Concord, Calif., June 12, 1985, 2.

35 **Allan boarded a schooner**: Wilson, *Chinatown Quest,* 3.

35 **"There weren't any roaming dangers"**: Remembrance from Caroline Bailey, box 8, folder 2, Martin Papers.

35 **To make the hours pass**: Author's transcription of Donaldina Cameron, interview by Martin, 1967, series 8, audiovisual materials, Martin Papers.

36 **rode back to his family**: Cameron, "Cameron Family History," 4.

36 **selling his remaining sheep**: Author's transcript of Caroline Bailey and Allan Cameron, interview by Mildred Martin, Sept. 23, 1971, Martin Papers.

36 **her mother's choice of a husband**: Cameron, "Cameron Family History," 3.

36 **Isabella died suddenly**: *Sacramento Daily Union,* May 27, 1874, 2.

37 **"I loved her"**: Box 4, folder 14, Martin Papers.

37 **all events are determined**: Pre-determinism is the belief that a supreme being has determined all events and outcomes in the universe. Thanks to the Reverend Barbara Rowe for clarifying this.

5. Victorian Compromise

38 **"I will give nothing"**: Condit, *Quarter of a Century,* 9.

38 **laws banning Chinese immigrants**: "Chinese: Immigration: Legislative Harassment," Library of Congress, www.loc.gov. See also Chen, *Chinese San Francisco.*

40   **a writ of habeas corpus:** Suchong Chan, "The Exclusion of Chinese Women, 1874–1943," Him Mark Lai Research Files, Chinese American History—Exclusion, 1882–1943, carton 22/7, Ethnic Studies Library, University of California, Berkeley.

41   **One early supporter:** A Presbyterian who would later join the Baha'i faith, Phoebe Hearst contributed to a wide variety of philanthropic causes involving women and children in the 1870s and 1880s. But her initial support of the Chinese Mission Home ended as Hearst's interests turned elsewhere, most notably to founding the Golden Gate Kindergarten Association.

41   **Phoebe Apperson Hearst:** Robbins, "Occidental Board of Foreign Missions of the Presbyterian Church," 8.

41   **a Presbyterian Sunday school:** Judith Robinson, *The Hearsts: An American Dynasty* (Newark: University of Delaware Press, 1991), 73.

41   **a group of like-minded women:** This was the case for Pauline Fowler Robbins, whose husband's financial misfortunes led them to move to the Bay Area, where they could rebuild their lives. She details this in Robbins, "Occidental Board of Foreign Missions of the Presbyterian Church," 3–7.

41   **Often, the donations:** Woman's Foreign Missionary Society of the Presbyterian Church (Presbyterian Church in the U.S.A.) et al., "Treasurer's Report," *Annual Report* (1878), 23.

41   **The many comings and goings:** Robbins, "Occidental Board of Foreign Missions of the Presbyterian Church," 24.

42   **"said many insulting things":** Ibid., 25.

42   **"You had to go up":** "Their New Home," *San Francisco Call,* May 12, 1893.

42   **that block of Sacramento Street:** Ibid.

42   **"by a mob":** Robbins, from an earlier handwritten draft of her history of the Occidental Board, Mrs. E. V. Robbins, "Our Forty Years, 1873–1913," San Francisco Theological Seminary Archive (hereafter cited as SFTS).

42   **the term "hoodlums":** Kevin J. Mullen, *Dangerous Strangers: Minority Newcomers and Criminal Violence in the Urban West, 1850–2000* (New York: Palgrave Macmillan, 2005), 53.

42   **Like the Chinese, the Irish:** Mrs. W. H. Hamilton, "Historical Sketch of the Occidental Board for First Seven Years," n.d., 10–11, SFTS, as cited in Pascoe, *Relations of Rescue,* 15.

42   **As tensions rose:** Robbins, "Occidental Board of Foreign Missions of the Presbyterian Church," 26.

43   **"I can't stand this!":** Ibid., 27.

43   **"They were unhappy":** Robbins, "Our Forty Years."

43   **"They had attempted":** Robbins, "Our Forty Years," "Occidental Board of Foreign Missions of the Presbyterian Church," 13–14.

43   **referred to Caucasians:** Peter Ward Fay, *The Opium War, 1840–1842* (Chapel Hill: University of North Carolina Press, 1997), 31.

43   **"exhausted nerves":** Robbins, "Our Forty Years."

44   **accused them of wasting time:** Robbins, "Occidental Board of Foreign Missions of the Presbyterian Church," 27.

44   **"Does it not seem marvelous":** Report of Mrs. Condit, *Woman's Work for Woman: A Union Magazine* (1879), 121–22, PHS.

44   **politicians balked:** Condit, *Quarter of a Century,* 9.

44 Victorian Compromise: Mullen, *Chinatown Squad,* 31.

45 these naive do-gooders: Chen, *Chinese San Francisco,* 76.

6. Inked Thumbprints

46 "Ah Ho distinctly agrees": Creed Haymond, *Chinese Immigration: Its Social, Moral, and Political Effect* (Sacramento, Calif.: F. P. Thompson, 1878), 63, as cited in Yung, *Unbound Feet,* 27 and elsewhere.

46 their thumbprints: California Legislature, Senate Special Committee on Chinese Immigration, and Creed Haymond, *Chinese Immigration: The Social, Moral, and Political Effect of Chinese Immigration: Testimony Taken Before a Committee of the Senate of the State of California, Appointed April 3d, 1876* (Sacramento, Calif.: State Printing Office, 1876), 27.

46 "In the sale of these girls": Ira Miller Condit, *The Chinaman as We See Him, and Fifty Years of Work for Him* (Chicago: F. H. Revell, 1900), 154.

48 "The women, as a general thing": Testimony Taken Before the Senate Committee of Rev. Otis Gibson, California Legislature, Senate Special Committee on Chinese Immigration, and Haymond, *Chinese Immigration,* 98.

48 Wong told the court: Ibid., 99–102.

48 In 1875, a "tong war": Eng Ying Gong and Bruce Grant, *Tong War! The First Complete History of the Tongs in America; Details of the Tong Wars and Their Causes; Lives of Famous Hatchetmen and Gunmen; and Inside Information as to the Workings of the Tongs, Their Aims and Achievements* (New York: Nicholas L. Brown, 1930), 14–23.

48 four tong members died: Mullen, *Chinatown Squad,* 78–79.

49 "Quite a number of Chinese": Gibson, *Chinese in America,* 315–23, as cited in *Chinese American Voices: From the Gold Rush to the Present,* ed. Judy Yung, Gordon H. Chang, and Him Mark Lai (Berkeley: University of California Press, 2006), 21.

49 the continuing economic downturn: John Bruce, *Gaudy Century: The Story of San Francisco's Hundred Years of Robust Journalism* (New York: Random House, 1948), 162–69.

51 "they were Jesus people": Cameron House Files, logbook, 10, Jan. 20, 1876.

51 "future housekeeping": Peggy Pascoe, "Gender Systems in Conflict: Marriages of Mission-Educated Chinese American Women," *Journal of Social History* 22, no. 4 (Summer 1989), doi.org/10.2307/3787541, citing M. H. F., "A Christian Chinese Wedding," *Occident,* May 1, 1878, 6.

51 the resolute Mary Ann Browne: Mary Ann Browne was better known by her married name, Mrs. P. D. Browne, and that is how she is identified in the reports of the Woman's Occidental Board of Foreign Missions.

51 When Culbertson first arrived: Robbins, "Occidental Board of Foreign Missions of the Presbyterian Church," 23–24.

51 A daily schedule: Pascoe, *Relations of Rescue,* 81.

52 hanging by a rope: "A Chinese Suicide," *Daily Alta California,* Nov. 18, 1889.

52 the wife of Judge George Barstow: Woman's Foreign Missionary Society of the Presbyterian Church (Presbyterian Church in the U.S.A.) et al., *Annual Report* (1919), 10.

52   **regular courtroom appearances:** Lately Thomas, *A Debonair Scoundrel: An Episode in the Moral History of San Francisco* (New York: Holt, Rinehart and Winston, 1962), 8.

52   **In a typical case, Ruef:** "The Chinese Slave Girl," *Daily Alta California,* Feb. 9, 1889.

7. The Celestial Quarter

55   **One such visitor:** Hodges was involved in a project called the Twenty Minutes' Society, a group that provided holiday gift boxes for domestic missionary schools. *Churchman* (Churchman Company, 1885), 612.

55   **braided with red silk:** [Ellen G. Hodges], *Surprise Land: A Girl's Letters from the West* (Boston: Cupples, Upham, 1887), 76.

55   **"After spending about twenty minutes":** Ibid., 78.

55   **Hodges was told that on different floors:** Ibid., 79–80.

55   **one of the opium dens:** "Opium Dens in Chinatown," *FoundSF,* accessed Sept. 19, 2017, www.foundsf.org.

56   **this time she was captivated:** [Hodges], *Surprise Land,* 84–85.

56   **"I have given as much time":** Ibid., 94–95.

57   **"There is much difficulty":** Ibid., 97.

57   **"We merely peered in":** Ibid., 99. Hodges was apparently moved enough by what she'd seen in Chinatown to make a large donation to the Woman's Occidental Board of Foreign Missions, the group that oversaw the Mission Home and the school. In the group's annual report from 1897, a Miss S. E. Hodges is listed as an honorary life member of the organization, a designation honoring those who had contributed at least $100 (some $2,800 in today's dollars) to its coffers.

58   **Against this backdrop, Hodges:** [Hodges], *Surprise Land,* 97–99.

58   **"scrupulously clean":** Woman's Foreign Missionary Society of the Presbyterian Church (Presbyterian Church in the U.S.A.), et al., *Annual Report* (1906–1907), 65.

58   **At the Oakland railroad station:** Margaret Belle Culbertson, "Diary of Margaret Belle Culbertson McNair" (1887), 14, Cameron House Archives.

58   **Some stalls specialized:** Charles Caldwell Dobie, *San Francisco's Chinatown* (New York: D. Appleton–Century, 1936), 260–61.

59   **To boost male potency:** Lisa See, *On Gold Mountain: The 100-Year Odyssey of a Chinese-American Family* (New York: St. Martin's Press, 1995), 11.

59   **shunned at the city's hospitals:** Guenter B. Risse, "Translating Western Modernity: The First Chinese Hospital in America," *Bulletin of the History of Medicine* 85, no. 3 (2011): 416, doi.org/10.1353/bhm.2011.0066.

59   **the smells of the waking neighborhood:** This might well have been the stables of Joseph Tape, who lived in a wood-framed cottage off Washington Street and near the Mission Home in the late 1880s. Ngai, *Lucky Ones,* 58–59.

59   **This exotic blend of aromas:** "Chinese in California Collection, circa 1851–1963," *Cornhill Magazine,* 1886, BANC MSS 2011/112, Bancroft Library, University of California. This description of Chinatown in 1895 is drawn from a number of sources, including nineteenth-century photographs of Chinatown from the San Francisco Historical Photograph Collection of the San Francisco Public Library, tourist brochures and magazine articles from the late nineteenth century, and Ellen G. Hodges's letters describing her visits to the quarter.

59 **service at the Congregational church:** Culbertson, "Diary of Margaret Belle Culbertson McNair," 15.

59 **transported to China:** Ibid., 15–16.

60 **Belle didn't seem frightened:** Ibid., 78.

60 **"Are You Ready?":** Ibid., 35.

60 **She'd sometimes chaperone couples:** Ibid., 34.

60 **Belle would shop for cakes:** Ibid., 26.

61 **For good luck:** Ibid., 27.

61 **Chinese men, accompanied by sheriffs and lawyers:** Ibid., 21.

61 **she refused to yield:** Ibid., 36.

8. "To Have a Little Chinaman"

62 **Through foreclosures:** Frances Dinkelspiel, *Towers of Gold: How One Jewish Immigrant Named Isaias Hellman Created California* (New York: St. Martin's Griffin, 2010), 91–92; Sandra Lee Snider, *Elias Jackson "Lucky" Baldwin: California Visionary* (Los Angeles: Dennis Landman, 1998), 8–9.

62 **"By gad! This is Paradise":** Carl Burgess Glasscock, *Lucky Baldwin: The Story of an Unconventional Success* (Indianapolis: Bobbs-Merrill, 1933), 176.

62 **When Cameron became too ill:** Cameron, "Cameron Family History," 3.

62 **Baldwin provided a comfortable home:** Ibid., 4.

62 **"Annie, Dolly & myself":** Allan Cameron to Jessie Cameron Bailey, Jessie Cameron Bailey Letters, 1884–1929, folder 1, March 5, 1884, Maui Historical Society.

64 **The senior Cameron:** Glasscock, *Lucky Baldwin*, 230–33.

64 **"He ruined me":** Ibid., 223.

64 **slowed down by his precarious health:** Allan Cameron, Jessie Cameron Bailey Letters, 1884–1929, folder 1.

64 **"all seeing eye":** Ibid.

65 **"I think it's a shame":** Mildred Crowl Martin, *Chinatown's Angry Angel: The Story of Donaldina Cameron* (Palo Alto, Calif.: Pacific Books, 1986), 31–32, citing Donaldina Cameron to Jessie Cameron Bailey, June 15, 1888.

65 **her sister Jessie, a teacher:** Jessie Cameron Bailey Letters, 1884–1929. Jessie taught at the Mauna'olu Seminary on Maui, and many of the letters in this collection are from her former students.

65 **"to have a little chinaman":** Martin, *Chinatown's Angry Angel*, 31; Donaldina Cameron to Jessie Cameron Bailey, June 15, 1888.

66 **one story titled "John":** Chen, *Chinese San Francisco*, 124.

66 **"You ask his mistress":** Charles Nordhoff, *California for Travellers and Settlers* (Berkeley, Calif.: Ten Speed Press, 1992), 85.

66 **Hearst spent part of his childhood:** Robinson, *Hearsts*, 76.

66 **George Hearst, who had:** Ben H. Procter, *William Randolph Hearst: The Early Years, 1863–1910* (New York: Oxford University Press, 1998), 16–17; Robinson, *Hearsts*, 113.

66 **"neat and smart":** Procter, *William Randolph Hearst*, 53.

67 **mapped every single building:** "Mapping Vice in San Francisco," *Mapping the Nation* (blog), accessed Sept. 21, 2015, www.mappingthenation.com.

67 **one in seven Chinese women:** Chinese Historical Society of America, *The Life, Influence, and the Role of the Chinese in the United States, 1776–1960: Proceedings,*

Papers of the National Conference Held at the University of San Francisco, July 10, 11, 12, 1975 (San Francisco: Society, 1976), 75–82.

67 **some 150 gambling dens:** Willard B. Farwell, *The Chinese at Home and Abroad, Together with the Report of the Special Committee of the Board of Supervisors of San Francisco on the Condition of the Chinese Quarter of That City* (San Francisco: A. L. Bancroft, 1885), 35.

67 **twenty-six opium "resorts":** Ibid., 27.

67 **"Descend into the basement":** Willard B. Farwell and John E. Kunkler, *Chinese in San Francisco* ([San Francisco: Published by order of the Board of Supervisors], 1885), 180.

68 **concerns about diseases:** Farwell, *Chinese at Home and Abroad,* 105–9.

68 **"if this evil of Chinese immigration":** Ibid., 111.

9. Baiting the Hook

70 **Ng Poon Chew had just become a teen:** Hyung-chan Kim, *Distinguished Asian Americans: A Biographical Dictionary* (Westport, Conn.: Greenwood Press, 1999), 56.

70 **an uncle had immigrated to the United States:** Him Mark Lai, "Summary of Interview of Mansie Chew (Daughter of Ng Poon Chew) by Ira Lee and Him Mark Lai," July 27, 1973, 1, AAS ARC 2010/1, carton 90, Him Mark Lai Research Files, Ethnic Studies Library.

70 **In addition to working on a ranch:** Condit, *Chinaman as We See Him,* 134.

70 **Sometimes torchlight parades:** Jean Pfaelzer, *Driven Out: The Forgotten War Against Chinese Americans* (Berkeley: University of California Press, 2008), 253.

72 **blow up Chinese laundries:** Ibid., 270.

72 **the wealthy Spreckelses:** "The Spreckels Vessel," *Daily Alta California,* Aug. 11, 1886.

72 **"We don't cut hair":** J. H. Laughlin, "What America Has Meant to One Immigrant," *Continent,* Jan. 28, 1915, 108.

72 **Not all of Chew's encounters:** Barbara L. Voss, "'Every Element of Womanhood with Which to Make Life a Curse or Blessing': Missionary Women's Accounts of Chinese American Women's Lives in Nineteenth-Century Pre-exclusion California," *Journal of Asian American Studies* 21, no. 1 (2018): 111.

72 **he absorbed both:** *Church at Home and Abroad* (Presbyterian Church in the U.S.A., 1916), 46.

72 **Traumatized by what happened:** "Ng Poon Chew," accessed Sept. 9, 2015, www .inn-california.com. This same anecdote was provided to me by the library of the San Francisco Theological Seminary, in a file compiled by the librarian Michael Peterson.

72 **From 1871 to 1885:** Joyce Kuo, "Excluded, Segregated, and Forgotten: A Historical View of the Discrimination of Chinese Americans in Public Schools," *Asian American Law Journal* 5 (Jan. 1998): 193, scholarship.law.berkeley.edu. In 1880, California passed a law that entitled all children in the state to public education, but San Francisco ignored it, according to Ngai, *Lucky Ones,* 49.

72 **a lawsuit in 1885:** For a fuller explanation of the case and the Tape family, see Ngai, *Lucky Ones,* 48–57.

72 **Her lawyer was William F. Gibson:** Charles J. McClain, *In Search of Equality: The Chinese Struggle Against Discrimination in Nineteenth-Century America* (Berkeley: University of California Press, 1994), 138–39.

72 **a separate school for Chinese:** Jonathan H. X. Lee, *Chinese Americans: The History and Culture of a People* (Santa Barbara, Calif.: ABC-CLIO, 2015), xxii.

72 **In its *Tape v. Hurley* decision:** Ngai, *Lucky Ones,* 142.

73 **white hoodlums stoned the house:** Pascoe, *Relations of Rescue,* 128.

73 **in a single house on Sullivan's Alley:** Farwell, *Chinese at Home and Abroad,* 9.

73 **"We have shown":** Farwell and Kunkler, *Chinese in San Francisco,* 204.

74 **"Desire to learn the English language":** Kuo, "Excluded, Segregated, and Forgotten," 194, citing Donald Nakanishi and Tina Yamano, *The Asian American Educational Experience: A Sourcebook for Teachers and Students* (New York: Routledge, 2014), 6.

74 **the seminary's first Chinese graduate:** Robert B. Coote and John S. Hadsell, *San Francisco Theological Seminary: The Shaping of a Western School of the Church, 1871–1998* (San Anselmo, Calif.: First Presbyterian Church, 1999), 158.

74 **"to do their countryman honor":** "Ng Poon Chew Ordained," *San Francisco Call,* Oct. 3, 1892.

74 **a plum assignment:** Condit, *Chinaman as We See Him,* 134.

75 **the gender ratio:** Pascoe, "Gender Systems in Conflict," 635.

75 **a charity formed in 1876:** "San Francisco History—Child-Saving Charities," accessed Sept. 10, 2015, www.sfgenealogy.org.

75 **"Well do we remember her":** Condit, *Chinaman as We See Him,* 141–42.

75 **In a standard ploy:** Jaschok and Miers, *Women and Chinese Patriarchy,* 211.

76 **The altar was festooned:** P. F. Robbins, *Occident,* May 18, 1892, 11.

76 **The Reverend Condit presided:** Jaschok and Miers, *Women and Chinese Patriarchy,* 212.

76 **"In this young Christian maiden":** Woman's Foreign Missionary Society of the Presbyterian Church (Presbyterian Church in the U.S.A.) et al., *Annual Report* (1892), 53–54.

76 **By 1901, in its annual report:** Pascoe, "Gender Systems in Conflict," 635.

77 **named their first child Mansie:** Lai, "Summary of Interview of Mansie Chew (Daughter of Ng Poon Chew) by Ira Lee and Him Mark Lai," 2.

77 **a formal photograph:** Kenneth H. Marcus and Yong Chen, "Inside and Outside Chinatown: Chinese Elites in Exclusion Era California," *Pacific Historical Review* 80, no. 3 (Aug. 2011): 388–89.

77 **"I feel so sad":** *Church at Home and Abroad,* 46.

77 **The church soon pulled its support:** "Ng Poon Chew: Chinese Statesman and Journalist," n.d., SFTS.

77 **offers of financial support:** Corinne K. Hoexter, *From Canton to California: The Epic of Chinese Immigration* (New York: Four Winds Press, 1977), 163–65.

77 **"The departure to San Francisco":** Arthur Judson Brown, diary of 1901–1902, n.d., 22–23, RG 02, box 11, Arthur Judson Brown Papers, Yale Divinity Library.

78 **One of Chew's daughters later recalled:** Lai, "Summary of Interview of Mansie Chew (Daughter of Ng Poon Chew) by Ira Lee and Him Mark Lai," 1.

78 **"I found the field too narrow":** "A Maker of New China," *Sunset,* May 1912.

78 **the Chinese-Western Daily:** "Rev. Ng Poon Chew Will Start a Daily Paper in San Francisco," *Los Angeles Herald,* Dec. 29, 1899.

78 **a leading advocate:** Chen, *Chinese San Francisco,* 3.

10. Life as a *Mui Tsai*

79 **The passage of the Chinese Exclusion Act:** Chang, *Chinese in America,* 144.

81 **He'd also learned to speak English:** Richard H. Dillon, *The Hatchet Men: The Story of the Tong Wars in San Francisco's Chinatown* (New York: Coward-McCann, 1962), 305.

81 **Some of his ploys included:** Hirata, "Free, Indentured, Enslaved," 12, citing Dillon, *Hatchet Men,* 319–21.

81 **Little Pete was put in charge:** "Little Pete in Control," *San Francisco Call,* Oct. 14, 1893.

81 **"How a Chinese Combine":** "Came to the Fair," *San Francisco Call,* June 6, 1894; also see "Cunning Little Pete," *San Francisco Call,* Dec. 24, 1895.

82 **poor families selling girls:** Jaschok and Miers, *Women and Chinese Patriarchy,* 11–12.

82 **within a patriarch's rights:** Ibid., 18.

82 **the law was relatively toothless:** Ibid., 175. This law was Article 313 of the Penal Code of 1928.

82 **For decades afterward:** Mary Backus Rankin, *Elite Activism and Political Transformation in China: Zhejiang Province, 1865–1911* (Stanford, Calif.: Stanford University Press, 1986), 54–60.

82 **close to a thousand years:** Gerry Mackie, "Ending Footbinding and Infibulation: A Convention Account," *American Sociological Review* 61, no. 6 (Dec. 1, 1996): 999–1000, doi.org/10.2307/2096305.

82 **throughout the nineteenth century:** Ibid., 1001.

82 **Tien's feet were bound:** Tien Fuh Wu, taped interview by Mildred Martin, 1969, Martin Papers.

83 **"Don't cry, Mother":** Victor Nee and Brett de Bary Nee, *Longtime Californ': A Documentary Study of an American Chinatown* (New York: Pantheon Books, 1973), 84. The Nees' story of "Lilac Chen," a pseudonym, was Tien Fuh Wu's story, according to Lorna Logan in letter to Mildred Martin in the early 1970s. Box 7, folder 12, Martin Papers. The Nees' account conveys the same information, in almost exactly the same words, as many of Tien Wu's own accounts in taped interviews.

83 **Tien began to kick and shout:** Tien Fuh Wu, interview by Him Mark Lai, n.d., Him Mark Lai Collection, box 26, folder 5, Ethnic Studies Library.

83 **Until the end of her life:** Tien Fuh Wu's employment records from the Presbyterian Church state her year of birth as 1886, which would have made her six or seven around the time of her sale.

83 **Because the strips used to bind feet:** Louisa Lim, "Painful Memories for China's Footbinding Survivors," NPR.org, accessed Nov. 2, 2015, www.npr.org.

83 **expand back to normal:** Tien Fuh Wu, taped interview by Martin, 1969, cassette box 20, audiocassette 1, Martin Papers.

83 **Tien's most lasting memory:** Nee and Nee, *Longtime Californ',* 85.

84 **deeds of sale:** "Establishing and Maintaining a Family in the Shadow of Chi-

nese Exclusion: A Case Study of the Fong Family of Santa Barbara County, California," World History in Context, 40–41, accessed Oct. 20, 2015.

84 **the term itself:** Yung, *Unbound Feet,* 37.

84 **"I'd get sleepy":** Kathleen Wong, "Quan Laan Fan: An Oral History," Winter 1974, 7, CT275, F3, A3, Ethnic Studies Library.

85 **"He was too poor!":** Ibid., 8.

85 **When Tien arrived in San Francisco:** U.S. immigration authorities searched for Tien Fuh Wu's landing records in later years but were unable to locate them. See Department of Justice, "Immigration Arrival Investigation Case Files, 1884–1944," case number 32737/005–02, National Archives and Records Administration.

85 **a groundbreaking ceremony:** Raymond H. Clary, *The Making of Golden Gate Park: The Early Years, 1865–1906* (San Francisco: California Living Books, 1980), 113.

85 **young Tien watched the prostitutes:** Tien Fuh Wu, interview by Him Mark Lai.

86 **Like Tien, these older girls:** Nee and Nee, *Longtime Californ',* 85.

86 **"Every time they were afraid":** Tien Fuh Wu, interview by Him Mark Lai. In 1889, three years before Tien's arrival in San Francisco, lawmakers raised the legal age of sexual consent in California, from ten to fourteen years old. Tien was much younger than fourteen, so that might have been why her owner concealed her behind a trunk. The brothel keeper's action could also have been motivated by a desire to protect her property from welfare workers. Although laws prohibiting child labor in the United States were not enacted until the early twentieth century, welfare workers had convinced the California legislature to pass a law protecting minors working in households or other forms of service. That included, of course, children like Tien who labored as servants in houses of prostitution.

86 **"I had no playmates":** Martin Papers.

86 **Tien's second owner:** Tien Fuh Wu, interview by Him Mark Lai.

86 **"Oh, this woman was so awful!":** Nee and Nee, *Longtime Californ',* 85.

11. "A Worse Slavery than Ever Uncle Tom Knew Of"

88 **never seen anything so cruel:** Woman's Foreign Missionary Society of the Presbyterian Church (Presbyterian Church in the U.S.A.) et al., *Annual Report* (1895), 53.

88 **"Much to our joy":** Woman's Foreign Missionary Society of the Presbyterian Church (Presbyterian Church in the U.S.A.) et al., *Annual Report* (1894), 38.

90 **"I was scared to death":** Nee and Nee, *Longtime Californ',* 85–86.

91 **One young physician:** Woman's Foreign Missionary Society of the Presbyterian Church (Presbyterian Church in the U.S.A.) et al., *Annual Report* (1894), 33.

91 **Worley, a single woman:** Risse, "Translating Western Modernity," 431.

91 **Her sister Florence:** "Fight for a Slave Girl," *San Francisco Call,* July 9, 1895.

91 **Tai Choie alias Teen Fook:** "Ledger of Inmates" (Presbyterian Mission Home, 1874), 198, Jan. 17, 1894, Cameron House Archives.

91 **the women collected donations:** Woman's Foreign Missionary Society of the Presbyterian Church (Presbyterian Church in the U.S.A.) et al., *Annual Report* (1891), 31.

92 **"our Oriental room"**: Woman's Foreign Missionary Society of the Presbyterian Church (Presbyterian Church in the U.S.A.) et al., *Annual Report* (1894), 35.

92 **The Chinese vice-consul**: "A House-Warming," *San Francisco Call,* Feb. 20, 1894, 9.

92 **"There was such an odd"**: Ibid.

93 **The sheer doggedness**: Abe Ruef, who had volunteered his legal services to the home for three years, had by then stepped aside and been replaced by an attorney named Henry Monroe.

93 **"slavery is not a thing of the past"**: "Chinese Slavery," *San Francisco Chronicle,* April 17, 1892, Judy Yung Collection, Ethnic Studies Library.

93 **whoever wrote it**: "Chinese Threats," *Evening Bulletin,* June 8, 1892, box 1, 1890s, Yung Collection.

94 **the price for a prostitute**: Clarence D. Long, "Wages by Occupational and Individual Characteristics," in *Wages and Earnings in the United States* (Princeton, N.J.: Princeton University Press, 1960), 99, accessed Nov. 3, 2015, www.nber.org.

12. Dynamite

95 **Her engagement to her brother's friend**: A family member would later suggest to the author that Sargent might have hoped to become intimate with Cameron before the wedding ceremony and that she, uncomfortable with his attentions, called it off.

98 **"She has often been threatened"**: "With Dynamite Sticks," *San Francisco Call,* April 21, 1895.

99 **Middle-class white women**: Jessica Ellen Sewell, *Women and the Everyday City: Public Space in San Francisco, 1890–1915* (Minneapolis: University of Minnesota Press, 2011), 4–6.

99 **"Oh yes. I have heard"**: Martin, *Chinatown's Angry Angel,* 40–43. Although the author interviewed Donaldina Cameron before she died as well as many of her closest colleagues, family members, and friends, she also acknowledges in her introduction that while some quotations are directly derived from her interviews with primary sources, "a few fictionalized scenes were confirmed as characteristic by those who knew her best." It is not clear whether the scene of her arrival at the home is one of these, but I have not found diaries, letters, or other primary sources to confirm this dialogue. Some of the details of the day of her arrival are also found in Wilson, *Chinatown Quest,* 8–12.

100 **"dens of vice"**: Woman's Foreign Missionary Society of the Presbyterian Church (Presbyterian Church in the U.S.A.) et al., *Annual Report* (1891), 44.

100 **She had enlisted**: Martin, *Chinatown's Angry Angel,* 40–43.

13. Devil's Playground

101 **Shooting guns was traditional**: "From a Chinese Pistol," *San Francisco Call,* July 6, 1895.

103 **The older girl**: "A Trip in Chinatown," *San Francisco Call,* April 20, 1895.

103 **number of violent deaths**: Mortuary Statistics, in *San Francisco Municipal Reports* (order of the Board of Supervisors, 1895), 917. The number of violent deaths had dropped to six in 1894–1895 compared with eighteen in 1891–1892.

The overall number of violent deaths in the city during that same time was essentially unchanged in the overall city, with 339 in 1894–1895 compared with 338 in 1891–1892.

103 **Violent crimes in the quarter:** Ibid. Violent deaths (Mongolian) rose from six in 1894–1895, to eleven in 1895–1896, to sixteen in 1896–1897.

103 **murders:** *San Francisco Municipal Reports for the Fiscal Year 1894–95, Ending June 30, 1895* (San Francisco: Published by order of the Board of Supervisors, 1895), 896, archive.org.

103 **"the sack":** Mullen, *Chinatown Squad,* 85.

103 **according to rumor:** Ibid., 80.

103 **multiple lawsuits against the squad:** Dillon, *Hatchet Men,* 292–93.

104 **Starting in the 1860s:** Ibid.

104 **A photograph taken that year:** *Chinatown Squad of the San Francisco Police Department Posing with Sledge Hammers and Axes in Front of August Pistolesi's Grocery Store at 752 Washington Street, 1895,* graphic.

105 **"This beating of Chinese":** Dillon, *Hatchet Men,* 294.

106 **So large were the crowds:** "Trouble in Chinatown," *San Francisco Call,* April 29, 1895.

106 **"Take Notice":** Ibid.

106 **on Baker Alley's:** "Murder in Chinatown," *San Francisco Call,* June 25, 1895.

106 **On Saturday night:** "Chinese New Year, 1645–1899," accessed Feb. 2, 2016, pinyin .info.

107 **A judge sentenced him:** Mullen, *Chinatown Squad,* 85.

107 **Little Pete himself became a victim:** "Foul Murder at San Francisco," *Sacramento Daily Union,* Jan. 24, 1897.

108 **A rival criminal tong:** One theory is that the gunmen were members of the See Yup tong, which had put a price of $3,000 on his head. The Chinese writer Eng Ying Gong claimed he interviewed Little Pete's killer in the See Yup District of China.

108 **who was tried before a jury:** "Little Pete's Murder," *Los Angeles Herald,* Nov. 7, 1897.

108 **a massive procession:** Dillon, *Hatchet Men,* 245.

108 **Handel's oratorio *Saul*:** Sue Fawn Chung and Priscilla Wegars, *Chinese American Death Rituals: Respecting the Ancestors* (Lanham, Md.: AltaMira, 2005), 226.

109 **"This was the last impression":** Frank Norris, "Passing of 'Little Pete,'" in *The Apprenticeship Writings of Frank Norris, 1896–1898,* ed. Joseph R. McElrath and Douglas K. Burgess (Philadelphia: American Philosophical Society, 1996), 241–43.

14. Chinatown in Tears

110 **a painful kick:** "She Gave Her Life to God," *San Francisco Call,* Aug. 1, 1897.

110 **Culbertson suffered badly:** Cassie Barrett and Danny Smith, "Recognition and Management of Abdominal Injuries at Athletic Events," *International Journal of Sports Physical Therapy* 7, no. 4 (Aug. 2012): 448–51.

110 **To gain custody:** Lorna E. Logan, *Ventures in Mission: The Cameron House Story* (n.p., 1976), 16.

112 **that court victory:** "The Slave Maiden: Fighting for Little Woon T'sun," *San Francisco Chronicle*, March 21, 1891, Yung Collection.

112 **a particularly demoralizing episode:** Missionary's Report, in Woman's Foreign Missionary Society of the Presbyterian Church (Presbyterian Church in the U.S.A.) et al., *Annual Report* (1897), 58–62.

112 **They rounded up sixty girls:** "Chinatown in Tears," *San Francisco Call*, March 23, 1897.

113 **"No, no, no":** Missionary's Report, in Woman's Foreign Missionary Society of the Presbyterian Church (Presbyterian Church in the U.S.A.) et al., *Annual Report* (1897), 60.

113 **the superintendent was a white devil:** Art Peterson, "Donaldina Cameron House," *FoundSF,* accessed Feb. 18, 2016, www.foundsf.org.

113 **"very rebellious subjects":** Missionary's Report, in Woman's Foreign Missionary Society of the Presbyterian Church (Presbyterian Church in the U.S.A.) et al., *Annual Report* (1897), 60–61.

114 **Since she'd become ill:** Ibid., 58.

114 **She was named Margaret:** Report of Rescue Work, in Woman's Foreign Missionary Society of the Presbyterian Church (Presbyterian Church in the U.S.A.) et al., *Annual Report* (1901), 77.

114 **The shadow of the superintendent's serious illness:** Woman's Foreign Missionary Society of the Presbyterian Church (Presbyterian Church in the U.S.A.) et al., *Annual Report* (1896), 22, 68–70. Describing her first year, Cameron wrote, "The darkest shadow which has fallen upon our Home has been the illness, and consequent absence for some months of our dear Miss Culbertson," adding that the matron's condition had helped to bring the residents and the young staffer closer together in their "common sorrow."

114 **"The Occidental Board":** Missionary's Report, in Woman's Foreign Missionary Society of the Presbyterian Church (Presbyterian Church in the U.S.A.) et al., *Annual Report* (1897), 60.

115 **nearly seven hundred girls:** "Culbertson, Margaret. Biographical File" (Presbyterian Office of History, n.d.).

115 **"serious breakdown":** Report of the Home, in Woman's Foreign Missionary Society of the Presbyterian Church (Presbyterian Church in the U.S.A.) et al., *Annual Report* (1898), 70–71.

15. Year of the Rat

116 **Shortly before midnight:** Guenter B. Risse, Plague, Fear, and Politics in San Francisco's Chinatown Research Files (SFH86), San Francisco History Center, San Francisco Public Library. These files contain translated stories from *Chung Sai Yat Po* (Chinese-Western Daily) published in Chinatown, including Danian Lu's translations of the stories from the early days of the plague.

116 **It looked like bubonic plague:** Marilyn Chase, *The Barbary Plague: The Black Death in Victorian San Francisco* (New York: Random House, 2003), 17–18. See also Guenter B. Risse, *Plague, Fear, and Politics in San Francisco's Chinatown* (Baltimore: Johns Hopkins University Press, 2012), 51.

116 **Only police and health officials:** "No. 21, [Cover]: On the Edge of the Quarantine, San Francisco: How Supplies Are Passed Under the Ropes, Down

Deserted Dupont Street," Chinese in California Collection, Bancroft Library, accessed March 15, 2016, www.oac.cdlib.org.

116   **The Chinese who supplied hotels:** "Seasonality Chart: Vegetables," CUESA, accessed March 13, 2016, cuesa.org.

118   **"The central telephone":** "Nothing but a Suspicion," *San Francisco Chronicle,* March 8, 1900.

118   **The cable cars:** "Transit in San Francisco: A Selected Chronology, 1850–1995," 13, accessed March 17, 2016, archives.sfmta.com.

118   **One of those interlopers:** Cameron House Files, 1939 1874, 267, March 18, 1900.

118   **an imbalance of yin forces:** Risse, Plague, Fear, and Politics in San Francisco's Chinatown Research Files, n.d., 41–50. See Risse's discussion of illness and folk religion.

118   **"killing airs":** Risse, *Plague, Fear, and Politics in San Francisco's Chinatown,* 57.

119   **The rainy weather cooperated:** Wilson, *Chinatown Quest,* 29–30.

119   **died "among friends":** Cameron House Files, 1939 1874, 267, March 11, 1900.

119   **"Little Ah Ching wished":** Cameron House Files, 267, March 1900.

119   **Eventually, she joined Cameron:** Martin, *Chinatown's Angry Angel,* 150.

119   **almost two thousand doses:** Chase, *Barbary Plague,* 49.

120   **jumped through a second-floor window:** Martin, *Chinatown's Angry Angel,* 78.

120   **"See what they do to you":** "Transcript of the Evidence Taken and Proceeding (Legislative Papers, Investigation of Vice in San Francisco's Chinatown)," § Assembly Committee, 448.

120   **hoping to avoid autopsies:** Risse, *Plague, Fear, and Politics in San Francisco's Chinatown,* 57–58.

120   **the fire burned for seventeen days:** "The Chinatown Fires," Hawai'i Digital Newspaper Project, accessed March 1, 2018, sites.google.com.

121   **From their perch:** Chase, *Barbary Plague,* 31.

121   **"I was slightly dizzy":** Ibid., 50.

121   **So he rented quarters:** Hoexter, *From Canton to California,* 162, 170.

121   **Printed in the lucky color:** Ibid., 171.

121   **on February 16, 1900:** This information was provided by the former SFTS archivist Michael Peterson.

122   **"If you will":** Hoexter, *From Canton to California,* 170.

122   **"plunged the town":** McClain, *In Search of Equality,* 247, citing various articles from *Chung Sai Yat Po* including "What Should We Do About Inoculation," May 18, 1900, and "The Background of Vaccination," May 19, 1900.

122   **"According to the epidemic":** Nayan Shah, *Contagious Divides: Epidemics and Race in San Francisco's Chinatown* (Berkeley: University of California Press, 2001), 132, citing *Chung Sai Yat Po,* March 8, 1900.

122   **Chew rolled up his sleeves:** Risse, *Plague, Fear, and Politics in San Francisco's Chinatown,* 123, citing "Health Officer Came to Our Offices," *Chung Sai Yat Po,* May 19, 1900, as well as *San Francisco Examiner,* June 1, 1900. This May 19 article in *Chung Sai Yat Po* implies that Ng Poon Chew got the vaccine but does not state it.

122   **more than half of its subscriber base:** Risse, *Plague, Fear, and Politics in San Francisco's Chinatown,* 123, citing *San Francisco Examiner,* May 31, 1900.

123   **"I certainly did":** "Quarantine," *San Francisco Examiner,* June 1, 1900.

123 **"the torture of medicine":** Risse, Plague, Fear, and Politics in San Francisco's Chinatown Research Files; "A Defense Proposed," *Chung Sai Yat Po,* May 22, 1900.

123 **A broad group of Protestant clergymen:** Risse, *Plague, Fear, and Politics in San Francisco's Chinatown,* 124, citing "Empathy, Kindness, and No Tolerance for Injustice," *Chung Sai Yat Po,* May 22, 1900.

16. Instant Fame

124 **They even got authorization:** McClain, *In Search of Equality,* 259–68. See also the Bancroft Library's Chinese in California Collection, specifically "The Barb-Wire Barricade," accessed March 15, 2016, www.oac.cdlib.org.

124 **He argued that the action:** McClain, *In Search of Equality,* 268.

124 **the Board of Health:** Ibid., 272–74.

124 **the first known outbreak:** Chase, *Barbary Plague,* 211.

126 **The Protestant churches:** Risse, Plague, Fear, and Politics in San Francisco's Chinatown Research Files.

126 **Chew and his staff:** Like many newspapers at the time, *Chung Sai Yat Po* generally did not run bylines with stories, but it is likely that Chew wrote many of the stories in the early years himself, because he had a very small staff.

126 **"Western doctors quarantined":** Yumei Sun, "From Isolation to Participation: Chung Sai Yat Po (Chinese-Western Daily) and San Francisco's Chinatown, 1900–1920" (Ph.D. diss., University of Maryland, College Park, 1999), citing *Chung Sai Yat Po,* Aug. 20, 1906.

127 **on March 29, 1900:** "Grave Charges Against Palo Alto Officials," *San Francisco Call,* March 31, 1900.

127 **"You have made a mistake":** Wilson, *Chinatown Quest,* 19.

127 **Dark corners behind sacks:** Tien Fuh Wu, interview by Him Mark Lai, 1971, Him Mark Lai Collection, box 26, folder 5, Ethnic Studies Library.

128 **three dozen residents:** The 1900 federal census naming all of the residents of 920 Sacramento Street in June. There were thirty-three Chinese and three Japanese "inmates," as the residents were called, plus Cameron and the matron in charge of housekeeping, Frances Thompson.

128 **Refusing to leave Kum alone:** "Alleged Abductors of Kim Quey on Trial," *San Francisco Call,* June 23, 1900.

128 **a primitive jail cell:** Missionary's Report, in Woman's Foreign Missionary Society of the Presbyterian Church (Presbyterian Church in the U.S.A.) et al., *Annual Report* (1901), 42.

128 **"dark and filthy cabin":** Cameron House Files, logbook, March 29, 1900.

129 **"This I refused":** "Chinese Abduction," *Palo Alto Times,* March 30, 1900. A first-person account by Cameron of the abduction and jailing was printed after this news story in the same edition of *The Palo Alto Times.*

129 **One man pulled:** "Chinese Abduction."

129 **Cameron fell into weeds:** Cameron House Files, 1939 1874, 269, logbook, March 29, 1900. See also "Kim Quey Testifies," *San Francisco Call,* June 24, 1900.

129 **was fined $5:** Wilson, *Chinatown Quest,* 20; Martin, *Chinatown's Angry Angel,* 55–59.

130 **"In the name of law":** "Chinese Abduction."

130 **a group of local supporters:** A. H. Tolman, "Obituary: Bernhard Ten Brink," *Modern Language Notes* 7, no. 6 (1892): 191–92; Jeannette Leonard Gilder and Joseph Benson Gilder, *Critic* 27 (1897): 58.

130 **Hundreds of university students:** "Palo Alto Historical Association Photograph Collection: Item Viewer," Nortree Hall, accessed March 10, 2016, archives .pahistory.org; Steve Staiger, "A Miscarriage of Justice in an Outraged Town," *Palo Alto Weekly,* April 23, 2000.

130 **burned an effigy:** Wilson, *Chinatown Quest,* 21.

131 **They also raised money:** "Mass Meeting," *Palo Alto Times,* April 3, 1900.

131 **"proved by her beauty":** Wilson, *Chinatown Quest,* 22, citing *San Francisco Chronicle,* April 3, 1900; see also "Palo Alto Abductors Denounced," *San Francisco Chronicle,* April 4, 1900, in Judy Yung Research Files.

131 **Chinatown's Baker's Alley:** Choy, *San Francisco Chinatown,* 153.

131 **despite intense pressure:** Cameron House Files, logbook, March 23, 1900. The entries suggest Kum Quai arrived at the Mission Home on the evening of March 23, 1900, after a Chinese man came to the home requesting that she be rescued. "There were many Chinese highbinders gathered in the house who tried to intimidate her and prevent her leaving," according to the logbook.

131 **"We admire the fearless":** "Citizens Denounce Kim Quey's Abduction," *San Francisco Call,* April 4, 1900.

131 **criminal indictments:** "Indicted for the Kidnaping of Kim Quey," *San Francisco Call,* April 28, 1900.

131 **Wearing American-style clothes:** "Kim Quey Testifies," *San Francisco Call,* June 24, 1900.

132 **Kum Quai, for one:** Missionary's Report, in Woman's Foreign Missionary Society of the Presbyterian Church (Presbyterian Church in the U.S.A.) et al., *Annual Report* (1901), 41.

132 **"Then, in the name":** Wilson, *Chinatown Quest,* 24–25. Wilson notes that John Endicott Gardner was the interpreter that day, but the Palo Alto Historical Association historian Steve Staiger, in a column he wrote about the case for the *Palo Alto Weekly* in 2016, states that the government appointed the Reverend David Charles Gardner as its representative in the case and that it was he who served as interpreter. Because of their shared surname, it is likely John Endicott Gardner was the interpreter and the Reverend Gardner took part in the buggy chase.

133 **dismissed the case:** "About the State," *Los Angeles Herald,* May 10, 1900.

133 **the accused men went free:** "Last of Indictments in Kim Quey Case Dismissed," *San Francisco Call,* July 10, 1900.

133 **"It is a matter of common knowledge":** "Public Appeal," *Mariposa Gazette,* April 7, 1900.

17. Municipal Storm

135 **the Weather Bureau:** "How the Storm Swept Down the Coast Line," *San Francisco Examiner,* Jan. 5, 1901.

135 **The flying wood:** Ibid.

137 **The paper's cartoonists:** Mullen, *Chinatown Squad,* 102.

137 **Sullivan was portrayed:** "Gambling Is Still Unchecked—Chief Sullivan Does NOTHING," *San Francisco Examiner,* Jan. 5, 1901.

137 "*Examiner* Detective Corps": Procter, *William Randolph Hearst,* 49–53.

137 the paper regularly voiced: Ibid., 53–54.

137 The *Examiner* trumpeted: "Legislature Votes to Investigate Corrupt Chinatown Conditions," *San Francisco Examiner,* Feb. 1, 1901.

137 On Monday, February 4: "SFPD History," Police Department, accessed May 29, 2016, sanfranciscopolice.org.

138 "the sweatbox": "Assembly Lexow Committee Hands In Voluminous Report," *San Francisco Call,* Feb. 22, 1901.

138 never read the penal code: Mullen, *Chinatown Squad,* 103; see also *Examiner* coverage of the hearings from February 6, 1901.

138 "Keep California White": *Densho Encyclopedia,* s.v. "James D. Phelan," accessed May 23, 2016, encyclopedia.densho.org.

138 In a courtroom packed: "Phelan Confesses to the Political Conspiracy in Which He and the Examiner Were Partners," *San Francisco Call,* Feb. 8, 1901.

138 The most pointed questions: Mullen, *Chinatown Squad,* 104, see map of Sullivan's Alley.

138 Jackson and Pacific Streets: There was no family relation between Phelan's brother-in-law Frank J. and the chief of police William P. Sullivan. See Selections from the James D. Phelan Papers: Correspondence: Outgoing Letters, May–Aug. 1907, Bancroft Library.

138 a lottery operation: "Transcript of the Evidence Taken and Proceeding (Legislative Papers, Investigation of Vice in San Francisco's Chinatown)," § Assembly Committee (n.d.), 156–59.

139 Lake, a single twenty-eight-year-old: Jeffrey L. Staley, "Contested Childhoods: The Pacific Society for the Suppression of Vice vs. the WHMS Methodist Oriental Home, 1900–1903," *Chinese America: History and Perspectives,* Jan. 2007. Margarita J. Lake (also sometimes referred to as Margaret) served as a missionary in the home, and her mother served as matron and a teacher.

139 "I disguised [myself]": "Transcript of the Evidence Taken and Proceeding (Legislative Papers, Investigation of Vice in San Francisco's Chinatown)," 442.

139 "I'm afraid I might be": Ibid., 445.

141 "Well, the police authorities": Ibid., 453.

141 the notorious thoroughfare: Ibid., 455.

141 "I have been told": Ibid., 456.

142 "Missionaries Describe": "Missionaries Describe to Investigators the Horrors of the Chinese Slave Trade," *San Francisco Call,* Feb. 12, 1901.

142 But after a contested custody battle: Staley, "Contested Childhoods," 46.

18. "Forcing Me into the Life"

143 they began hearing the testimony: "Transcript of the Evidence Taken and Proceeding, Legislative Papers, Investigation of Vice in San Francisco's Chinatown," 485. John Endicott Gardner, the government official who had appeared during the Kum Quai case in Palo Alto, served as translator during the hearings. He was born in China to an American missionary father and a half-Chinese mother. For more information on Gardner and the U.S. Treasury Department's Chinese bureau, see Ngai, *Lucky Ones,* 75–76.

143   **Lake jumped in to explain:** "Transcript of the Evidence Taken and Proceeding, Legislative Papers, Investigation of Vice in San Francisco's Chinatown," 487.

145   **purchased for $2,200:** Ibid., 489.

145   **eight months in the brothel:** Ibid., 490–91.

145   **"who lets them know":** Ibid., 492.

146   **"If there was ever slavery":** Ibid., 495.

146   **"that Chinese women":** "Assembly Lexow Committee Hands In Voluminous Report."

147   **a new section to the penal code:** California, *The Codes and Statutes of California: As Amended and in Force at the Close of the Thirty-Fourth Session of the Legislature, 1901, with Notes Containing References to All the Decisions of the Supreme Court Construing or Illustrating the Sections of the Codes, and to Adjudications of the Courts of Other States Having Like Code Provisions: Penal Code* (San Francisco: Bancroft-Whitney, 1901), 330–31.

147   **And Chief Sullivan:** "Chief of Police Sullivan's Life Ends at Early Hour This Morning," *San Francisco Call,* Nov. 11, 1901.

19. "I May Go to Sleep Tonight and Then Find Myself in Hell!"

148   **her birthday:** Logan, *Ventures in Mission,* 21. All of the personnel documents that Tien Fuh Wu filled out for her Presbyterian employers cite January 17 as her birthdate.

148   **"carefree":** "Wu, Tien Fuh," personnel file from 1934, PHS.

150   **Slipping off their shoes:** Tien Fuh Wu, taped interview by Mildred Martin, part B, 1969, Martin Papers.

150   **back down to the kitchen:** Nee and Nee, *Longtime Californ',* 83–90. Also "Tien Fu Wu [*Sic*] 1983," n.d., 1–10, Him Mark Lai Research Files, Ethnic Studies Library.

151   **the home's backyard:** The backyard is now covered by Cameron House's parking lot.

151   **"Aiya! Aiya!":** Nee and Nee, *Longtime Californ',* 89.

151   **"The big girls, you know":** "Tien Fu Wu [*Sic*] 1983," 8–10. Interestingly, Tien's answer to the question of how she became a Christian was left out of the Nees' published book, in which they used the pseudonym "Lilac Chen" for Tien Fuh Wu. This section on her decision to get baptized comes from the transcript of the interview with Wu.

151   **"I just cried and cried":** Ibid., 9.

152   **"happy-go-lucky":** Tien Fuh Wu, interview by Martin, part B, cassette 2, 1969, Martin Papers.

152   **Cameron never forgot:** Martin, *Chinatown's Angry Angel,* 45–46.

152   **"She was born honest":** Donaldina Cameron, interview by Mildred Martin, part 2, cassette 20, Martin Papers.

152   **"You don't need to tell me":** Martin, *Chinatown's Angry Angel,* 66.

152   **an effort to catch pneumonia:** Tien Fuh Wu, interview by Martin, part B, cassette tape, 1969, Martin Papers.

153   **in mid-November 1890:** Cameron House Files, Registry of Inmates, Nov. 16, 1890, 142.

153   **Leung's father had borrowed:** Woman's Foreign Missionary Society of the Presbyterian Church (Presbyterian Church in the U.S.A.) et al., *Annual Report* (1890), 46–48.

154   **seventeen court hearings:** Cameron House Files, Registry of Inmates, 142.

154   **That legal battle attracted:** Woman's Foreign Missionary Society of the Presbyterian Church (Presbyterian Church in the U.S.A.) et al., *Annual Report* (1890), 47.

154   **a quiet student:** Tien Fuh Wu, Personnel File, Jan. 1934, Biographical Vertical File, Tien Fuh Wu, PHS.

154   **A photograph of her:** Martin, *Chinatown's Angry Angel*, 69.

154   **"She was different from me":** "Wu, Tien Fuh," 1934 personnel document, PHS.

155   **sobbing uncontrollably:** Tien Fuh Wu, interview by Martin, part B, cassette 5, 1969, Martin Papers.

155   **"Don't cry, Mama":** Tien Fuh Wu, taped interview by Mildred Martin, parts A and B, 1969, Martin Papers.

20. A Deathbed Promise

156   **"I offered to help":** Wu, Personnel File, June 11, 1943.

156   **"I was hungry":** Tien Fuh Wu, taped interview by Mildred Martin, parts A and B, 1969, Martin Papers.

158   **"watching over them":** Woman's Foreign Missionary Society of the Presbyterian Church, *Annual Report* (1903), 55.

158   **She earned $5 a month:** Letter from Tien Fuh Wu, Sarah Refo Mason Papers, Record Group 175, Special Collections, Yale Divinity School Library.

158   **"The darkest shadow":** Woman's Foreign Missionary Society of the Presbyterian Church (Presbyterian Church in the U.S.A.) et al., *Annual Report* (1901), 47.

158   **arcane legal terms:** Wu, Personnel File, fig. June 11, 1943, personnel document.

159   **educational segregation continued:** Chen, *Chinese San Francisco*, 167–68.

160   **Horace C. Coleman:** Cameron House Files, 386, a page at the end of the "Registry of Inmates" that lists the "Girls supported in the Home by churches or individuals." The second entry is "Teen Fook" (Tien's alias) and Margaret (Foon Ying) by Mr. H. C. Coleman, 83 E. Main Street, Morristown, Montgomery Co., Pennsylvania.

160   **fund a scholarship:** Tien Fuh Wu, taped interview by Mildred Martin, parts A and B, 1969, Martin Papers.

160   **Neither the scar:** Martin, *Chinatown's Angry Angel*, 68. The caption reads, "The photograph that Tien Wu, about 16, sent to 'my American Papa,'" 1900.

161   **"Oh, Mr. Coleman":** Tien Fuh Wu, interview by Martin, cassette recording, Martin Papers. Also, Tien Fuh Wu, interview by Him Mark Lai, 1971, box 26, folder 5, Him Mark Lai Collection, Ethnic Studies Library.

161   **Grace Kelly:** The records of the now-closed Stevens School are held at the Chestnut Hill Historical Society in Philadelphia. The holdings from 1900 to 1905, the period in which Tien would have enrolled, are scarce and limited to only a few administrative records. No enrollment or class records or class photographs exist in the holdings that could have confirmed Tien's attendance.

161   **"I thank God":** Wu, Personnel File, fol. personnel document, 1934. "Worldly" is misspelled in the document as "wordly."

21. Taking Public Stands

162 **"young, well bred"**: "A Real Missionary," *San Francisco Chronicle,* May 5, 1901.

164 **"It took only four years"**: Woman's Foreign Missionary Society of the Presbyterian Church (Presbyterian Church in the U.S.A.) et al., *Annual Report* (1902), 38.

164 **Congress began debating**: "Exclusion Will Have the Floor," *San Francisco Chronicle,* April 4, 1902.

165 **Stanton died in the fall**: "Elizabeth Cady Stanton Dies at Her Home," *New York Times,* Oct. 27, 1902, accessed Nov. 8, 2016, archive.nytimes.com.

166 **a growing number of women**: Estelle B. Freedman, *Feminism, Sexuality, and Politics: Essays by Estelle B. Freedman* (Chapel Hill: University of North Carolina Press, 2006), 21–36.

166 **"I am weary and discouraged"**: Series 2, box 4, folder 75, Burton/Lake/Garton Family Papers, Coll. 301, Special Collections and University Archives, University of Oregon Libraries, Eugene. This is a handwritten address by Margarita (Margaret) Lake possibly intended for the Woman's Home Missionary Society's California convention in the summer of 1902.

166 **a bungled rescue attempt**: Staley, "Contested Childhoods." See Staley's account for a detailed and fascinating account of the interaction between Kane and Margarita Lake during that time.

166 **it was Margarita Lake**: *The San Francisco Examiner* on Feb. 5, 1901, reported that it was Lake who urged the California state legislators to look into the Chinese slave traffic and "brought the resolution" to J. R. Knowland, the state assemblyman who chaired the committee to investigate the conditions of enslaved Chinese women and girls.

167 **she wrote letters**: George C. Pardee Papers, 1903, Bancroft Library.

167 **testified before a congressional committee**: *Reports of the Industrial Commission on Immigration: Including Testimony, with Review and Digest, and Special Reports* (Washington, D.C.: U.S. Government Printing Office, 1901), 786–89.

167 **once, after preparing**: "President McKinley Changes All Engagements Owing to the Critical Condition of His Much Beloved Wife," *San Francisco Call,* May 16, 1901.

167 **"Even the babies"**: Matron's Report, in Missions, *Annual Report of the Board of Foreign Missions of the Presbyterian Church of the United States of America* (1902), 49.

168 **a late-night visit**: It is not clear from the Matron's Report who made up the "Presidential Party" that visited the home, though based on the seriousness of Ida McKinley's illness, it is more likely that some of the president's representatives, rather than the president himself, visited the home that night.

22. Pink Curtain

169 **By the turn of the century**: Woman's Foreign Missionary Society of the Presbyterian Church (Presbyterian Church in the U.S.A.) et al., *Annual Report* (1903), 15.

169 **the fifth of eight children**: Kazuhiro Oharazeki, *Japanese Prostitutes in the North American West, 1887–1920* (Seattle: University of Washington Press, 2016), 3.

169   **near the mouth of Tokyo Bay:** Tomoko Yamazaki, *The Story of Yamada Waka: From Prostitute to Feminist Pioneer* (Tokyo: Kodansha International, 1985), 13–14, 42–43. This account of her life is largely drawn from this source, which is the sole English-language biography of her. The author draws on Yamada Waka's many short stories and essays as well as his own research to piece together her life.

169   **the marriage was unhappy:** Ibid., 52.

171   **stepped off the boat:** Oharazeki, *Japanese Prostitutes in the North American West,* 4.

171   **a procuress's convincing promises:** Yamazaki, *Story of Yamada Waka,* 53–54.

171   **two hundred or so other Japanese women:** Kazuo Itō, *Issei: A History of Japanese Immigrants in North America* (Seattle: Japanese Community Service, 1973), 768–69.

171   **"pink curtain":** Kazuhiro Oharazeki, "Japanese Prostitutes in the Pacific Northwest, 1887–1920" (Ph.D. diss., State University of New York at Binghamton, 2008), 111.

171   **where Yamada worked:** Yamazaki, *Story of Yamada Waka,* 71–72. Although this book says she worked out of the Eastern Hotel on King Street, that structure wasn't built until several years after she'd left Seattle. See also "If These Walls Could Talk: Historic Buildings in the Heart of Seattle's API Community," *International Examiner,* July 7, 2011, accessed Nov. 1, 2016, www.iexaminer.org.

171   **"white man's bird":** Yuji Ichioka, "Ameyuki-San: Japanese Prostitutes in Nineteenth-Century America," *Amerasia Journal* 4, no. 1 (Jan. 1977): 12, doi .org/10.17953/amer.4.1.h1543r885t12668p.

171   **more Japanese men than women:** Yamazaki, *Story of Yamada Waka,* 15.

171   **the columnist compared:** Oharazeki, "Japanese Prostitutes in the Pacific Northwest, 1887–1920," 120. See also "Takao," *The Honest Courtesan* (blog), March 24, 2015, maggiemcneill.wordpress.com.

172   **"Yae cherry blossom":** Oharazeki, *Japanese Prostitutes in the North American West,* 4.

172   **pimps were said to have killed:** Ibid., 95.

172   **"I lived in a corner":** Ibid., 108, citing Yamada Waka, "America no fujin e" (To an American lady), in Waka Yamada, *Ren'ai no shakaiteki igi* (Social meanings of love).

172   **The man who eventually helped:** Ichioka, "Ameyuki-San," 8.

172   **a makeshift rope:** Yamazaki, *Story of Yamada Waka,* 80.

172   **He squeezed money:** Ibid., 81.

173   **leaving Tachii emotionally distraught:** Yamada Waka's biographer suggests that Tachii might have been truly in love with her and that she had spurned his sexual advances. A different account of what happened is provided in Oharazeki, *Japanese Prostitutes in the North American West,* 4. The author states that Tachii sold her for $150 to a brothel in San Francisco.

173   **according to the home's tally:** Report of the General Corresponding Secretary, in Woman's Foreign Missionary Society of the Presbyterian Church (Presbyterian Church in the U.S.A.) et al., *Annual Report* (1903), 16.

173   **four other Japanese residents:** Ibid., 15.

173   **"house of ill repute":** Oharazeki, *Japanese Prostitutes in the North American West,* 89.

173   **Yamada and Tachii were arrested:** Cameron House Files, 289, Registry of Inmates. Yamada Waka's entry is listed under the name "Hanna Mori

or Maka Asaba." She later became known as Asaba Waka and then Yamada
Waka.

173 **upcoming midterm elections:** "Local Council of Women Hears R. H. Webster,"
San Francisco Call, Nov. 2, 1902.

174 **"never see the likes of you":** Yamazaki, *Story of Yamada Waka,* 86.

174 **carbolic acid:** "Unrequited Love Leads to Suicide," *San Francisco Chronicle,* Dec.
16, 1903.

174 **"please take good care":** Ibid.

174 **"Tomb of Tachii Nobusaburo":** Yamazaki, *Story of Yamada Waka,* 106–8.

23. Courage to Fight Evil

175 **"When I emerged":** Yamazaki, *Story of Yamada Waka,* 76.

177 **"I fled into a sort of nunnery":** Ibid., 95. Yamada wrote and published her essays
in Japanese.

177 **She learned quickly:** Woman's Foreign Missionary Society of the Presbyterian
Church (Presbyterian Church in the U.S.A.) et al., *Annual Report* (1902), 51–53.

177 **"We had always hoped":** Yamazaki, *Story of Yamada Waka,* 96.

178 **"The more I studied the Bible":** Ibid., 95.

178 **"When I met him":** Ibid., 100.

179 **a friend made coffee:** Ibid., 101–2.

179 **Eleanor Roosevelt:** Ibid., 23, 149. The author notes that Waka was used by the
Japanese military government of the 1930s for propaganda purposes.

24. The Chinese Mark Twain

180 **"She is petite but ambitious":** Judy Yung, "Social Awakening of Chinese American Women as Reported in *Chung Sai Yat Po, 1900–1911," Chinese America: History and Perspectives* (1988): 92–93.

180 **Sieh wore a fashionable silk robe:** "Leads Her Sisters out of Bondage," *San
Francisco Chronicle,* Nov. 3, 1902.

180 **she'd delivered a rousing speech:** Yung, *Unbound Feet,* 54.

182 **she proclaimed feminist ideas:** Judy Yung, *Unbound Voices: A Documentary History of Chinese Women in San Francisco* (Berkeley: University of California Press,
1999), 181.

182 **"being of the weaker sex":** Ibid., 184, citing a translated speech printed in *Chung
Sai Yat Po,* Nov. 3, 1902.

182 **"like zealots":** "Leads Her Sisters Out of Bondage."

182 **Sieh's progressive views:** American women missionaries, in particular, helped
spur on some of the rapid advances Chinese women were making during this
period through education and by providing role models of independent women.
John Pomfret, *The Beautiful Country and the Middle Kingdom: America and
China, 1776 to the Present* (New York: Henry Holt, 2017), 98.

182 **"It is imperative":** Yung, *Unbound Voices,* 185.

183 **It had a circulation:** James Philip Danky and Wayne A. Wiegand, *Print Culture
in a Diverse America* (Urbana: University of Illinois Press, 1998), 87.

183 **known as Dr. Chew:** Chew is Ng Poon Chew's given name and Ng was his
surname, but he became known as Dr. Chew in the United States, an honorific

referring to his ordination as a Presbyterian minister. His children came to use Chew as their surname.

183 **Illnesses spread through the facility:** Erika Lee and Judy Yung, *Angel Island: Immigrant Gateway to America* (Oxford: Oxford University Press, 2010), 10–11.

183 **One prominent Chinese visitor:** Hoexter, *From Canton to California,* 184.

184 **a 1905 Supreme Court decision:** *United States v. Ju Toy,* 198 U.S. 253 (1905).

185 *A Statement for Non-exclusion:* Patrick J. Healy and Ng Poon Chew, *A Statement for Non-exclusion* (San Francisco, 1905), 1.

185 **The book also implied:** Ibid., 196–97.

185 **Chinese American leaders:** Hoexter, *From Canton to California,* 191.

185 **"U.S. government is attempting":** Ibid., 189.

185 **dramatic drop in numbers:** Delber L. McKee, "The Chinese Boycott of 1905–1906 Reconsidered: The Role of Chinese Americans," *Pacific Historical Review* 55, no. 2 (May 1986): 168, doi.org/10.2307/3639528.

185 **An outpouring of plays:** Chen, *Chinese San Francisco,* 149.

185 **trim Western-style haircut:** Hoexter, *From Canton to California,* 197.

186 **"I am here to plead":** "Conference Indorses Chinese Exclusion," *New York Times,* Dec. 9, 1905.

25. "'Ell of a Place!"

188 **"It is not advisable":** Arnold Genthe, *As I Remember* (New York: Reynal & Hitchcock, 1936), 32.

188 **"Canton of the West":** Ibid., 45.

188 **a camera small enough:** Ibid., 34–38.

188 **six-foot-two:** Marina Kaneti, "Arnold Genthe," in *Immigrant Entrepreneurship: German-American Business Biographies, 1720 to the Present,* German Historical Institute, Aug. 28, 2014, www.immigrantentrepreneurship.org.

188 **A photograph of him:** Anthony W. Lee, *Picturing Chinatown: Art and Orientalism in San Francisco* (Berkeley: University of California Press, 2003), 102, plate 3.1.

190 **"For my first experiment":** Genthe, *As I Remember,* 35.

190 **some of the street characters:** Ibid., 36.

191 **"Miss Cameron was not":** Ibid., 39–40.

191 **In another image, young Minnie Tong:** It is not clear whether Arnold Genthe set up his camera on a timer to snap this photograph of himself and Tea Rose or if Cameron or an assistant took it.

191 **portrait of her in profile:** Arnold Genthe and John Kuo Wei Tchen, *Genthe's Photographs of San Francisco's Old Chinatown* (New York: Dover, 1984), 104–5.

192 **"for the poetry":** Genthe, *As I Remember,* 40.

193 **All four levels:** Photograph from the San Francisco Public Library's History Center of the Grand Opera House on the night of April 17, 1906, in *Three Fearful Days: San Francisco Memoirs of the 1906 Earthquake and Fire,* ed. Malcolm E. Barker (San Francisco: Londonborn, 1998), 65.

193 **one of the most extravagant displays:** "Fashionable Society Comes Out Radiantly on the Second Night," *San Francisco Call,* April 18, 1906.

193 **After ten minutes:** Philip Fradkin, *The Great Earthquake and Firestorms of 1906* (Berkeley: University of California Press, 2005), 47.

193 **"The whole house":** Genthe, *As I Remember,* 87.

193   "earthquake attire": Ibid., 88.

193   **Genthe spotted Enrico Caruso:** "The Candid Friend," *San Francisco Call,* March 13, 1910.

193   **"'Ell of a place!":** Genthe, *As I Remember,* 89.

193   **Fortified with the bread:** Recollections of James W. Byrne of having breakfast in the Palace Palm Court, in Barker, *Three Fearful Days,* 104–7.

194   **across from the *Call* building:** Ibid., 71. This is an excerpt from the recollections of the police officer Michael J. Brady, who had reached Market Street after patrolling Chinatown during the morning of the earthquake.

194   **Smoke rose from fires:** "New York Sun on the San Francisco Earthquake—1906," accessed Feb. 21, 2017, nationalcenter.org.

194   **The new Fairmont hotel:** Walt Crowley and Robert Courland, *The Fairmont: The First Century of a San Francisco Landmark* (History Link, 2007), 18–19.

194   **The Mission Home can be seen:** A print of this photograph is housed at the Bancroft Library at UC Berkeley. On the back of the print is a handwritten note: "Looking down Sacramento Street (from Powell St. towards the Bay), on the morning of September 18th, 1906." Banc pic 2004.004–1.

194   **"the flames shooting upward":** Fradkin, *Great Earthquake and Firestorms of 1906,* 51.

195   **it resembled a dollhouse:** Gladys C. Hansen and Emmet Condon, *Denial of Disaster* (San Francisco: Cameron, 1989), 111.

195   **a blackened body:** Second set of photo inserts, picture credit Arnold Genthe, Fine Arts Museums of San Francisco, in Fradkin, *Great Earthquake and Firestorms of 1906.*

195   **a lone Chinese man:** *Photo by Arnold Genthe of San Francisco Chinatown: Chinaman Overlooking Earthquake Ruins, 1906,* Library of Congress, Washington, D.C., accessed Feb. 20, 2017, www.loc.gov.

26. The Lord Is My Shepherd

196   **a new matron:** Woman's Foreign Missionary Society of the Presbyterian Church (Presbyterian Church in the U.S.A.) et al., *Annual Report* (1906–1907), 65.

196   **The net, which they draped:** Donaldina Cameron, "The Passing of the Occidental Mission Home," MSS Collection, Cameron House/SF Chinese Mission, box 1 Loc-35, SFTS.

196   **"During the never-to-be-forgotten moments":** Ibid., 3.

198   **heard crackling noises:** Report of General Corresponding Secretary, in Woman's Foreign Missionary Society of the Presbyterian Church (Presbyterian Church in the U.S.A.) et al., *Annual Report* (1906–1907), 56.

198   **ordered troops into the city:** Fradkin, *Great Earthquake and Firestorms of 1906,* 62–63.

198   **her large household:** Woman's Foreign Missionary Society of the Presbyterian Church (Presbyterian Church in the U.S.A.) et al., *Annual Report* (1906–1907), 67.

198   **the home's family physician:** *Crocker-Langley San Francisco Business Directory . . .* (San Francisco: H. S. Crocker, 1899), 974. Based on this listing from the directory, Dr. Kibbe practiced at 422 Ellis Street, which was about a twenty-minute walk from the Mission Home.

198 **bring the tiny ones to safety:** Cameron, "Passing of the Occidental Mission Home," 4–5.

199 **small mementos:** *Sunday School Scholars' Bible,* n.d.

199 **Thursday, April 19:** Cameron, "Passing of the Occidental Mission Home," 6–8. It appears that Cameron was accompanied by someone else as she returned to the home, but it is not clear who came with her.

200 **Tying torn sheets to broom handles:** Ibid., 7–8.

200 **Skipping breakfast:** "The Occidental Board After Earthquake and Fire," *Woman's Work for Woman,* June 1906, 128.

200 **rubble-strewn Market Street:** Cameron, "Passing of the Occidental Mission Home," 8.

200 **felt intense anxiety:** Woman's Foreign Missionary Society of the Presbyterian Church (Presbyterian Church in the U.S.A.) et al., *Annual Report* (1906–1907), 67.

201 **a black bowler hat:** Hansen and Condon, *Denial of Disaster,* 82, from a photograph of refugees and their belongings in front of the Ferry Building.

201 **The group crossed the bay:** Bob Battersby and Susan Nielsen, eds., *Ross, California: The People, the Places, the History* (Ross, Calif.: Ross Historical Society, 2007), 75. The San Francisco Theological Seminary is close to the border between Ross and San Anselmo.

201 **In 1892, the school:** "History of SFTS," SFTS, accessed Feb. 3, 2017, sfts.edu.

201 **Romanesque-style:** Coote and Hadsell, *San Francisco Theological Seminary,* 96. See also photographs of the campus from 1895 and 1905.

201 **"Life in an empty barn":** Cameron, "Passing of the Occidental Mission Home," 9.

201 **in the unheated structure:** A. W. Halsey, "The Rescue Home for Chinese Girls in San Francisco," *Assembly Herald,* Aug. 1906, 404. Halsey excerpts from Donaldina Cameron's writing.

202 **"kept the valley clean":** Edward A. Wicher, "The San Francisco Theological Seminary" (1906), 2, SFTS.

202 **"Do not worry about me":** Donaldina Cameron to Jessie, Charley, and Caroline Bailey, April 1906, Martin Papers.

202 **more than three thousand people:** "Casualties and Damage After the 1906 Earthquake," accessed Feb. 3, 2017, earthquake.usgs.gov.

202 **"Occidental Board of Foreign Missions":** Cameron, "Passing of the Occidental Mission Home," 1.

203 **thousands of negatives:** Genthe, *As I Remember,* 95.

203 **the most important negatives:** Ibid., 96–97.

203 **And in a photograph:** Wilson, *Chinatown Quest.* This is a photograph after page 80 in the 1950 revised edition, with the caption "Lo Mo and Some of Her 'Children' Camping in the Marin Hills." It appears to have been taken from the hill near the San Francisco Theological Seminary's chapel.

203 **a "Fairy Palace":** The address of the home in San Rafael was 3 Bayview Street, which is in the Gerstle Park neighborhood of the city.

203 **The front door:** Barry Spitz, *Marin: A History* (San Anselmo, Calif.: Potrero Meadow, 2006), 158, photograph from the Anne T. Kent California Room Collection of the Marin County Free Library. Also, Cameron, "Passing of the Occidental Mission Home," 10.

27. "The Stress of Circumstances"

204 **The couple loaded:** Hoexter, *From Canton to California,* 206.

204 **He was nearly finished:** Ibid., 201.

206 **a five-cent loaf of bread:** Judy Yung, oral history transcripts, 1990, 5, Ethnic Studies Library, accessed May 4, 2017, www.oac.cdlib.org.

206 **roughly a tenth of the city:** "Casualties and Damage After the 1906 Earthquake."

206 **"brooding or weeping softly":** Erica Ying Zi Pan, *The Impact of the 1906 Earthquake on San Francisco's Chinatown* (New York: P. Lang, 1995), 38, citing *Chung Sai Yat Po,* May 10, 1906.

207 **"Fire has reclaimed":** *Overland Monthly,* vol. XLVII, April 1906, 400.

207 **between fourteen thousand:** Pan, *Impact of the 1906 Earthquake on San Francisco's Chinatown,* 105.

207 **By some counts, four thousand:** Ibid., 41. Pan cites the *Oakland Tribune*'s coverage of Chinese earthquake refugees.

207 **the shivering Chinese:** Fradkin, *Great Earthquake and Firestorms of 1906,* 182–83.

208 **paint the characters backward:** Hoexter, *From Canton to California,* 208.

208 **engraved for printing:** "Annual Report of the Board of Home Missions," May 16, 1907, 449, PHS.

208 **"Everyone believes":** Hoexter, *From Canton to California,* 209.

208 **They held classes:** Woman's Foreign Missionary Society of the Presbyterian Church (Presbyterian Church in the U.S.A.) et al., *Annual Report* (1906–1907), 68.

209 **seek relief outdoors:** "Annual Report of the Board of Home Missions" (1907), 455.

209 **Supporters sent money:** A separate receipt dated May 2, 1906, in the file of the Earthquake Relief Funds at the San Francisco Theological Seminary indicates Cameron, who was the fund's coordinator, received another $100 from Dr. McAfee. Whether the $10 in her letter was a mistake or the $10 was in addition to the $100 is unclear.

209 **"Dear Dr. McAffee":** Donaldina Cameron, "1906 Letter to Dr. McAfee Regarding Earthquake Funds," June 3, 1906, MSS collection, 2016-06-74 San Francisco Earthquake, Presbyterian SFTS 1906, box 1, Loc-MPs, SFTS.

210 **soaring rents:** "Annual Report of the Board of Home Missions" (1907), 448.

210 **"much negotiating":** Woman's Foreign Missionary Society of the Presbyterian Church (Presbyterian Church in the U.S.A.) et al., *Annual Report* (1906–1907), 68, 70. The address of the house was 477 East Eleventh Street in Oakland.

210 **swelled to some seven thousand:** Pan, *Impact of the 1906 Earthquake on San Francisco's Chinatown,* 42.

210 **"slave girl traffic":** "Rescue Chinese Slave and Baby from Orientals," *Oakland Enquirer,* Jan. 11, 1907, Him Mark Lai Research Files, Ethnic Studies Library.

210 **Only one, a seventeen-year-old:** The *Oakland Enquirer* names the seventeen-year-old as Sun Lean.

210 **To Cameron's joy:** Missions, *Annual Report of the Board of Foreign Missions of the Presbyterian Church of the United States of America,* 454.

211 **"The police department":** "Rescue Chinese Slave and Baby from Orientals."

211 **injured by gunfire:** "Highbinder War Is Opened in Oakland," *San Francisco Call,* Jan. 12, 1907.

28. Homecomings

212 **Chew found a way:** In neighboring Berkeley, very close to where the Chews bought their home, Chinese could buy property, and their children were not segregated in public schools. Ngai, *Lucky Ones,* 68.

212 **a two-story house:** Hoexter, *From Canton to California,* 212. The house was located at 3765 Shafter Avenue, and the name Dr. N. P. Chew, according to Hoexter, was identical with that of an old Philadelphia family.

212 **quickly blended in:** Judy Yung, Oral history transcripts, 1990, 7.

212 **"It wasn't long":** Hoexter, *From Canton to California,* 213, citing Jessie Juliet Knox, "A Chinese Horace Greeley," *Oakland Tribune Magazine,* Dec. 3, 1922.

214 **estimated eight thousand Chinese:** Pan, *Impact of the 1906 Earthquake on San Francisco's Chinatown,* 62.

214 **stoned to death:** Chen, *Chinese San Francisco,* 164, citing *Chung Sai Yat Po,* June 15, 1906.

214 **Rebuilding without permits:** Pan, *Impact of the 1906 Earthquake on San Francisco's Chinatown,* 67–69.

215 **lawyers informed them:** Translation of *Chung Sai Yat Po* editorial from April 29, 1906, by Danny Loong, which appeared in the Chinese Historical Society of America's 2006 exhibition on the earthquake and its impact on Chinatown.

215 **Look, who was secretary:** Choy, *San Francisco Chinatown,* 43.

215 **incandescent bulbs:** Ibid., 113–14.

215 **Tiny lights and the exuberant use:** Ibid., 44–45.

215 **"the fantasy of the Far East":** Pan, *Impact of the 1906 Earthquake on San Francisco's Chinatown,* 98.

216 **many prominent donors:** Wilson, *Chinatown Quest,* 83.

216 **more than $50,000:** "Dedicate New Mission Home," *San Francisco Call,* April 15, 1908.

216 **"teeming" Chinatown:** L. Eve Armentrout and Jeong Huei Ma, The Chinese of Oakland, Oakland Chinese History Research Committee (1982), 31.

216 **"In Peking, we have a daily":** "Dedicate New Mission Home."

29. Municipal Crib

218 **an irreproachable champion:** In later years, the attorney Robert H. Borland also assisted the home. Both Monroe and Borland often volunteered their services.

220 **a permit for construction:** "Favored Contractors: The Dineen Case Typical of Administration Graft," *San Francisco Chronicle,* Oct. 23, 1905.

220 **ties to the mayor:** Fremont Older, *My Own Story* (San Francisco: Call, 1919), 48.

220 **buried the report:** Walton Bean, "Boss Ruef's San Francisco," n.d., 62–63, citing *Bulletin* articles from 1904 and 1905, Bancroft Library. See also Thomas, *Debonair Scoundrel,* 27.

220 **The brothel opened:** Asbury, *Barbary Coast,* 268–69.

221 **calling herself Lily:** Older does not provide a last name for Lily, who was presumably a prostitute working in the municipal crib, in his autobiography and does not name the second woman whom Lily introduced him to.

221 **To Older's dismay:** Older, *My Own Story,* 48–52.

221 **the Pup, his headquarters:** Peter Booth Wiley, *National Trust Guide/San Francisco: America's Guide for Architecture and History Travelers* (New York: John Wiley & Sons, 2000), 61.

221 **$10,000 annually:** Franklin Hichborn, *"The System," as Uncovered by the San Francisco Graft Prosecution* (San Francisco: Press of the James H. Barry Company, 1915), 114–15.

221 **five counts of extortion:** Ibid., 118–19.

222 **Older returned to San Francisco:** Older, *My Own Story,* 74–75.

222 **stories on the graft probe:** "Ruef's Graft from the Houses of Ill Fame: Witnesses Testify as to Money He Secured from Vile Resorts," *San Francisco Chronicle,* Dec. 1, 1906.

222 **The slaver's testimony:** "Secret Service Enmeshes Ruef in Chinese Slave Traffic," *San Francisco Call,* April 27, 1907.

223 **"the sale of human beings":** "Government Agents Glean Evidence to Show Guilt of Arch Grafter," *San Francisco Call,* April 26, 1907.

223 **"All out for the whorehouse!":** Asbury, *Barbary Coast,* 269.

223 **Ruef was sentenced:** "Ruef Found Guilty on Sixth Ballot After 24 Hours," *San Francisco Call,* Dec. 11, 1908.

223 **Older cheered:** Evelyn Wells, *Fremont Older* (New York: Arno, 1970), 203.

224 **asked Ruef to forgive him:** Walton Bean, *Boss Ruef's San Francisco: The Story of the Union Labor Party, Big Business, and the Graft Prosecution* (Berkeley: University of California Press, 1952), 310.

30. Paper Son

225 **nicknamed "the Professor":** "The Professor" was apparently a long-standing honorific given to McChesney. "Death Summons Aged Educator," *Oakland Tribune,* Feb. 26, 1912, ohsmemorial.com.

225 **"wooden house":** H. Mark Lai, Genny Lim, and Judy Yung, *Island: Poetry and History of Chinese Immigrants on Angel Island, 1910–1940* ([San Francisco]: Hoc Doi, 1980), 13.

225 **His paperwork indicated:** Many of the descriptions of the immigrant known as Leung Foo, a.k.a. Wong See Duck, as well as the dialogue and investigation details in this chapter are based on his immigration case files spanning from 1908 until the late 1950s, as well as partnership investigation files of the company he later established. A typed transcript of the Chinese Division inspector McChesney's interview notes from November 17, 1908, as well as affidavits, photographs, and correspondence are contained in NARA file 12017/45620 in its San Bruno, California, offices.

225 **denied entry:** Lucy Salyer, "Captives of Law: Judicial Enforcement of the Chinese Exclusion Laws, 1891–1905," *Journal of American History* 76, no. 1 (June 1989): 91–117, www.jstor.org.

227 **U.S. Immigration Service's Chinese Division:** *California Blue Book, or State Roster* (Sacramento: State Printing Office, 1907), 832.

227 **a dialect:** In Leung's immigration case file from 1908, the dialect he spoke is referred to as "See Yip," but it was likely to have been Sze Yup, which is a form of Cantonese from the Pearl River delta in China's southern province of Guangdong.

229 **Hundreds, perhaps thousands:** Many more Chinese immigrants might have come over the Canadian and Mexican borders. See Kenneth Chew, Mark Leach, and John M. Liu, "The Revolving Door to Gold Mountain: How Chinese Immigrants Got Around U.S. Exclusion and Replenished the Chinese American Labor Pool, 1900–1910," *International Migration Review* 43 (2009): 410–30, doi:10.1111/j.1747–7379.2009.00770.x.

229 **so-called earthquake exemption:** Ibid., 414.

230 **Arthur Spencer:** "Arthur Spencer Confesses," *San Francisco Call,* March 2, 1901.

230 **left his government appointment:** "The County News," *Marin County Tocsin,* Nov. 18, 1899. McChesney also married into the wealthy Jewett family, but it is unclear why he would have become a Chinese inspector so late in his career.

31. *Dragon Stories*

232 **Under the pseudonym:** Teen Fook is the name that Wu was first registered under in the Mission Home's Registry of Inmates in 1894, and she is referred to by this name over the years in the Mission Home's annual reports.

232 **in the fall of 1908:** The full title of the booklet is *Dragon Stories: The Bowl of Powfah, The Hundredth Maiden: Narratives of the Rescues and Romances of Chinese Slave Girls, Pacific Presbyterian,* 1908, Bancroft Library. It was written by an unnamed author and illustrated with photos by Arnold Genthe and R. E. Wales.

232 **pre-earthquake photographs:** Lee, *Picturing Chinatown,* 311. Genthe might have donated these photographs to Cameron for publication in the booklet based on their long-standing friendship.

232 **Wu was in Philadelphia:** The papers of the Stevens School, which was founded in 1868 and operated until 1982, are located at the Chestnut Hill Historical Society in Philadelphia. There are no records of Wu's attendance at the school, though the employment records Wu filled out and filed with the Presbyterian Church's Board of National Missions cite her attendance at the Stevens School's high school from 1905 to 1909 and state she received her diploma.

232 **the Reverend Henry W. Frost:** *Woman's Work* (1912): 125.

232 **China Inland Mission:** The China Inland Mission was founded in 1865 by an American missionary named James Hudson Taylor as a Christian mission aimed at reaching inland and rural areas of China. "James Hudson Taylor— OMF International (U.S.)," *OMF International (U.S.)* (blog), accessed April 30, 2017, omf.org.

232 **a large, busy household:** Thomas Gold Frost and Edward Lysander Frost, *Frost Family in England and America, with Special Reference to Edmund Frost and Some of His Descendants* (Buffalo: Russell Printing Company, 1909), 98, 109, plate 313 for photograph of the children.

232 **"so sultry":** Tien Fuh Wu, interview by Him Mark Lai.

232 **"not easy for a poor orphan girl":** Ibid.

234 **"excited little maidens":** It is not clear whether the stories are factual or composite accounts of rescues that took place at the Mission Home, but they bear a strong resemblance to cases related in Cameron's annual reports and might have been written by Cameron herself. Almost exactly the same rescue stories are related in the first biography of Cameron, Carol Green Wilson's *Chinatown*

Quest, 59–60, although neither Wu's real name nor pseudonym is used: there is only mention of an interpreter.

236   **Her sponsor:** *Woman's Work* 27 (1912): 124–25.

236   **more than a thousand girls:** E. French Strother, "Setting Chinese Slave Girls Free," *California Weekly,* Feb. 26, 1909, Martin Papers. The number of twelve hundred residents cited by Strother is correct. It is not accurate, however, that he states all of these girls were rescued from slavery: some were placed in the home by immigration authorities; others were fleeing difficult domestic situations, though not necessarily slavery.

236   **tuitions were paid:** Coleman's sponsorship of Tien Fuh Wu is noted toward the back of the Mission Home's Register of Inmates (page 386), and it notes that he also sponsored Margaret (Foon Ying).

236   **"native helpers":** Pascoe, *Relations of Rescue,* 113.

236   **"Tien Fook, stinking sow":** Anonymous threatening letter to Miss Wu, Chinese and English translation, n.d., Cameron House Archives.

237   **"Miss Cameron was more fearful":** Nee and Nee, *Longtime Californ'.* From a transcribed interview with Tien Fuh Wu with Victor Lee kindly provided by the historian Judy Yung.

237   **"men are very useful":** Lorna Logan, taped interview by Sarah Refo Mason, 1991, Mason Papers.

237   **"Some of them become ambitious":** Mrs. E. V. (Pauline) Robbins, "Chinese Slave Girls: A Bit of History," *Overland Monthly,* Jan. 1908.

32. Tiny

239   **As a nine-year-old:** Background material on Tye Leung Schulze came from an unprocessed collection of materials donated by her family to U.C. Berkeley's Asian Studies Library, as well as primary material provided by historian Judy Yung.

239   **Three years later:** Yung, *Unbound Feet,* 170. Leung's own account states that "Miss Donaldina Cameron and my school teacher Miss Crather rescue me and took me to Miss Cameron's home at 920 Sacramento St." (Yung, *Unbound Voices,* 286).

239   **Her teacher taught her:** Yung, *Unbound Voices,* 285–88.

241   **Wu was away at school:** Cameron's diary for 1909 shows that she worked closely with Leung during this period. If Cameron kept diaries for other years, they have disappeared. The 1909 diary, which is small and handwritten, is in the Martin Papers at Stanford University.

241   **$720 a year:** *Far West* 2, no. 15 (March 1910).

241   **"capable young interpreter":** Missions, *Annual Report of the Board of Foreign Missions of the Presbyterian Church of the United States of America* (1909–1910), 62.

241   **"distinguished her as the only":** "Chinese Girls Appear in Oriental Splendor," *Los Angeles Herald,* March 17, 1910.

242   **"were the only result":** *Far West* 2, no. 15 (March 1910).

242   **In 1912, the newspapers featured Leung:** Yung, *Unbound Feet,* 162–63.

242   **"the first Chinese woman":** "Orientals, Riding on Wave of Progress, Lose No Time in Adopting Motor Car," *San Francisco Call,* May 19, 1912.

242 **the state's antimiscegenation laws:** "Chinese American Women: A History of Resilience and Resistance," accessed April 26, 2017, www.womenshistory.org.

243 **work as a night-shift operator:** Yung, *Unbound Voices,* 283.

33. Missionaries of the Home

244 **largest number of girls:** Woman's Foreign Missionary Society of the Presbyterian Church (Presbyterian Church in the U.S.A.) et al., *Annual Report* (1908–1909), 71.

246 **"Some of us are old fashioned":** Ibid., 77.

247 **San Francisco pediatrician:** A medical institute at the University of California at San Francisco is now named after Langley Porter.

247 **Chinese patients:** Ibid.; Missions, *Annual Report of the Board of Foreign Missions of the Presbyterian Church of the United States of America* (1908–1909). Also "History: Chinese Hospital," Sf.Org, accessed June 2, 2017, www.chinesehospital -sf.org.

247 **"Alice and Ida saw the man":** Cameron, Nov. 14, 1909, diary entry, box 6, folder 5, Martin Papers.

248 **After she had lived through:** "Another Yee Falls, Victim of Tong Feud," *San Francisco Call,* Nov. 15, 1909.

34. Matchmaking

249 **"Book of Lamentations":** Martin, *Chinatown's Angry Angel,* 153.

249 **"a stern taskmaster":** Logan, taped interview by Mason.

251 **married in the 1890s:** Pascoe, "Gender Systems in Conflict," 640.

251 **"Dear Lo Mo":** Wu to Cameron, May 23, 1915, Quie Gee no. 970, Cameron House Archives.

251 **The crowded conditions:** Bertha M. Smith, "They Call Her Fahn Quai 'the White Spirit,'" 1915, Martin Papers.

251 **sleep on cots:** Martin, *Chinatown's Angry Angel,* 172.

252 **Cantonese profanities:** Wilson, *Chinatown Quest,* 99.

252 **"Lean hard":** Martin, *Chinatown's Angry Angel,* 152. Cameron's first biographer, Carol Green Wilson, does not mention the engagement with Nathaniel Tooker in her book, nor do any of the remaining personal papers of Cameron note or allude to such an engagement.

252 **Nathaniel Tooker had passed away:** "Nathaniel Tooker (1830–1911)," Find a Grave, accessed May 10, 2017, www.findagrave.com.

252 **architect Julia Morgan:** Eva Armentrout Ma, *Hometown Chinatown: A History of Oakland's Chinese Community, 1852–1995* (New York: Routledge, 2014), 72.

253 **"had encountered in their own lives":** Pascoe, "Gender Systems in Conflict," 634.

253 **"old maids and widows":** "Employment Files of Ethel V. Higgins, 1884–1971," n.d., 3, Oct. 5, 1933. This was a description later omitted from her official files. At the time she wrote it, Higgins was the director of the Ming Quong Home, after working alongside Cameron for many years. Her answer to the query "Tell one funny incident in mission experience" is this: "The staff of Ming Quong Home is made up of old maids and widows. The children have evidently observed that, in either case, it is a manless existence. Children from homes broken by divorce

or legal separation evidently associate all troubles with the men of the family. One day a little girl from such a home, who was living at Ming Quong because her parents were divorced remarked to a staff member:—'We children have been talking things over and we have made up our minds that we are never going to marry; we're always going to be widows!'" H5 Higgins, Ethel V., PHS.

253 **Cameron had befriended:** Martin, *Chinatown's Angry Angel*, 70.

253 **young ring bearer:** Logan, taped interview by Mason.

253 **266 of the Chinese women:** Pascoe, "Gender Systems in Conflict," 637.

253 **marital and family circumstances:** Logan, taped interview by Mason.

254 **one Chinese woman for every:** Pascoe, "Gender Systems in Conflict," 635, citing "The Ratio of Chinese Women to Men Compared to the Ratio of Women to Men in the Total Population of California, 1850–1970," Hirata.

254 **"Everybody is after me":** Pascoe, "Gender Systems in Conflict," 639, citing Cameron, June 13, 1915, inmate file 269, Cameron House Archives.

254 **doors remained guarded:** Pascoe, "Gender Systems in Conflict," 636, citing Woman's Occidental Board of Foreign Missions, *Annual Report* (1903 and 1895).

254 **"I am their mother":** Strother, "Setting Chinese Slave Girls Free."

255 **named their children Donaldina:** Logan, taped interview by Mason.

255 **"You will be glad":** Tien Fuh Wu, "Letter to Donaldina Cameron on Ah Ying and Suie Cum," June 20, 1915, Ah Ying, Cameron House Archives.

255 **"It is well known in Chinatown":** Ibid., Tien Fuh Wu.

255 **The missionary who received:** Ibid., Tien Fuh Wu.

256 **"I shall send you this letter":** Mary E. Banta, "Letter Reporting Ah Ying's Whereabouts in San Francisco," July 25, 1915, Ah Ying, Cameron House Archives.

256 **the astronomical sum:** Wu wrote that Ah Ying was sold for $6,000, but in Cameron's report to her board that year she stated she was sold for $3,400, which is a figure more in line with other reported slave prices at the time.

256 **"such a coward":** Tien Fuh Wu, "Letter to Donaldina Cameron Reporting on Ah Ying."

256 **The teenager was shuttled:** Woman's Foreign Missionary Society of the Presbyterian Church (Presbyterian Church in the U.S.A.) et al., *Annual Report* (1916), 65.

256 **"You know mother":** "Tien Wu to Donaldina Cameron Saying Ah Ying Had Been Taken to San Francisco and Sold for $6,000," June 26, 1915, Ah Ying 1915 no. 1022, Cameron House Archives.

257 **The two former slaves:** Woman's Foreign Missionary Society of the Presbyterian Church (Presbyterian Church in the U.S.A.) et al., *Annual Report* (1916), 66–67.

35. The "Joy Zone"

258 **gorgeous world's fair:** Laura A. Ackley, "Gem of the Golden Age of World's Fairs," in *Jewel City: Art from San Francisco's Panama-Pacific International Exposition*, ed. James A. Ganz (Oakland: University of California Press, 2015), 43.

258 **opening day:** Laura A. Ackley, *San Francisco's Jewel City: The Panama-Pacific International Exposition of 1915* (Berkeley, Calif.: Heyday, 2014), 142.

260 **"There are more things":** Frank Norris, *The Third Circle* (London: John Lane, Bodley Head, 1909), 13.

260 **existing basements:** Raymond W. Rast, "The Cultural Politics of Tourism in San Francisco's Chinatown, 1882–1917," *Pacific Historical Review* 76, no. 1 (2007): 19–20, doi.org/10.1525/phr.2007.76.1.29.

260 **"Hello, Doc":** Genthe, *As I Remember,* 36.

260 **miniature "Forbidden City":** Frank Morton Todd, *The Story of the Exposition: Being the Official History of the International Celebration Held at San Francisco in 1915 to Commemorate the Discovery of the Pacific Ocean and the Construction of the Panama Canal* (New York: G. P. Putnam's Sons, 1921), 3:288–89.

261 **the Chinese Pavilion:** Ackley, *San Francisco's Jewel City,* 183–84.

261 **"Opium Den":** Ibid., 266, see caption to photograph of signs for the exhibit.

261 **Cameron and Wu both saw:** No letters or diary entries exist to document whether Cameron or Wu visited the fair or the exhibit, but the fact that both women signed protest letters against "Underground Chinatown" suggests they did.

261 **nineteen million people:** Ackley, *San Francisco's Jewel City,* 197.

261 **other entertainments:** Ibid., 265–72.

261 **actors pretending:** Lee, *Picturing Chinatown,* 171.

261 **white woman forced:** Clarissa A. Chun, "Spectacle and Spectators: The European American View of the Chinese at the Panama-Pacific International Exposition (San Francisco, 1915)" (Harvard University, 1995), 57, citing Chen Chi to C. C. Moore, March 19, 1915, "Underground Chinatown—Protest Against Concession," Him Mark Lai research files, carton 23, Records of the P-PIE, Ethnic Studies Library, box 97, folder 14.

261 **offensive scenario:** Chen Chi (commissioner general of China to the Panama-Pacific International Exposition) to Charles C. Moore, Panama-Pacific International Exposition Papers, Bancroft Library (hereinafter referred to as P-PIE), March 19, 1915, carton 33, folder 36, Bancroft Library.

262 **Red Light Abatement and Injunction Act:** Alice Smith (Prostitute), *Alice: Memoirs of a Barbary Coast Prostitute,* ed. Ivy Anderson and Devon Angus (Berkeley, Calif.: Heyday, 2016), xli–xliii.

262 **sedate landscape paintings:** Todd, *Story of the Exposition,* 3:290.

262 **White Slave Traffic Act:** Ruth Rosen, *The Lost Sisterhood: Prostitution in America, 1900–1918* (Baltimore: Johns Hopkins University Press, 1983), 15–17.

262 **women held in bondage:** Marlene D. Beckman, "The White Slave Traffic Act: The Historical Impact of a Criminal Law Policy on Women," *Georgetown Law Journal* 72 (Feb. 1984): 1111.

262 **England's early industrial era:** Rosen, *Lost Sisterhood,* 116.

262 **In 1905, a conference:** Beckman, "White Slave Traffic Act."

263 **1,057 persons were convicted:** Rosen, *Lost Sisterhood,* 118, citing Maude Miner, *Slavery of Prostitution* (New York: Macmillan, 1916).

263 **"Underground Chinatown is a disgrace":** Chen Chi (commissioner general of China to the Panama-Pacific International Exposition) to Charles C. Moore.

263 **"indecency and horror":** Chinese Chamber of Commerce to Charles C. Moore, March 19, 1915, Records of the P-PIE, Bancroft Library.

263 **"repulsive and disgraceful":** Chinese Consolidated Benevolent Association (Chinese Six Companies) to Charles C. Moore, March 19, 1915, carton 33, folder 36, Bancroft Library.

263 **"When the debris"**: Chinese Press of San Francisco to Charles C. Moore, including Ng Poon Chew as one of the signatories, March 24, 1915, carton 33, folder 36, Bancroft Library.

263 **former slave Tien Fuh Wu**: Representatives of Christian Chinese Churches in Chinatown to Charles C. Moore, March 24, 1915, carton 33, folder 36, Bancroft Library.

264 **unpopular stand**: Representatives of the Christian Missions of Chinatown (including Donaldina Cameron) to Charles C. Moore, March 24, 1915, carton 33, folder 36, Bancroft Library.

264 **letters of complaint**: Ackley, *San Francisco's Jewel City*, 251.

264 **By June 1915**: "New Concession Shows Evils of Drug Habit: 'Underground Slumming' Offers Effective Lesson in Effects of Illicit Traffic," *San Francisco Chronicle*, June 9, 1915.

265 **"Go slumming"**: Ackley, *San Francisco's Jewel City*, 268.

265 **the fair's closing**: Chun, "Spectacle and Spectators," 61–63, citing Memorandum, "American-Oriental Concessions," carton 95, Records of the P-PIE.

265 **Chinese Theatre**: Ackley, *San Francisco's Jewel City*, 268.

38. Fruit Tramps

266 **One person who understood**: John H. Laughlin, "Charles C. Moore," March 20, 1915, P-PIE, Bancroft Library.

266 **more than a decade**: Wesley S. Woo, "Presbyterian Mission: Christianizing and Civilizing the Chinese in Nineteenth Century California," *American Presbyterians* 68, no. 3 (1990): 176.

266 **Her name was Ethel Higgins**: "Employment Files of Ethel V. Higgins, 1884–1971."

268 **unassuming appearance**: Ibid.

268 **mainline Protestantism**: Pascoe, *Relations of Rescue*, 197–98.

268 **welcoming, maternal feel**: Woman's Foreign Missionary Society of the Presbyterian Church (Presbyterian Church in the U.S.A.) et al., *Annual Report* (1874), 12. Wu's title is generally cited as Chinese assistant, but it does appear occasionally as assistant superintendent as well. See 1920 annual report and 1915 signature on letter opposing "Underground Chinatown."

268 **"Mrs. Young's [*sic*] mission"**: Woman's Foreign Missionary Society of the Presbyterian Church (Presbyterian Church in the U.S.A.) et al., *Annual Report* (1917), 35.

269 **strides toward equality**: Yung, "Social Awakening of Chinese American Women as Reported in *Chung Sai Yat Po*," 88–89.

269 **"I never found"**: Tien Fuh Wu, interview by Him Mark Lai.

269 **"had helped to rear me"**: Nee and Nee, *Longtime Californ'*, 86.

269 **"Now don't think"**: Cameron correspondence, 1914–1918, Martin Papers. The year of this letter is undated, but it might have been from May 1917.

270 **ordered the brothels closed**: Smith, *Alice*, lxxiii–lxxv, citing San Francisco *Bulletin* coverage, Feb. 14 and 15, 1917.

270 **"I hope you are being"**: Elizabeth Feung to Cameron, April 22, 1917, Cameron Family private collection.

270 **"made over" by her vacation:** Woman's Foreign Missionary Society of the Presbyterian Church (Presbyterian Church in the U.S.A.) et al., *Annual Report* (1917), 34.

270 **farmers needed help:** George H. Nash, *The Life of Herbert Hoover: Master of Emergencies, 1917–1918* (New York: W. W. Norton, 1996), 153–54.

271 **leftover funds:** Martin, *Chinatown's Angry Angel,* 178–79.

271 **"starting a wee bank account":** Mrs. Rawlins Cadwallader, "Assorted Board Papers, Speeches, and Letters," SFTS.

271 **donated $100:** Ibid.

271 **risen over the years:** Ibid.

37. "Are You Wearing a Mask and Taking Precautions?"

272 **raised nearly $4,500:** Cadwallader, "Assorted Board Papers, Speeches, and Letters," 1925 1919, SFTS. The $6,000 "general living expenses" cited comes from a Campaign Survey that Cadwallader signed with estimated costs for the years 1920–1925, item no. 6 (see note).

272 **generation of women:** Woman's Foreign Missionary Society of the Presbyterian Church (Presbyterian Church in the U.S.A.) et al., *Annual Report* (1919), 49. In her tribute to him, Cameron wrote that "Shepherd" was the tender name by which he was called in the family circle of the Mission Home, where he was deeply loved and honored.

272 **major changes:** Ibid., 10. Cadwallader, who had been a vice president on the board, became its president in 1919.

274 **Ethel and her sister:** Missions, *Annual Report of the Board of Foreign Missions of the Presbyterian Church of the United States of America* (1920), 25.

274 **annual fund-raising bazaar:** Logan, taped interview by Mason.

274 **Gifts to the homes:** Missions, *Annual Report of the Board of Foreign Missions of the Presbyterian Church of the United States of America* (1918), 17.

274 **Others donated food:** Missions, *Annual Report of the Board of Foreign Missions of the Presbyterian Church of the United States of America* (1919), 53.

274 **Indeed, Margaret Dollar:** Woman's Foreign Missionary Society of the Presbyterian Church (Presbyterian Church in the U.S.A.) et al., *Annual Report* (1920), 88.

274 **"Not one death":** Woman's Foreign Missionary Society of the Presbyterian Church (Presbyterian Church in the U.S.A.) et al., *Annual Report* (1919), 45.

275 **"tireless and faithful":** Missions, *Annual Report of the Board of Foreign Missions of the Presbyterian Church of the United States of America* (1919), 49.

275 **fear of contagion:** Woman's Foreign Missionary Society of the Presbyterian Church (Presbyterian Church in the U.S.A.) et al., *Annual Report* (1919), 18.

275 **"Are you wearing a mask":** Nora K. Baukes to Donaldina Cameron, ca. 1918, Martin Papers.

275 **known as Captain Dollar:** "Captain Dollar" was an honorific title. Robert Dollar was not a sea captain, but did own many ships.

275 **room for study:** "Study of Tooker School for Chinese Girls," Dec. 1919, Cadwallader Papers, SFTS.

275 **"Tell your board":** Martin, *Chinatown's Angry Angel,* 187.

275 **"castle" at San Simeon:** "Hearst Castle Architect Julia Morgan," accessed June 6, 2017, hearstcastle.org.

276 **rats would jump:** Sara Holmes Boutelle, *Julia Morgan: Architect* (New York: Abbeville Press, 1988), 78.

276 **buildings for women's organizations:** Ibid., 88.

276 **a safe place:** Ackley, *San Francisco's Jewel City,* 332–33.

276 **won the assignment:** Boutelle, *Julia Morgan,* 55–59.

276 **"like an icebox":** Copy of letter from Mary R. Tooker to Hodge, Sept. 5, 1920, Cadwallader, "Assorted Board Papers, Speeches, and Letters."

38. Quiet Defiance

279 **The Chinese rug:** Wilson, *Chinatown Quest,* 119–20. See also Martin, *Chinatown's Angry Angel,* 189–90.

279 **"Dolly, will you wear":** Martin, *Chinatown's Angry Angel,* 191–92.

279 **a mysterious package:** Ibid., 192–93. These items cannot be located. There is a similar account of the twenty-fifth anniversary celebration for Cameron in her biographer Carol Green Wilson's *Chinatown Quest,* 117–21.

280 **dates its establishment:** "History of the Church," PHS, accessed March 7, 2018, www.history.pcusa.org.

280 **scenes from the Mission Home's history:** Woman's Foreign Missionary Society of the Presbyterian Church (Presbyterian Church in the U.S.A.) et al., *Annual Report* (1920), 33.

281 **"The high cost of living":** Ibid., 38.

281 **"we have these children":** Mrs. Cadwallader to Dr. A. W. Halsey, Oct. 23, 1919, Cadwallader Papers, SFTS.

281 **The residents mostly ate:** "Study of Tooker School for Chinese Girls."

281 **"monthly *written* report":** Handwritten copy of "Instructions for Tooker Memorial School (from) Directors meeting," Aug. 2, 1918, Cadwallader, "Assorted Board Papers, Speeches, and Letters."

281 **"none of the girls":** Typed memo titled "Action of Board, December 9, 1919," Cadwallader, "Assorted Board Papers, Speeches, and Letters."

282 **nine Protestant groups:** By Cadwallader's count, there were fourteen denominations working within Chinatown's twelve-block area.

282 **"There seemed to be":** Charles Reginald Shepherd, *The Story of Chung Mei: Being the Authentic History of the Chung Mei Home for Chinese Boys up to Its Fifteenth Anniversary, October, 1938* (Philadelphia: Judson Press, 1938), 6.

282 **"There are so many":** Ibid., 9–10.

283 **make some changes:** Logan, *Ventures in Mission,* 40.

283 **"District" operation:** Cadwallader to Margaret E. Hodge, Oct. 4, 1920, and Hodge to Cadwallader, Sept. 20, 1920, Cadwallader, "Assorted Board Papers, Speeches, and Letters."

283 **"a really happy time":** Donaldina Cameron's handwritten diary, Jan. 1921, Cameron Family Papers. Private family papers courtesy of Ann F. Cameron.

283 **The following weeks:** Ibid.

283 **"the real number":** See Cadwallader to W. Reginald Wheeler, Sept. 27, 1921, Cadwallader, "Assorted Board Papers, Speeches, and Letters."

284 **"off the books"**: Cadwallader to F. S. Bennett, July 20, 1921, 3, Cadwallader, "Assorted Board Papers, Speeches, and Letters."

39. "Sargy"

285 **white handkerchief**: Wilson, *Chinatown Quest*, 121.
285 **long-troubled Chinatown Squad**: Mullen, *Chinatown Squad*, 146.
287 **A photograph from that meeting**: "Jesse Brown Cook Scrapbooks Documenting San Francisco History and Law Enforcement, ca. 1895–1936," accessed Aug. 2, 2017, www.oac.cdlib.org. Description of the scene from a photograph in the Bancroft Library titled *Peace Meeting in Chinatown, February 1921,* Banc Pic 1996.003, vol. 10 of the Jesse Cook Scrapbooks.
287 **murder rate**: Mullen, *Dangerous Strangers*, 78–79.
288 **largest rescues**: Inspector John J. Manion, "Lo Mo: Mother of Chinatown," *Women and Missions*, Jan. 1932, 388.
288 **"Good morning"**: Wilson's account of this raid in *Chinatown Quest* (213–15) says that Wu and Higgins also accompanied Cameron. The newspaper story did not mention this, but it is highly likely Wu would have been there because Cameron and Manion would have needed her as an interpreter. Manion's first-person account of this states that Wu and Higgins were present.
288 **"You stay across the street"**: Ernest Lenn, "Dong Lai—Slave Girl," *San Francisco News*, Aug. 24, 1933, Martin Papers. This raid is also related in *Chinatown Quest* and *Chinatown's Angry Angel*.
288 **A big man**: Mullen, *Chinatown Squad*, 146.
288 **Manion had scouted the building**: Wilson, *Chinatown Quest*, 213–15.
289 **nickname "Sargy"**: "Sergeant Manion Five Years in Chinatown," *Douglas 20, Police Journal*, July 1926, Bancroft Library; Opie L. Warner, "White Man Rules Chinatown for 20 Years," *Police and Peace Officers' Journal*, Feb. 1941.
289 **Mass at Old St. Mary's**: Jerry Flamm, *Good Life in Hard Times: San Francisco's '20s and '30s* (San Francisco: Chronicle Books, 1978), 94.
289 **"I feared that we might"**: Manion, "Lo Mo," 389.

40. Bessie

290 **best-known image of Cameron**: With thanks for his guidance on this photograph to Professor Lee, *Picturing Chinatown*.
292 **"Oh, I'm ready for the auction block"**: Dr. Bessie Jeong, oral history interview by Suellen Cheng and Munson Kwok, Feb. 25, 1983, Chinese Women of America, 1848–1942, Research Project, Chinese Historical Society of Southern California, Los Angeles (courtesy of Judy Yung).
292 **Typically, a matchmaker**: Yung, *Unbound Feet*, 165.
293 **"you would be a sort of slave"**: Ibid., citing Bessie Jeong, "Story of a Chinese Girl Student," Survey of Race Relations Collection, Hoover Institution on War, Revolution, and Peace, Stanford University.
293 **"He had a horrible disposition"**: Bessie Jeong, "Story of a Chinese Girl Student," Survey of Race Relations Collection, Hoover Institution on War, Revolution, and Peace, Stanford University, 3.
293 **Bessie was a fast learner**: Ibid., 4.

293 **"I wasn't insulted"**: Dr. Bessie Jeong, oral history interview by Suellen Cheng and Munson Kwok.

293 **"were being sold"**: Ibid., 13.

294 **"to kill me again"**: May Louie Wong to Cameron, June 29, 1916, Cameron House Files.

294 **"There is no use in talking"**: Jeong, "Story of a Chinese Girl Student," 5.

294 **rather homely teen**: Photograph of Jeong from Stanford yearbook, 1927, 148.

294 **forced into matrimony**: Jeong, "Story of a Chinese Girl Student."

294 **She left the boardinghouse**: Cameron House Files. Much of the following material on Bessie Jeong comes from the private archives at Cameron House on Bessie Jeong a.k.a. Jeong Yoke Yeen.

295 **"I knew that if I went"**: Jeong, "Story of a Chinese Girl Student," 5–6.

11. Heavens for Courage

296 **judge Frank Murasky**: Evarts I. Blake, *San Francisco: A Brief Biographical Sketch of Some of the Most Prominent Men Who Will Preside over Her Destiny for at Least Two Years* (San Francisco: Press Pacific, 1902), 137.

296 **kidnapped by bandits**. Cameron House Files. One of the brothers managed to escape and return to the United States, where he came up with money required to free them. The family remained divided, because the father stayed in China and Jeong, her sister, and at least one brother were in America.

296 **"You have no idea"**: Mae Louie Wong to Donaldina Cameron, Feb. 2, 1917, Cameron House Files.

296 **"I give you the heavens"**: Dr. Bessie Jeong, oral history interview by Suellen Cheng and Munson Kwok.

298 **they enrolled her**: Ethel Higgins, "Letter to Mrs. C. S. Wright Regarding Bessie Jeong," Jan. 26, 1926, Bessie Jeong case file 982, Cameron House Files.

299 **"she may continue"**: Donaldina Cameron, "Recommendation Letter to Stanford University," July 18, 1925, Bessie Jeong case file 982, Cameron House Files.

300 **"In all this time"**: Ethel Higgins to Mrs. C. S. Wright Regarding Bessie Jeong, Jan. 26, 1926, Cameron House Files.

300 **David Starr Jordan**: Jordan was called by Clarence Darrow as an expert witness for the defense in the Scopes Trial the year that Jeong was admitted to Stanford.

300 **"I believe that she"**: Donaldina Cameron, "Letters Requesting Help in Obtaining a Tutor for Bessie Jeong," Nov. 13, 1925, Cameron House Files.

300 **In June 1927**: *The Stanford Quad (Year Book of Stanford University)* (1927), 148.

300 **to graduate from Stanford**: "Noted Chinese Woman to Address Y.W. Committee," *Stanford Daily*, Feb. 3, 1933.

301 **"It was a happy reward"**: Donaldina Cameron, "New Lives from Old Chinatown," *Missionary Review of the World* (1934): 330, Mason Papers.

301 **Cameron wrote to congressmen**: Mildred C. Martin, "Eulogy for Dr. Bessie Jeong," 1992, 3–4, Martin Papers; Cameron House Files. See also Dr. Bessie Jeong, oral history interview by Suellen Cheng and Munson Kwok, 36.

301 **"If they see 'Bessie'"**: Yung, *Unbound Feet*, 142.

301 **"I hate to say this"**: "Story of a Chinese Girl Student," box 25, folder 54, Survey of Race Relations, Hoover Institution Archives.

42. The Thwack of Bouncing Balls

303 **largest luxury liners:** Department of Justice, "Wu, Tien Fuh."

303 **nearly a thousand passengers:** Kenneth J. Blume, *Historical Dictionary of the U.S. Maritime Industry* (Lanham, Md.: Scarecrow Press, 2012), 400.

303 **jobless rate:** "Unemployment Relief Distribution in the Bay Area During the Depression," Cliometric Society, accessed Aug. 9, 2017, www.cliometrics.org.

303 **two million people:** *Chronicle of America* (New York: Dorling Kindersley, 1995), 654.

305 **porcelain "foo dogs":** These were temple-guarding lion figures, often referred to as foo dogs by American tourists and others.

305 **The sounds of children playing:** For more detail, see Wendy Rouse Jorae, *The Children of Chinatown: Growing Up Chinese American in San Francisco, 1850–1920* (Chapel Hill: University of North Carolina Press, 2009).

305 **Built into the hillside:** Choy, *San Francisco Chinatown*, 102–3. It is now named the Willie "Woo Woo" Wong Playground, named in 2009 after a five-foot-five basketball phenomenon from the neighborhood.

305 **"This Is a Private Family":** Pardee Lowe, "Chinatown in Transition," 1938, 7, Pardee Lowe Papers, Hoover Institution on War, Revolution, and Peace, Stanford University. Lowe was a Chinese merchant born in San Francisco. He wrote this unpublished manuscript about Chinatown in the 1930s for a travel magazine, which turned it down.

306 **open segregation continued:** Choy, *San Francisco Chinatown*, 179–83.

306 **safety net:** Yung, *Unbound Feet*, 180–81.

306 **crowded conditions:** Community Chest of San Francisco Social Work Department, "Survey of Social Work Needs of the Chinese Population of San Francisco," March 19, 1930, 3, Chinese Baby Home Correspondence, 1924–1930, PHS.

306 **free herb dispensary:** Lowe, "Chinatown in Transition," 10.

306 **"In recent years":** Community Chest of San Francisco Social Work Department, "Survey of Social Work Needs of the Chinese Population of San Francisco," 15.

307 **"You will see Tien Wu":** Cameron to Mrs. Bennett, May 20, 1931, Martin Papers.

307 **a better alternative:** Robert Eric Barde, *Immigration at the Golden Gate: Passenger Ships, Exclusion, and Angel Island* (Westport, Conn.: Praeger, 2008), 205. See also Lee and Yung, *Angel Island*.

307 **official-looking letters:** Carol Green Wilson, "A Vital Need," *Women and Missions*, Aug. 1931, 172, Cameron Family private collection.

308 **"far better to go back":** Logan, taped interview by Mason.

308 **"The fate of these helpless girls":** Wilson, "Vital Need." This is an "as told to" commentary from Cameron to Wilson, who would become her first biographer.

308 **"The thought of Miss Cameron":** Ibid. The article quotes from a letter to Cameron from a missionary named Mrs. Hinckey, and the rescued young woman is named Li Ah King.

309 **"I am sure Miss Wu":** Donaldina Cameron, "To Edna R. Voss, Secretary, on the Need for a South China Affiliate," June 23, 1931, Martin Papers, 4–13, Cameron-Logan letters, 1922–1936, Stanford Special Collections.

309 **Stone had founded:** Daniel H. Bays, *Christianity in China: From the Eighteenth Century to the Present* (Stanford, Calif.: Stanford University Press, 1999), 315.

43. Little General

311 **turned down several suitors:** Martin, *Chinatown's Angry Angel*, 242.
311 **"They are congenial and gentlemanly":** Donaldina Cameron, "Exodus from 920 to China," ca. 1933, 2, citing a letter from Tien Fuh Wu, Martin Papers.
313 **"how God supplied":** Ibid.
313 **Bethel mission:** Photographs of the Gospel Hall and Bible Seminary of the Bethel Mission are located at the Yale Divinity School Library.
313 **apparently lovers:** Jane Hunter, *The Gospel of Gentility: American Women Missionaries in Turn-of-the-Century China* (New Haven, Conn.: Yale University Press, 1984), 74–75.
314 **"Ladder Streets":** Department of Justice, "Wu, Tien Fuh."
314 **Wu's forceful personality:** Logan, taped interview by Mason.
314 **"Please tell your Dr. Bessie":** Cameron, "Exodus from 920 to China," 5.
315 **tensions between the two countries:** "The Road to Pearl Harbor: The United States and East Asia, 1915–1941," EDSITEment, accessed Aug. 10, 2017, edsitement.neh.gov.
315 **"loyalty and integrity":** The files include a letter from Cameron referencing Wu's mailing address in Hong Kong, which was 5 Ladder Street.
315 **Her permit to reenter:** Department of Justice, "Wu, Tien Fuh."
315 **home in southern China:** Logan, *Ventures in Mission*, 46. Logan, who was Cameron's successor at the Mission Home, wrote about Wu's trip: "She was able to return in the following year, disappointed that her hoped-for plan had not materialized, but grateful to God for His provision for each one of the girls."

44. Shangri-La

316 **Shopkeepers had replaced:** Lowe, "Chinatown in Transition," 4–6.
316 **hand-carved camphor chests:** Choy, *San Francisco Chinatown*, 203. The Eastern Bakery was established in 1924.
318 **hardware store:** A 1930 partnership list of the Wing Lee Co. named forty-five members, twelve of whom were active, and a total capitalization of $30,000. Leong Chong Po (a.k.a. Wong See Duck) is named as the manager of the group, with the largest capital position in the firm of $2,000. Partnership Investigation Case file 13502–900-B, Wing Lee Co., 900 Grant Avenue, National Archives, San Bruno, Calif.
318 **a well-fed man:** Immigration and Naturalization Service, Immigration case files of Lee Lon Ying a.k.a. Wong So, No. 12016/5916 (n.d.). Photographs included in letter to INS Seattle district director dated March 27, 1935.
319 **Wong See Duck for many years:** Because Wong See Duck and one of the women who testified against him, Wong So, share surnames, the merchant will generally be referred to by his full name and the woman will be referred to by her full name.
319 **syndicate of investors:** Alfonso J. Zirpoli, *Faith in Justice: Alfonso J. Zirpoli and the United States District Court for the Northern District of California*, 35, an oral history conducted 1982–1983 by Sarah L. Sharp, Regional Oral History Office, Bancroft Library, accessed Aug. 13, 2017, archive.org.

320   **average new house:** "1930s Important News and Events, Key Technology, Fashion, and Popular Culture," The People History, accessed Aug. 16, 2017, www.thepeoplehistory.com. According to this, the average cost of a new home in the United States in 1930 was $7,145.

320   **during that passage:** Zirpoli, *Faith in Justice,* 36.

320   **"Smoking rooms":** Flamm, *Good Life in Hard Times,* 84.

322   **Harvard Business School graduate:** "East and West Meet in San Francisco Home of K. L. Kwong, New Chinese Consul General," *San Francisco News,* Jan. 24, 1935, Yung Collection.

322   **turkey dinner:** Unknown, but possibly Evelyn Browne Bancroft, "Description of Christmas Celebrations at the Mission Home in the Early 1930s," 4–14, Personal letters, Martin Papers.

322   **Jeung gave birth:** "Birth Certificate for Wong Jeong David," May 18, 1934, U.S. District Court SF No. 25295 U.S. vs. Fong Shee, Dept. Exhibit B, National Archives and Records Administration.

322   **Zirpoli, prosecutor of the case:** Zirpoli, *Faith in Justice,* iv.

322   **Jeung's courageous flight:** Valentine C. Hammack as told to Dean S. Jennings, "Broken Blossoms: Exposing San Francisco's Vice Marts," *Famous Detective Cases,* Oct. 1935, 95, Donaldina Cameron biographical file, PHS. Hammack was an assistant U.S. district attorney at the time of this case, and the details in this article are largely supported by the extensive case files in the National Archives and Records Administration.

323   **The only person authorized:** Ibid. This bank statement was entered into evidence during the trial and is now part of the National Archives and Records Administration's case files.

323   **threatened tong war:** Edward Wong, "The 1935 Broken Blossoms Case—Four Chinese Women and Their Fight for Justice," 43, accessed Aug. 16, 2017, edward wong.atavist.com.

324   **"In the course":** Ibid., 37.

324   **a strong enough case:** Prosecutors discovered this was the same apartment at 826 Jackson Street that one of Wong See Duck's daughters had listed as her home address with her school, helping them to further link Wong See Duck and his wife to the transaction.

45. Broken Blossoms

327   **Unable to speak:** Martin, *Chinatown's Angry Angel,* 258.

327   **The holdouts, Zirpoli believed:** Zirpoli, *Faith in Justice,* 36.

327   **Jeung clung to Cameron:** Martin, *Chinatown's Angry Angel,* 258–59.

327   **block Cameron and Wu:** Tien Fuh Wu, "Dear Friends of the Women's Missionary Society," Feb. 20, 1936, box 6, folder 6, Martin Papers.

327   **"Even this trying experience":** "'920' News Letter," March 1935, SFTS.

327   **another enslaved woman:** "Case of Lee Choy Ying," typed transcript of interview with Wong So.

329   **At three in the morning:** "S.F. Slave Girl Names High Ups," *San Francisco Examiner,* April 18, 1935, Cameron House Archives.

329   **the ring led by Wong See Duck:** Ibid.

330 **"Such a heart I'd bear"**: Donaldina Cameron's *Sunday School Scholars' Bible*, Cameron Family Papers.

330 **"And such wisdom"**: Julia Ward Howe, "A Vision of Palm Sunday," in *The Julia Ward Howe Birthday Book: Selections from Her Works* (Boston: Lee and Shepard, 1889), 234.

330 **"We feel quite limp"**: Martin, *Chinatown's Angry Angel*, 261, citing letter from Lorna Logan to her family, May 3, 1935.

330 **daily transcripts**: Zirpoli, *Faith in Justice*, 36.

331 **discovered in New York**: "Louie Gin Leung Aka Lee Gim Gook," 1930s, Cameron House Files.

331 **"baby cottage"**: "'920' News Letter," 3.

331 **a black-and-white photograph**: Donaldina Cameron's *Sunday School Scholars' Bible*, Cameron Family Papers. The photograph is undated; it remained in the Bible even after Cameron's death.

331 **"Now little David and Alice"**: Tien Fuh Wu, "Dear Friends of the Women's Missionary Society," 2.

332 **the couple was married**: Wong, "1935 Broken Blossoms Case," 47.

332 **Lois Qui Wong**: Ibid.

332 **a fictitious name**. The birth certificate lists her name as Lois Jeong and the father's name as Wong Kwong. However, it did accurately note that Jeung lived at the Mission Home at 920 Sacramento Street.

Epilogue: "Blessed Tien"

333 **Mother's Day cards**: Tien Fuh Wu et al., "God Bless You on Mother's Day," n.d., Martin Papers.

333 **her employer's**: Her employer was the Presbyterian Church in the United States, headquartered in New York City, under the Board of National Missions.

333 **mishandling of a case**: Case 1311, Cameron House Files, including extensive correspondence and trial testimony, and newspaper clippings.

335 **Chinese Peace Association**: Adam McKeown, *Chinese Migrant Networks and Cultural Change: Peru, Chicago, and Hawaii, 1900–1936* (Chicago: University of Chicago Press, 2001), 185.

335 **settle disputes**: Cameron to Chinese Peace Association of San Francisco, April 1937, Cameron House Files.

335 **an alarming handwritten letter**: Case 1311, 1937, Cameron House Files. There are about a dozen newspaper clippings in this file, although not all of them are identified or fully dated. They appear to be mostly from the Sacramento papers and appeared between February and April 1937.

335 **"Surely no man"**: Cameron House Files, 1937. Cameron's typed notes for speaking before the Chinese Peace Association, dated April of that year.

335 **Cameron was widely credited**: The teen's baby died shortly after it was born, 335 Sacramento's district attorney probed the death as a suspected murder. See "Babcock Probes Murder Theory in Death of Baby Who Caused Tong Feud," Cameron House Files.

336 **"She heard of the case"**: Cameron House Files, 1937. Report of Investigation Case of *People of the State of Cal. v. Chan Bong Yen*. The report is signed by

F. Louis and may be the result of Cameron's entreaties to the state's attorney general to look into the matter.

336   **Higgins had been:** Ethel Higgins, Personnel File, October 5, 1933, Biographical Vertical file, PHS.

336   **"First, owing to the fact":** Wu to Voss, Aug. 14, 1934, RG 414, PHS.

336   **"one of the sweetest":** Voss to Wu, Aug. 21, 1934, RG 414, PHS.

337   **a confidential report:** Logan to Katherine E. Gladfelter, Feb. 26, 1948, Mason Papers.

337   **forced to rely on Wu:** Unlike Cameron, Lorna Logan succeeded in learning Chinese and immersing herself more deeply in Chinese culture by living in China during a sabbatical, visiting her sister who was a missionary working in China. Lorna Logan correspondence, Mason Papers, and recollections of Doreen Der-McLeod.

337   **couldn't carry a tune:** Logan, taped interview by Mason.

337   **"It is almost a tragedy":** Cameron to Logan, Feb. 24, 1937, Martin Papers.

337   **Cameron objected:** Logan, taped interview by Mason.

338   **entertained visitors:** Details on Cameron and Wu in their old age come from a panel discussion attended by the author and held on the evening of December 5, 2015, at Cameron House with four of Cameron's relatives: her grandnieces Ann Cameron and Catherine Cameron, her grandnephew Scott Cameron, and Donaldina (Donny) Cameron Klingen, another grandniece. During the discussion that evening, Catherine Cameron noted that it was her experience with the woman she called her "Auntie Wu" that helped lead to her scholarship on slavery. She dedicated her book *Captives: How Stolen People Changed the World* (Lincoln: University of Nebraska Press, 2016) to "Tien Fuh Wu (1886–1973) and other women who have survived slavery."

338   **After Cameron died:** With thanks to Ann Cameron for providing an eight-track audio recording of Donaldina Cameron's January 14, 1968, memorial service.

338   **barred Chinese:** Ching-Ching Ni, "The Site Where Chinese Laborers Were Interred, Their Graves Later Forgotten, Gets a Memorial," *Los Angeles Times,* March 9, 2010, articles.latimes.com.

339   **"It is going to be VERY hard":** Cameron to Miss Goddard, Oct. 16, 1941, RG 414, PHS.

A Note on Names and Language

353   **refers to heaven or sky:** In Wade-Giles Romanization, T'ien can mean "heaven" or "sky" or refer to a deity. www.britannica.com.

Index

PMH indicates Presbyterian Mission Home.
Page numbers in *italics* refer to illustrations.

abolitionists, 25, 93, 164
Achoy, *see* Ah Toy
Addams, Jane, xi
Ah Ching, 114, 119
Ah Fah, 50–51, 350
Ah Gum, 143, 145
Ah Ho, 46
Ah Toy, 30, 32–34, 347, 365
Ah Tsun, 216
Ah Ying, 255–57, 395
American Exchange Hotel, 20–21, 22
Angel Island Immigration Station, 241,
    242, 298, 306, 307–8, 352
Annals of San Francisco, The, 32, 33
anti-Chinese legislation
    Chinese Exclusion Act, *see* Chinese
        Exclusion Act
    Page Act, 40, 70, 349
anti-Chinese sandlot riots, *47*, 49–50
anti-Chinese violence
    increase in early 1880s, 70, 72, 73
    sandlot riots, *47*, 49–50
antimiscegenation laws, 11, 75, 242–43,
    346
Arabian Oyae, *see* Yamada Waka
Asaba Waka, *see* Yamada Waka
Atoy, *see* Ah Toy
auctioning of women, 13, 223, 362

Babcock, Eleanor Olney, 97, 244, 279
Bailey, Charles Alden ("Charley"), 65,
    202, 246
Baldwin, Elias J. ("Lucky"), 62, 64, 350
Bancroft, Evelyn (née Browne), 95, 199,
    283
Banta, Mary E., 255, 256
Barbary Coast (district bordering
    Chinatown), 11, *219*, 270
Barstow, George, 52
Baskin, Miss, 76
Bethel Mission in Shanghai, 309, 313
Board of Education, Brown v., 73
bound feet, custom of, 30, 82, 83–84,
    182
Boxer Rebellion, 180, 182
Bray, Mrs. J. G., 41
Broken Blossoms trials, 327, 329, 330–31,
    332, 333, 347, 352
brothels, 8, *31*
    conversion into family housing, 305
    female ownership of, 33–34
    Kane's assistance to missionaries in
        rescues from, 140, 141, 142, 166
    in Oakland, 210–11
    Peking (Chinatown brothel), 85–86
    police crackdowns on, 45, 270
    raids in 1897 on, 112–13

brothels (continued)
    rumors spread about Mission Home
        by, 113
    tourists' visits to, 139, 140, 141
    white watchmen used by, 145
Brown, Arthur Judson, 77–78
Browne, Mary Ann, 51, 91, 95, 367
Browne, Mrs. P. D., 305, 306
Brown v. Board of Education, 73
Brun, S. J., 130–31
bubonic plague epidemic
    in Chinatown, 119–21, 124, 125, 126
    in Honolulu, 120, 122
    mass vaccination program in
        Chinatown for, 119–20, 121,
        122–23
    in other parts of San Francisco, 126
    quarantine in Chinatown for, 116, 118,
        121, 125, 351
Buffalo Bill Cody, 261
Bulletin, The, 218, 221, 222, 224, 346
Burns, William J., 222

Cadwallader, Mrs. Rawlins, 272, 280, 281,
        283, 284
California Society for the Prevention of
        Cruelty to Children, 75, 85, 103
Calvary Presbyterian Church, 25, 28
Cameron, Allan (Donaldina's brother),
        18, 37, 64, 65
    at Berenda ranch, 36
    death of, 253, 325, 352
    in New Zealand, 35
    as ranch foreman at La Puente, 62
Cameron, Allan (Donaldina's father),
        18–19
    death of, 64, 95
    financial crisis of, 34–35, 191
    pneumonia after pursuit of rustlers, 36
    ranch at Berenda, 35
    as ranch foreman at La Puente, 62,
        64, 350
Cameron, Annie, 18, 37, 62
Cameron, Catherine, 18
Cameron, Donaldina ("Dolly"), 345, 353
    after earthquake and fires of 1906, 196,
        198–203, 205, 208–10, 216, 241, 351

anniversary celebration for, 277, 279–80
annual reports to Presbyterian board,
        140, 158, 161, 164
appointment as PMH's
        superintendent, 120, 127, 351
bedroom at PMH, 277, 279
as Bessie Jeong's advocate, 294–95, 296,
        298, 299–301
biography of, 337
birth of, 19, 35, 349
breakdown in 1898, 115
Chinese Peace Association and,
        335–36
on conversion of rescued women to
        Christianity, 162
Culbertson as mentor to, 99–100, 115,
        118, 199
during Culbertson's illness, 114, 376
custody of girls, 127–33, 132, 139, 296,
        333
death of, 338, 339, 352
diary from 1909, 244, 246–48
in Dragon Stories, 234, 236
early life of, 18–19, 20, 21, 35–37, 62, 64,
        349, 350
effect of Leung Yuen Qui's death on,
        155, 158, 162
enemies' nicknames for, xi, 289, 354
engagement to George Sargent, 64–65,
        95, 374
engagement to Nathaniel Tooker, 252,
        394
evolving perspective of, 164–66, 178–79
fame of, 131, 133–34, 139, 164, 165–67,
        168, 283–84
family background of, xi, 18–19, 191
first day at PMH, 95, 97–100, 101
during flu pandemic of 1918, 274–75,
        298
fund raising by, 216, 272, 274, 283–84
Genthe's friendship with, 190–92, 246,
        345
health of, 246, 251–52
hiring of Higgins, 268, 270
imprisonment in Palo Alto in 1900,
        127, 128–29
internal rift between Occidental
        Board and, 281

interpreters for, 152–53, 154–55, 158, 178,
236, 239, 241
Kane and, 140–41
legal battles for PMH, 127–33, *132*, 139,
296
Manion and, 285, 288–89
photographs of, *96*, *97*, *163*, *165*, *287*,
312, *334*
PMH renamed in honor of, 337
recruitment of Shepherd as new ally,
282–83
relationship with Wu, 152, 156, 158, 236,
307, 337–39, 352, 354
rescue work of, xi, 118–19, 140–41,
210–11, 283–84, 285, 288–90, *291*
retirement of, 333, 335–36, 337–38, 352
return from La Puente in 1900, 118, 127
role in arranging marriages, 249, *250*,
251, *253–55*, *332*
role in furthering education of
residents, 178
support for bubonic plague
vaccinations, 120, 123
testimony at Fisk Commission
hearings, 138, 139–41
Tooker Home and, 252, 274, 275–76, 281
on "Underground Chinatown" exhibit,
264
at Wong See Duck's trial, 325, 327
Cameron, Ewen, 191
Cameron, Helen, 18, 36, 37
Cameron, Isabella MacKenzie, 18–19, 20,
21, 34, 36–37, 64, 349
Cameron, Jessie, 18, 35, 64, 65, 202, 369
Cameron family, 18–19
grief over Isabella's death, 36–37
journey to San Francisco, 18–19, 349
life in New Zealand, 19, 35
ranch at Berenda, 34, 35–36
at Rancho La Puente, 62, *63*, 64
short stay in San Francisco, 18, 19–22
Wu's burial in family plot of, 338
Cameron House, ix, 337
see also Presbyterian Mission Home
Carey, Mary S., 72
Carnegie, Andrew, 167, 351
Caruso, Enrico, 193
Cassatt, Mary, 53

Chew, Mansie, 77
Chew, Ng Poon, 79, 215, 345, 353, 385–86,
390
after earthquake and fire of 1906, 198,
204, 206, 208
children of, 77, 121
death of, 318
education of, 70, 73–74, 201, 350
founding of *Chung Sai Yat Po*, 78,
121–22
immigration to San Francisco, 70
integration into white Oakland
neighborhood, 212, 214, 390
as a journalist, 77–78, 378
as a pastor, *71*, 74–75, 77
photograph of, *184*
prejudice encountered by, *72*
reporting on plague epidemic in
Chinatown, 121, 122–23, 126, 377
on residence certificates requirement,
184
speaking tour across the United States,
185–87, 188
support of Presbyterian Mission
Home, 78, 183, 216–17, 274
threatening note sent to, 93
wedding of, 76, 350
China Inland Mission, 232, 392
China's 1898 Reform Movement, 182
Chinatown
brothels in, *see* brothels
bubonic plague epidemic in, 119–21,
124, *125*, 126
mass vaccination program for,
119–20, 121, 122–23
quarantine for, 116, 118, 120, 121, *125*,
351
corruption in, 101, 103–5, 135, *136*,
137–39, 223, 351
destruction of, in fires of 1906, 202,
204, 206, *207*, 207
district associations in, 10
Farwell's report on, 67–69, *68*, 73
Genthe's photographs of, 188, *189*, 190,
191
Grant Avenue in, 215, 316, *317*
herbalists in, 59
as largely a society of men, 10–11, *17*

Chinatown *(continued)*
  photographs of
    after dark, *102*
    alley in early 1930s in, *4*
    children in, *89, 157, 304*
    crowded condition in tenement
      houses, *117*
    Sacramento Street in 1866, *24*
  population of, 305
  prostitution in, xi–xii
    after gold rush, 30, 32
    as blamed for outbreaks of venereal
      diseases, 45
    in Farwell's report, 67, *68,* 73
    intense demand for, 11–12, 79
    "tong war" over, 48–49
    white customers of, 11
  rebuilding of, after fire of 1906, 208,
    214–15
  reformed Police Squad in, 103–6, *104,*
    135, *136,* 137–38, 285, 287–89, 319,
    346
  rivalry between missionaries in, 23
  sexual slavery in, *see* sexual slavery
  stereotypes about, in world's fair, 258,
    259, 260–62, 263–65
  tourists' visits to, 53, *54,* 55–58, 103,
    108–9, 139, 140, 141
  violent crimes in, 101, 103, 106, 108, 112,
    374–75
Chinatown Quest (Wilson), 337
Chinese Consolidated Benevolent
    Association, *see* Six Companies
    (Chinese Consolidated
    Benevolent Association)
Chinese Exclusion Act, 84, 94, 350
  debates in Congress to extend,
    164–65
  Examiner's support for extension of,
    137
  extension of, 137, 164–65, 183
  increase in trafficking from China
    after, 165
  indefinite extension of, 183
  lopsided gender ratio between
    Chinese immigrants due
    to, 75
  passage of, 69, 70, 79, 350

"paper sons" methods of skirting the,
    228–30
  repeal of, 187
Chinese immigrants, *9, 23*
  burial in cemeteries, barred from, 338
  children in *mui tsai* system, *80,* 83,
    84–85
  in Chinatown, *see* Chinatown
  civil rights of, 78, 126, 184, 185–87, 188
  female
    in late 1860s, 8, 10, 11–12
    missionaries' efforts directed toward,
      27–29
    trafficking of, *see* sexual slavery
  gender imbalance among, 10–11, 79,
    254
  health fears raised by Farwell's report
    relating to, 68–69
  institutionalized harassment and
    racism against, 38, 40, 72–73, 370
  legislation restricting, 40, 69, 70, 79,
    349; *see also* Chinese Exclusion
    Act
  male, hair and clothing of, 22
  programs offered by missionaries to,
    73–74
  residence certificates requirement for,
    184, 187, 350
  tensions between working-class Irish
    Catholics and, 42, 43, 49
  violence toward, 22, 23, 25, 40, 49–50,
    70, 72, 73
  see also specific immigrants
Chinese Peace Association, 335
Chin Jun, 55
Chin Mooie, 56
Choy, Philip P., 215
Chun Fah, 79, 217, 305, 318, 345, 350
  after earthquake of 1906, 198, 204, 212,
    214
  as an interpreter, 75
  arrival at PMH, 75
  children of, 77
  nickname of "Spring Flower," 76
  threatening note sent to, 93
  wedding of, 76
Chung Mei Home for Chinese Boys,
    283

Chung Sai Yat Po (Chinese-Western Daily), 214, 318, 330, 376, 377, 378
advocacy for Chinese American women's rights, 183
circulation of, 183
coverage of Wong See Duck's trials, 330
founding of, 78, 121–22
on mass inoculations for bubonic plague, 122, 377
office of, after fires of 1906, 204, 206
plague epidemic and, 126
post-earthquake publication of, 208, *213*
on racially motivated attacks after fires, 214
on Sieh King King, 180
support for economic boycott in 1905, 185
Chy Lung, 40, 350
Chy Lung v. Freeman, 40, 350
City of Paris, 41
civil rights
of Chinese Americans, Chew's role in defending, 78, 126, 184, 185–87, 188
concerning lawful search and seizure, in rescues, 141
Clark, John A., 33
Cohn, Newton E., 230
Cole, Caroline Hubbell, 27–28
Coleman, Horace C., 160–61, 232, 236, 393
Collins, Wilkie, 53
Condit, Ira, 46, 48, 74, 76, 77
Condit, Samantha, 27, 28–29, 38, 44, 46, 318
Cook, Jesse Brown, 105, 351
criminal tongs
Chinese Peace Association and, 335
in Oakland, 211
payoffs to police, 103
peace meeting between rival leaders in 1921, 287, *287*
role in prostitution and trafficking, 46, 48–49, 79, 81
violence between, 107–8, 375
see also Little Pete (Fung Jing Toy)
Crocker, Mrs. H. J., 272
Crowley, Patrick, 103, 106

Culbertson, Margaret, *111*, 345, 350
background of, 51
as Cameron's mentor, 99–100, 115, 118, 199
custody of girls, 75, 154
death of, 114–15, 156, 351
extended medical leave from PMH, 88, 92
financial sponsorship arranged for Wu, 159–60
frustration with not being able to stop trafficking, 112–14
health of, 52, 88, 92, 95, 99, 110, 114–15, 376
legal battles of, 52, 60, 61, 93, 110, 112, 154, 374
reliance on translators, 76, 152–53, 154
threats to, 52, 93–94, 97–98, 99, 112
transformation of PMH, 51–52
Culbertson, Margaret Belle (niece), 58, 59–60, 61
Cummings, Miss, 43

Daily Alta California, 18, 20, 67
Daily Examiner, The, 14
Davis, Jefferson, 25
Degas, Edgar, 53
de Young, Michael, 193
Dodge, Grace, 216
"Doe, Mary," 143
Dollar, Margaret, 274
Dollar, Robert, 274, 275, 345
Donn Quai Yuen Theater, 180, *181*
Doors of Hope, 309
Dragon Stories (Genthe and Wales), 232, 234–35, 236, 256, 392
Dred Scott decision, 185
Dreim Farm, 34
due process clause, 185
Dyer, Edgar G., 128, 129, 133

education
programs offered to Chinese students by missionaries, 73–74
segregation in public schools, 72–74, 159, 351, 370

education *(continued)*
  Supreme Court rulings on
    in *Brown v. Board of Education,* 73
    in *Tape v. Hurley,* 72–73
Eighteenth Amendment, 352
equal protection clause, 73
Evergreen Cemetery, 338

F. C. Peters & Co., 107
Fahn Quai, 289, 354
Famous Detective Cases, 330
Farwell, William B., 67–69, *68,* 73
Federal Bureau of Investigation, 104
feet, binding of, 30, 82, 83–84, 182
Field, Mary H., 115, 351
Fifth Amendment, 185
First Presbyterian Church, 199, 200
Fisk, Arthur G., 137, 351
Fisk Commission, 147, 351
  hearings
    Cameron's testimony at, 139–41, 142
    girls' testimony at, 143, 145
    Lake's testimony at, 138–39, 142
    Phelan's testimony at, 138
    Sullivan's testimony at, 137–38
  legislation resulting from, 147
  visit to Methodist Mission Home, 143, 145–46
Flood, Mrs. James, 193
flu pandemic of 1918, 274–75, 298, 352
Fourteenth Amendment, 73
Freeman, Chy Lung v., 40, 350
Freeman, John H., 40
Freeman, Mrs. J. A., 272
Frost, Henry W., 232
Fung Jing Toy, *see* Little Pete (Fung Jing Toy)
Funston, Frederick, 198

gambling dens, 67, *68,* 103, 137, 138, 139
Gardner, David Charles, 130, 133, 379
Gardner, John Endicott, 131–32, 379, 380
Geary Act of 1892, 69, 350
Genthe, Arnold, 232, 260, 345
  Cameron's friendship with, 190–92, 246, 345

items lost in fire, 202–3
photographs after earthquake, 194–95, *197*
photographs after fires, *207*
photographs of Chinatown, 188, *189,* 190, 191
photographs of rescued girls from PMH, 191, *192,* 386
Unsuspecting Victim, Chinatown San Francisco, An, 189
Gibson, Otis, 16, 23, 25, 27, 48, 72, 362
Gibson, William F., 72, 73
Gilbert, W. S., 53
Gilchrist, Mrs., 299
gold, discovery of, 10
Golden Gate Bridge, 352
"Golden Peach," *see* Xijiao ("Golden Peach")
Gompers, Samuel, 186, 187
graft probe, 220–24, 351
Grant, Ulysses S., 49
Grauman, Sidney, 260, 262, 264
Great Britain, end of slavery in, 25
Great Depression, 3, 303, 305
Gulick, Emily, 26, 28
Gulick, John, 26

Hansen's disease, 68
Harper's, 66
Harper's Weekly, 125
Harrison, William Greer, 19
Harte, Bret, 27, 32, *39,* 207
Healy, Patrick, 185
Hearst, George, 41, 66
Hearst, Phoebe Apperson, 41, 66, 274, 276, 366
Hearst, William Randolph, 41, 66, 135, 137, 147, 186, 275
"Heathen Chinee, The" (Harte), *39,* 207
Heney, Francis J., 221–22, 223
Herrington, Bert A., 130, 132, 133
Higgins, Ethel, 276, 277, 345, 394
  as Cameron's aide, 268
  as director of Ming Quong Home, 336
  education of, 266
  financial gift to PMH, 274

during flu pandemic, 275
on Jeong, 300
at jubilee festivities, 280
in rescues, 288–89
World War I and, 270–71
Him Mark Lai, 232
Hip Yee Tong, 46, 79
Hodges, Ellen G., 55–58, 368
Hong Tong, 68
Honolulu, bubonic plague outbreak in, 120, 122
Hoover, Herbert, 305
Houseworth, Annie, 88, 90, 91, 92, 97
Howe, Julia Ward, 329–30
Hughes, Jennie, 309, 313, 314, 315
Hull House, founding of, xi
human trafficking, *see* sexual slavery
Hung Mooie, 200
Hurley, Tape v., 72–73

immigrants, Chinese, *see* Chinese immigrants
interracial marriage, 11, 75, 242–43, 346
Irish Catholics, working-class, tensions between Chinese immigrants and, 42, 43, 49
Irish laborers, importation and demonization of, 69

Japanese women
at PMH, 169, 173–74, 175, 177, 347
prostitutes, photograph of, 170
trafficking of, 169, 171
Yamada Waka, 169, 171–75, 176, 177–79, 347, 353–54
Jeong, Bessie, 297, 314, 346, 401, 405
Cameron's custody of, 296
education of, 293, 296, 298, 299–301
escape to PMH, 294–95, 296
family background of, 292–94
private medical practice of, 301
role in PMH's "baby cottage," 331
on slave trade, 301–2
Jeong Yoke Ying, *see* Jeong, Bessie

Jeung Gwai Ying, 321, 346, 353
children of, 321, 322, 327, 331, 332
escape to Mission Home, 6–7, 320–21, 352, 360
journey to the United States, 3, 4, 360
marriage of, 332
pregnancy of, 6, 320, 322
sexual slavery of, 3, 5, 319, 320, 324
testimony against Wong See Duck, 325, 327, 330, 346
Jim (Chinese cook), 36
Jin Ho, 16, 18, 23
"John" (Nordhoff), 66
Jordan, David Starr, 300, 401
Ju Toy, United States v., 184–85

Kane, Frank J., 140, 141, 142, 166
Kearney, Denis, 47, 49, 50, 69
Keller, Helen, 261
Kelly, Grace, 161
Key, Francis Scott, 42
Kibbe, Minora E., 198, 199
Kim Quey, *see* Kum Quai
Kipling, Rudyard, 53
Kum Mah, 153, 154
Kum Quai, 127–33, 132, 139, 379, 380
Kwong, K. L., 322
Kwong Dock Tong, 48

Lake, Margarita J., 138–39, 140, 142, 143, 145–46, 166, 380
Langdon, William H., 223
language, note on, 354
Laughlin, John H., 266, 268, 274, 276
Lee Book Dong, 211
Lee Long Ying, *see* Jeung Gwai Ying
leprosy, *see* Hansen's disease
Leung Bing Chung, 227, 228–29, 230
Leung Foo, *see* Wong See Duck
Leung Kai Ming, 256
Leung Kum Ching, 118–19
Leung Louie Gin, 331
Leung Yuen Qui, 119, 153, 153–55, 156, 158, 161, 162
Light House Mission Band, 76

Little Pete (Fung Jing Toy), 79, 103, 110, 112, 346
  criminal enterprises of, 81, 107, 132
  final portrait of, *107*
  funeral for, 108–9
  murder of, 106–8, 351, 375
Logan, Lorna, 337, 406
Longfellow, Henry Wadsworth, 26, 35
Look Tin Eli, 215
Loomis, Mrs. Henry, 41
"Love in Our Society" (Yamada), 177

MacArthur, Walter, 187
MacKenzie, Donald, 37
MacKenzie, Isabella, *see* Cameron, Isabella MacKenzie
Manchuria, 315
Manion, John J. "Jack," 321, 346, 352
  as head of Chinatown Squad, 285, *286*, 287, *287*, 319, 321, 346, 352
  rescues with Cameron, 285, 288–89, 321
Mann Act, 262
marriage
  for Chinese women fleeing slavery, 61
  interracial, 11, 75, 242–43, 346
Marshall, James, 10
McAfee, Lapsley A., 209, 389
McChesney, Joseph Burwell, 225, 227, 229–31, 391, 392
McCormick, Cyrus, 216
McKinley, Ida, 167, 168, 383
McKinley, William, 167–68, 383
McLaren, John Hays, 253
Menzel, Adolph, 192–93
Methodist Mission Home
  dismissal of Lake and her mother from, 166
  girls' testimony to Fisk committee at, 143, 145
  Jin Ho at, 18
  physical threats to, 93, 101
  Sing Kum at, 18
Midwinter Fair (1894), 81, 85
Mikado, The, 53
Mills family, 51
Ming Quong Home, 301, 331, 336, 394
"Ministry Program," 73–74

missionaries, Christian
  conversion of rescued women to, 162, 164, 177–78
  in forming new social movement against sex slavery, 25–26, 27
  increase in women's missionary societies, 26–27
  initial housing offered to rescued women, 18, 27–29, 40–44
  Kane's assistance in rescues on behalf of, 140, 141, 142, 166
  programs offered to Chinese students by, 73–74
  rivalry between Presbyterians and Methodists, 23, 27
  see also Methodist Mission Home; Presbyterian Mission Home
Mission Home
  Methodist, *see* Methodist Mission Home
  Presbyterian, *see* Presbyterian Mission Home
Monet, Claude, 53
Monroe, Henry E., 218, 374
Moore, Charles, 264
Morgan, Julia, 252, 275–76, 305
Mott, Lucretia, 165
mui tsai system, *80*, 83, 84–85
Murasky, Frank, 296

names, Chinese, 353–54
Nation, Carry, 131
Nebraska, 18, 19, 362
New York Evening Post, The, 66
New York Times, The, 187
Ng Noy, 50, 350
Ng Poon Chew, *see* Chew, Ng Poon
Nineteenth Amendment, 281
Nordhoff, Charles, 66
Norris, Frank, 108–9, 260

Oakland
  Chews' integration into white neighborhood of, 212, 214
  Chinese Americans' migration to, after fire in 1906, 207–8

criminal tongs in, 211, 323
Ming Quong Home in, 336
PMH's temporary home in, 210, 351
Oakland Enquirer, 210
Occidental Board
internal threats within, 281
Presbyterian Mission House of, *see*
Presbyterian Mission Home
Oceanic Steamship Co., 72
Octopus, The (Norris), 108
Older, Cora, 218
Older, Fremont, 218, 220, 221, 222, 223–24,
346, 351
Olney, Eleanor, *see* Babcock, Eleanor
Olney
Omaha Exposition (1898), 132
One Ho, 34
opium
dens in San Francisco, 55–56, 57–58,
67, 68
smuggling into the United States, 361
Overland Monthly, The, 27, 207, 237
Owyang, King, 92

Pacific Society for the Suppression of
Vice, 85, 140, 166
Page Act, 40, 70, 349
Palace Hotel, 116, 193
Palo Alto kidnapping case, 127–33, 132,
139, 154, 379, 380
Palo Alto Times, The, 129
Palo Alto Weekly, 379
Panama-Pacific International Exposition,
258, 259, 260, 268, 276, 352
Pardee, George, 351
Peking (Chinatown brothel), 85–86
Phelan, Arthur J., 322
Phelan, James D., 137, 138, 147, 380
Pigtail Parade in Chinatown, 157
Pistolesi, August, 105
plague epidemic, *see* bubonic plague
epidemic
Porter, R. Langley, 247
Powderly, Terence V., 186, 187
predeterminism, 37, 365
prejudice against the Chinese, racial,
38–39, 72

Presbyterianism, Scottish, 37
Presbyterian Mission Home
after 1906 earthquake, 196, 198–203,
205, 208–10, 351
attorneys for, 52, 218, 346, 350, 374
baby cottage at, 331
Cameron as superintendent of, *see*
Cameron, Donaldina ("Dolly")
children at, 149, 161, 167–68
conversion of rescued women, 177–78
court cases of, 52, 110, 112, 130–33, 154
Culbertson as superintendent of, *see*
Culbertson, Margaret
custody battles of, 52, 93, 110, 112,
127–33, 139, 154, 296, 379, 380
daily schedule of residents at, 51, 148
damage from fire in 1906, 202, 206,
207
deaths at, 52, 91, 156
education at, 169, 177
flu pandemic of 1918 and, 274–75, 298
founding of, ix, xi–xii, 44, 360
fund-raising by, 53, 56, 91, 216, 272, 274
Industrial Department of, 273, 274
Japanese residents at, 169, 173–74, 175,
177, 347
jubilee celebrations at, 280, 352
Logan as superintendent of, 337
main entrance to, x
marriages from, 50–51, 60–61, 76–77,
178, 179, 246, 331–32
after earthquake, 203
arranging of, 51, 249, 250, 253–55
for Broken Blossoms, 331–32
prospective bridegrooms in,
requirements for, 110, 112, 178
merchants in neighborhood of, 58–59
original location of, 40–44, 57
overcrowding at, 91–92, 251
oversight of, 283, 359
portraits of residents of, 165, 191, 192,
267, 273, 386
purchase of new location, 91
rebuilding of, after fire damage, 216,
245, 351
renaming of, in 1942, 337
reports to board of, 151
reputation for being haunted, ix, xi

Presbyterian Mission Home *(continued)*
  residents in 1920s and 1930s of,
      changing nature for, 283–84, 290,
      306–7
  security at, 7, 56–57, 97, 98–99, 127–28,
      237, 254
  struggle to gain initial support for, 38,
      42–44
  threats against residents of, 52, 56–57,
      61, 93–94, 97–99, 112, 127–28, 236,
      350
  total number of residents at, 360
  tourists visiting, 167
  translators at, 119, 153, *153*, 154
  World War I and, 270–72
Prohibition, 280, 281, 316, 352
prostitution
  antimiscegenation law and, 11
  in Chinatown, xi–xii
    after gold rush, 30, 32
    as blamed for outbreaks of venereal
        diseases, 45
    in Farwell's report, 67, *68*, 73
    intense demand for, 11–12, 79
    "tong war" over, 48–49
    white customers of, 11
  criminal tongs control of trafficking
      and, 46, 48
  law banning trafficking for the
      purposes of, 14–15
  in New Orleans's Storyville, 220
  police officers' role in, 8–10, 13–14
  in Seattle, 169, *170*, 171–72
  Victorian Compromise on, 44–45

Quan Laan Fan, 84–85
Queen's Room, 13, 15
Qui Ngun, 249, 251, 255

racial prejudice against the Chinese,
    38–39, 72
racism, institutionalized, 38, 40, 72–73, 370
rape, 3, 145, 146, 185, 262, 283, 333
Real Detective, 330
Red Light Abatement and Injunction
    Act, 262, 281, 290, 352, 361

residence certificates, requirement for, 184
"rice Christians," 151
Rinaldo, Isidor, 230
Robbins, Pauline Fowler, 41–42, 43, 280,
    346, 366
Robinson, William, 191
Roosevelt, Eleanor, 176, 179
Roosevelt, Franklin D., 305
Roosevelt, Theodore, 186, 187, 214, 221, 222
Ruef, Abraham, 214, 225, 346
  corruption and, 218, 220, 221, 222–23,
      351
  imprisonment of, 224, *224*
  as PMH's attorney, 52, 350, 374

Sam Yups, 107
sandlot riots, anti-Chinese, *47,* 49–50
San Francisco
  ban on opium dens, 55
  Chinatown, *see* Chinatown
  Chinese immigrants in, *see* Chinese
      immigrants
  constant construction in, after 1868
      earthquake, 20
  earthquake of 1906, 193–96, *197,* 198,
      202
  employment of Chinese servants, by
      middle- and upper-class families
      in, 65–66, 68
  graft probe in, 220–24
  hard economic times in the 1870s in,
      38, 40, 42
  legal brothels in, until 1917, 361
  police in, *see* San Francisco Police
      Department (SFPD)
  rivalry between Methodists and
      Presbyterians in, 23
  violent crimes in 1895, escalation of,
      103, 375
  Woman's Missionary Society of the
      Methodist Episcopal Church
      in, 16
San Francisco Call, 74, 92, 98, 101, 113, 121,
    222
San Francisco Chronicle, 121, 222
  exposé on "Chinese slavery," 93
  on the graft probe, 222

profiles of Cameron in, 131, 162, 164
on quarantine of Chinatown, 118
on Sieh's progressive views, 182
stories on Tachii's dramatic suicide, 174
on treatment of sick prostitutes, 14
San Francisco Examiner, 329, 383
exposé on SFPD's Chinatown Squad
and Sullivan, 135, *136,* 137, 138, 351
on vaccination program for bubonic
plague, 121, 122
San Francisco Police Department
(SFPD)
Chinatown Squad
corruption in, 101, 103
Manion as head of, 285, *286,* 287,
288–89, 319, 346
reformed, 103–6, *104,* 135, *136,* 137–38,
285, 287–89, 319, 346
Morals Squad of, so called, 270
role in prostitution in 1869, 8–10,
13–14, 45
San Francisco Theological Seminary, 74,
201, 345, 350
Sargent, George, 64–65, 95, 246, 350, 374
scarlet fever, 246–47
Schmitz, Eugene, 214, 218, 219–20, 221,
222, 223, 346, 351
Schmitz, Herbert, 220
Schulze, Charles Frederick, 242–43
Scott, William Anderson, 25
Scottish Presbyterianism, 37
Seattle, human trafficking of Japanese
women in, 169, 170–72
Second Great Awakening, 26
segregation
in public education, 72–74, 159, 351, 370
in YWCA, 306
Seneca Falls convention (1848), 164, 165
sexual slavery, xi–xii, 5, 13, *144,* 362
failed rescue of women in 1897 from,
112–13
Jeong's escape from, xii, 6–7, 320–21,
352, 360
rape and, 3, 145, 146
Sieh's condemnation of, 182
trafficking of girls for, 8, 10, 11–14, 26
broadening of antislavery law to
include penalties against, 147

Cameron's criticism of, 131, 133–34,
164–67, 168
criminal tongs control of, 46, 48,
81–82
from Japan, 169, 170–72, 179
Jeong, 3, 5, *319,* 320, 324
law in 1870 banning, 14–15
missionaries in forming new social
movement against, 25–26, 27
police officers' role in, 8–10,
13–14
from poor families, 11, 26, 81–82
by Wong See Duck, 288, 319, *319,*
323–24, 327–29, 331, 347
written contracts for, 46, 48
SFPD, *see* San Francisco Police
Department (SFPD)
Shepherd, Charles R., 282–83, 352
Shi Meiyu, *see* Stone, Mary
Shreve & Co., 41
Sieh King King, 180, 182–83
Sieu Cum, 255
Sing Chong Bazaar, 215
Sing Kum, 18
Six Companies (Chinese Consolidated
Benevolent Association), 10
Little Pete's smuggling scheme's
with, 81
public stand against trafficking and
prostitution, 11, 49
request for Chew to go on speaking
tour about boycott, 185
SFPD Chinatown Squad's corruption
and, 106
slavery
of African Americans
Thirteenth Amendment's
abolishment of, xii, 12, 349
in Great Britain, end of, 25
mui tsai system as, *80,* 83, 84–85
sexual, *see* sexual slavery
Smith, Emery E., 130
Song of Hiawatha, The (Longfellow), 35
Spencer, Arthur, 230
Spreckels, Rudolph, 222, 223
Spreckels family, 72
Staiger, Steve, 379
Standard Lodging House, 220, 221

Stanford University
  founding of, 129
  Jeong's admission to, 299, 300
  support for Cameron and Kum Quai
    and, 130–31, 133
Stanton, Elizabeth Cady, 165
"Star-Spangled Banner, The" (Key), 42
Statement for Non-exclusion, A (Healy
    and Chew), 185
Steinbeck, John, 329
Stevens School, 161, 232, 382, 392
Stone, Mary, 309–10, 313–14, 315, 352
Stowe, Harriet Beecher, 93
Straus, Isidor, 186
Suey Sing tong, 46, 48, 287, 318–19, 323
Sullivan, Arthur, 53
Sullivan, Frank J., 138
Sullivan, William P., 135, 136, 137–38, 147
Sun Yat-sen, 184, 269
Supreme Court
  ruling on Brown v. Board of
    Education, 73
  ruling on Chy Lung v. Freeman, 40, 350
  ruling on Tape v. Hurley, 72–73
  ruling on United States v. Ju Toy,
    184–85
Sutro, Adolph, 161
Sutter's Mill, 10
syphilis, 45

Tachii Nobusaburo, 172–74, 384
Taiping Rebellion, 82
Tape, Mamie, 72–73
Tape v. Hurley, 72–73
Taylor, James Hudson, 392
Tea Rose, see Tong, Minnie ("Tea Rose")
"Third Circle, The" (Norris), 260
Thirteenth Amendment, xii, 12, 349
Thompson, Frances, 167, 196, 378
Tien Fuh Wu, see Wu, Tien Fuh
Tong, Minnie ("Tea Rose"), 191, 192, 192,
    386
tongs, criminal, see criminal tongs
Tooker, Mary, 252, 276
Tooker, Nathaniel, 252, 394
Tooker Home, 252, 274, 275–76, 281, 298,
    301

Tooker sisters, 252, 269, 274
Toynbee Hall, xi
True magazine, 330
Turner, Anna A. Key, 42
"22 Lewd Chinese Women," 40, 48, 350
Tye Leung ("Tiny"), 237, 239, 240, 241–43,
    242, 346

Uncle Tom's Cabin (Stowe), 93
"Underground Chinatown" exhibit,
    261–62, 263–65, 266, 396
unemployment, 42, 49
United States v. Ju Toy, 184–85
Unsuspecting Victim, Chinatown, San
    Francisco, An (Genthe), 189
U.S. vs. Wong See Duck, 319

Van Gogh, Vincent, 53
Van Pelt, Mrs., 41
venereal diseases, 45
Victoria, Queen, 60, 137
Victorian Compromise, 44–45
Voss, Edna, 336–37

Ways of Ah Sin, The (Shepherd), 352
white slavery, as a term, 262–63
Williams, Miss E., 41
Willows Camp, 207
Wilson, Carol Green, 337
Wilson, Woodrow, 270–71
Wing, Muriel, 216
Wing Lee Co., 318–19, 323, 403
Wing Quong Hing, 320, 332
Woman's Foreign Missionary Society
    (Methodist), 313
    (Presbyterian), 26, 28–29, 349, 359
Woman's Missionary Society of the
    Methodist Episcopal Church in
    San Francisco, 16
women's missionary societies, increase
    in, 26–27
women's suffrage, 165, 179, 281, 352
Won Fore, 251
Wong, Anna May, 329
Wong, Ben, 48

Wong, Lois Qui, *see* Jeung Gwai Ying
Wong, May Louise, 299
Wong Hee, *see* Wong See Duck
Wong See Duck
  hardware store used as front by, 318–19,
    323, 403
  immigration to America, 225, *226,*
    227–28, 231, 287, *326*
  photograph of, *226*
  threats to Jeung, 5
  trafficking ring of, 288, 319, *319,* 323–24,
    327–29, 331, 347
  trials of, 325, 327, 329, 330
Wong See Duck, U.S. vs., 319
Wong Su, 327–29, 328, 330, 331, 347, 352
Woo, Margaret, 241
Woon Tsun, *see* Leung Yuen Qui
Workingmen's Party, 47, 50, 69
World War I, 270–71
Worley, Florence, 91
Worley, Minnie G., 91, 247
Wu, Tien Fuh, 347, 353
  anniversary surprises for Cameron,
    277, 279–80
  birthdate of, 148, 381
  bound feet of, 82–84
  burial in Cameron family plot, 338
  burns/abuse from owner, 88, 90
  as a child at PMH, 148, 150–51, 156,
    160, 161
  Chinese Peace Association and, 335
  as a Christian, 151–52
  death of, 352
  on death of Leung Yuen Qui, 154–55,
    156, 161
  delight in youngest members of
    PMH, 331
  in *Dragon Stories,* 232, 234, 235, 236,
    256, 392
  early confrontations with Cameron,
    152
  education of, 148, 159, 161, 232, 234, 236,
    237
  family background of, xi, 82–83
  father's sale of, 83, 156, 169, 372
  financial sponsor of, at PMH, 159–60
  during flu pandemic, 275
  lack of interest in suitors, 237
  life as a *mui tsai,* 84, 85–88, 90, 148
  marriages arranged by, 249, 251, 253,
    254, 255
  portraits of, *159, 312, 334*
  public appearances of, 307
  relationship with Cameron, 152, 156,
    158, 236, 307, 337–39, 352, 354
  relationship with Cameron's family,
    338
  relationship with Cameron's successor,
    337
  rescue of, 88, 90–91, 148
  rescue work of, xi, 255–57, 288–290
  retirement of, 337, 352
  search for family in China, 268–69
  threats received by, 236–37
  transit to San Francisco, 84
  trip with deported women back to
    China, 303, 307–8, 309–11, 313–15
  on Wong See Duck's trials, 325, 330
  World War I and, 270–71

Xijiao ("Golden Peach"), 48, 349

Yamada Kakichi, 178, 179
Yamada Waka, 347
  education of, 178, 179
  family background of, 169
  forced prostitution of, 171–72
  marriage of, 178–79
  meeting with Eleanor Roosevelt, *176,*
    179
  at Presbyterian Mission Home, 169,
    173–74, 175, 177, 347
  various names of, 353–54, 385
Yamazaki, Tomoko, 354
Yee Mar, *319*
Yuen Kum, 203
Yum Gue, 289

Zirpoli, A. J., 322, 327, 328

Illustration Credits

Page

x. Courtesy of the author

4. San Francisco History Center, San Francisco Public Library

9. Library of Congress

17. Library of Congress

24. Arnold Genthe, Library of Congress

31. Theodore C. Marceau, Courtesy of the Bancroft Library, University of California, Berkeley

39. Library of Congress

47. California Historical Society

54. Arnold Genthe, Library of Congress

57. Courtesy of Cameron House

63. Courtesy of the Cameron Family

68. San Francisco History Center, San Francisco Public Library

71. Courtesy of Huntington Library

80. Stanford Special Collections

89. Arnold Genthe, Library of Congress

96. Courtesy of Cameron House

102. Willard E. Worden, San Francisco History Center, San Francisco Public Library

104. San Francisco History Center, San Francisco Public Library

107. Courtesy of the Bancroft Library, University of California, Berkeley

111. Courtesy of Cameron House

117. I. W. Taber, Courtesy of the California History Room, California State Library, Sacramento, California

125. Library of Congress
132. Courtesy of the Palo Alto Historical Association
136. Periodicals, San Francisco Public Library
144. Courtesy of the Bancroft Library, University of California, Berkeley
149. Arnold Genthe, Library of Congress
153. Courtesy of Cameron House
157. Arnold Genthe, Library of Congress
159. Courtesy of Cameron House
163. Courtesy of Cameron House
165. Louis J. Stellman, Courtesy of the California History Room, California State Library, Sacramento, California
170. Library of Congress
176. Library of Congress
181. Courtesy of the Museum of Performance and Design, Performing Arts Library, San Francisco, California
184. Louis J. Stellman, Courtesy of the California History Room, California State Library, Sacramento, California
189. Library of Congress
192. Library of Congress
197. Arnold Genthe, Library of Congress
205. Anne T. Kent California Room, Marin County Free Library
207. Arnold Genthe, Library of Congress
213. Louis J. Stellman, Courtesy of the California History Room, California State Library, Sacramento, California
219. San Francisco History Center, San Francisco Public Library
224. Courtesy of the Bancroft Library, University of California, Berkeley
226. National Archives and Records Administration
233. Courtesy of Cameron House
240. Ethnic Studies Library, Berkeley
242. Courtesy of Judy Yung
245. Courtesy of Cameron House
250. Courtesy of Cameron House
259. Anne T. Kent California Room, Marin County Free Library
267. Courtesy of Cameron House
273. Courtesy of Cameron House
278. Courtesy of Cameron House
286. San Francisco History Center, San Francisco Public Library
287. Courtesy of the Bancroft Library, University of California, Berkeley
291. Courtesy of Cameron House

297. San Francisco History Center, San Francisco Public Library
304. California Historical Society
312. Louis B. Stellman, Courtesy of the California History Room, California State Library, Sacramento, California
317. San Francisco History Center, San Francisco Public Library
319. National Archives and Records Administration
321. Courtesy of Cameron House
326. National Archives and Records Administration
328. Courtesy of Cameron House
334. Courtesy of Cameron House

A NOTE ABOUT THE AUTHOR

Julia Flynn Siler is a *New York Times* best-selling author and journalist. Her most recent book is *Lost Kingdom: Hawaii's Last Queen, the Sugar Kings, and America's First Imperial Adventure.* Her first book, *The House of Mondavi: The Rise and Fall of an American Wine Dynasty,* was a finalist for a James Beard Award and a Gerald Loeb Award for distinguished reporting. A veteran journalist, Siler is a longtime contributor and former staff writer for *The Wall Street Journal* and has been a guest commentator on the BBC, CNBC, and CNN. She lives in the San Francisco Bay Area with her husband and their two sons.

A NOTE ON THE TYPE

This book was set in a modern adaptation of a type designed by the first William Caslon (1692–1766). The Caslon face, an artistic, easily read type, has enjoyed more than two centuries of popularity in the English-speaking world. This version, with its even balance and honest letterforms, was designed by Carol Twombly for the Adobe Corporation and released in 1990.

Composed by North Market Street Graphics,
Lancaster, Pennsylvania

Printed and bound by Berryville Graphics,
Berryville, Virginia

Designed by Cassandra J. Pappas